W9-ATP-424

DAVID GLENN HUNT
MEMORIAL LIBRARY
GALVESTON COLLEGE

GUSTAVE FLAUBERT

Modern Critical Views

Chinua Achebe
Henry Adams
Aeschylus
A. R. Ammons
Sherwood Anderson
Aristophanes
John Ashbery
Margaret Atwood
W. H. Auden
Jane Austen
Isaac Babel
Charles Baudelaire
Simone de Beauvoir
Samuel Beckett
Saul Bellow
Thomas Berger
John Berryman
The Bible
Elizabeth Bishop
William Blake
Giovanni Boccaccio
The Brontës
John Bunyan
Anthony Burgess
Italo Calvino
Albert Camus
Canadian Poetry: Modern
    and Contemporary
Canadian Poetry through
    E. J. Pratt
Louis-Ferdinand Céline
Miguel de Cervantes
Geoffrey Chaucer
John Cheever
Anton Chekhov
Kate Chopin
Joseph Conrad
Contemporary Poets
Stephen Crane
e. e. cummings
Dante
Charles Dickens
James Dickey
Emily Dickinson
John Donne & the
    Seventeenth-Century
    Metaphysical Poets
John Dryden
W. E. B. Du Bois
Lawrence Durrell
George Eliot
T. S. Eliot
Elizabethan Dramatists
Ralph Ellison
Ralph Waldo Emerson
Euripides
William Faulkner
Henry Fielding
F. Scott Fitzgerald
Sigmund Freud
Robert Frost
Northrop Frye

J. W. von Goethe
Nikolai Gogol
William Golding
Thomas Hardy
Nathaniel Hawthorne
William Hazlitt
H. D.
Seamus Heaney
Lillian Hellman
Ernest Hemingway
Hermann Hesse
Homer
Langston Hughes
Ted Hughes
Victor Hugo
Zora Neale Hurston
Henry James
Dr. Samuel Johnson and
    James Boswell
Ben Jonson
James Joyce
Carl Gustav Jung
Franz Kafka
Yasonari Kawabata
John Keats
Søren Kierkegaard
D. H. Lawrence
Frederico García Lorca
Robert Lowell
Malcolm Lowry
Norman Mailer
Bernard Malamud
Thomas Mann
Katherine Mansfield
Christopher Marlowe
Gabriel García Márquez
Andrew Marvell
Carson McCullers
Herman Melville
Arthur Miller
Henry Miller
John Milton
Marianne Moore
Alberto Moravia
Toni Morrison
Alice Munro
Iris Murdoch
Robert Musil
Vladimir Nabokov
Friedrich Nietzsche
Frank Norris
Joyce Carol Oates
Sean O'Casey
Flannery O'Connor
Joe Orton
George Orwell
Ovid
Cynthia Ozick
Grace Paley
Harold Pinter
Luigi Pirandello
Sylvia Plath

Plato
Plautus
Edgar Allan Poe
Poets of Sensibility & the
    Sublime
Poets of the Nineties
Ezra Pound
Anthony Powell
Pre-Raphaelite Poets
Marcel Proust
Adrienne Rich
Samuel Richardson
Philip Roth
Jean-Jacques Rousseau
John Ruskin
William Shakespeare
    (3 vols.)
    Histories & Poems
    Comedies & Romances
    Tragedies
George Bernard Shaw
Mary Wollstonecraft
    Shelley
Percy Bysshe Shelley
Sam Shepard
Alexander Solzhenitsyn
Sophocles
Wole Soyinka
Edmund Spenser
Wallace Stevens
Robert Louis Stevenson
Tom Stoppard
August Strindberg
Jonathan Swift
Henry David Thoreau
James Thurber and S. J.
    Perelman
J. R. R. Tolkien
Leo Tolstoy
Jean Toomer
Lionel Trilling
Anthony Trollope
Ivan Turgenev
Mark Twain
Virgil
Voltaire
Kurt Vonnegut
Derek Walcott
Alice Walker
Robert Penn Warren
Edith Wharton
Patrick White
Walt Whitman
Oscar Wilde
Tennessee Williams
Virginia Woolf
William Wordsworth
Jay Wright
Richard Wright
William Butler Yeats
A. B. Yehoshua
Emile Zola

These and other titles in preparation

Modern Critical Views

GUSTAVE FLAUBERT

Edited and with an introduction by
Harold Bloom
Sterling Professor of the Humanities
Yale University

CHELSEA HOUSE PUBLISHERS
New York ◊ Philadelphia

DAVID GLENN HUNT
MEMORIAL LIBRARY
GALVESTON COLLEGE

© 1989 by Chelsea House Publishers, a division of Main Line Book Co.

Introduction © 1988 by Harold Bloom

All rights reserved. No part of this publication may be reproduced or transmitted in any form or by any means without the written permission of the publisher.

Printed and bound in the United States of America

10 9 8 7 6 5 4 3 2 1

∞ The paper used in this publication meets the minimum requirements of the American National Standard for Permanence of Paper for Printed Library Materials, Z39.48–1984.

Library of Congress Cataloging-in-Publication Data
Gustave Flaubert / edited and with an introduction by
Harold Bloom.
    p. cm.—(Modern critical views)
    Bibliography: p.
    Includes index.
    Summary: A collection of fourteen critical essays on the
French writer, arranged in chronological order of their original
publication.
    ISBN 1–55546–302–9
    1. Flaubert, Gustave, 1821–1880—Criticism and
interpretation. [1. Flaubert, Gustave, 1821–1880—Criticism
and interpretation. 2. French literature—History and
criticism.] I. Bloom, Harold. II. Series.
PQ2249.G84   1988
843'.8—dc19   87–15488
                                                           CIP
                                                           AC

Contents

Editor's Note

This book brings together a representative selection of the best modern critical views of Gustave Flaubert's work. The critical essays are reprinted here in the chronological order of their original publication. I am grateful to Karin Cope for her erudite assistance in editing this volume.

My introduction centers upon *Madame Bovary*, read here as a prophecy of the Impressionist critics, novelists, and painters who were influenced by Flaubert. Hugh Kenner commences the chronological sequence of criticism with his analysis of *Bouvard et Pécuchet* as a comedy of the European Enlightenment, with its amiable lust for dictionaries and encyclopedias.

In Victor Brombert's reading of *Madame Bovary*, we are given an exegesis of how "the cycles of ennui and spatial monotony . . . are brought into contrapuntal tension with an underlying metaphoric structure suggesting limits." Michel Foucault, master of the archives (in a Borgesian sense), reads *The Temptation of Saint Antony* in its three versions as a perpetual influence upon all of Flaubert's other ongoing works.

Sartre's Flaubert is the subject of Neil Hertz's lucid account of Flaubert's "conversion" to the religion of art. The luridly splendid *Salammbô* is read by Veronica Forrest-Thomson as a ritual that paradoxically celebrates the limitations of the power of language.

Hayden White, deft historian of consciousness, contrasts Marx and Flaubert as stylists of reality. *Hérodias*, the neglected story of the *Trois Contes,* is defended by Jane Robertson as the most poetically allusive of the three tales. *Bouvard et Pécuchet* returns in a retrospective study by Andrew J. McKenna, who traces the comic pattern of their dilemma and their failure.

The early works of Flaubert are examined in their mimetic procedures by Michal Peled Ginsburg. In Shoshana Felman's advanced reading, *The Legend of Saint Julian the Hospitable* is seen as "Flaubert's signature," the semantically overloaded and problematic portrait of a profoundly evasive and masterful self, or fiction of a self. Eugenio Donato's investigation of Flaubert's proper name may be read as a coda to Felman's more complex meditation.

The Temptation of Saint Antony is described by Peter Starr as an instance of the knowing disintegration of Flaubert's quest to find a "science" or a "method" for his narrative art. Emma Bovary returns in Lawrence Rothfield's analysis of how well or badly semiotics and Marxism can render a reading of its salient difficulties. In this book's final essay, Milad Doueihi studies the *Sentimental Education* as an interplay between Frédéric's inability to express his love for Madame Arnoux and his obsession with her costumes.

Introduction

At six o'clock this evening, as I was writing the word "hysterics,"
I was so swept away, was bellowing so loudly and feeling so
deeply what my little Bovary was going through, that I was afraid
of having hysterics myself. I got up from my table and opened
the window to calm myself. My head was spinning. Now I have
great pains in my knees, in my back, and in my head. I feel like
a man who has ———ed too much (forgive me for the expression)—a kind of rapturous lassitude.

(Flaubert to Louise Colet, letter of 23 December 1853)

I will not echo the Lycanthrope [Petrus Borel], remembered for
a subversiveness which no longer prevails, when he said: "Confronted with all that is vulgar and inept in the present time, can
we not take refuge in cigarettes and adultery?" But I assert that
our world, even when it is weighed on precision scales, turns out
to be exceedingly harsh considering it was engendered by Christ;
it could hardly be entitled to throw the first stone at adultery. A
few cuckolds more or less are not likely to increase the rotating
speed of the spheres and to hasten by a second the final destruction of the universe.

(Baudelaire on *Madame Bovary*)

The societal scandal of *Madame Bovary* is as remote now as the asceticism
of the spirit practiced by Flaubert and Baudelaire, who seem almost self-
indulgent, in the era of Samuel Beckett. Rereading *Madame Bovary* side-by-
side with say *Malone Dies* is a sadly instructive experience. Emma seems as
boisterous as Hogarth or Rabelais in the company of Malone and Macmann.

1

And yet she is their grandmother, even as the personages of Proust, Joyce, and Kafka are among her children. With her the novel enters the realm of inactivity, where the protagonists are bored, but the reader is not. Poor Emma, destroyed by usury rather than love, is so vital that her stupidities do not matter. A much more than average sensual woman, her capacity for life and love is what moves us to admire her, and even to love her, since like Flaubert himself we find ourselves in her.

Why is Emma so unlucky? If it can go wrong, it will go wrong for her. Freud, like some of the ancients, believed there were no accidents. Ethos is the daimon, your character is your fate, and everything that happens to you starts by being you. Rereading, we suffer the anguish of beholding the phases that lead to Emma's self-destruction. That anguish multiplies despite Flaubert's celebrated detachment, partly because of his uncanny skill at suggesting how many different consciousnesses invade and impinge upon any single consciousness, even one as commonplace as Emma's. Emma's *I* is an other, and so much the worse for the sensual apprehensiveness that finds it has become Emma.

"Hysterics suffer mainly from reminiscences" is a famous and eloquent formula that Freud outgrew. Like Flaubert before him, he came to see that the Emmas—meaning nearly all among us—were suffering from repressed drives. Still later, in his final phase, Freud arrived at a vision that achieves an ultimate clarity in the last section of *Inhibitions, Symptoms, and Anxiety*, which reads to me as a crucial commentary on Emma Bovary. It is not repressed desire that ensues in anxiety, but a primal anxiety that issues in repression. As for the variety of neurosis involved, Freud speculated that hysteria results from fear of the loss of love. Emma kills herself in a hysteria brought on by a fairly trivial financial mess, but underlying the hysteria is the terrible fear that there will be no more lovers for her.

The most troubling critique of *Madame Bovary* that I know is by Henry James, who worried whether we could sustain our interest in a consciousness as narrow as Emma's:

> The book is a picture of the middling as much as they like, but does Emma attain even to *that*? Hers is a narrow middling even for a little imaginative person whose "social" significance is small. It is greater on the whole than her capacity of consciousness, taking this all round; and so in a word, we feel her less illustrational than she might have been not only if the world had offered her more points of contact, but if she had had more of these to give it.

That *sounds* right enough, yet rereading the novel does not make us desire a larger or brighter Emma. Until she yields to total hysteria, she incarnates the universal wish for sensual life, for a more sensual life. Keats would have liked her, and so do we, though she is not exactly an Isabel Archer or a Millie Theale. A remarkable Emma might have developed the hardness and resourcefulness that would have made her a French Becky Sharp, and fitted her for survival even in mid-nineteenth century Paris. But James sublimely chose to miss the point, which Albert Thibaudet got permanently right:

> She is more ardent than passionate. She loves life, pleasure, love itself much more than she loves a man; she is made to have lovers rather than a lover. It is true that she loves Rodolphe with all the fervor of her body, and with him she experiences the moment of her complete, perfect and brief fulfillment; her illness, however, after Rodolphe's desertion, is sufficient to cure her of this love, but from weakness and total inability to look ahead, a naivete which makes her an easy prey to deceit in love as well as in business. She lives in the present and is unable to resist the slightest impulse.

I like best Thibaudet's comparison between Flaubert's attitude towards Emma and Milton's towards his Eve: "Whenever Emma is seen in purely sensuous terms, he speaks of her with a delicate, almost religious feeling, the way Milton speaks of Eve." One feels that Milton desires Eve; Flaubert indeed is so at one with Emma that his love for her is necessarily narcissistic. Cervantes, not Milton, was in some sense Flaubert's truest precursor, and Emma (as many critics have remarked) has elements of a female Quixote in her. Like the Don, she is murdered by reality. Milton's Eve, tough despite her yielding beauty, transcends both the order of reality and the order of play. Emma, lacking a Sancho, finds her enchanted Dulcinea in the paltry Rodolphe. Flaubert punished himself harshly, in and through Emma, by grimly mixing in a poisonous order of provincial social reality and an equally poisonous order of hallucinated play, Emma's fantasies of an ideal passion. The mixing in is cruel, formidable, and of unmatched aesthetic dignity. Emma has no Sublime, but the inverted Romantic vision of Flaubert persuades us that the strongest writing can represent ennui with a life-enhancing power.

Sartre, very early in his endless meditations upon Flaubert, sensibly observed that "Flaubert despised realism and said so over and over throughout his life; he loved only the absolute purity of art." *Madame Bovary* has little to do with realism, and something to do with a prophecy of impressionism, but in a most refracted fashion. All of poor Emma's moments are at once drab and privileged; one remembers Browning's Andrea del Sarto intoning: "A common grayness silvers everything." The critical impressionism of Walter Pater is implicit in *Madame Bovary;* imagery of hallucinatory intensity is always a step away from suddenly bursting forth as secularized epiphanies. The impressionist painters and Proust lurk in the ironies of Flaubert's style, but the uncanny moral energy remains unique:

> The priest rose to take the crucifix; then she stretched forward her neck like one suffering from thirst, and glueing her lips to the body of the Man-God, she pressed upon it with all her expiring strength the fullest kiss of love that she had ever given. Then he recited the *Misereatur* and the *Indulgentiam,* dipped his right thumb in the oil, and began to give extreme unction. First, upon the eyes, that had so coveted all worldly goods; then upon the nostrils, that had been so greedy of the warm breeze and the scents of love; then upon the mouth, that had spoken lies, moaned in pride and cried out in lust; then upon the hands that had taken delight in the texture of sensuality; and finally upon the soles of the feet, so swift when she had hastened to satisfy her desires, and that would now walk no more.

This is Flaubert's elegy for Emma and ultimately transcends its apparent ironies, if only because we hear in it the novelist's deeper elegy for himself. He refuses to mourn for himself, as befits the high priest of a purer art than the novel knew before him, yet his lament for Emma's sensual splendor is an authentic song of loss, a loss in which he participates.

HUGH KENNER

Gustave Flaubert:
Comedian of the Enlightenment

The Enlightenment lingers in our intellectual histories as a puzzling phenomenon, puzzling because it is so hard to say briefly what it was. It lacks
chronology, it lacks locality, it lacks identity. It is personified by no conve-
nient heroes, being by definition antiheroic. Diderot and D'Alembert are
rather examples than exemplars. It perhaps hardly knew that it was happening, or not much more than the Middle Ages knew that they were happening,
and we may perhaps speculate that the romantic movement was the first such
event that did know that it was happening, and that this was where the
romanticism lay. The Enlightenment seems in retrospect a sort of mystical
experience through which the mind of Europe passed, and by which the
memory of Europe remains haunted. We carry with us still one piece of
baggage from those far-off days, and that is the book which nobody wrote
and nobody is expected to read, and which is marketed as the Encyclopaedia:
Britannica, Americana, Antarctica or other.

The Encyclopaedia, like its cousin the Dictionary, takes all that we know
apart into little pieces, and then arranges those pieces so that they can be
found one at a time. It is produced by a feat of organizing, not a feat of
understanding. No Bacon, no Aquinas, is tracing the hierarchies of a human
knowledge which he has assumed the responsibility of grasping. If the Encyclopaedia means anything as a whole, no one connected with the enterprise
can be assumed to know what that meaning is. A hundred contributors, or

From *Flaubert, Joyce and Beckett: The Stoic Comedians.* © 1962 by Hugh Kenner.
Beacon Press, 1962.

a thousand, each responsible for squinting at creation through a single knot-hole, can work in utter isolation, very likely in a hundred different cities, each on his self-contained packet of knowledge; and these packets an editor with a flow-chart may coordinate, if at all, by appending cross-references, and organize only by filing each in its alphabetical place. That the great *Encyclopédie* contained cross-references to articles which did not exist is not surprising under the circumstances, nor is the presence of wholesale contra-diction within the covers of any such bound set; nor, finally, the nearly surrealist discontinuity of the final product. The compendia of which Pliny's *Natural History* is the first extant example have a discursive plan, and later compilations have a hierarchic plan, like the Arts Curriculum. Thus Bartho-lomew de Glanville, an English Franciscan friar, wrote about 1360 a most popular work, *De proprietatibus rerum,* in nineteen books, beginning with God and the angels and ending with colors, scents, flavors, and liquors, with a list of thirty-six eggs; and in the next century "A very popular small encyclopaedia, *Margarita philosophica* (1496), in twelve books, was written by Georg Reisch, a German, prior of the Carthusians of Freiburg, and con-fessor of the emperor Maximilian I. Books 1–7 treat of the seven liberal arts; 8, 9, principles and origin of natural things; 10, 11, the soul, vegetative, sensitive and intellectual; 12, moral philosophy." (I am quoting from the *Encyclopaedia Britannica* article on Encyclopaedias.) But open the *Encyclo-paedia Britannica* itself, and the first topic on which you will receive instruc-tion is the letter A, and the second is the meaning of the term "A–1 at Lloyd's," and the fourteenth is the Aardvark. This is sublimely nonsensical, like conversation in Wonderland, and when G. K. Chesterton remarked at the opening of this century that Nonsense was the literature of the future, we may be sure that he had not only the "Alice" books in the back of his mind but the *Britannica,* 9th edition, at his elbow. (Chesterton later wrote the article on Humor for the 11th edition. I find it curious that there is no article on Nonsense.)

The mark of the Encyclopaedia, then, is its fragmentation of all that we know into little pieces so arranged that they can be found one at a time. Nothing, except when a cross-reference is provided, connects with or entails anything else; nothing corrects anything else, or affords perspective on any-thing else. And nobody, consequently, is talking to anyone else. Least of all is the contributor talking to the reader, for there is no way in which the contributor can form the least idea who the reader is. The only entrance requirement is that he be able to use the alphabet; beyond that, his credentials are anybody's guess. Is he the master of his subject, looking for a handy digest of one portion of it? The author of the article on Quaternions prefers to think so. Is his general knowledge extensive, except for the particulars of the subject under discussion? So supposes the expert on the Renaissance. Is he, however, perhaps the veriest tyro, stuffed with just such general notions as will enable him to read a column of moderately undemanding prose, with constant exclamations of astonishment? That is what the authority on Waterfalls has clearly decided. Above all, is he going to relate one subject to another? It is devoutly to be hoped that he is not; for were any diligent soul to attempt a correlation between "Eliot, T. S.," "English Literature—Twentieth Century," and "Poetry, American," all concerned might find themselves saddled with some exceedingly awkward correspondence. Or perhaps not; there is always the hope that the reader will exhibit Pécuchet's syndrome, and give it up.

II

Pécuchet and his friend Bouvard invariably do give it up, but they never lack energy for a new beginning. Flaubert himself gave up, after thirteen months of inventing and chronicling their researches, but in two years he resumed this most exacting of labors, with a ferocity that did not again flag until his death. The truncated *Bouvard et Pécuchet* survives, a Pyrrhic victory over Gutenberg's empire. "As for Molière's comedies," declaimed Augustine Scribe before the Académie Française, "what have they to tell us of the great events of the age of Louis XIV? Have they a word to say about the errors, the weaknesses, the failings of the king? Do they so much as mention the revocation of the Edict of Nantes?" And taking in his hand the printed transcript of this oration, Flaubert wrote in the margin:

> Revocation of the Edict of Nantes: 1685.
> Death of Molière: 1673.

He conceived Bouvard and Pécuchet as two men who should enact, in all innocence, on a heroic scale, just such a reduction to zero of universal, of encyclopaedic, nullity.

And with what Odyssean zest do they read, mark and regurgitate, burning through libraries like a prairie fire! They are the Questing Heroes of an age that is still ours; a Duplex Hercules assaulting jungles, clearing swamps; a bipartite Theseus venturing into the Labyrinth with transit and theodolite. Chimera after chimera they confront, exhaust, drain, discard. Seven dragons are slain of a morning, and the land is bare after their passing. They dispose of Ancient History in three hundred words; it is obscure from lack of documents. They turn to modern history, where the documents are so numerous they grow confused "through their ignorance of dates." Undaunted, they engorge a mnemonic system which has the advantage of combining three other systems; thus "Fenaigle divides the universe into houses, which contain rooms, each having four walls with nine panels, each panel bearing an emblem. Thus, the first king of the first dynasty will occupy the first panel in the first room. A beacon on a hill will tell how he was named 'Phar-a-mond,' according to the system of Pâris. By Allevy's method, in placing above a mirror, which stands for 4, a bird 2 and a hoop 0, one will obtain 420, the date of that prince's accession."

Now mark the heroism of their total commitment, suffering all their surroundings to dissolve into a vast mnemono-technic edifice:

> For greater clearness, they took, as a mnemonic base, their own house, where they were living, attaching to each one of its parts a distinct event—and the courtyard, the garden, the surroundings, the entire district, had no other meaning than to jog their memory. The boundary-posts in the country limited certain epochs, the apple-trees were genealogical trees, the bushes were battles, the world became a symbol.

It is the sacramental universe of the new learning, run up in a fortnight. "They sought, on the walls, a quantity of things that were not there, and ended by seeing them, but no longer knew the dates they represented."

But as the wave topples, watch them snatch truth from the wreck of method; for even as they lose hold on the means of recalling dates, they learn that the dates themselves are not worth recalling:

> Besides, dates are not always authentic. They learnt, in a student's manual, that the date of the birth of Jesus must be put back five years earlier than is usual, that with the Greeks there were three ways of reckoning the Olympiads, and with the Romans eight ways of dating the beginning of the year. So many opportunities for mistakes, besides those that result from the signs of the zodiac, eras, and different sorts of calendars.
>
> And from disregard of dates they passed to contempt for facts.
> What is important is the philosophy of history.

This in turn they speedily discard; and having exhaustively proved the total impossibility of writing history, they set out to write one.

So much in three pages, less than one per cent of the book; never was zeal so disinterested, so unflagging. Weaving ropes of sand and carving monuments in water, they undo with fantastic thoroughness the work of three thousand years, dismembering Solomon's house stone by stone and bringing the New Atlantis level with the waves, during thirty years (thirty years!) sojourn inside the world of the Encyclopaedia, where most of us have not the heart to venture for more than a few minutes at a time. At seventy-five they are as dauntless as at fifty. Their very despairs—as when they arrive at the certainty that nothing exists—are but stages of the illuminative way, "into the desolation of reality." And when all else has failed; when they have plumbed to the uttermost the follies of a hundred systems; discarded

    agriculture, arboriculture and formal gardening;
    chemistry, medicine, astronomy, archaeology and geology;
    prehistory, history and the philosophy of history;
    literature, grammar and aesthetics;
    politics;
    love, gymnastics;
    mesmerism, magnetism, spiritualism and the evocation of the
        dead;
    metaphysics, suicide, Christianity, even Buddhism;

why then, having retraced the history of the human race from the tilling of the fields to theology the queen of sciences and seen all these crumble to dust, then still dauntless they take up pedagogy, so that they may reclaim two waifs from brutality and instill in them the love of learning. Odysseus himself was less heroic; he was succored by the memory of an Ithaca he had known.

Yet it seems clear that Pécuchet and his friend Bouvard lack the ideal qualifications for their high calling; for one thing, they are both getting old. They are just old enough, however, for Flaubert's purposes, and born moreover, according to their author's careful determinations, precisely in the nick of time to inherit the ages. For their great experiment commences toward the end of 1840, when each of them has lived half a hundred years; which means that they were born in the first months of the new heaven and the new earth, about 1790, when the Revolution had decreed the obsolescence of cant, superstition and custom. Like Russians born in the year 1918, they are untainted by the least memory of a time when knowledge, which is power, was the preserve of the few. Their very life in the womb commenced after the fall of the Bastille, and was transacted in utter innocence of clerical tyranny or the insolence of hereditary office. "Memories almost their own," we are told, enlivened accounts of "the highroads covered with soldiers singing the Marseillaise. On the doorsteps sat women sewing the canvas for the tents. Sometimes there came a stream of men in red caps, carrying on the end of a slanted pike a bloodless head with hanging locks. The lofty tribune of the Convention towered above a cloud of dust, where enraged faces were howling cries of death. As one passed at midday near the lake of the Tuileries, one heard the shock of the guillotine, as though sheep were being axed."

Of all this, contemporaneous with their infancy, they are the inheritors, so that in the summer of 1845 they shudder under no tyranny, but take their ease in the garden, under the arbor, savoring the freedom to know. "Pécuchet, with a little stool beneath his feet, was reading aloud in his hollow voice, tirelessly, and only stopping to plunge his fingers in his snuff-box. Bouvard was listening to him with his pipe in his mouth, his legs apart, the top of his trousers unbuttoned."

For if there is one thing certain about the Enlightenment it is this, that the Revolution has democratized its benefits, and released, for any pair of copying-clerks, the assurances, the freedom for the intellect to play, that were once monopolies of the salon. And this is a capital fact, that Flaubert locates their enterprise so exactly at the semicentenary of civilization's new frontier, like a solemn commemorative ritual. Every man is at liberty now to be his own polymath. The mind of Europe has disclosed its secret contents and become a vast Coney Island in which all France is entitled to play.

And are they not all France? They are all France's notion of all France. Flaubert, the great connoisseur of received ideas, does not omit to register the most pervasive idea of all, that Frenchmen are by turns sensual and rational; worldly, lecherous and suave, or else rigorous, logical, prickly; the fat and the thin, the optimist and the pessimist; the Mediterranean and the Roman temperament, respectively. In dividing this vast cliché neatly into its elements, he commenced with their names, by which he set great store: Bouvard, a full round sound for the lips to caress; Pécuchet, crackling with the percussives of disciplined enunication. And their full names, each once recorded, each an absurd thundering litany of emblems and rallying-cries: François Denys Bartholomée Bouvard; Juste Romain Cyrille Pécuchet! See how Rome and la Belle France answer one another; Juste Romain Cyrille— justice, Roman law, and a saint celebrated (says the *Encyclopaedia Britannica*) for his "furious zeal"; François Denys Bartholomée—France, the patron saint of France, and the apostle with the most orotund name of all, whose Day, moreover, is intertwined with the most intimate processes of pre-Revolutionary French history. Of so much past do they bear the stamp; the one, therefore, "confident, irresponsible, open-handed; the other cautious, thoughtful, sparing."

All this has the mad precision of farce; and farce, sure enough, supplies the decor of page one. The empty street is described like an empty stage:

"Lower down, the Canal St. Martin, enclosed by two locks, showed the straight line of its inky water. Midway, there was a boat filled with timber, and on the banks two rows of barrels." Two men appear, simultaneously, from opposite sides, one tall, one short; one plump, one stringy; the hair of one curly blond, of the other straight and black. They reach the middle of the boulevard, and as if on cue sit down simultaneously on the same bench. And as if on cue, the machinery of recognition commences:

> In order to wipe their brows they removed their headgear, which each placed by his side; and the smaller man saw written in his neighbor's hat, "Bouvard"; while the latter easily made out in the cap of the individual wearing the frock-coat the word "Pécuchet."
>
> "Fancy that," he said. "We've both had the idea of writing our names in our hats."
>
> "Good heavens, yes; mine might be taken at the office."
>
> "The same with me; I work in an office too."

So insidiously plausible is this encounter that we are hardly sure whether we are in the domain of burlesque or not.

But burlesque of what? Why, of fiction. For behind that half-page we are to imagine a writer racking his brains for a plausible way to get the story started; we are to imagine the fussing over point of view; the agonizing over probabilities, since your French bourgeois does not, without some occasion, simply start talking to a total stranger; the wrestling with the sequence in which the characters are to be named, described, and set talking. We are to fancy (to transpose into modern terms) Jamesian beginnings, Faulknerian beginnings; the five-hundred-word draft crumpled in a melodrama of despair; the eight-thousand-word draft composed, pruned, retouched, ripped up; the half-written circuitous opening, with its easy meditations on chance and destiny, never completed; the dismal brooding; and the joy. For in a transport of joy our author has realized with what efficiency he can manage the recognition scene if only each character does something on which the other may remark; and what more plausible than the doffed hat; and what better calculated to promote the doffed hat from plausibility to certainty than a temperature of 90 degrees (precisely 33 degrees Centigrade; odd numbers look more authentic). And to ensure that the doffed hat initiates talk, let there be something written inside it (masterstroke!); and to kill more than one bird with this pellet, let exposition be combined with mechanism, and let what is written inside the hat be the wearer's name. For otherwise, the characters would have to volunteer their names, and it is difficult to devise a way of managing this.

Or perhaps we are to imagine nothing of this sort; but to imagine instead a writer of demotic cunning, by nature so perfectly attuned to idiocy that his imagination, the moment it is set the problem of introducing two characters, spontaneously stages the scene in this way. For postulate a mind which functions out of habit on a certain plane of plausible unreality, the plane for example on which the business of detective novelettes is transacted, and it will be effortlessly fecund in such devices for maneuvering personages and information over the page.

At any rate, this is what was concocted for us, in August 1874, by the most meticulous craftsman of prose fiction the world had ever seen, the man for whom a tale of provincial adultery had been the labor of five years. "I flounder," he wrote six days after beginning the writing of *Bouvard*, "I flounder, I erase, I despair. Last night I was violently sick to my stomach. But it will go forward; it *must* go forward! The difficulties of this work are petrifying. No matter; by hard labor I can vanquish them." And petrifying they were; for the task he had set for himself was nothing less than to achieve by labor effects comparable to those of appalling incompetence: the incompetence that supposes the mirror held up to nature when two lay figures seat themselves simultaneously and take off in synchrony their hats: the incompetence, in short, of fiction itself, which is endlessly *arranging* things. He will use fiction itself to vanquish fiction; he will arrange, and maneuver, and contrive, to such bland effect that no one will ever afterward be quite sure where contrivance began and serendipity left off. He will use with cunning every device of the merely facile novelist; and the result will be such a compendium of unreality that it will seem real.

What happens, then, when the timeless pair have completed their exchange on hats? Why, what would happen? thinks the skilled hack. They would look into each other's faces; and this is plainly our cue for personal descriptions, which Sir Walter Scott inserted so awkwardly (but we know better now). And so:

> Then they inspected one another.
> Bouvard's pleasant appearance quite charmed Pécuchet.
> His blue eyes, always half closed, smiled out of a rosy face. His trousers, buttoning at the side and wrinkling down over buckskin shoes, took the shape of his stomach.

And such are the resources of literary skill, we divine immediately that Bouvard is fat. These are sophisticated times; once Bouvard would have been

introduced as the stout man. It is the same with the conversation that soon
commences:

> Suddenly a drunken man zigzagged across the pavement, and they
> began a political discussion on the subject of the working classes.
> Their opinions were alike, except that Bouvard was perhaps more
> liberal-minded.

Or,

> The sight of this wedding-party led Bouvard and Pécuchet to talk
> of women, whom they declared flighty, perverse and obstinate.
> All the same, they were often better than men; though at other
> times they were worse. In short, it was best to live without them;
> and Pécuchet had remained single.

Or later, when the prostitute has strutted by with the soldier,

> Bouvard indulged in a smutty remark. Pécuchet grew very red
> and, doubtless to avoid replying, indicated with a glance that a
> priest was approaching.
> The ecclesiastic stalked down the avenue of thin young elms
> that studded the pavement, and when the three-cornered hat was
> out of sight Bouvard expressed his relief, for he hated Jesuits.
> Pécuchet, without absolving them altogether, showed some re-
> spect for religion.

We are given barely ten words of their dialogue; we can reconstruct it,
though, with ease. Our reconstruction will depend on the prime convention
of commercial fiction: that there is a little stock of standard dialogues on
given subjects—politics, domesticity, religion—which the reader by this time
knows as well as the author; and that a drunken man is a political object,
a wedding party a domestic object, and a priest a religious object, the mere
sight of which will initiate the dialogue appropriate to it. Flaubert, busily at
work behind this subversive enterprise of his, is leaving us the blanks to fill
in, by way of making three points: (1) that we know how to fill them in;
hence (2) that prose fiction consists of standard passages which the reader
soon learns to negotiate as he does a familiar stairway; and (3) that the
dimmest novel cannot compete, in obviousness, with middle-class life itself,
middle-class life in which people exchange responses a Flaubert can calculate
with Newtonian precision, and exchange these under the impression that
they are making conversation, by which man is distinguished from the brutes.

And this completes the Flaubertian circle, which being a circle brings together irreconcilable extremes: actual life, gravid, numinous, authentic; and, jejune, simian, rampant in the abeyance of all but the contriving faculty, commercial literature. The hack writer it seems, he is the supreme realist.

III

Flaubert's patient aping of commercial formulas is of course not confined to *Bouvard et Pécuchet*. Consider the dialogue between Emma Bovary and Léon:

> "I think there is nothing so admirable as sunsets," she resumed, "but especially by the side of the sea."
>
> "Oh, I adore the sea!" said Monsieur Léon.
>
> "And then, does it not seem to you," continued Madame Bovary, "that the mind travels more freely on this limitless expanse, the contemplation of which elevates the soul, gives ideas of the infinite, the ideal?"

In the *Dictionnaire des idées reçues* for which Flaubert amassed material over some three decades, we find:

> MER: N'a pas de fond. Image de l'infini.—Donne des grandes pensées.

A page later Emma has reached music:

> Emma continued: "And what music do you prefer?"
>
> "Oh, German music; that which makes you dream."

Again their conversation echoes the *Dictionnaire:*

> ALLEMANDS: Peuple de rêveurs (vieux).

Here, finally, are Emma and Léon on Poetry:

> "Has it ever occurred to you," Léon went on, "to come across some vague idea of your own in a book, some dim image that comes back to you from afar, and as the completest expression of your own slightest sentiment?"
>
> "I have experienced it," she replied.
>
> "That is why," he said, "I especially love the poets. I think verse more tender than prose, and that it moves far more easily to tears."
>
> "Still in the long run it is tiring," continued Emma. "Now I,

on the contrary, adore stories that rush breathlessly along, that frighten me. I detest commonplace heroes and moderate sentiments, such as there are in nature."

"In fact," observed the clerk, "these works, not touching the heart, miss, it seems to me, the true end of art. It is also sweet, amid all the disenchantments of life, to be able to dwell in thought among noble characters, pure affections, and pictures of happiness."

This happens not to echo the *Dictionnaire,* the entries in which, when they pertain to Literature or Poetry, are of the most curt and impatient description. It is easy to identify the kind of thing it does echo: it is a veritable checklist of things it is fashionable to think about literary enchantment. It is not, in fact, a really convincing bit of dialogue, so aware are we of the author's checklist. Emma and Léon are meant to be talking completely out of books, and Flaubert's dialogue is at its best when the books are at a little distance.

This is the unfailing charm of the *Dictionnaire des idées reçues,* that the books lie generally at a distance. The ideas there conveniently codified have been *reçues*—received, accepted—because of their inherent resonance with the honest middle-class soul, *anima naturaliter inepta.* "Vox populi, vox Dei," runs its portentous subtitle; and in 1850, the very year in which he was much later to place Bouvard and Pécuchet's speculations on the Social Contract and the Divine Right, he was explaining to a correspondent, how this book, "equipped with a fine preface to show how it was undertaken in order to guide the public back to tradition, order, and convention, and so arranged that the reader could never be sure if he was being made a fool of or not," had in fact a good chance of success; "car elle serait toute d'actualité." This "Catalogue des idées chic" admits different sorts of material, the author never having quite delimited its scope. Some of the entries reflect his private irritations; we can imagine the savagery with which he noted "PROSE: Easier to write than verse." Some reflect simple fatigue with the thing too often said: "FUNERAL: Of the deceased: And to think that I had dinner with him only a week ago!" Some codify medical lore: "NIGHTMARE: Comes from the stomach." But it is when it touches on the rhetoric of bourgeois omniscience that the conception grows transcendent. Thus of "EXTIRPATE" we are told that this verb is used only of heresies and corns, and of "ERECTION" that it is used only of monuments. Whether these remarks are descriptive or prescriptive we cannot tell. "MALEDICTIONS" are "given only by fathers." "MESSAGE" is "more noble than letter."

"IVORY" is used only of teeth, and "ALABASTER" of "the finest parts of the female body." And honest indignation makes for its target with untrammeled certainty. Certain things are to inspire our indignation: "s'indigner contre": waltzes, for example, and New Year's gifts. Others, a notch higher, we are to fulminate against: Flaubert's fine idiom is "tonner contre," though of "FULMINER" he remarks, "joli verbe." "Tonner contre" is the order whenever we are confronted with, for instance, the Baccalaureate, the Cuisine of the Midi, Duelling, Sybarites, Eclecticism and "EPOQUE (la nôtre)." At least twice, Flaubert brings our capacity for indignation to untranslatable apotheosis. Of "HIATUS" we receive his categorical imperative, "ne pas le tolerer." And as for the Pyramids, cunningly exploiting the placement of the French adjective to apotheosize Johnson's meditation on one stone to no purpose laid upon another, he levels them with a single blast of republican scorn: "PYRAMIDE: Ouvrage inutile."

The idea of arranging such things alphabetically came to Flaubert as early as 1843. Alphabetical arrangement suggests at once a useful book, a guide to conversation as the usual Dictionary is a guide to writing. We confront at once this difficulty, however, that when you are writing you can stop to look up words and no one will be the wiser, whereas when you are conversing it is hardly *comme il faut* to be referring constantly to a handbook as various subjects present themselves. We have thus the most useless useful book imaginable, since it is precisely when you need it that you cannot possibly consult it. So there inheres in the very conception a sort of Heisenberg's Principle, and a Platonic characterization of the supreme bourgeois, the very *Idea* of a bourgeois, equipped with this work in which he has invested a portion of his capital, but which can only benefit him on some pure plane of theory where the act of conversing is as abstract and timeless as the act of writing an Encyclopaedia article. So the first thing that the alphabetical arrangement does is plunge the entire work into absurdity. The second thing it does is supply just the discontinuity of surface that gave Flaubert such trouble in writing prose, permuting with dreary labor the three forms of the French past tense, balancing period against epigram, narrative with reflection. And the third thing we gather from the alphabetical arrangement is the scientific character of the work; it is finally, says M. Descharmes,

a sheaf of notes to which Flaubert has distilled his psychological and moral observations, the stupidities he heard repeated all around him, the characteristic gestures of people in given circumstances, all the lacunae and all the pretensions of cautious good sense, of bourgeoisdom in its most general form.

For Art, Flaubert wrote to George Sand, is not meant to portray exceptions; like Science itself, it is meant to portray things as they *always* are, in themselves, in their general nature, disengaged from all ephemeral contingency; and each article in the *Dictionary,* M. Descharmes notes, is the synthesized result of an indefinite number of particular observations, isolated presentations, phrases repeated on the same subject by people of different social and intellectual classes. Each definition supposes a vast documentation, amassed during years of patient listening (René Descharmes, *Autour de Bouvard et Pécuchet*).

It is therefore, finally, a handbook for novelists; Art tending toward the general and human behavior tending toward the cliché, we are back again to the fact that the supreme artist is the cliché expert and cannot do better than to imitate, as closely as he can, the procedures of the hack. If the *Dictionary* is useless for guiding conversation, it is useful for the writer; and the writer who used it was Flaubert himself, turning, it would seem from entry to entry precisely like a correspondence-school novelist. It was one of the tenets of the Enlightenment, that Art can be systematized, its long traditions having yielded a store of images and turns of phrase which we cannot do better than imitate. In the *Spectator* for May 28, 1711, there appeared an advertisement for a book of which three editions had sold out: "The Art of English Poetry, containing, I. Rules for making Verses. II. A Collection of the most natural, agreeable and sublime Thoughts, viz. Allusions, Similes, Descriptions and Characters of Persons and Things that are to be found in the best English Poets. III. A Dictionary of Rhymes." It is true that Flaubert's own *Dictionnaire* contains under "DICTIONARY" the entry, "Put together only for the ignorant," and under "DICTIONARY OF RHYMES," "S'en servir? honteux!" But he himself, on causing Bouvard to awaken from a deep slumber, would seem to have consulted his own compilation: "DORMIR (trop): épaissit le sang," and accordingly wrote, "Bouvard . . . was nervous on waking, since prolonged sleep may bring on apoplexy." Or, having Pécuchet lecture on Astronomy ("belle science très utile pour la marine"), Flaubert has him broach the topic by stating that sailors employ it on their voyages. Nor was it only *Bouvard and Pécuchet* that he composed in this way; M. Descharmes gives many pages of examples culled from *Madame Bovary* and *L'Education sentimentale,* and intimates that he could have done the same for *Un Coeur simple* as well.

Once we have seen *Le Dictionnaire des idées reçues* as a scientific compilation, only gathered, unlike the eighteenth-century poets' manuals, from the life rather than from other books, we are in a position to notice a highly peculiar phenomenon, to which Flaubert pointed the way in proposing to publish the *Dictionnaire* itself as a book. For clothed in the authority of print, complete with an elaborate preface, it would serve to authorize what it had begun by merely collecting. To set before the middle classes exactly what they think and say, in codified form, is to establish a feedback loop, and feedback may have either a positive sign, encouraging the phenomena it transmits, or a negative, diminishing them. It pleased Flaubert to imagine a nation of readers no one of whom would ever dare open his mouth again, for fear of uttering one of the phrases the Dictionary contained. But the book would have depended, for its comic effect, on flirting with the other possibility, positive feedback, a gloriously efficient standardization of bourgeois behavior, confirmed, launched, invested in Print, bursting with confidence, fulminating as never before against Sybarites, Eclecticisme and Epoque (la nôtre), or exchanging with now indestructible conviction its affirmations on Health (too much of it, cause of sickness), Homer (never existed; famous for his laughter) and Humidity (cause of all illness).

For already a surprising amount of this lore has leaked into the popular mind out of printed pages; the non-existence of Homer, for example, was a scholarly notion before it became the property of the Vox Populi. We may go further; Emma Bovary herself would have been impossible without books, quantities of books, books of the very sort that *Madame Bovary* itself approximates, and filled with dialogue very like her dialogues with her husband and her several lovers. *Madame Bovary* is a novel about a woman who has read novels, kept as close as possible to the plot, the characterization, and the dialogue of the sort of novels she has read.

IV

Once again we have returned to the center of the maze, where life and art are uncertain which copies the other. We note the continuity of Flaubert's themes; from first to last he is the great student of cultural feedback, writing books about what books do to the readers of books, one eye always on the sort of thing his own book is going to do to its own reader. We note too that in *Madame Bovary* the conception is still essentially primitive. Emma has transposed the themes and sentiments of novels into life, with the lack of success one might expect. Flaubert's narrative, that is, assigns causes; if the hack is the supreme realist, it may be because real people have been modeling their actions on the imaginative products of hacks. Certainly, for the *Dictionary* entries on which he based the discourses of Emma and Léon, Flaubert need not have listened to thousands of Emmas and Léons; he could have gotten "Sea: image of the infinite" directly out of other novels, and perhaps did.

In *Bouvard et Pécuchet,* however, there is no question of making a scapegoat out of second-rate fiction. On the contrary, as we have seen, the book itself aspires *directly* to the idiot accuracy of second-rate fiction. The two heroes, furthermore, aspire directly to the utter insanities of scientific genius. We have not before us a travesty of anything. We have the thing itself. We hear of them, for example, checking by experiment the assertion that animal heat is developed by muscular contraction. Bouvard enters a tepid bath, armed with a thermometer:

> "Move your limbs!" said Pécuchet.
> He moved them without any effect on the temperature. "It's decidedly cold."
> "I'm not warm myself," replied Pécuchet, also starting to shiver. "But work your pelvic members! Make them stir!"
> Bouvard opened his thighs and waggled his buttocks, rocked his stomach, puffed like a whale, then looked at the thermometer, which all the time was falling.
> "I can't make it out; yet my limbs are moving."
> "Not enough."
> And he went on with his gymnastics.

He keeps this up for three hours, while the thermometer falls to 53 degrees.

This seems imbecilic; but certainly, if the temperature of the bath had risen, even fractionally, they would not seem imbecilic at all; they would have been the co-discoverers of Bouvard's Law. Equal absurdity menaced the researches of the man who inserted brass wires into the spinal marrow of dead frogs, and allowed their feet to touch an iron plate, to see if the dead legs would move. But they did move, and the phenomenon was called Galvanism, and Charlotte Brontë was enabled to write of a melancholy hero that the heroine's approach "always galvanized him into a new and spasmodic life"; so Galvani and his dead frog contributed to literature as well as to science.

That Bouvard and Pécuchet are easily dismissed as absurd just because they fail is a highly important principle. Aesthetically considered, Galvani with his dead frogs, all hanging by brass hooks from an iron wire, their legs twitching in concert, is equally absurd, irremediably absurd, dismally open to the charge that man created in God's image is on this occasion passing his time in a very strange way. It is facts that are absurd; nothing is more absurd than the very conception of a *fact,* an isolated datum of experience,

something to find out, isolated from all the other things that there are to be
found out; the twitch, under certain conditions, of a dead frog's legs, or the
presence, in an optimum Galvanic Battery, of thirty pieces of silver. Before
encyclopaedias were invented, facts had to be invented, the very concept of
a fact: fact as the atom of experience, for the encyclopaedist to set in its
alphabetical place, in dramatic testimony to the realization that no one knows
in what other place to set it, or under what circumstances it may be wanted
again. The *N.E.D.* does not find the word "fact" used in this way before
1632. Before then, a fact was a thing done, *factum,* part of a continuum of
deed and gesture.

And it is facts, at last, that Flaubert sets out to wither. The critic Anthony Thorlby has described very well how Flaubert isolates detail from
detail to this end:

> Each fact is isolated in turn, with sufficient detachment from the
> next to emphasize the absence of any real perspective between
> one kind of fact and another. And since facts presented all from
> the same point of view inevitably fall into some kind of perspec-
> tive and assume a real meaning as a whole, this has required a
> constant interruption of stylistic continuity, by means of change
> in tense, person, subject, tone, direct and reported speech, and
> whatever other device of syntax and vocabulary Flaubert could
> muster. That is why virtually every phrase set him a new problem
> in expression: how to turn it aesthetically to bring out its essential
> sameness as a fact.

(Gustave Flaubert)

For he is busily reproducing in a fabulous narrative the inanity of the Encyclopaedia; and Mr. Thorlby ends by comparing the whole heroic book to
"an immensely complex and comprehensive mathematical formula which
makes everything equal zero."

Scholars and thinkers have been butts of satire ever since Aristophanes
disclosed Socrates suspended in a basket, to bring him nearer the clouds. It
is not, however, with facts that the comic Socrates trifles, since the very
notion of a fact is not to be invented for two thousand years. He trifles with
Reason, making the worse argument appear the better. By the time of the
next great academic satire, the third book of *Gulliver's Travels,* humanity
has encountered Facts; indeed Gullliver's mind is totally given over to fact,
and so is the ant-like energy of Swift's prose, moving crumbs of information
hither and thither with an activity exactly proportioned to their magnitude.
The scientists in Lagado, however, are not, for better or worse, preoccupied

with Facts but with Projects. Swift ridicules their activities, not their methods: their proposals to extract sunlight from cucumbers, or food from excrement, seeking to reverse the direction of processes that have flowed in their present direction since the world was made, with the inevitibility of great rivers. These people are doing something foolish; it remains open to learning to do things that are wise. Another century and a half, however, and Flaubert will be suggesting that nothing remains open to learning at all, nothing but the cataloguing of its own inanities.

Having failed to lead their pupils Victor and Victorine into paths of virtue and contemplation, Bouvard and Pécuchet determine on schemes of adult education, so grandiose that their speedy ruin brings total disgrace; and everything having come to pieces in their hands, they resolve to copy as in the old days. So, at a two-seated desk, specially constructed, Flaubert meant them to live out their days, side by side, making up out of all the books that they have read what can best be described as an Encyclopaedia. Hear Descharmes's description of the unwritten second volume:

> They would copy above all for the pleasure of copying, and the high comedy of their labor they would doubtless never suspect. Thence would come peace, even intellectual tranquillity, for this mechanical labor would serve to disentangle the confusion of their ideas, to classify the contradictory notions with which their narrow minds buzz, to supply them with ready-made judgments, generally vouched for by some authoritative name. And in their inexhaustible desire to learn, they would make daily additions to this *Encyclopédie grotesque* with further reading and new annotations, happy at last to be safe from the perils of putting theory into practice, and to be storing up, with no notion of using it, an archive of misdirected learning.

Here the serpent commences to swallow his tail; for *Bouvard and Pécuchet* was at last to commence displaying, in ordered form, its own vast materials, distilled from Flaubert's eleven thousand pages of notes. It is a book made of facts, and facts reduced, by every artifice Flaubert could devise, to an extraordinary blank plane of autonomous factuality; and it was finally to spew forth again its own sources, summarized, digested, annotated. Under "CONTRADICTIONS," we should have read seven opinions on the time it takes a body to putrefy completely, ranging from forty years to fifteen months; under "BELLES IDEES," Bernardin St. Pierre's statement that the melon was divided into slices by nature to facilitate its consumption by families; under "ANECDOTES" the case history of a Marine Officer's twenty years' constipation; and under I do not know what heading, the declaration of the Bishop of Metz, in December 1846, that the floods of the Loire in that year were due to the excesses of the Press and the imperfect observation of the Sabbath.

So fact, eleven thousand pages of fact, having buttressed fiction, fiction was at length to issue in fact, the very characters in the novel perfecting and completing their author's researches. So, with the classic simplicity which like everything classic verges on the banal, the clerks were to come full circle, copying as they had begun by copying, and the generic novel full circle, a cliché of plot superintending their immense amassement of clichés. So the scientific character of the novel, its quest for the ideal type, the general law, was to turn upon itself like a haruspex scrutinizing his own entrails. And so, finally, the intellectual progress of the human race was to be completed in miniature during the thirty-odd years of Bouvard and Pécuchet's researches; for having commenced, like the Greeks, heroic men, nearly mythological in their zeal, a new Cadmus, a new Pisistratus, they were to finish like neo-Christians, monastic men, in a new dark ages of the intellect, side by side at their manuscripts, sifting, preserving; and having commenced, like the first men, tilling the fields, they were to end like the last men, making Encyclopaedias: inheriting, so, the new heaven and the new earth of the Enlightenment.

VICTOR BROMBERT

Madame Bovary:
The Tragedy of Dreams

Ah! que notre verre est petit, mon
Dieu! que notre soif est grande!
—Par les Champs et par les grèves

THE MYTH OF THE "PENSUM"

Several myths continue to distort our perspective on *Madame Bovary*. Flaubert set so much store by technical perfection, he so vociferously denied the intrinsic merits of a "subject" and proclaimed instead the supreme importance of style, he complained so bitterly of the tortures of composition and of the desperate baseness of his Norman setting, that it is only too easy to believe that the novel was for him primarily an exercise in self-discipline, perhaps even a much needed therapy to rid himself of his disheveled romanticism. The subject had supposedly been suggested to Flaubert ("Why don't you write the story of Delaunay?") to help him achieve literary sanity, after Louis Bouilhet and Maxime Du Camp, summoned for a solemn consultation, advised him to throw the manuscript of *La Tentation de saint Antoine* into the fire.

Many comments in Flaubert's *Correspondance* seem to substantiate these views. His ideal, as he confided it to Louise Colet, was to write a "livre sur rien," a book "about nothing at all," with almost no subject—a book, in short, which would exist by virtue of the "inner strength of its style." In thus posing as an axiom the nonexistence of intrinsically "beautiful" or

From *The Novels of Flaubert: A Study of Themes and Techniques.* © 1966 by Princeton University Press.

"ugly" subjects, and in affirming his conviction that style, all by itself, is "an absolute way of seeing things," Flaubert heralded significant modern notions, and seemed to point the way to some of the truly original achievements of later fiction. His own technical prowess, his supreme dedication to his art, his exigent standards all explain why he has assumed an almost exemplary stature. *Madame Bovary* came indeed to be considered a paragon of the genre. Writers admired it as one admires a lesson. For Henry James, Flaubert was the "novelist's novelist." For Zola, *Madame Bovary* represented the *roman type.*

To be considered a "novelist's novelist" is of course an enviable reputation. But the very expression seems to imply a somewhat theoretical, overly deliberate and even "cold" or lifeless creation. Henry James was filled with professional admiration for Flaubert, but he also found *Madame Bovary* morally shallow. This indeed seems to have been the slowly acquired fame of the novel: it was considered an astonishing feat of literary organization, displaying an unusual mastery of structure and texture, but a work that did not spring from the author's heart, whose subject even ran counter to the author's temperament—in short, a self-imposed task! And here again, numerous remarks in Flaubert's letters seemed to confirm these feelings. "One must write more coldly," he explains to Louise Colet, who was herself rather given to effusive writing. "Let us beware of this kind of over-excitement which is called inspiration." His cult of impassibility led him to paradoxes: "The less one feels a thing, the better one is able to express it." And still while writing *Madame Bovary:* "I am truly tired of this work; it is a real *pensum* for me now." This feeling of self-inflicted, yet stubbornly continued punishment is one of the strongest impressions left by Flaubert's letters. Thus it can be said that the *Correspondance,* admirable though it is, ultimately rendered the author a disservice. Not taking into account that most of these letters which evoke the drudgery of his work were written late at night, when Flaubert was exhausted by the unending battle with words, readers have all too easily adopted the stereotyped view of a stubborn and masochistic novelist engaged in an impressive but sterile literary exercise.

The truth is somewhat different. Not only are there sources other than the Delamare story (the *Mémoires de Madame Ludovica,* for instance, which tell of the adulteries and financial difficulties of Mme Pradier, whom Flaubert frequented long before the unfavorable verdict against *La Tentation de saint Antoine*), but the theme of *Madame Bovary,* and in particular the central motif of adultery, had been a major obsession of Flaubert ever since his adolescence. *Passion et vertu,* written at the age of sixteen years, is indeed a striking miniature version of *Madame Bovary.* Based on an actual case history reported in the *Gazette des Tribunaux,* this short "conte philosophique" tells of the adulterous Mazza and of her seducer Ernest, who is clearly a first version of Emma Bovary's lover Rodolphe. Mazza surrenders to her passion with such a total frenzy that Ernest, almost afraid (in this he announces Léon) decides to abandon her. Desperate, Mazza kills her husband and her children, and finally takes her own life by poison. The story was written in 1837, some fifteen years before Flaubert set to work on *Madame Bovary.* The subject can therefore hardly be called new or alien to the author's more permanent preoccupations.

But it is not so much the subject as it is the themes and the psychological drama which sharply prefigure the later novel. In *Passion et vertu,* literature also serves as a purveyor of illusions. The lover also plans his seduction cold-bloodedly, and almost cruelly. As for the adulterous Mazza, her "immense desires" obviously transcend the mere gratification of the senses. A metaphysical malaise is at the root of her yearning for excess. The flesh and its pleasures turn out to be an immense disappointment. The ennui she experiences stems from a hunger which can never be satisfied. Flaubert in fact compares Mazza to those "starved people who are unable to nourish themselves." Her longing for the inaccessible ultimately leads to dehumanization ("Elle n'avait plus rien d'une femme"), to madness and to an inescapable attraction to the ultimate absolute, death.

The significance of a text such as this can scarcely be stressed too much. Not only were some of the key themes of *Madame Bovary* (sterile but frenetic eroticism, sensuous longing for the absolute, flirtation with death) already fully sketched out in Flaubert's mind in 1837, but this long gestation should encourage critics to subordinate considerations of sheer technical accomplishments to the deeper meanings of the work. *Madame Bovary* is hardly an artificial or arbitrary exercise—even though Flaubert himself claimed that the subject was unpalatable to him. It corresponds in fact to some of the basic patterns of his imagination.

FIRST IMPRESSIONS

The opening chapter describes Charles Bovary's first day at school. The young boy is so clumsy, his attire so ludicrous, that he almost automatically provokes the cruel hilarity of the other students. The author stresses the boy's pathetic inelegance, his timidity, his ineffectual good will, his trancelike docility and resignation. All the physical details of the scene serve to bring out Charles's ineptness as he enters into the somnolent classroom atmosphere. He at first remains in the corner behind the door, almost invisible:

the first impression is one of unredeemed insignificance and self-effacement. His hair cut short on his forehead suggests obtuseness. His jacket, which seems too tight around the armholes, suggests constriction and limitations. His stout, unshined hob-nailed shoes express the boy's dullness and awkwardness. His stiff countenance—he does not dare to cross his legs or lean on his elbows, and he listens "attentive as if at a sermon"—conveys an almost servile submissiveness to authority. But it is above all the boy's headgear, a pitiful, unsightly combination of shako, bearskin, billycock hat and cotton nightcap, which sums up, in its tiers and superstructure, the layers and monumentality of the wearer's unintelligence. The scene ends when Charles, as a punishment for having innocently provoked mirth and class disorder, is told to conjugate twenty times "*ridiculus sum.*"

Readers have often wondered why Flaubert began his novel as though Charles Bovary were the central character. The opening scene seems to have no bearing on Emma's tragedy, and Emma herself, of course, does not yet exist on Charles's horizon. Moreover, the very point of view of this first scene remains puzzling. The collective personal pronoun *nous* ("We were in class when . . .") evidently communicates the proper tone of childhood reminiscences. But this point of view is not sustained, and very soon an anonymous author's perspective replaces this most personal voice. It seems hardly conceivable that so careful a craftsman as Flaubert should not have noticed the discrepancy, and that the curiously oblique approach should be the result of inadvertence.

The mere fact that the novel does not end with Emma's death, and that once again, in the final pages, Charles comes to stand out in the foreground, should be sufficient indication that he is not a peripheral character. He is not only the permanent victim of a fate he cannot control any more than he can control the cruel laughter which greets his first appearance at school, he also serves to bring out the basic themes of blindness and incommunicability. For Charles "sees" Emma (the structure of the novel ensures that our first glimpse of Emma passes through Charles's consciousness), but he is constitutionally unable to *understand* her. Flaubert denies himself the facile prerogatives of the omniscient author. We are gradually led to the unique perspective of Emma. But this is achieved progressively: Charles serves as a transition. The mysterious "nous" can thus be considered part of those subtle modulations whereby Flaubert guides our vision to the very center of tragedy, while exploiting all the possibilities of an ironic distance.

It would be a mistake, however, to reduce Charles to a purely functional role. A careful reading of the text, as well as of the available scenarios, reveals an intrinsic interest in the character. His early courtship of Emma, at the

Bertraux farm, is treated with obvious warmth. His nascent sensations of love—associated with the sights and smells of country life—are almost touchingly presented. The various drafts, moreover, insist on human traits which are far from ludicrous. Young Charles is a "gentle nature, sensitive as a young man should be." His love for his wife is deep and tragic, and it bestows upon him an undeniable stature: "ADORES his wife, and of the three men who sleep with her, he is certainly the one who loves her most [—This is what has to be stressed]." Remarks such as these clearly indicate that the very conception of the character justified his central position in the opening chapter.

More important, however, than either the technical function (transitional perspective) or the human interest of Charles Bovary, is the thematic value of his initial appearance in the schoolroom. The systematic use of character in the service of themes is indeed one of the salient traits of Flaubert's work. And not only characters, but objects also assume a primary thematic importance. Charles's cap is thus not merely an absurd personal appendage, but its heteroclite aspect, its senseless accumulation and confusion of styles, symbolize an abdication of the human spirit in the face of pure phenomena. The cap, in its very multiplication of shapes, represents the essence of meaninglessness and incongruity. Such an extension of meaning to objects is clearly one of Flaubert's conscious methods. In the description of the cap which appears in one of the earliest drafts, Flaubert states that it was a "synthesis" of all the ugly and uncomfortable headgears in existence, that it was one of those pitiful things "in which matter itself seems sad." And the cap is far from an isolated example. The *pièce montée* served as a dessert at the wedding (with its porticoes, colonnades, nutshell boats, lakes of jam, and its cupid balancing itself in a chocolate swing) or the improvised therapeutic apparatus for curing club feet (with its eight pounds of iron, wood, leather, nuts and screws) fulfill similar functions.

The opening scene of the novel is thus not so much an introduction into a given character's private world, as an indirect statement of motifs and themes. The pathos of incommunicability (the teacher at first cannot even understand Charles's name), the constriction of a narrow world here symbolized by school routines, the loneliness of the individual in the face of a harassing group, and above all, the themes of inadequacy and failure, are all set forth in these first pages. The entire beginning is under the triple sign of inadequacy, drowsiness and a passively accepted necessity. The work which ends with Charles's lamentable thought, "It is the fault of fatality!" appropriately begins on a note of resignation.

RHYTHM AND SYMBOLIC DETAILS

Two Flaubertian characteristics stand out immediately: the importance of significant details and a blocklike composition involving a double rhythm. The first chapter typically provides a *scene* (the arrival of Charles in school), and then immerges the reader into a continuum of time: Charles's youth, his adolescence, his education, his career, his first marriage. This double perspective, dramatic and narrative, constitutes the basic Flaubertian unit, and these units, in turn, provide the permanent tension between temporal immediacy and the denseness and elasticity of time. Flaubert may not have thought in terms of chapter units (the chapter divisions appear only in the final manuscript sent to the printer), but he did plan his novel around a series of key scenes and episodes: the agricultural show; the first seduction scene or *baisade,* as he crudely puts it in his outlines; the visit to the priest. The staggering number of outlines, the infinite patience with which Flaubert copied and elaborated them, is clear testimony to the importance of careful plotting in *Madame Bovary.* "*All depends on the outline,*" he asserts to Louise Colet. And, even more significantly, he has this advice to give to his friend Ernest Feydeau: "books are not made like babies, but like pyramids, with a premeditated plan, by placing huge blocks one above the other."

Thus each chapter centers on one major subject and could easily be given a relevant title: chapter 1: the childhood and studious youth of Charles; chapter 2: the meeting with Emma; chapter 3: the marriage proposal; chapter 4: the wedding; chapter 5: the Bovary house in Tostes; chapter 6: the education of Emma; chapter 7: the routine of married life; chapter 8: the Vaubyessard ball; chapter 9: Emma's nervous illness. And the same double rhythm of narration and description is maintained throughout. Almost every chapter contains a central scene or tableau: the visit to the sick farmer, the first impression of Emma, the wedding feast, the famous ball scene, the description of the daily meals. The unique act is thus juxtaposed with the daily routine, until the two seem to merge in a pattern of repetition and uniformity. Percy Lubbock's distinction between "scenic" and "panoramic" elements in *Madame Bovary* conveniently points to the author's binocular vision; but it is a simplification, for it fails to take into account the more profound rhythmic patterns which are concerned not only with spatial, but with temporal perspectives. Georges Poulet's phenomenological approach, stressing alternating movements of contraction and expansion, brings us closer to the fundamental movements of the novel.

As for Flaubert's love of descriptive detail, it is probably the one element in his work that has met with the most misunderstanding. Barbey d'Aurevilly summed up many contemporary reactions when he termed Flaubert an "enragé descripteur." The brothers Goncourt similarly were disturbed by the importance of "props" which, they felt, choked his characters and were largely responsible for the soulless quality of the novel. Such reactions cannot be attributed merely to professional jealousy or critical nearsightedness. Many readers continue to be disturbed by Flaubert's apparently gratuitous fascination with material realities, and particularly with the life of objects.

The functional nature of the Flaubertian "detail" is perhaps best illustrated, early in the novel, in the pages which provide our first glimpses of Emma. During Charles's first visit she pricks her fingers while sewing, and repeatedly puts them to her mouth to suck them. In another characteristic pose, she stands motionless, with her forehead against the window, looking into the garden. The two basic traits of her character are clearly brought out: sensuousness and the propensity to dream. (The act of sucking a bleeding finger obviously had strong erotic associations for Flaubert: in his scenarios, he has Emma suck Léon's slightly wounded finger, and this gesture supposedly characterizes her increasing sexual frenzy.) Thus a number of details, during Charles's first encounters with her, betray Emma's temperament: her full, fleshy lips that she has a habit of biting when silent (the French verb *mordillonner* is far more suggestive); the soft down on the back of her neck which the wind seems to caress; the small beads of perspiration on her bare shoulders; her particular way of throwing her head back in order to drink the almost empty glass of curaçao, her lips pouting, her neck straining, while with the tip of her tongue she attempts to lick in feline fashion the few remaining drops.

Even her languorous manner of speaking, the modulations of her voice which seem to lead to a murmur, her half-closed eyelids as her thoughts appear to wander—all these suggest a strong erotic potential which finds its first symbolic awakening during the dance ritual at the Vaubyessard ball. The waltz (considered immoral by the Imperial prosecutor) sweeps Emma into a whirlwind of sensations, as she surrenders to the promiscuity of the dance. Here too, the details are all chosen with care: the dance begins slowly, but soon the tempo increases; Emma's dress catches against the trousers of her partner as their feet "commingled"; a torpor seizes her, and the movement becomes increasingly accelerated, until Emma, panting, almost faints, and has to lean back against the wall "covering her eyes with her hand." The obvious sexual symbolism is proof not only of the purposefulness with which Flaubert selects his detail, but reveals the extremely powerful sexual undertones of the novel which—if one is to judge by the outlines and scenarios—Flaubert prudently toned down in his final draft. For in his scenarios, he stresses almost obsessively, and with considerable crudeness of thought and of language, the increasingly morbid sensuality of Emma. This sensuality extends beyond her character, it invades the entire world of *Madame Bovary*. According to Flaubert's sketches, Charles—after Emma's death—was to suffer from an "unhealthy love," whipped on by retrospective sexual jealousy: "amour malsain—excité par celui des autres—d'actrice—envie de la baiser."

The significant, carefully plotted detail is, however, not limited to character analysis. Indeed, this is one of its lesser functions. From the very outset, it serves as a "relative" symbol. The flat fields around the Bertaux farm, stretching their great surfaces until they fade into the gloom of the sky, represent the very monotony of experience to which Emma seems condemned. The horse's movement of fright as Charles reaches the farm almost assumes the value of a warning. One may prefer to call these "relative" symbols, because symbolism as practiced by Flaubert is rarely absolute in kind (pointing to a system of universal correspondences), but almost always of a strictly literary nature, fulfilling a dramatic or thematic role. Its function can be premonitory or proleptic, as when Emma, watching the dark clouds from her window, sees them gather and roll ominously in the direction of Rouen. Similarly, when Charles carries his former wife's bridal bouquet up to the attic, Emma wonders what would happen to her own after she died. (Later she herself destroys her bouquet.) An entire moral climate can be evoked by means of such details. The street organ brings to Emma airs played "elsewhere" (in elegant theaters and salons), but transposed to the constricted atmosphere of Tostes. The unglamorous contrast is further stressed by the coarseness of the man who turns the handle, by his well-aimed long squirts of brown saliva.

The exploitation of details for ironic contrasts seems almost a perverse pleasure with Flaubert; he sometimes carries it to cruel extremes. Thus Homais, when a proper tomb for Emma is discussed, suggests a temple of Vesta or a "mass of ruins." Charles finally opts in favor of a mausoleum which on the two main sides is to have "a spirit bearing an extinguished torch." It is easy to see, however, how close the use of such contrasts comes to a moral commentary. When Flaubert refers to the mud on Emma's boots as the "crotte des rendez-vous" (the "mud of the rendezvous"); when he has the beadle, in the cathedral, point out to the lovers a piece of statuary which is supposedly "a perfect representation of nothingness" and exhort them to look at the "Last Judgment" and the "condemned" in Hell-flames—one can hardly speak of the author's lack of intervention, of his impassibility! At times, the symbolic detail serves as an ironic punctuation, as it almost graphically plots the stages of a moral evolution. The plaster statue of a priest which adorns the Bovary garden in Tostes soon loses its right foot; later, white scabs appear on its face where the plaster has scaled off; and during the moving to their new home in Yonville, the plaster priest falls from the cart and is dashed into a thousand fragments. The gradual destruction of the ecclesiastical figure parallels the gradual disintegration of their marriage. Finally, the apparently gratuitous detail can have both a prophetic and a seductive value: on her trip to the convent, young Emma eats from painted plates that tell the story of Mademoiselle de La Vallière, the famous favorite of Louis XIV. Even the seemingly insignificant fact that the explanatory legends of this glamorous destiny are chipped by the scratches of knives (how many travelers have stopped at the same inn and eaten from the same plates!) tends to orient the reader's mind toward a "moral" interpretation.

"One eats a great deal in Flaubert's novels," observes Jean-Pierre Richard in his brilliant essay. It would seem indeed that Flaubert had an alimentary obsession. In an amusing letter to his friend Louis Bouilhet, he himself comments on this gastronomic imagination. "It is a strange thing how the spectacle of nature, far from elevating my soul toward the Creator, excites my stomach. The ocean makes me dream of oysters, and last time I crossed the Alps, a certain leg of chamois [antelope] I had eaten four years earlier at the Simplon, gave me hallucinations." Food plays an extraordinary role in his novels: feasts, orgies, bourgeois meals, peasant revels. This concern for appetite and digestion corresponds unquestionably, as Richard suggests, to the larger themes of his work: the "appetite" for the inaccessible, the voracious desire to *possess* experience, the preoccupation with metamorphoses, the tragedy of indigestion, and ultimately the almost metaphysical sense of nausea as the mind becomes aware that not to know everything is to know nothing. The very essence of *bovarysme* seems involved in this frustrated gluttony.

In *Madame Bovary,* food, the ritual of meals, deglutition and rumination play a particularly important role. One would almost be tempted to explicate the entire novel in terms of its gastronomic and digestive imagery. Sensuousness (old Rouault's taste for rare legs of lamb), a penchant for debauched sexuality (Emma licking the drops of curaçao, the drops of sauce dripping from the senile lips of the lecherous old duc de Laverdière), but above all a certain quality of vulgarity are conveyed. The Rabelaisian wedding feast—sixteen hours of eating and drinking, coarse jests and bawdy songs—is a true festival of rustic rowdiness and bad taste, the crowning symbol of which is the pretentious and utterly grotesque wedding cake. Similarly, the feast of the agricultural show, with its dirty plates and animal-like promiscuity, serves primarily to describe an atmosphere of chaos and gross inelegance.

In contrast to these plebeian *ripailles* stands the gastronomic supper at the Vaubyessard ball, with its delicately blended emanations of truffles, aromatic viands, rare flowers and fine linen. The silver dish-covers, the cut crystal, the champagne—all contribute here to the impression of urbane refinement, and sets up in Emma, through whose consciousness the entire scene is viewed, the basic tension of the novel. Her background and her lofty dreams come into such evident clash that she is almost compelled to *negate* the one or the other. Emma's choice is typical: "in the refulgence of the present moment, her entire past life, so distinct until then, faded away completely, and she almost doubted having lived it." The entire episode at the Vaubyessard ball has—we are told—made "a hole" in her life. And it is revealing that the awareness of this sudden disappearance of a given reality coincides with the degustation of a maraschino ice which voluptuously melts in her mouth.

The common onion soup which awaits her upon her return to Tostes is an ironic reminder of a reality which refuses to be thus negated. After merging with, and even symbolizing, Emma's growing dreams of luxury and passion, alimentary images point again to the vulgarity and triteness of her environment. And it is not only a specific ugliness, but the odious quality of existence itself which is brought out through images of rumination. Flaubert—witness the names of *Bov*ary and *Bouv*ard—is haunted by the bovine image. Repeatedly, Emma is repelled by her husband's eating habits, by the gurgling noises he makes when taking soup, or by his way of cleaning his teeth with his tongue. Just as his mastication seems to make impossible any contact between his love and her needs, so Bournisien's laborious digestion stresses his inadequacy as a priest when he fails to intuit her desperate condition.

Meals and digestive processes thus punctuate a monotonous existence which condemns Emma to an imprisonment in the self. The very rhythm of mediocrity is conveyed by cycles of alimentation, until finally the process of eating becomes a symbol of habit: "It was a habit among other habits, like a predictable dessert after the monotony of dinner." The act of setting the table is the drab ritual of life itself, with its eternal repetition and sameness. And, as if to emphasize the meaninglessness of this routine, Homais interrupts the Bovary meals regularly every evening, at 6:30, with his pompous presence and preposterous chatter.

Ultimately, the mealtimes come to symbolize Emma's utter dejection, as all the "bitterness of existence" seems served up on her plate. The smell of the boiled beef mixes with the whiffs of sickliness that arise from her soul. The image of the plate combines, in this context, the finite and the infinite:

"toute l'amertume de l'existence"—but reduced to, and confined within the petty circle of her own monotonous life. All living becomes an endless erosive consumption. Food and waste (or disease) are indeed repeatedly brought into juxtaposition: the kitchen smells penetrate into the consulting room, and the coughing of the patients can be heard in the kitchen. The alimentary metaphor conveys the reality of life itself:

> Puisque la portion vécue avait été mauvaise, sans doute ce qui restait à *consommer* serait meilleur.

> Il connaissait l'existence humaine tout du long, et il s'y *attablait* sur les deux coudes avec sérénité.

The verb *consommer* has, of course, a double meaning: beyond the alimentary image there is also the idea of waste and destruction. Ironically, Emma's very death is provoked by *swallowing* poison, and the first symptoms of her agony are those of major indigestion.

Even more ironic is the victory of Existence over Tragedy itself: life simply continues, mediocre and indifferent. Flaubert exploits alimentary images with the same bitterness that makes him grant Homais the Legion of Honor at the end of the novel. After Emma almost throws herself out the attic window following Rodolphe's desertion, she is caught again by the sickening routine of life: "she had to go down to sit at the table." She tries to eat, but the food chokes her. "Et il fallut descendre"—the very dreariness of life's continuity is conveyed by this call to join her husband at the dinner table. So also, life continues during her very agony: Homais, who cannot let slip by an occasion to entertain a celebrity, invites Doctor Larivière for lunch. (The very pedantry of Homais manifests itself earlier through his love for all manners of "recipes.") And at the end of the wake, Homais and Bournisien enjoy cheese, a large roll and a bottle of brandy in the very presence of the corpse ("puis ils mangèrent et trinquèrent, tout en ricanant un peu"). The novel ends with old Rouault's reassurance that, despite Emma's death, Charles will continue to receive his yearly turkey!

PATTERNS OF IMAGERY: HER DREAMS TOO HIGH, HER HOUSE TOO NARROW

Flaubert takes cruel satisfaction in ironic contrasts. Many of them are set up in a somewhat obvious fashion: the Bovary dog-cart and the elegant carriages of the guests at the Vaubyessard ball; Charles's smugness and Emma's frustration; her exaltations and her moments of torpor; the alternations of ardor and frigidity; Emma's vibrating body still tingling from the caresses, while her lover, a cigar between his lips, is mending a broken bridle! At times, the antithesis tends to be more subtle: the knotty articulations of a peasant hand appear on the very page where the lovers' fingers intertwine.

These planned juxtapositions do, however, point to the heart of the subject. They emphasize the basic theme of incompatibility. Their implicit tensions stress a fundamental state of *divorce* at all levels of experience. But they also fulfill a dramatic function. If Charles's father happens to be a squanderer and an almost professional seducer, if Charles himself, while still married to his first wife, is drawn to Emma because she represents a forbidden and inaccessible love, these ironies are part of an effective technique of "preparation." And these very anticipatory devices—whether prophetic in a straightforward or an ironic fashion—are in turn related to the theme of "fate" which Flaubert propounds with characteristic ambiguity. "C'est la faute de la fatalité!" is Charles's pathetic, yet moving final comment. But the notion of "fatality" is of course one of the most belabored Romantic clichés; Charles's exclamation carries its own condemnation, at the same time that it implies a debunking of the tragic ending of the novel. Rodolphe, writing his cowardly letter of rupture to Emma, hits upon the expression: "accuse only fate"—and he congratulates himself on his skillful use of a word "which is always effective"! The expression coincides with the very devaluation of love. Similarly, Charles blames the pitiful outcome of the club-foot operation on a malevolent destiny ("La fatalité s'en était mêlée"), when in reality only his hopeless incompetence is at fault. Yet who is to deny that, in addition to elements of pathos, the novel constantly suggests an all-pervasive determinism: Emma's temperament, the character of Charles, the effects of heredity, the erosive quality of small-town life, the noxious influence of books, the structure of the novel itself?

Flaubert significantly devotes an entire chapter to Emma's education in the convent. Her private symbolism of love, mysticism and death is determined by this experience. The "mystic languor" provoked by the incense, the whisperings of the priest, the very metaphors comparing Christ to a celestial lover, predispose her to confuse sensuous delights and spiritual longings. The convent is Emma's earliest claustration, and the solicitations from the outside world, whether in the form of books which are smuggled in, or through the distant sound of a belated carriage rolling down the boulevards, are powerful allurements. As for Emma's reactions to the books she reads, the image of a female Quixote comes to mind. She too transmutes reality into fiction. Here, as in Cervantes's novel, literature itself becomes one of the strongest determinants.

Yet there is, in *Madame Bovary*, a necessity stronger even than the temperamental, social and intellectual pressures to which the protagonist is subjected. It is a necessity inherent in the inner logic and progression of Flaubert's own images. The very chapter on Emma's education reveals a characteristic pattern. The primary images are those of confinement and immobility: the atmosphere of the convent is protective and soporific ("elle s'assoupit doucement"); the reading is done on the sly; the girls are assembled in the study, the chapel or the dormitory. Very soon, however, images of escape begin to dominate. These images are at first strictly visual: ladies in castles (typically also claustrated, and dreamily expecting in front of a window the cavalier with a white plume); madonnas, lagoons, gondoliers and angels with golden wings; illustrations in books depicting English ladies kissing doves through the bars of a Gothic cage (still the prison theme). Soon, however, the images become less precise, giving way to vaporous dreams ("pale landscapes of dithyrambic lands"), and to an increasingly disheveled exoticism: sultans with long pipes, Djiaours, Bayadères, Greek caps and Turkish sabres. The suggested confusion of these images rapidly degenerates into indifferentiation and ultimately even chaos, as palm trees and pine trees, Tartar minarets and Roman ruins, crouching camels and swimming swans are brought into senseless juxtaposition. Escape seems inevitably to lead to a manner of disintegration, even to images of death (perhaps even a suggested death-wish), as the swans are transformed into dying swans, singing to the accompaniment of funereal harps, and Emma, infinitely bored by it all, but unwilling to admit it to herself, continuing her dreams by habit or by vanity, finally withdraws into herself, "appeased."

The chapter on Emma's education is revealing, not merely because it proposes a parable of the entire novel, but because the progression of images corresponds to a pattern repeated throughout the book: from ennui to expectation, to escape, to confusion, back to ennui and to a yearning for nothingness. But whereas the symbolic detail is often, with Flaubert, part of a deliberate technique, this logic of imagery associations, these recurrent patterns depend on the spontaneous life of images, on their mutual attractions and irremediable conflicts, on a causality which operates at an unconscious, *poetic* level. The novel as a whole is thus constructed around recurrent clusters of images, all of which are part of definable, yet interrelated cycles. These cycles, or cyclic themes, do parallel on a massive canvas the inevitable movement, from boredom to self-destruction, which characterizes *Madame Bovary* in its overall conception as well as in its detailed execution.

First the patterns of ennui. This begins early in the novel. The eternal sameness of experience is already suggested by the weekly letters to his

mother which the boy Charles writes regularly every Thursday evening with
the same red ink, and which he seals with the same three wafers. Charles's
working habits are moreover compared to those of a mill-horse. The primary
means for suggesting an anesthetizing routine are temporal. Emma gets into
the habit of taking strolls in order to avoid the "eternal" garden. The days
resemble each other ("the same series of days began all over"); the future
seems like an endlessly dark corridor. And repeatedly, the mournful church
bell punctuates the return of the monotonous hours and days with its characterless lament. The repeated use of the imperfect tense, with its suggestions
of habitual action, further stresses the temporal reality of Flaubertian boredom. Even comic effects contribute to an impression of sameness (Flaubert's
sense of comedy constantly exploits repetitions): on the day of the agricultural show, the local national guardsmen and the corps of firemen are being
drilled endlessly up and down the Yonville square. "Cela ne finissait pas et
toujours recommençait."

The underlying sense of hopelessness and monotony is also conveyed by
means of liquid images. There is a great deal of oozing, dripping and melting
in Flaubert's fictional world. During Charles's early courtship of Emma, the
snow is melting, the bark of the trees is oozing, one can hear drops of water
falling one by one. Later, when the bitterness of her married existence seems
to be served up to her nauseatingly during their daily meals, Emma is aware
that the walls are "sweating." These liquid images, suggesting erosion and
deterioration, are of course bound up with a sense of the emptiness of Time.
A steady *écoulement,* or flow, corresponds to feelings of hopeless waste and
vacuity. These liquid images of an annihilating temporality will be even more
pervasive in *L'Education sentimentale.* But *Madame Bovary* also brings out
this immense sadness of time's undoing. Old Rouault explains that, after his
wife died, grief itself dissolved ("ça a coulé brin à brin"). The steady flow
becomes the very symbol of a chronic despair. After Léon's departure, Emma
is plunged again into a life of spiritual numbness: "The river still flowed on,
and slowly pushed its ripples along the slippery banks." Finally, the monotony of existence is conveyed through a series of spatial images. The Norman
landscape near Yonville is "flat," the meadow "stretches," the plain broadens
out and extends to the very horizon—"à perte de vue." This colorless landscape is in harmony with the lazy borough sprawling along the river banks.
Emma, throughout the novel, scans the horizon. But nothing appears which
would relieve the deathlike evenness.

This spatial imagery clearly constitutes the bridge between the theme of
ennui and the theme of escape. Once again, the series of images can be traced
back to the early pages of the novel which deal exclusively with Charles.

Repeatedly, he opens his window, either to stare at the muddy little river which in his mind becomes a wretched "little Venice" and to dream of a yearned-for elsewhere, or to indulge in love reveries as he leans in the direction of the Bertaux farm. The window becomes indeed in *Madame Bovary* the symbol of all expectation: it is an opening onto space through which the confined heroine can dream of escape. But it is also—for windows can be closed and exist only where space is, as it were, restricted—a symbol of frustration, enclosure and asphyxia. Flaubert himself, aware that Emma is often leaning out the window, explains that "the window in the provinces replaces the theater and the promenade." More, however, is involved than a simple taste for spectacle. Jean Rousset, in a brilliant essay, quite rightly suggests that the open window unleashes "mystical velleities." In fact, the symbolic uses of the window reveal not only a permanent dialectic of constriction and spatiality, but an implicit range of emotions embracing the major themes of the novel.

Emma's characteristic pose is at, or near, a window. This is indeed one of the first impressions Charles has of her: "il la trouva debout, le front contre la fenêtre." Windows which are "ajar" are part of her literary reveries in the convent. The image, from the very outset, suggests some manner of imprisonment as well as a longing for a liberation. After her marriage, her daily routine brings her to the window every morning. When she goes through one of her nervous crises, she locks herself up in her room, but then, "stifling," throws open the windows. Exasperated by a sense of shame and contempt for her husband, she again resorts to the typical gesture: "She went to open the window . . . and breathed in the fresh air to calm herself." The sense of oppression and immurement is further stressed after Rodolphe abandons her: the shutter of the window overlooking the garden remains permanently closed. But the imprisonment in her own boundless desire is intolerable. Emma's sexual frenzy, which reaches climactic proportions during her affair with Léon, is probably the most physical manifestation of her need to "liberate" herself. The window, as symbol, offers an image of this release. It is revealing that she first glimpses her future lover, Rodolphe, from her window. Similarly, she watches Léon cross the Yonville square. And it is characteristic also that, upon Léon's departure from Yonville, Emma's first gesture is to open her window and watch the clouds. The space-reverie at first corresponds to a sense of hope: either the surge toward emancipation, as after the Vaubyessard ball (Emma "opened the window and leant out"); or the process of convalescence (Emma, recovering from her nervous depression, is wheeled to the window in her armchair). But the space-hope is even more fundamentally a space-despair. From the garret where she reads Rodolphe's letter and almost commits suicide, all the surrounding plain is visible. The garret window offers the broadest panorama. But it is a dreary view; the endless flat expanse provides a hopeless perspective.

Chronic expectation turns to chronic futility, as Emma's élans toward the elsewhere disintegrate in the grayness of undifferentiated space. Daydreams of movement and flight only carry her back to a more intolerable confinement within her petty existence and her unfulfilled self. But expectation there is. Just as the chatelaines in her beloved Gothic romances wait for the dashing cavalier on his black horse, so Emma lives in perpetual anticipation. "At the bottom of her heart . . . she was waiting for something to happen." Flaubert insists, somewhat heavily at times, on this compulsive expectance of the conclusive event. The frustrated local barber, dreaming of a shop in the theater district of some big town, thus walks up and down "like a sentinel on duty" waiting for customers. And Emma, casting despairing glances upon her life's solitude, interrogates the empty horizon. Each morning, as she wakes up, she hopes that this day will bring a three-decker, laden with passion to the portholes. Every evening, disappointed, she again longs for the morrow.

Images of movement reinforce the theme of escapism. Emma enjoys taking lonely walks with her greyhound and watching the leaps and dashes of the graceful animal. Restlessness and taste for aimless motion point to the allurement of a mythical *elsewhere*. Once again, the theme is ironically broached early in the novel, in pages concerned with Charles. "He had an aimless hope." Images of space and motion—the two are frequently combined—serve, throughout the novel, to bring out the vagrant quality of Emma's thoughts. Departure, travel and access to privileged regions are recurring motifs. The "immense land of joys and passions" exists somewhere beyond her immediate surroundings: the more accessible things are, the more Emma's thoughts turn away from them. Happiness, by definition, can never be *here*. "Anywhere out of the World"—the title of Baudelaire's prose poem—could sum up Emma's chronic yearning for the exotic. "It seemed to her that certain places on earth must yield happiness, just as some plants are peculiar to certain places and grow poorly anywhere else." By a skillful, and certainly far from gratuitous touch, Flaubert concludes Emma's initiatory stay at the Vaubyessard residence with a visit to the hothouses, where the strangest plants, rising in pyramids under hanging vases, evoke a climate of pure sensuality. The exotic setting becomes the very symbol of a yearned-for bliss. The "coming joys" are compared to tropical shores so distant that they cannot be seen, but from where soft winds carry back an intoxicating sweetness.

Travel and estrangement come to symbolize salvation from the im-murement of ennui. Emma believes that change of abode alone is almost a guarantee of happiness. "She did not believe that things could be the same in different places." The unseen country is obviously also the richest in promises of felicity. Paris remains sublimely alluring precisely because—contrary to his original intentions—Flaubert does not grant Emma access to this promised land. Her first conversation with Léon typically exploits the Romantic cliché of the "limitless" expanse of the ocean, which "elevates the soul" through suggestions of the ideal and of infinity. And Léon's blue eyes seem beautiful to Emma because they appear more limpid than "those mountain-lakes where the sky is mirrored." The culmination of the travel imagery coincides with plans for Emma's elopement with Rodolphe ("il fera bon voyager") and with her visions of life in gondolas or under palm trees, to the accompaniment of guitars, in far-off countries with splendent domes and women dressed in red bodices. The very concept of emancipation is bound up with the notion of voyage. During her pregnancy Emma hopes to have a son, because a man is free: "he can travel over passions and over countries, cross obstacles, taste of the most far-away pleasures." And part of Rodolphe's prestige when she meets him is that he appears to her like a "traveler who has voyaged over strange lands." As early as her disappointing honeymoon (which, she feels, ought to have led to "those lands with sonorous names"), she knows that Charles did not, and could not, live up to her ideal of man as initiator to remote mysteries. She yearns for the inaccessible with a naïve but pungent lyricism: "she was filled with desires, with rage, with hate." Her desperate escapism, which ultimately alarms and alienates both her lovers, is of an almost sacrilegious nature. It is significant that sex is repeatedly associated with mystico-religious images (the remarkable death scene pushes the association to its logical conclusion), and that the assignation with Léon takes place in the Rouen cathedral, which Emma's distorted sensibility views as a "gigantic boudoir." Emma's tragedy is that she cannot escape her own immanence. "Everything, including herself, was unbearable to her." But just as her walks always lead back to the detested house, so Emma feels thrown back into herself, left stranded on her own shore. The lyrical thrust toward the inaccessible leads back to an anesthetizing confinement.

The cycles of ennui and spatial monotony, the images of escape (window perspectives, motion, insatiable desire for the elsewhere), are thus brought into contrapuntal tension with an underlying metaphoric structure suggesting limits, restriction, contraction and immobility. The basic tragic paradox of *Madame Bovary* is unwittingly summed up during Emma's first conversation

with Léon. They discuss the pleasures of reading: "One thinks of nothing
. . . the hours slip by. One *moves motionless* through countries one imagines
one sees" (italics mine). As for the sense of limitation, the very site of
Yonville (the diminutive conglomeration in the midst of a characterless, undifferentiated landscape) suggests a circumscribed and hopelessly hedged-in
existence. As soon as one enters the small market town, "the courtyards
grow narrower, the houses closer together, and the fences disappear." The
entire first chapter of part 2, which introduces the reader to Yonville, plays
on this contrast between expanse and delimitation. The very life of Yonville
suggests constriction. Viewed from a distance—for instance during Emma's
promenade on horseback with Rodolphe—the small community appears even
more jammed in. "Emma half closed her eyes to recognize her house, and
never had this poor village where she lived seemed so small to her." The
same feeling of constriction is experienced inside her house, as Emma bewails
"her too exalted dreams, her narrow home." The entire tragic tension of the
novel seems to be summed up in this experience of spiritual claustrophobia.
The sitting-room where Emma, in her armchair, spends hours near the window, is distinguished by its particularly "low ceiling." The predominant
impression is one of entrapment or encirclement. In a somewhat labored but
telling simile, Flaubert compares Emma's married life to a complex strap
which "buckles her in" on all sides.

This imagery of restriction and contraction is intimately related to the
disintegrating experiences of sameness, interfusion and confusion of feelings,
indiscrimination, abdication of will and lethal torpor. Space is lacking even
in the Yonville cemetery, which is so full of graves that the old stones, completely level with the ground, form a "continuous pavement." This absence
of a hiatus has its stylistic counterparts in the tight verbal and dramatic
juxtapositions. There is no solution of continuity between the platitudinous
official speeches, the lowing of the cattle and Rodolphe's talk of elective
affinities. The seduction scene at the *comices agricoles*—a chapter of which
Flaubert was particularly proud—is almost a continuous exercise in tele-
scoping of levels of reality. Everything tends to merge and become alike. Even
the villagers and the peasants present a comical and distressing uniformity.
"Tous ces gens-là se ressemblaient."

Confusion, whether due to oppressive monotony, moral drowsiness or
spiritual anesthesia, is one of the leitmotifs in *Madame Bovary*. Once more,
the opening pages are revealing. When Charles reads the list of course of-
ferings at the medical school, he experiences a spell of "dizziness." Riding
toward the Bertaux farm, he falls into a characteristic doze wherein his most
recent sensations "blend" with old memories: the warm odor of poultices

"mingled" in his brain with the fresh smell of dew. *Confondre, se mêler* are among Flaubert's favorite words. "Et peu à peu, les physionomies se confondirent dans sa mémoire." As the Vaubyessard ball recedes into the past, the sharp outlines dissolve and all the figures begin to merge. Emma's ability to distinguish between levels of values dwindles as the novel progresses. "She confused in her desire the sensualities of luxury with the delights of the heart." Later, this commingling of sensations becomes increasingly habitual, until no clear notions at all can be distinguished.

Emma's lust, her longing for money and her sentimental aspirations all become "confused" in one single, vague and oppressive sense of suffering. While listening to Rodolphe's seductive speeches, she conjures up other images: the viscount with whom she waltzed at Vaubyessard, his delicately scented hair, Léon who is now far away. The characteristic faintness ("mollesse") which comes over her induces an overlapping and a blurring of sensations which is not unlike a cinematographic fadeout. ("Puis tout se confondit.") But this psychological strabismus is not here a technique whereby the author creates suspense or modestly veils the action. It corresponds to an abdication of choice and will, and points to the very principle of disintegration. As she is about to seek solace from the priest, Emma longingly recalls her sheltered life in the convent where she was "lost" ("confondue") in the long line of white veils. The memory makes her feel faint ("molle"); and she yearns for anything which would submerge and absorb her existence. The latent yearning for annihilation or nothingness is probably the most fundamental tragic impulse of Flaubertian protagonists. Not only does Emma dream of dissolving herself in an all-absorbing whole, but approaching death is described as a "confusion de crépuscule." Ultimately, not only all desire but all pain is absorbed in an all-embracing and all-negating woe. Thus Charles's retrospective jealousy, when he discovers Emma's infidelities, becomes "lost in the immensity of his grief." The frustration of all desire and of all hope is so great that nothing short of total sorrow and total surrender to nonbeing can bring relief.

A state of numbness or even dormancy is one of the chronic symptoms of *bovarysme*. *Mollesse, assoupissement* and *torpeur* are other favorite words of Flaubert. They refer most generally to a vague sensuous well-being, to a condition of nonresistance and even surrender. When Emma hears Rodolphe's flattering, if not original love declaration (he compares her to an angel), her pride "like one who relaxes in a bath, expanded softly" ("mollement"). The almost untranslatable *mollement* appears again, a few pages later, when Rodolphe puts his arm around Emma's waist and she tries "feebly" to disengage herself. Numbness and drowsiness occur almost regularly in a sexual context. During the nocturnal trysts in the garden, Emma, her eyes half closed, feels her emotion rise with the softness ("mollesse") of the perfume of the syringas. Her physical submissiveness to Rodolphe is termed a "beatitude that benumbed her" ("une béatitude qui l'engourdissait"). And when she meets Léon again at the opera in Rouen, she is assailed by the "torpor" of her memories.

The pathological nature of such torpid states is strongly suggested. Early in the novel, her torpor follows moments of "feverish" chatter, and corresponds to periods when Emma suffers from heart palpitations. But the real pathology is of the spirit, not of the body. Just as the somnolence of the listeners at the agricultural show reflects the dullness of the speeches and the intellectual indolence of the townspeople, so Charles's congenital yawning symbolizes his inadequacy. When the coach arrives in Yonville, Charles is still asleep. During the evening at the Homais, he regularly falls asleep after playing dominoes. Such drowsiness seems contagious. Only Emma's takes on a more symbolic aspect. She suffers from an "assoupissement de sa conscience": her very conscience is made numb. And in this numbness there is not only the principle of despair, but of death. All desire, like Baudelaire's *ennui,* leads to an omnivorous yawn. After Léon leaves Yonville, Emma's sensuous and sentimental frustration expresses itself through an infinite lassitude, a "numb despair." Her blinds are now kept closed (recurrence of the window motif), while she herself spends her days stretched out on her sofa, reading a book. The very atmosphere of Emma's burial will be one of monotony and sickening tedium. As Charles leads the funeral procession, he feels himself growing faint at this unending repetition of prayers and torches, surrounded by the insipid, almost nauseating smell of wax and of cassocks. A liturgical torpor invests him, and reduces all pain to a blurred feeling of weariness.

The very movement of the imagery in *Madame Bovary* thus leads from desire to frustration and failure, and ultimately to death and total undoing. Images of liquefaction and flow, which will be central to *L'Education sentimentale,* here also serve to convey the processes of dissolution. Emma almost perversely savors the slow disintegration of her being. The maraschino ice melting in her mouth corresponds to an entire past she wishes to negate. But the present, no matter how much one counts on it to beget change, never really disrupts the hopeless continuity of life. The tiny river near Yonville symbolizes a "time" which knows neither alteration nor respite ("La rivière coulait toujours"). This temporal symbolism is bound up with the experience of loss and erosion: the great love with Rodolphe is like "the water of a river absorbed into its bed" until Emma begins to see the mud. During her convalescence, the falling rain is the background to the sick woman's daily anticipation of the "inevitable return" of the same petty events. But it is above all morbidity of spirit or body which is suggested through fluid or soluble metaphors. From the empty and bloody orbits of the Blind Man flow "liquids" which congeal into green scales. Similarly, a "black liquid" oozes from the blisters on Hippolyte's leg. And after Emma dies, a "rush of black liquid" issues from her mouth, as though she were still vomiting. Even the soil thrown up at the side of her grave seems to be "flowing" down at the corners. This fluent quality of life points not only to mortality, but to decomposition. "Whence came this insufficiency in life, this instantaneous rotting of everything on which she leant?" Emma's question goes to the very heart of the book. For life, in the Flaubertian context, is a steady process of decay.

This relentless deterioration of everything is very different from the Balzacian wear and tear which is most often the price man pays for his tragic energy. Flaubert's heroes not only have a vocation for failure, but they fail independently of any investment of fervor. Charles's early fiasco at his examination foreshadows his entire career. Paradoxically, it could be said that unsuccess precedes the act of living. In Flaubert's world, life is not fought out and lost, but *spent*. It is only appropriate that Emma should be congenitally improvident. For she is a squanderer not only of money. In a strained but revealing simile, Flaubert compares her loss of illusions to a steady act of "spending." "Elle en avait dépensé à toutes les aventures de son âme." But it is, in reality, her own self that she is dissipating, as though urged on by the desire to fade or melt away. Flaubert elsewhere speaks of death as a "continuous swooning away" (an "évanouissement continu"). The death-wish is a permanent reality in the fictional world of Flaubert; it most often reveals itself through an almost mystical desire to vanish or be absorbed by a larger whole. On her way to Father Bournisien, Emma dreams of the "disappearance" of her entire existence. The longing for nothingness is often linked to religious or pseudo-religious images. In Emma's mind, it is most often associated with memories of the convent, with a desire to return to it, as one might to a maternal womb. The desire to stop living ("She would have liked not to be alive, or to be always asleep") corresponds to a quasi-metaphysical fatigue, to the immedicable pain of having been betrayed by life itself. In the face of universal abandon, the Flaubertian heroine is driven to dissipation. She becomes the willing accomplice of all the forces of disbandment.

MICHEL FOUCAULT

Fantasia of the Library

The Temptation of Saint Anthony was rewritten on three different occasions: in 1849, before *Madame Bovary;* in 1856, before *Salammbô;* and in 1872, while Flaubert was writing *Bouvard et Pécuchet.* He published extracts in 1856 and 1857. Saint Anthony accompanied Flaubert for twenty-five or thirty years—for as long, in fact, as the hero of the *Sentimental Education.* In these twin and inverted figures, the old anchorite of Egypt, still besieged by desires, responds through the centuries to a young man of eighteen, seized by the apparition of Madame Arnoux while travelling from Paris to Le Havre. Moreover, the evening when Frédéric—at this stage, a pale reflection of himself—turns away, as if in fear of incest, from the woman he continues to love, recalls the shadowed night when the defeated hermit learns to love even the substance of life in its material form. "Temptation" among the ruins of an ancient world populated by spirits is transformed into an "education" in the prose of the modern world.

The Temptation was conceived early in Flaubert's career—perhaps after attending a puppetshow—and it influenced all of his works. Standing alongside his other books, standing behind them, *The Temptation* forms a prodigious reserve: for scenes of violence, phantasmagoria, chimeras, nightmares, slapstick. Flaubert successively transformed its inexhaustible treasure into the grey provincial reveries of *Madame Bovary,* into the sculpted sets of *Salammbô,* and into the eccentricities of everyday life in *Bouvard. The*

From *Language, Counter-Memory, Practice,* edited by Donald F. Bouchard and translated by Sherry Simon. © 1977 by Cornell University. Cornell University Press, 1977.

Temptation seems to represent Flaubert's unattainable dream: what he wanted his works to be—supple, silky, delicate, spontaneous, harmoniously revealed through rapturous phrases—but also what they must never be if they were to see the light of day. *The Temptation* existed before any of Flaubert's books (its first sketches are found in *Mémoires d'un fou, Rêve d'enfer, Danse des morts,* and, particularly, in *Smahr*), and it was repeated—as ritual, purification, exercise, a "temptation" to overcome—prior to writing each of his major texts. Suspended over his entire work, it is unlike all his other books by virtue of its prolixity, its wasted abundance, and its overcrowded bestiary; and set back from his other books, it offers, as a photographic negative of their writing, the somber and murmuring prose which they were compelled to repress, to silence gradually, in order to achieve their own clarity. The entire work of Flaubert is dedicated to the conflagration of this primary discourse: its precious ashes, its black, unmalleable coal.

II

We readily understand *The Temptation* as setting out the formal progression of unconfined reveries. It would be to literature what Bosch, Breughel, or the Goya of the *Caprichos* were at one time to painting. The first readers (or audience) were bored by the monotonous progression of grotesques: Maxime Du Camp remarked: "We listened to the words of the Sphinx, the chimera, the Queen of Sheba, of Simon the Magician. . . . A bewildered, somewhat simpleminded, and, I would even say, foolish Saint Anthony sees, parading before him, different forms of temptation" (*Souvenirs littéraires*). His friends were enraptured by the "richness of his vision" (François Coppée), "by its forest of shadows and light" (Victor Hugo), and by its "hallucinatory mechanism" (Hippolyte Taine). But stranger still, Flaubert himself invoked madness, phantasms; he felt he was shaping the fallen trees of a dream: "I spend my afternoons with the shutters closed, the curtains drawn, and without a shirt, dressed as a carpenter. I bawl out! I sweat! It's superb! There are moments when this is decidedly more than delirium." As the book nears completion: "I plunged furiously into *Saint Anthony* and began to enjoy the most terrifying exaltation. I have never been more excited."

In time, we have learned as readers that *The Temptation* is not the product of dreams and rapture, but a monument to meticulous erudition. To construct the scene of the heresiarchs, Flaubert drew extensively from Tillemont's *Mémoires ecclésiastiques,* Matter's four-volume *Histoire du gnosticisme,* the *Histoire de manichée* by Beausobre, Reuss's *Théologie chré-*

tienne, and also from Saint Augustine and, of course, from Migne's *Patrologia* (Athanasius, Jerome, and Epiphanus). The gods that populate the text were found in Burnouf, Anquetil-Duperron, in the works of Herbelot and Hottinger, in the volumes of the *Univers pittoresque,* in the work of the Englishman, Layard, and, particularly, in Creuzer's translation, the *Religions de l'antiquité.* For information on monsters, he read Xivrey's *Traditions tératologiques,* the *Physiologus* re-edited by Cahier and Martin, Boaïstrau's *Histoires prodigieuses,* and the Duret text devoted to plants and their "admirable history." Spinoza inspired his metaphysical meditation on extended substance. Yet, this list is far from exhaustive. Certain evocations in the text seem totally dominated by the machinery of dreams: for example, the magisterial Diana of Ephesus, with lions at her shoulders and with fruits, flowers, and stars interlaced on her bosom, with a cluster of breasts, and griffins and bulls springing from the sheath which tightly encircles her waist. Nevertheless, this "fantasy" is an exact reproduction of plate 88 in Creuzer's last volume: if we observe the details of the print, we can appreciate Flaubert's diligence. Cybele and Atys (with his languid pose, his elbow against a tree, his flute, and his costume cut into diamond shapes) are both found in plate 58 of the same work; similarly, the portrait of Ormuz is in Layard and the medals of Oraios, Sabaoth, Adonaius, and Knouphus are easily located in Matter. It is indeed surprising that such erudite precision strikes us as a phantasmagoria. More exactly, we are astounded that Flaubert experienced the scholar's patience, the very patience necessary to knowledge, as the liveliness of a frenzied imagination.

Possibly, Flaubert was responding to an experience of the fantastic which was singularly modern and relatively unknown before his time, to the discovery of a new imaginative space in the nineteenth century. This domain of phantasms is no longer the night, the sleep of reason, or the uncertain void that stands before desire, but, on the contrary, wakefulness, untiring attention, zealous erudition, and constant vigilance. Henceforth, the visionary experience arises from the black and white surface of printed signs, from the closed and dusty volume that opens with a flight of forgotten words; fantasies are carefully deployed in the hushed library, with its columns of books, with its titles aligned on shelves to form a tight enclosure, but within confines that also liberate impossible worlds. The imaginary now resides between the book and the lamp. The fantastic is no longer a property of the heart, nor is it found among the incongruities of nature; it evolves from the accuracy of knowledge, and its treasures lie dormant in documents. Dreams are no longer summoned with closed eyes, but in reading; and a true image is now a product of learning: it derives from words spoken in the past, exact recensions, the amassing of minute facts, monuments reduced to infinitesimal fragments, and the reproductions of reproductions. In the modern experience, these elements contain the power of the impossible. Only the assiduous clamor created by repetition can transmit to us what only happened once. The imaginary is not formed in opposition to reality as its denial or compensation; it grows among signs, from book to book, in the interstice of repetitions and commentaries; it is born and takes shape in the interval between books. It is a phenomenon of the library.

Both Michelet (in the *Sorcière*) and Edgar Quinet (in *Ahasvérus*) had explored these forms of erudite dreams, but *The Temptation* is not a scholarly project which evolved into an artistically coherent whole. As a work, its form relies on its location within the domain of knowledge: it exists by virtue of its essential relationship to books. This explains why it may represent more than a mere episode in the history of Western imagination; it opens a literary space wholly dependent on the network formed by the books of the past: as such, it serves to circulate the fiction of books. Yet, we should not confuse it with apparently similar works, with *Don Quixote* or the works of Sade, because the link between the former and the tales of knight-errantry or between the *Nouvelle Justine* and the virtuous novels of the eighteenth century is maintained through irony; and, more importantly, they remain books regardless of their intention. *The Temptation,* however, is linked in a completely serious manner to the vast world of print and develops within the recognizable institution of writing. It may appear as merely another new book to be shelved alongside all the others, but it serves, in actuality, to extend the space that existing books can occupy. It recovers other books; it hides and displays them and, in a single movement, it causes them to glitter and disappear. It is not simply the book that Flaubert dreamed of writing for so long; it dreams other books, all other books that dream and that men dream of writing—books that are taken up, fragmented, displaced, combined, lost, set at an unapproachable distance by dreams, but also brought closer to the imaginary and sparkling realization of desires. In writing *The Temptation,* Flaubert produced the first literary work whose exclusive domain is that of books: following Flaubert, Mallarmé is able to write *Le Livre* and modern literature is activated—Joyce, Roussel, Kafka, Pound, Borges. The library is on fire.

Déjeuner sur l'herbe and *Olympia* were perhaps the first "museum" paintings, the first paintings in European art that were less a response to the achievement of Giorgione, Raphael, and Velasquez than an acknowledgment (supported by this singular and obvious connection, using this legible reference to cloak its operation) of the new and substantial relationship of painting to itself, as a manifestation of the existence of museums and the particular reality and interdependence that paintings acquire in museums. In the same period, *The Temptation* was the first literary work to comprehend the greenish institutions where books are accumulated and where the slow and incontrovertible vegetation of learning quietly proliferates. Flaubert is to the library what Manet is to the museum. They both produced works in a self-conscious relationship to earlier paintings or texts—or rather to the aspect in painting or writing that remains indefinitely open. They erect their art within the archive. They were not meant to foster the lamentations—the lost youth, the absence of vigor, and the decline of inventiveness—through which we reproach our Alexandrian age, but to unearth an essential aspect of our culture: every painting now belongs within the squared and massive surface of painting and all literary works are confined to the indefinite murmur of writing. Flaubert and Manet are responsible for the existence of books and paintings within works of art.

III

The presence of the book in *The Temptation,* its manifestation and concealment, is indicated in a strange way: it immediately contradicts itself as a book. From the start, it challenges the priority of its printed signs and takes the form of a theatrical presentation: the transcription of a text that is not meant to be read, but recited and staged. At one time, Flaubert had wanted to transform *The Temptation* into a kind of epic drama, a *Faust* capable of swallowing the entire world of religion and gods. He soon gave up this idea but retained within the text the indications marking a possible performance: division into dialogues and scenes, descriptions of the place of action, the scenic elements, and their modifications, blocking directions for the "actors" on stage—all given according to a traditional typographical arrangement (smaller type and wider margins for stage directions, a character's name in large letters above the speeches, etc.). In a significant redoubling, the first indicated setting—the site of all future modifications—has the form of a natural theater: the hermit's retreat has been placed "at the top of a mountain, on a platform rounded in the form of a half-moon and enclosed by large boulders." The text describes a stage which, itself, represents a "platform" shaped by natural forces and upon which new scenes will in turn impose their sets. But these indications do not suggest a future performance (they are largely incompatible with an actual presentation); they simply designate the specific mode of existence of the text. Print can only be an unobtrusive aid to the visible; an insidious spectator takes the reader's place and the act of reading is dissolved in the triumph of another form of sight. The book disappears in the theatricality it creates.

But it will immediately reappear within a scenic space. No sooner have the first signs of temptation emerged from the gathering shadows, no sooner have the disquieting faces appeared in the night, than Saint Anthony lights a torch to protect himself and opens a "large book." This posture is consistent with the iconographic tradition: in the painting of Breughel the Younger, the painting that so impressed Flaubert when he visited the Balbi collection in Genoa and that he felt had incited him to write *The Temptation,* the hermit, in the lower right-hand corner of the canvas, is kneeling before an immense volume, his head slightly bowed, and his eyes intent on the written lines. Surrounding him on all sides are naked women with open arms, lean Gluttony stretching her giraffe's neck, barrel-like men creating an uproar, and nameless beasts devouring each other; at his back is a procession of the grotesques that populate the earth—bishops, kings, and tyrants. But this assembly is lost on the saint, absorbed in his reading. He sees nothing of this great uproar, unless perhaps through the corner of his eye, unless he seeks to protect himself by invoking the enigmatic powers of a magician's book. It may be, on the contrary, that the mumbling recitation of written signs has summoned these poor shapeless figures that no language has ever named, that no book can contain, but that anonymously invade the weighty pages of the volume. It may be, as well, that these creatures of unnatural issue escaped from the book, from the gaps between the open pages or the blank spaces between the letters. More fertile than the sleep of reason, the book perhaps engenders an infinite brood of monsters. Far from being a protection, it has liberated an obscure swarm of creatures and created a suspicious shadow through the mingling of images and knowledge. In any case, setting aside this discussion of the open folio in Breughel's painting, Flaubert's Saint Anthony seizes his book to ward off the evil that begins to obsess him and reads at random five passages from Scriptures. But, by a trick of the text, there immediately arises in the evening air the odors of gluttony, the scent of blood and anger, and the incense of pride, aromas worth more than their weight in gold, and the sinful perfumes of Oriental queens. The book—but not any book—is the site of temptation. Where the first passage read by the hermit is taken from "Acts of the Apostles," the last four, significantly, come from the Old Testament (Acts of the Apostles 10:11; Daniel 2:46; 2 Kings 20:13; 1 Kings 10:1)—from God's Scripture, from the supreme book.

The two earlier versions of *The Temptation* excluded the reading of sacred texts. Attacked by the canonical figures of evil, the hermit immediately seeks refuge in his chapel; goaded by Satan, the Seven Deadly Sins are set against the Virtues and, led by Pride, they make repeated assaults upon the protected enclosure. This imagery of the portal and the staging of a mystery are absent from the published text. In the final version, evil is not given as the property of characters, but incorporated in words. A book intended to lead to the gates of salvation also opens the gates of Hell. The full range of fantastic apparitions that eventually unfold before the hermit—orgiastic palaces, drunken emperors, unfettered heretics, misshapen forms of the gods in agony, abnormalities of nature—arise from the opening of a book, as they issued from the libraries that Flaubert consulted. It is appropriate, in this context, that Flaubert dropped from the definitive text the symmetrical and opposing figures of logic and the swine, the original leaders of the pageant, and replaced them with Hilarion, the learned disciple who was initiated into the reading of sacred texts by Saint Anthony.

The presence of the book in *The Temptation,* initially in a theatrical spectacle and then more prominently as the source of a pageant, which, in turn, obscures its presence, gives rise to an extremely complicated space. We are apparently presented with a frieze of colorful characters set against cardboard scenery; on the edge of the stage, in a corner, sits the hooded figure of the motionless saint. The scene is reminiscent of a puppet theater. As a child, Flaubert saw *The Mystery of Saint Anthony* performed numerous times by Père Legrain in his puppet theater; he later brought George Sand to a performance. The first two versions of *The Temptation* retained elements from this source (most obviously, the pig, but also the personification of sin, the assault on the chapel, and the image of the virgin). In the definitive text, only the linear succession of the visions remains to suggest an effect of "marionnettes": sins, temptations, divinities, and monsters are paraded before the laconic hermit—each emerging, in turn, from the hellish confines of the box where they were kept. But this is only a surface effect constructed upon a staging in depth (it is the flat surface that is deceptive in this context).

As support for these successive visions, to set them up in their illusory reality, Flaubert arranged a limited number of stages, which extends, in a perpendicular direction, the pure and straightforward reading of the printed phrases. The first intersection is the reader (1)—the actual reader of the text—and the book lies before him (1a); from the first lines (*it is in the Thebaid . . . the hermit's cabin appears in the background*) the text invites the reader to become a spectator (2) of a stage whose scenery is carefully described (2a); at center stage, the spectator sees the hermit (3) seated with his legs crossed: he will shortly rise and turn to his book (3a) from which disturbing visions will gradually escape—banquets, palaces, a voluptuous

queen, and finally Hilarion, the insidious disciple (4). Hilarion leads the saint
into a space filled with visions (4a); this opens a world of heresies and gods,
and a world where improbable creatures proliferate (5). Moreover, the heretics are also capable of speech and recount their shameless rites; the gods
recall their past glories and the cults that were devoted to them; and the
monsters proclaim their proper bestiality. Derived from the power of their
words or from their mere presence, a new dimension is realized, a vision
that lies within that produced by the satanic disciple (5a), a vision that
contains the abject cult of the Ophites, the miracles of Apollonius, the temptations of Buddha, and the ancient and blissful reign of Isis (6). Beginning
as actual readers, we successively encounter five distinct levels, five different
orders of language (indicated by a): that of the book, a theater, a sacred
text, visions, and visions that evolve into further visions. There are also five
series of characters, of figures, of landscapes, and of forms: the invisible
spectator, Saint Anthony in his retreat, Hilarion, the heretics, the gods and
the monsters, and finally, the shadows propagated by their speeches or
through their memories.

This organization, which develops through successive enclosures, is
modified by two others. (In actuality, it finds its confirmation and completion
in two others.) The first is that of a retrospective encasement. Where the
figures on the sixth level (visions of visions) should be the palest and least
accessible to direct perception, they appear forcefully on the scene, as dense,
colorful, and insistent as the figures that precede them or as Saint Anthony
himself. It is as if the clouded memories and secret desires, which produced
these visions from the first, have the power of acting without mediation in
the scenic space, upon the landscape where the hermit pursues his imaginary
dialogue with his disciple, or upon the stage that the fictitious spectator is
meant to behold during the acting out of this semi-mystery. Thus, the fictions
of the last level fold back upon themselves, envelop the figures from which
they arose, quickly surpass the disciple and the anchorite, and finish by
inscribing themselves within the supposed materiality of the theater. Through
this retrospective envelopment, the most ephemeral fictions are presented in
the most direct language, through the stage directions, indicated by the author, whose task is an external definition of the characters.

This arrangement allows the reader (1) to see Saint Anthony (3) over
the shoulder of the implied spectator (2) who is an accomplice to the dramatic presentation: the effect is to identify the reader with the spectator.
Consequently, the spectator sees Anthony on the stage, but he also sees over
his shoulder the apparitions presented to the hermit, apparitions that are as
substantial as the saint: Alexandria, Constantinople, the Queen of Sheba,

Hilarion. The spectator's glance dissolves into the hallucinated gaze of the hermit. Anthony then leans over Hilarion's shoulder, and sees with his eyes the figures evoked by the evil disciple; and Hilarion, through the arguments of the heretics, perceives the face of the gods and the snarling monsters, contemplates the images that haunt them. Developed from one figure to another, a wreath is constructed which links the characters in a series of knots independent of their proper intermediaries, so that their identities are gradually merged and their different perceptions blended into a single dazzling sight.

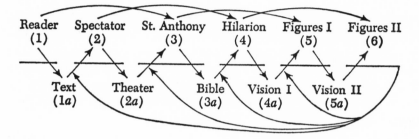

An immense distance lies between the reader and the ultimate visions that entrance the imaginary figures: orders of language placed according to degrees of subordination, relay-characters gazing over each other's shoulders and withdrawing to the depths of this "text-representation," and a population abounding in illusions. But two movements counter this distance: the first, affecting the different orders of language, renders the invisible elements visible through a direct style, and the second, which concerns the figures, gradually adopts the vision and the light fixed upon the characters and brings forward the most distant images until they emerge from the sides of the scene. It is this double movement that makes a vision actually tempting: the most indirect and encased elements of the vision are given with a brilliance compatible with the foreground; and the visionary, attracted by the sights placed before him, rushes into this simultaneously empty and overpopulated space, identifies himself with this figure of shadow and light, and begins to see, in turn, with unearthly eyes. The profundity of these boxed apparitions and the linear and naive succession of figures are not in any way contradictory. Rather, they form the perpendicular intersections that constitute the paradoxical shape and the singular domain of *The Temptation*. The frieze of marionnettes and the stark, colored surface of these figures who jostle one another in the shadows offstage are not the effects of childhood memories or the residue of vivid impressions: they are the composite result of a vision that develops on successive and gradually more distant levels and a temptation that attracts the visionary to the place he has seen and that suddenly envelops him in his own visions.

IV

The Temptation is like a discourse whose function is to maintain not a single and exclusive meaning (by excising all the others), but the simultaneous existence of multiple meanings. The visible sequence of scenes is extremely simple: first, the memories of the aging monk, the hallucinations and sins summarized by the figure of an ancient queen who arrives from the Orient (chapters 1 and 2); then, the disciple who initiates the rapid multiplication of heresies through his debate on Scripture (3 and 4); followed by the emergence of the gods who successively appear on the stage (5); with the depopulation of the earth, Anthony is free to return to it guided by his disciple who has become both Satan and Knowledge, free to gauge its expanse and to observe the tangled and infinite growth of monsters (6, 7). This visible sequence is supported by a number of underlying series.

1. Temptation is conceived in the hermit's heart; it hesitantly evokes his companions during his retreat and the passing caravans; from this, it extends into vaster regions: overpopulated Alexandria, the Christian Orient torn by theological conflicts, all those Mediterranean civilizations ruled by gods who emerged from Asia, and, finally, the limitless expanses of the universe—the distant stars at night, the imperceptible cell from which life awakens. But this ultimate scintillation only serves to return the hermit to the material principle of his first desires. Having reached the limits of the world, the grand and tempting itinerary returns to its point of departure. In the first two versions of the text, the Devil explained to Anthony "that sins were in his heart and sorrows in his mind." These explanations are now inessential: pushed to the limits of the universe, the arching waves of the temptation return to those things that are nearest. In the minute organism where the primordial desires of life are awakened, Anthony recaptures his ancient heart, his badly controlled appetites, but no longer experiences their charged fantasies. Before his eyes, there lies the material truth. Under this red light, the larva of desire is gently formed. The center of temptation has not shifted: or rather, it has been displaced very slightly from the top to the bottom—passing from the heart to the sinews, from a dream to the cell, from a bright image to matter. Those things that haunted the imagination of the hermit from inside can now become the object of enraptured contemplation; and where he had pushed them aside in fear, they now attract and invite him to a dormant identification: "to descend to the very depths of

matter, to become matter." It is only in appearance that the temptation wrenches the hermit from his solitude and populates his field of vision with men, gods, and monsters, for, along its curved expanse, it gives rise to a number of distinct movements: a progressive expansion to the confines of the universe; a loop bringing desire back to its truth; a shift that causes a violent phantasm to subside in the soft repose of matter; a passage from the inside to the outside—from heartfelt nostalgia to the vivid spectacle of life; the transformation of fear into the desire for identification.

2. Sitting on the doorstep of his cabin, the hermit is obsessed by the memories of an old man: formerly, isolation was less painful, work less tedious, and the river not as distant as now. He had enjoyed his youth—the young girls who congregated at the fountain—and also his retreat, and the opportunity for companionship, particularly with his favorite disciple. His memories flood back upon him in this slight wavering of the present at the hour of dusk. It is a total inversion of time: first, the images of twilight in the city humming with activity before dark—the port, shouting in the streets, the tambourines in the taverns; followed by Alexandria in the period of the massacres, Constantinople during the Council; this suddenly gives way to the heretics whose affronts originated with the founding of Christianity; behind them are the gods who once had a following of faithful and whose temples range from India to the Mediterranean; and finally, the appearance of figures as old as time itself—the distant stars, brute matter, lust and death, the recumbent Sphinx, chimeras, all those things that, in a single movement, create life and its illusions. Further, beyond this primordial cell from which life evolved, Anthony desires an impossible return to the passive state prior to life: the whole of his existence is consequently laid to rest where it recovers its innocence and awakens once again to the sounds of animals, the bubbling fountain, and the glittering stars. The highest temptation is the longing to be another, to be all others; it is to renew identifications and to achieve the principle of time in a return that completes the circle. The vision of Engadine approaches. (Engadine is an Alpine valley in Switzerland where Nietzsche spent his summers between 1879 and 1888—Translator.).

An ambiguous figure—simultaneously a form of duration and eternity, acting as conclusion and a fresh start—introduces each stage of this return through time. The heresies are introduced by Hilarion—as small as a child and withered like an old man, as young as awakening knowledge and as old as well-pondered learning. Apollonius introduces the gods: he is familiar with their unending metamorphoses, their creation and death, but he is also able to regain instantly "the Eternal, the Absolute, and Being." Lust and Death lead the dance of life because they undoubtedly control the end and new beginnings, the disintegration of forms and the origin of all things. The larva-skeleton, the eternal Thaumaturge, and the old child each function within the book as "alternators" of duration; through the time of history, myth, and the entire universe, they guarantee the hermit's recapture of the cellular principle of life. The night of *The Temptation* can greet the unchanged novelty of a new day, because the earth has turned back upon its axis.

3. The resurgence of time also produces a prophetic vision of the future. Within his recollections, Anthony encountered the ancient imagination of the Orient: deep within this memory, which no longer belongs to him, he saw a form arising that represented the temptation of the wisest of the kings of Israel—the Queen of Sheba. Standing behind her, he recognized in the shape of an ambiguous dwarf, her servant and his own disciple, a disciple who is indissociably linked to Desire and Wisdom. Hilarion is the incarnation of all the dreams of the Orient, but he possesses as well a perfect knowledge of Scriptures and their interpretation. Greed and science are united in him—covetous knowledge and damnable facts. This gnome increases in size throughout the course of the liturgy; by the last episode, he has become gigantic, "beautiful as an archangel and luminous as the sun." His kingdom now includes the universe as he becomes the Devil in the lightning flash of truth. Serving as an embryonic stage in the development of Western thought, he first introduces theology and its infinite disputes; then, he revives ancient civilizations and their gods whose rule was so quickly reduced to ashes; he inaugurates a rational understanding of the world; he demonstrates the movement of the stars and reveals the secret powers of life. All of European culture is deployed in this Egyptian night where the spectre, the ancient history, of the Orient still haunts the imagination: the theology of the Middle Ages, the erudition of the Renaissance, and the scientific bent of the modern period. *The Temptation* acts as a nocturnal sun whose trajectory is from east to west, from desire to knowledge, from imagination to truth, from the oldest longings to the findings of modern science. The appearance of Egypt converted to Christianity (and with it Alexandria) and the appearance of Anthony represent the zero point between Asia and Europe; both seem to arise from a fold in time, at the point where Antiquity, at the summit of its achievement, begins to vacillate and collapses, releasing its hidden and forgotten monsters; they also plant the seed of the modern world with its promise of endless knowledge. We have arrived at the hollow of history.

The "temptation" of Saint Anthony is the double fascination exercised upon Christianity by the sumptuous spectacle of its past and the limitless acquisitions of its future. The definitive text excludes Abraham's God, the Virgin, and the virtues (who appear in the first two versions), but not to save them from profanation; they were incorporated in figures that represent them—in Buddha, the tempted god, in Apollonius the thaumaturge who resembles Christ, and in Isis the mother of sorrows. *The Temptation* does not mask reality in its glittering images, but reveals the image of an image in the realm of truth. Even in its state of primitive purity, Christianity was formed by the dying reflections of an older world, formed by the feeble light it projected upon the still grey shadows of a nascent world.

4. The two earlier versions of *The Temptation* began with the battle of the Seven Deadly Sins against the three theological virtues (Faith, Hope, and Charity), but this traditional imagery of the mysteries disappears in the published text. The sins appear only in the form of illusions and the virtues are given a secret existence as the organizing principles of the sequences. The endless revival of heresies places Faith at the mercy of overpowering error; the agony of the gods, which makes them disappear as glimmers of imagination, transforms Hope into a futile quest; and nature in repose or with its savage forces unleashed reduces Charity to a mockery. The three supreme virtues have been vanquished; and turning away from Heaven, the saint "lies flat on his stomach, and leaning upon his elbows, he watches breathlessly. Withered ferns begin to flower anew." At the sight of this small palpitating cell, Charity is transformed into dazzling curiosity ("O joy! O bliss! I have seen the birth of life; I have seen motion begin."), Hope is transformed into an uncontrollable desire to dissolve into the violence of the world ("I long to fly, to swim, to bark, to shout, to howl."), and Faith becomes an identification with brute nature, the soft and somber stupidity of things ("I wish to huddle upon these forms, to penetrate each atom, to descend to the depths of matter—to become pure matter.")

This book, which initially appears as a progression of slightly incoherent fantasies, can claim originality only with respect to its meticulous organization. What appears as fantasy is no more than the simple transcription of documents, the reproductions of drawings or texts, but their sequence conforms to an extremely complex composition. By assigning a specific location to each documentary element, it is also made to function within several simultaneous series. The linear and visible sequence of sins, heresies, divinities, and monsters is merely the superficial crest of an elaborate vertical structure. This succession of figures, crowded like puppets dancing the farandole, also functions as: a trinity of canonical virtues; the geodesic line of a culture born in the dreams of the Orient and completed in the knowledge of the West; the return of History to the origin of time and the beginning of things; a pulsating space that expands to the outer limits of the universe and suddenly recedes to return to the simplest element of life. Each element and each character has its place not only in the visible procession, but in the organization of Christian allegories, the development of culture and knowledge, the reverse chronology of the world, and the spatial configurations of the universe.

In addition, *The Temptation* develops the encapsulated visions in depth as they recede, through a series of stages, to the distance; it constitutes a volume behind the thread of its speeches and under its line of successions. Each element (setting, character, speech, alteration of scenery) is effectively placed at a definite point in the linear sequence, but each element also has its vertical system of correspondences and is situated at a specific depth in the fiction. This explains why *The Temptation* can be the book of books: it unites in a single "volume" a series of linguistic elements that derive from existing books and that are, by virtue of their specific documentary character, the repetition of things said in the past. The library is opened, catalogued, sectioned, repeated, and rearranged in a new space; and this "volume" into which Flaubert has forced it is both the thickness of a book that develops according to the necessarily linear thread of its text and a procession of marionnettes that, in deploying its boxed visions, also opens a domain in depth.

V

Saint Anthony seems to summon *Bouvard et Pécuchet,* at least to the extent that the latter stands as its grotesque shadow, its tiny, yet boundless, double. As soon as Flaubert completed *The Temptation,* he began his last book. It contains the same elements: a book produced from other books; the encyclopedic learning of a culture; temptation experienced in a state of withdrawal; an extended series of trials; the interplay of illusions and belief. But the general shape is altered. First, the relationship of the Book to the indefinite series of all other books has changed. *The Temptation* was composed of fragments drawn from invisible volumes and transformed into a display of pure phantasms: only the Bible—the supreme Book—shows the sovereign presence of the written word in the text and on the center of its stage; it announced, once and for all, the powers of temptation possessed by the Book. Bouvard and Pécuchet are directly tempted by books, by their endless multiplicity, by the frothing of works in the grey expanse of the library. In *Bouvard et Pécuchet,* the library is clearly visible—classified and analysed. It can exert its fascination without being consecrated in *a* book or transformed into images. Its powers stem from its singular existence—from the unlimited proliferation of printed paper.

The Bible has become a bookstore, and the magic power of the image has become a devouring appetite for reading. This accounts for the change in the form of temptation. Saint Anthony had withdrawn into idle seclusion in his desire to avoid the disturbing presence of others; yet, neither a living grave nor a walled fortress are sufficient protection. He had exorcised every living form but they returned with a vengeance, testing the saint by their proximity but also by their remoteness. These forms surround him on every side, possess him, but disappear as he extends his hand. Their operation places the saint in a state of pure passivity: his only function was to localize them in the Book through happy memories or the force of imagination. All of his gestures, every word of compassion, and any show of violence, dissipate the mirage—proving that he had suffered a temptation (that only in his heart did an illusory image take on reality). Bouvard and Pécuchet, on the other hand, are indefatigable pilgrims: they try everything, they touch and are drawn to everything; they put everything to the test of their marginal industry. If they withdraw from the world as the Egyptian monk did, it is an active retreat, an enterprising use of their leisure where they summon, with constant recourse to their extensive reading, all the seriousness of science and the most solemnly printed truths. They wish to put into practice everything they read, and if success eludes them, as the images dissipate before Saint Anthony, it is not as a result of their initial gesture but of their persistent search. Their temptation arises from zealousness.

For these two simple men, to be tempted is to believe. It is to believe in the things they read, to believe in the things they overhear; it is to believe immediately and unquestioningly in the persistent flow of discourse. Their innocence is fully engaged in this domain of things already said. Those things that have been *read* and *heard* immediately became things *to do*. But their enterprise is so pure that no setback can alter their belief: they do not measure their truths by their success; they do not threaten their beliefs with the test of action. Possible disasters always remain outside the sovereign field of belief and their faith remains intact. When Bouvard and Pécuchet abandon their quest, they renounce not their faith but the possibility of applying their beliefs. They detach themselves from works to maintain the dazzling reality of their faith in faith. They repeat, for the modern world, the experiences of Job; stricken through their knowledge and not their possessions, abandoned by science and not by God, they persist, like him, in their fidelity—they are saints. For Saint Anthony, unlike these modern-day saints, temptation lies in the sight of the things without belief: it is to perceive error mixed with truth, the spectre of false gods resembling the true God, a nature abandoned with providence to the immensity of its spaces or the unleashing of its vital forces. And paradoxically, as these images are relegated to the shadows from which they emerged, they carry with them some of the belief that Saint Anthony had invested in them, if only for an instant—a part of the faith he had invested in the Christian God. The disappearance of those fantasies that seemed most inimical to his faith does not forcefully reinstate his religion, but gradually undermines it until it is completely taken from him. In their fanatical bloodshed, the heretics dissolve the truth; and the dying gods gather into their darkness part of the image of the true God. Anthony's saintliness was broken in the defeat of those things in which he had no faith; and that of Bouvard and Pécuchet triumphs in the downfall of their faith. They are the true elect. They were given the grace denied the saint.

The relationship between sainthood and stupidity was undoubtedly of fundamental importance for Flaubert; it can be found in Charles Bovary; it is visible in *Un Coeur simple,* and perhaps as well, in the *Sentimental Education;* it is essential to *The Temptation* and *Bouvard,* but it adopts symmetrically opposite forms in these books. Bouvard and Pécuchet link sainthood to stupidity on the basis of the will-to-act, the dimension where they activate their desires: they had dreamed of being rich, of being men of leisure and independent means, men of property, but in achieving these goals, they discover that these new roles necessitate an endless cycle of tasks and not a pure and simple existence; the books that should have taught them how to exist dissipated their energies by telling them what they must do. Such is the stupidity and virtue, the sanctity and simplemindedness of those who zealously undertake to make of themselves what they already are, who put into practice received ideas, and who silently endeavor throughout their lives to achieve union with their inner selves in a blind and desperate eagerness. On the other hand, Saint Anthony links simplemindedness to sainthood on the basis of a will-to-be: he wished to be a saint through a total deadening of his senses, intelligence, and emotions, and by dissolving himself into the images that come to him through the mediation of the Book. It is from this that the temptations increase their hold upon him: he refuses to be a heretic, but takes pity on the gods; he recognizes himself in the temptations of Buddha, secretly shares the raptures of Cybele, and weeps with Isis. But his desire to identify with the things he sees triumphs when faced with pure matter: he wishes to be blind, drowsy, greedy, and as stupid as the "Catoblepas"; he wishes that he were unable to lift his head higher than his stomach and that his eyelids would become so heavy that no light could possibly reach his eyes. He wishes to be a dumb creature—an animal, a plant, a cell.

He wishes to be pure matter. Through this sleep of reason and in the innocence of desires that have become pure movement, he could at least be reunited to the saintly stupidity of things.

As Anthony is about to accomplish his desire, the day returns and the face of Christ shines in the sun: the saint kneels and returns to his prayers. Has he triumphed over his temptations; has he been defeated and, as a punishment, must the same cycle be indefinitely repeated? Or has he achieved purity through the dumbness of matter; is this the moment when he achieves a true saintliness by discovering, through the dangerous space of books, the pulsation of innocent things; is he now able to *perform,* through his prayers, prostrations, and readings, this mindless sanctity he has become?

Bouvard and Pécuchet also make a new start: having been put to the test, they are now made to abandon the performance of those actions they had undertaken to become what they were initially. They can now be purely and simply themselves: they commission the construction of a large double desk to reestablish the link to their essential nature, to begin anew the activity which had occupied them for over ten years, to begin their copying. They will occupy themselves by copying books, copying their own books, copying every book; and unquestionably they will copy *Bouvard et Pécuchet.* Because to copy is *to do* nothing; it is *to be* the books being copied. It is to be this tiny protrusion of redoubled language, of discourse folded upon itself; this invisible existence transforms fleeting words into an enduring and distant murmur. Saint Anthony was able to triumph over the Eternal Book in becoming the languageless movement of pure matter; Bouvard and Pécuchet triumph over everything alien to books, all that resists the book, by transforming themselves into the continuous movement of the book. The book opened by Saint Anthony, the book that initiated the flight of all possible temptations is indefinitely extended by these two simple men; it is prolonged without end, without illusion, without greed, without sin, without desire.

NEIL HERTZ

Flaubert's Conversion

In the *Search for a Method,* in various interviews, and again in a brief preface, Sartre has laid out clearly enough his reasons for writing *L'Idiot de la famille.* To begin with, he has set himself an intellectual problem conceived in the most general terms: he would like to answer the question "What can be known about a man?"—that is, to what extent is it possible to construct a single, coherent and truthful account of a life, what Sartre likes to call a "totalization," out of the various kinds of data (socioeconomic, psychoanalytic, etc.) that can be gathered about any given person? Isn't there a risk, he asks in his preface, that no such totalization is possible, that at best all we can produce is a collection of "heterogeneous and irreducible layers of meaning"? Perhaps, but Sartre would forestall such scepticism, and in the next sentence he makes his project explicit, in language whose tone shifts slightly as one reads it, from that of a modest working hypothesis to something more like that of a confession of faith: "This book attempts to prove that the irreducibility is only apparent and that each bit of information, once set in place, becomes a portion of a whole which never ceases building itself up [*la portion d'un tout qui ne cesse de se faire*]." It is the use of the reflexive in that last phrase that is both metaphysically exciting and somewhat puzzling: what is this entity which never ceases building itself up? It cannot be either a person's actual life or his own comprehension of his life—in the case of Flaubert, at least, we can be sure that those ongoing totalizations have come to a halt. Is it then, perhaps, the "Life" we hold in our hands, a

From *Diacritics* 2, no. 2 (Summer 1972). © 1972 by Diacritics, Inc.

book that is both ample and as yet incomplete? I don't mean to worry a sentence in Sartre's preface, but I do want to call attention to the tinge of the absolute that colors his prose whenever he refers to the activity of totalizing, and to a certain ambiguity about the status and location of this totalizing agent or self-creating whole. For I believe that such moments of tonal heightening best reveal the connection between Sartre's most general formulation of his aims as a biographer and his choice of his particular subject, Flaubert.

Sartre would assert that in one sense the choice of a subject doesn't matter—anyone would do, provided we had a certain amount of information about him at our disposal—but he is thoroughly aware that he had his reasons for choosing Flaubert. In his preface he mentions a number of these: his well-known fascination with (and antipathy to) Flaubert, the fact that the novelist had already "objectified himself" in his works, the availability of so much material for interpretation in the early writings and in the correspondence, the centrality of Flaubert "at the crossroads of all our contemporary literary problems." But still another reason, the most strikingly worded Sartre has produced, does not appear in the preface: it is to be found in his conversation with the editors of the *New Left Review:* Why Flaubert? "Because he is the imaginary. With him, I am at the border, the barrier of dreams." (The interview appeared in the *New Left Review,* no. 58. An abridged version was reprinted in *The New York Review of Books,* 26 March 1970. The entire text, in French, may be found in *Situations 9* [Paris: NRF, 1972].) Here again the language rises, this time to a lyrical rendering of a moment of absolute confrontation across the threshold that divides two realms. The encounter between the biographer and the life he would rehearse and interpret, between Sartre and his subject, is figured here as an allegory of encounter between the real and the imaginary, because of the nature of this particular subject. Sartre takes this as a challenge that calls forth his efforts as a would-be totalizing biographer: one writes about Flaubert in order to understand the relation between the real and the imaginary. Yet there is something oddly static about that image of confrontation; it feels more like an end of the line than it does like the beginning of a work-in-progress. Perhaps even too much like an end of the line: for it could be taken as a figure for the impossibility of the sort of totalization Sartre desires. Seen in this light, *L'Idiot* would seem to be an attempt to deny the implications of that figure; the work's declared purpose—to prove that the "irreducibility" of "heterogeneous layers of meaning" is only apparent—becomes part of a more fundamental attempt to prove that "real" and "imaginary" are not themselves heterogeneous and irreducible categories, that, in fact, the imaginary is reducible to the real. In the pages that follow I would like to consider one of the ways in which Flaubert both lends himself to this project—for the Flaubert of the letters, far from being Sartre's great antagonist, is in many ways in complicity with him—and, ultimately, frustrates it. I shall be concerned chiefly with the interpretation of Flaubert's collapse at Pont l'Evêque in January 1844, the event Sartre refers to as the novelist's conversion, and with the fictional representation of that event in the 1845 *Sentimental Education*.

Flaubert himself was the first to take the incident at Pont l'Evêque as a key to the understanding of his life: two years later, in what has become a famous letter, he wrote that it marked the division between "two distinct existences," the moment when his "active life" ended and "something else" began. What did he mean by this? Sartre devotes the last 350 pages of *L'Idiot* to answering that question, and what he sets forth is not merely the most elaborate but in places the most convincing interpretation we have, a sustained analysis that is patient, tactful and steadily shrewd. By locating his account of Pont l'Evêque at the turning-point of his own narrative, he endorses Flaubert's sense of the event's unique importance; the first and second major divisions of *L'Idiot* have followed the novelist through his childhood and adolescence, tracing his development into what Sartre calls a "passive agent" and arriving with him at a dead-end, where the contradictions inherent in his position are brought to bear, with intolerable pressure, on his life. On the last page of part 2 the dilemma is formulated: Flaubert finds himself incapable of continuing his work as a law student but equally incapable of speaking out against his father's wish that he continue. What will he do? Sartre insists that he cannot "do" anything, yet that something had to be "done." Part 2 ends on this note of somewhat melodramatic suspense; when the narration is taken up again we are presented with a spare, but no less melodramatic, account of what took place at Pont l'Evêque:

> One night in January '44, Achille and Gustave are returning from Deauville, where they had gone to look over the chalet. It is dark out, as dark as the inside of a furnace; Gustave himself is driving the cabriolet. Suddenly, somewhere near Pont l'Evêque, as a wagon overtakes them on the right, Gustave drops the reins and falls thunderstruck at his brother's feet.

For Flaubert, Sartre claims, this was "a moment in which a life totalizes itself and realizes the destiny it has been bearing within itself"; the rest of part 3 will unfold the meaning of this totalization. Sartre proceeds by stages. First he considers the collapse as the epitome of Flaubert's neurosis—that is, as the conversion of the psychological into the somatic, a maneuver that allows the novelist to win his quarrel with his father without actually putting anything into words. For indeed the collapse, and the subsequent milder seizures in the months that followed, had the effect of absolving Flaubert of any further responsibilities as a law student, of focusing his family's concerned attention on him, and of leaving him free to read and write. Sartre sees in this Flaubert's "immediate, negative, and tactical response to an emergency." But now a further question arises: is there a fundamental and necessary relation between Flaubert's neurosis and his art? Sartre believes that there is, and sets out next to demonstrate that this tactical response, which a psychoanalyst would take as a symptom of "conversion-hysteria," can be interpreted "*at the deepest level* as a strategic and positive response to . . . the necessity and the impossibility . . . of being an Artist" (the italics are Sartre's); to this aspect of the maneuver Sartre gives the name of "the conversion to optimism," using the word "conversion" now no longer in its psychoanalytic but in its religious or metaphysical sense.

Sartre is now in a position to reinterpret the collapse in the light of that principle of total compensation which he likes to call the "*Qui perd gagne*"; when Flaubert falls senseless at his brother's feet he is, according to Sartre, betting that "he who loseth his life shall find it" and thus placing himself in a tradition of Augustinian transformation. But what is it Flaubert hopes to gain, in return for his "active life"? Sartre uncovers two layers of intention. There is, first of all, the most obvious hope: that Flaubert will see his powers as an artist emerge out of the wreckage of his life. This wish Sartre finds most fully elaborated in the last chapters of the 1845 *Sentimental Education*, chapters that were added to the novel in the months following Pont l'Evêque. But there is something a bit strident and schematic about the end of that novel, in which Flaubert's hero is abruptly transformed from a moody young man with conventional literary yearnings into someone we are told is now a serious writer; Sartre is led to suspect that the ease with which the hero is consolidated in his new role as Artist masks a certain uneasiness on his creator's part, and that the "real meaning of the '*Qui perd gagne*'" may lie at a still deeper level. The final section of *L'Idiot* sets out in search of that "real meaning" and discovers it to be ultimately religious: despite his proclaimed and no doubt sincere agnosticism, "what the convert of Pont l'Evêque is trying to recover is that identification of the Father with God which once guaranteed his personal identity."

This is but the barest account of the richly detailed and energetic interpretative activity at work in *L'Idiot de la famille;* what I hope to have suggested is that the structure (although certainly not the tone) of Sartre's book is basically that of a certain kind of hagiography: the narrative of a life whose meaning is disclosed through the progressively deepened understanding of a single, decisive moment of conversion. Sartre is anxious to insist both on the uniqueness of Flaubert's conversion as a moment in time (e.g., Sartre tries to fix the exact date of Flaubert's first seizure and to privilege it over its subsequent repetitions) and on its structural unity as a "fundamental and *single* conversion in which the tactical level and the strategic level reciprocally symbolize each other" (the italics are Sartre's). Why this insistence? I believe that it is because the conversion is meant to serve as that prior act of synthesis whose (real) existence underwrites the totalization Sartre aims at in his biography: the interpreter need no longer fear that he is faced with the merely tautological "unity" of an individual life if that life has already caught up its own threads and, in effect, totalized itself. It is in this way that Flaubert's letter serves Sartre's purposes: when the novelist writes of his "two distinct existences" and orders them in an irreversible sequence he is telling a story Sartre wants to hear, for it is a story whose burden is the possibility of totalization. Sartre may wish to introduce qualifications into his own rehearsal of that story—to catch Flaubert out in moments of self-mystification, to distinguish and stratify the levels at which the life discloses itself, etc.— but the unity of Flaubert's sense of his life and, more importantly, its organization in time, leading up to and away from a point of conversion, is never seriously challenged in *L'Idiot de la famille*.

Yet there are signs that Flaubert himself had a more complex understanding of the meaning of Pont l'Evêque—not in the letters, which substantiate Sartre's view, but in those very last chapters of the 1845 *Sentimental Education* which Sartre reads as corroborating evidence. It is worth looking more closely at those chapters, for while they offer themselves to Sartre's interpretation they also raise questions about that central link—between conversion and totalization—upon which Sartre's project seems to depend. We shall see that in order to interpret the novel as he does Sartre must ignore or minimize the effect of this questioning.

No one is sure exactly how far along in his manuscript Flaubert had come before his seizure obliged him to put it aside, but it is certain that chapters 26 and 27 were not composed until sometime late in 1844. A radical change in tone and in conception is apparent in the opening lines of chapter 26, where one of the two main characters, Jules, is seen walking through the countryside; it is very quickly obvious that he is a much more interesting figure than he was when he last appeared in the novel. Some twenty pages earlier he was hardly more than a poet manqué; now we find him involved in a wavering but progressive and increasingly complex meditation. The language of these pages is often strongly articulated, the turns of thought are subtle, and the concerns very clearly Flaubert's own; there can be no doubt that he is writing out of the experience of Pont l'Evêque. What is at issue is precisely the question of totalization: the first of these chapters dramatizes Jules's attempts to locate himself in relation to his own past, to his conception of art and to the world at large, and it moves towards two climactic moments, one presented as a sublime but fleeting vision of totality, the other as a grotesque complement to that vision, an uncanny encounter with a hideous dog. It is as a result of this encounter, we are meant to feel, that Jules's life is transformed; in Sartre's account the meeting with the dog represents the "symbolic" equivalent of Pont l'Evêque, "the instant in which the convert, in fear and trembling, sees his life totalized, in all its ugliness." What follows, in chapter 27, is a lengthy and at times rhapsodic presentation of Jules in his new incarnation as Artist: "He has become a grave and great artist, whose patience is untiring and whose devotion to the ideal is no longer intermittent; by taking his form from a study of the masters, and by drawing out of himself the matter that it should contain, he found that he had naturally acquired a new manner, a real originality."

But here a curious problem of interpretation arises. Sartre locates the moment of "definitive rupture," the dividing-line between Jules's old and new lives, in the space between the last lines of chapter 26 and the beginning of chapter 27. But, as I've already suggested, Jules is portrayed as a changed man even in the opening pages of chapter 26. He is first seen wondering at his own "serene immobility," a self-imposed "calm" which has succeeded in distancing him "so abruptly from his youth, and had required of him so harsh and so sustained an effort of will, that he had hardened himself to tenderness and had almost petrified his heart." This self-discipline was intended to separate him not only from his past emotions but from his present feelings as well: "Even while stimulating his sensibility with his imagination, his mind worked to annul the effects of this, so that the importance of the sensation (*le sérieux de la sensation*) would vanish as rapidly as the sensation itself." Despite certain "lapses and relapses," this program of "superhuman stoicism" has, we are told, been a thorough, almost a too-thorough success: "if [Jules] hadn't felt each day obliged, as an artist, to study [his passions] and to seek them out in others, then to reproduce them in the most concrete and salient form . . . he might have come almost to despise them." Jules's state of mind here is, it would seem, indistinguishable from what it will become after his encounter with the dog; if anything the language in these pages is more convincing, because considerably less inflated, than that of chapter 27. And indeed Sartre, in the course of a discussion of how Jules is represented *after* his conversion, draws repeatedly on these earlier pages. Each of the quotations above reappears in *L'Idiot* side-by-side with passages from chapter 27, as though there were no compelling reason to differentiate the two moments in Jules's progress (e.g., where Sartre constructs a long question out of a medley of fragments from both sections of the novel). But if no such differentiation is necessary, what becomes of the notion of conversion, of that "definitive rupture" that Sartre would locate in the lives of both Jules and his creator?

Sartre does not raise the question as explicitly as this, but his interpretation of the novel suggests what his answer might be: Jules is indeed transformed at the *end* of chapter 26, he would insist, but he was "already well on his way to conversion" before the episode of the dog. His movement along this path has been progressive but not steadily so: rather it is spoken of as a series of humiliating falls from which Jules "rebounds" each time to a higher position, only to fall still deeper the next time. "The last and deepest (fall)," Sartre notes, "evidently corresponds to the crisis of January '44." This is a plausible account of the structure of these chapters, but I don't find it a convincing one. What Flaubert's text presents, it seems to me, is at once a subtler and a more equivocal temporal scheme, whose implications are richer than the overt pattern of Jules's conversion can quite deal with. Chapter 26 makes sense when it is seen to be organized around two distinct time-schemes, one (Jules's) moving forward to a "conversion" at the end of the chapter, the other (Flaubert's) looking backward to a "conversion" that had already taken place in January 1944. Sometimes the two rhythms seem to be consonant, sometimes not, and out of this play there emerges a telling uncertainty. But it is not the uncertainty that Sartre finds in the novel, turning on the question of the "real meaning" of Pont l'Evêque; rather it is an uncertainty in Flaubert's understanding of what it means to write autobiographical fiction, that is, of what it means to invent (or to revive) a character named Jules, who can be made, more or less obliquely, to "represent" oneself at a moment of critical experience. The novel does not succeed in resolving this uncertainty, and if we look once more at the last chapters we can perhaps see why.

The "serenity" Jules experiences in the opening paragraphs of chapter 26 is not as "immobile" as he could wish; it soon dissolves into feelings of wonder and fear at the effects of his own detachment. Moving through a landscape that reminds him of various sentimental moments in his past, he finds himself unable to connect his thoughts and memories with one another; turning inwards he finds nothing but a painful "confusion, a whole world whose secret, whose unity, he could not understand." In Sartre's terms, we might say that Jules is confronted by all that is apparently "heterogeneous and irreducible" in his life. But within the space of a few intensely active paragraphs his thought begins to move into a more hopeful vein as he imagines the possibility that, through "art, pure art," the scattered elements of his life might be arranged in a meaningful sequence, then that this ordering may correspond to some benign, though hidden, principle: "Perhaps, therefore, everything that he had felt, endured, suffered had come for purposes he knew nothing about, directed towards a fixed and constant goal, unperceived but real." And it is at this point that Jules is granted his vision of totality:

> And then he thought that all that had once seemed to him so miserable might well have its own beauty and harmony; by synthesizing it and by bringing it back to first principles, he perceived a miraculous symmetry in the mere fact of the periodic return of the same ideas when confronted with the same things, the same sensations in the presence of the same facts; Nature lent itself to this concert and the entire world appeared to him, reproducing the infinite and reflecting the face of God; Art drew all those lines, sang out all those sounds, sculpted all those forms, seized their respective proportions and in unknown ways drew them to that beauty more beautiful than Beauty itself. . . .
>
> He lifted up his head, the air was pure and penetrated with the scent of briars; he breathed it in deeply and something fresh and vivifying entered his soul; the cloudless sky was as white as a veil, the sun, which was setting, sent out no rays, showed its face, luminous and easy to contemplate. It seemed to him that he was emerging from a dream, for he felt the freshness that one experiences on waking, and the naive surprise that takes hold of us on seeing again objects which seem to us new, lost as we were, just a moment before, in a world that has vanished. Where was he? in what place? at what time of day? what had he done? what had he thought? He tried to get hold of himself and to reenter the reality he had left behind.

The first of these paragraphs describes a sublime moment of totalization; but the effect of all such moments is to suspend and dissimulate the powerful expansive pressures that have generated them—like Wordsworth in "Tintern Abbey." Jules is "laid asleep" so that "with an eye made quiet by the power of harmony" he may "see into the life of things." Perhaps it would be more accurate to say that it is Jules's activity that is suspended and Flaubert's that is dissimulated, for it is out of that difference—between the author and his surrogate, however closely identified they may be—that the instability of such passages is developed. The precariousness of the moment can be felt in the shift from the first paragraph to the second, from "the entire world appeared to him, . . . reflecting the face of God" to "the sun . . . showed its face, luminous and easy to contemplate," a gentle shift that brings Jules back to a fuller consciousness just as the vision is fading. His reappearance is evoked in language that blends a sense of innocence and renewal with hints of imaginative imperialism: we are reminded that Jules's consciousness, like Flaubert's, is both the scene of this vision and a supplementary and disturbing element within that scene. And, significantly, Flaubert's scene immediately darkens: Jules comes to himself to the sound of the barking of a dog, and the rest of the chapter details the bizarre encounter with an animal that is recurrently described as repulsively ugly but in some horrid way fascinating.

Like the familiar details of the landscape in the chapter's opening pages, the dog reminds Jules of his past—is this creature, he wonders bathetically, perhaps the same spaniel he had once given to the woman he loved?—and he is again led into a meditative sequence, although this time the rhythm of his thoughts is more desperate and their content more lugubrious. Now the world appears to him not as a vision of totality or even as a confused series of impressions, but as sheer repetition: the dog keeps trailing him, barking steadily, and Jules strains to interpret this literally inarticulate speech:

> Jules tried to discover some difference in the monotony of these furious, plaintive and frenetic sounds; he forced himself to guess at and seize the thought, the thing, the prognostic, the tale or the complaint that they were trying to express; but his ear could hear nothing but the same vibrations, almost continuous, strident, always alike.

Into this void of meaning Jules's thought expands in morbid fantasy: he recalls suicidal broodings of his own, then fears that perhaps the dog's mistress has killed herself, and then, in what can be read as a sketch for the end of *Madame Bovary,* conjures up an image of "her corpse, the mouth half-opened, the eyes shut." His thought is approaching a point at furthest remove from his earlier vision; from what had seemed at the moment like a poised reconciliation of his imaginative powers with a fresh and sunlit world he has been led to an encounter in which the dog figures those same powers, but now seen as alien and threatening. The presentation is Gothic, deliberately excessive:

The clouds parted and . . . the moonlight lit up the accursed dog
who was still barking; . . . it seemed, in the night, as if two
threads of fire were issuing from its eyes and coming straight
towards Jules's face and meeting his gaze; then the beast's eyes
suddenly grew larger and took on a human form, a human feeling
palpitated within them, issued from them; out of them poured a
sympathetic effusion which grew and grew, always increasing and
invading you with an infinite seduction. . . .

There were no more cries, the beast was mute and did nothing
but widen that yellow pupil in which it seemed to Jules that he
could see his reflection; astonishment was exchanged, they confronted each other, each asking of the other things that cannot
be spoken. Quivering at this mutual contact, they were both ter-
rified, they were frightening each other; the man trembled under
the gaze of the beast, in which he believed he could see a soul,
and the beast trembled under the gaze of the man, in which it
saw, perhaps, a god.

Enlarging more rapidly than flame, Jules's thought had turned
into doubt, the doubt into certitude, the certitude into fear, the
fear into hatred. "Then die!" he screamed, shaking with anger
and smashing the dog's face with a violent and sudden kick; "Die!
die! get out of here! leave me alone!"

"He is the imaginary. With him, I am at the border, the barrier of
dreams." Sartre's characterization of Flaubert is to the point; Jules could
properly say the same thing of the dog, another figure of "the imaginary"
as a projected creature of the self. The encounter, in this case, is experienced
as a moment of mad expansiveness and uncertain exchange, followed by
panic: Jules's thought tailspins into murderous action. Yet his fall is simply
an accelerated and lurid sequel to the milder declension we noticed earlier,
when the image of the world reflecting the face of God was displaced by one
of Jules gazing easily at the sun. I have suggested that the instability of that
moment of plenitude and totalization was not accidental but inherent, a
function of the difference between an imagining self and whatever it seeks
to totalize. What is presented in the episode of the dog is someone experiencing that difference as madness and seeking to reduce it by violence. Jules
calms down, but his next act—his "conversion"—is no less a domestication:
it is still another attempt to reduce the anxious, vibratory temporality that
is figured so melodramatically in his exchange of glances with the dog, this
time not by eliminating the dog but by orienting his own life in a time-

scheme that offers a clear and reassuring sense of "before" and "after." This is what gives the novel the linear structure Sartre finds there. There is no doubt that he is in touch with one of Flaubert's intentions when he places Jules's conversion at the end of chapter 26 and sees in it a representation of Pont l'Evêque, for Flaubert himself has a stake in imagining Jules's life in these reassuring terms.

But Flaubert is also responsible for constructing the chapter in such a way that this linear pattern is blurred and cast in doubt. Jules may already be "saved" in its opening pages; if so, we see him fall again and again experience a conversion; conversion comes to seem less an act of totalization than what one repeatedly does when in despair of totalization. The crucial difference comes to seem not that between an old life and a new life— whether Jules's or Flaubert's—but that between Jules and Flaubert. And the discovery of the novel may be that that relationship is both irreducible and perpetually subject to disorientation. Flaubert's relation to Jules—that is, to an imagined self—is as shifty, as open to dislocating fantasy, as is Jules's to the dog.

Or as Sartre's to Flaubert, for that matter, if we turn and read L'Idiot de la famille in the light cast by the 1845 Education. To say that Flaubert "is" the imaginary is to grant him the prestige of an object of absolute ambivalence, by turns repulsive and seductive, like Jules's dog. The biographer then sets out to totalize that figure. The hope is not simply that another man's life, with all its contingent differences, will be truthfully interpreted, or even that the possibility of such a totalization will be vindicated, but that a more radical difference will be reduced. There is a passage in The Words that shows Sartre at work on this project at an early age:

> The dining-room would be bathed in shadow. I would push my little desk against the window. The anguish would start creeping up again. The docility of my heroes, who were unfailingly sublime, unappreciated and rehabilitated, would reveal their unsubstantiality. Then it would come, a dizzying, invisible being that fascinated me. In order to be seen, it had to be described. I quickly finished off the adventure I was working on, took my characters to an entirely different part of the globe, generally subterranean or underseas, and hastily exposed them to new dangers: as improvised geologists or deep-sea divers, they would pick up the Being's trail, follow it, and suddenly encounter it. What flowed from my pen at that point—an octopus with eyes of flame, a twenty-ton crustacean, a giant spider that talked—was I myself,

a child monster; it was my boredom with life, my fear of death, my dullness and my perversity. I did not recognize myself. No sooner was the foul creature born than it rose up against me, against my brave speleologists. I feared for their lives. My heart would race away; I would forget my hand; penning the words, I would think I was reading them. Very often things ended there: I wouldn't deliver the men up to the Beast, but I didn't get them out of trouble either. In short, it was enough that I had put them in contact. I would get up and go to the kitchen or the library. The next day, I would leave a page or two blank and launch my characters on a new venture. Strange "novels," always unfinished, always begun over or, if you like, continued under other titles, odds and ends of gloomy tales and cheery adventures, of fantastic events and encyclopedia articles. I have lost them and I sometimes think it's a pity. If it had occurred to me to lock them up, they would reveal to me my entire childhood.

L'Idiot takes its place in that series of "strange 'novels' . . . continued under other titles" which Sartre accurately names as perpetually displaced versions of autobiography. The final encounter with the Beast, the ultimate totalizing moment, is deferred, perhaps for reasons that may be more respectable than Sartre believes them to be. Flaubert's fascination is partly that of the Beast, but partly that of another writer, one who has, at certain points in his work, made it clear that he has understood the entire project more thoroughly than Sartre and who thus threatens Sartre with the possibility that both the melodrama and the wistfulness that suffuse this childhood memory are somewhat unnecessary.

VERONICA FORREST-THOMSON

The Ritual of Reading Salammbô

SPEECH AND VISION

When we are trying to organize our reading of *Salammbô*, looking for a framework in which to integrate the objects, persons, and events which confront us, we find two opposing principles which may be called speech and vision. These two elements create a dialectic between the terms of which the novel constitutes its possibilities of action and personality. Speech belongs to the level of action in war and politics where the characters attempt to gain power over each other by manipulating forms of behaviour that derive from a collective consciousness. On this level the relationship between characters and between characters and the world in which they act is conditioned by the forms of understanding associated with such limited and illusion-ridden consciousness. Vision presents us with another kind of understanding, often mediated through religion and ritual, but present also when the characters simply stand gazing mutely in the presence of another, or of a scene which cannot be accommodated by any preestablished method of making sense. Because of the inadequacy in modes of translating into forms of action and speech this other kind of understanding, the two levels remain dissociated from each other. Further, since the norm of intelligibility is given by the social action of the level of speech and since also this norm is criticized by being juxtaposed with the presentation of its inadequacy, there is no principle which will make the novel as a whole intelligible, either to the characters or to the reader.

From *Modern Language Review* 67, no. 4 (October 1972). © 1972 by the Modern Humanities Research Association.

We may, however, see the possibility of such a principle in the act of narration itself which, together with myth and ritual, provides for a transformation of unmediated experience into organized patterns. This gives considerable importance to narrations by the characters within the text, especially when these occur in the context of myth and ritual. For narration as an action within the text acts as an analogue for two extratextual activities: the novelist's ordering of his material, and the reader's attempt to make sense of this ordering. The reader must see certain elements within the novel as metaphors for his own activity because it is only thus that some overall principle of understanding may be included in the structure of the work. If the order imposed by the novelist on his material does not provide such a principle, the reader is forced to try to do so himself. In a sense then, it can only be the reader's narration—his idea that narration implies an intelligible organization of language—that synthesizes the two disparate levels of the text. We have here an illustration of Barthes's statement that "l'enjeu du travail littéraire . . . c'est de faire du lecteur, non plus un consommateur, mais un producteur du texte" (S/Z).

In his search for a new pattern, the reader will seize upon any pretext to make the situation of certain characters into a symbol for this attempt to re-order the work; he will also tend to give importance to themes in the book that seem metaphors for such an activity. Thus arises the centrality of myth and ritual and of the figures who try to use the forms of these available to them to integrate their actions and experiences more fully than do the other characters. Such figures are Mâtho, the priest Schahabarim, and, of course, Salammbô herself. These characters lack a framework of understanding in which their actions (speech) and their vision of different kinds of being than their actions allow them, may be made to relate. The whole plot of the novel may be seen as a series of attempts to construct such a framework; and from the failures and illusions to which this gives rise appear the famous effects of Flaubertian irony. The fictions of the imagination, here represented by religion, do not accord with the facts of the world in terms of which these fictions must be realized.

If, however, such attempts are regarded by the reader as metaphors for his own activity, they cannot be treated entirely ironically. If the reader is aware that, in reading, he is creating a new pattern which includes his processes of understanding, he will have to recognize that, as this new pattern is identified with certain elements in the text, it now forms part of the world of the text. In the text, all kinds of understanding are shown as provisional and relative; so that any discovery of the "reality" of a situation misunderstood by the characters, for example that Salammbô's mystical fervour is motivated by sexual desire, is immediately undercut. But this means that there is no consistent factual element against which the characters' fictions may be exposed as illusory.

The reader is in no better position than the characters to discover the "reality" behind their situations. Or rather, he is only quantitatively better off, in that he has access to all situations and all points of view; but this does not provide him with an overall principle for making the situations intelligible. The only reality behind the chaotic appearances of the novel is the reality of the activity of reading it. Hence the pattern which takes most account of the resemblance between the situation of the reader and that of the characters seems the nearest approach to what is really happening in the novel. Such a pattern is, in Barthes's sense of the term, a "simulacrum" of the work: "il manifeste une catégorie nouvelle de l'objet, qui n'est ni le réel ni le rationnel, mais le fonctionnel" ("L'activité structuraliste," in *Essais critiques*). *Salammbô* is a very clear case of a literary work in which the notion of reality is entirely dependent on the notion of functionality, of "how we make an object understandable." Far from our interpretation of the novel being measured against a standard of reality presented in it, it is our interpretation itself that provides the standard.

With the appearance of Spendius this pattern of interpretation begins to emerge. In the first pages we are presented with a confusion of objects, crowds, and actions which appear incomprehensible except in terms of the simplest identifications provided by the Flaubertian "c'était. . . ." Spendius is the first to differentiate himself from the crowd, and he does so by speaking, looking at the sky, holding a cup, and invoking the gods. These three elements recur constantly when a character is brought into focus as the incarnation of an organizing principle. Speech, vision, and drinking—which is related to speech, on the one hand, with absorption as a metaphor for dominance, and to vision, on the other, through its association with ritual— are among the "rites" of narration which, through our arrangement of them, structure the novel.

Spendius attempts to incorporate ritual with a story that has political purposes: "Il laissa tomber la coupe et conta son histoire." This kind of narration, which synthesizes speech and vision by accommodating the latter to the world of the former, represents a perverted understanding. Nevertheless it does provide the reader with a provisional solution to the mystery associated with both these activities when they occur separately.

Speech is ordinarily confined to imperatives and ejaculations; its association with the level of action involves it in illusion. The characters do not know why they act; the chaos of possible explanations, like the excess of religious interpretations, makes any consistent motivation impossible. Speech, then, belongs to the area of chance and delusion. It is also the means by which the characters try to dominate each other in political or strategic intrigues; when they use it for this purpose they must comply with the forms of speech that are collectively comprehensible; thus speech represents the constriction of preformulated modes of understanding, and denies the characters any extension in the kinds of sense they may make of their world.

The principle of vision is mysterious in a different way. It is associated—naturally enough, since scenes form the background to action—with descriptive passages and with the imperfect tense. It belongs to the area in which the characters are trying to extend their understanding and to integrate more elements of their experience, both of others and of the world, than are necessary to action; hence vision frequently incapacitates a character for understanding his own functioning on the level of action; for there he is still trapped in the chaotic corruption of the collective consciousness. This is the case with Mâtho and Salammbô until the end of the novel. Vision is also associated with the religious rites in which the characters try to extend their understanding of the nature of the gods, rather than simply to placate them according to social formulae.

Narration combines speech and vision, the level of action and the level of expanded understanding; for it is not only in itself a physical and social act implying an audience of other characters which the narrator wishes to influence by his story, it also presents access to a world where human actions have a coherent meaning which the speaker understands and wishes to communicate as something distinct from the single limited situation in which his narration takes place. It is the only access to a world of coherently understood action that the novel provides. So that when a character narrates a story—as also when he performs a religious rite proper, instead of merely acting in accordance with a religious convention—he temporarily dominates the organization of the text. In this way he acts as a surrogate for the author—the invisible "narrator," who is in fact a by-product of the reader's idea that narration guarantees the intelligibility of the world it presents.

However great, then, may be our awareness that the character is insincere, limited, or deluded in his attempt to combine speech and vision, we find it difficult to dissociate ourselves from his view of the situation. For what he is doing is so similar to our own attempt, in reading, to repeat the process of ordering that the author has performed—which we believe the author to have performed—before us. It could not, therefore, be true, as R. J. Sherrington claims (in *Three Novels by Flaubert: A Study of Techniques*), that the collective point of view is predominant in *Salammbô;* for it is not what we are looking for to help us find a thematic integration for the work. The collective point of view presents us with nothing but chaos and the perversions of understanding which cause cruelty and intrigue.

I should also disagree with Sherrington's acceptance of the ironic devaluation of the characters' attempts to see their actions as in some way related to the gods. In the case of Mâtho and Salammbô this attempt involves a view of their actions and identities as a metaphor for the divine. And, once again, this need to construct metaphoric relations is too similar to the reader's activity of re-ordering to be dismissed. The exotic environment is not strange simply to the modern reader; the central characters themselves find it strange. And what they find strange in it is the framework through which it forces them to interpret their own actions and their relation to other human beings. This, on another level, is exactly what puzzles the reader, who is unsure of the concept of personality appropriate in the world of the novel.

Despite our reservations about Spendius's viewpoint as an organizing principle, then, it is accepted as such in the first two chapters of the novel. We know that his invocation of the gods is insincere, that he uses social and religious rituals as a means of power rather than of understanding, and that the story he tells—his own past history—is a way of directly influencing his present situation. The outcome of his prominence is simply trouble, caused, first, by the demand for the ceremonial goblets of the Sacred Legion, and later, by his use of Mâtho's vision of Salammbô to the end of provoking war. Because he is at this stage the only character who is presented as understanding his actions, purposes, and relation to others, with any consistency, he does, all the same, provide a support for the reader.

Spendius's prominence here both prepares for, and contrasts with, the first appearance of Salammbô later in the same chapter. She is distinguished by a relationship of vision with the mercenaries: "Immobile et la tête basse, elle regardait les soldats" and "elle marchait lentement entre les tables des capitaines, qui se reculaient un peu en la regardant passer." She answers her own question "Qu'avez-vous fait!"—a question which relates to more important matters than the eating of the sacred fish, for none of the characters (except Spendius) knows what he is doing or what is his relation to the sacred—by a retreat into her own world of religious ritual. This retreat is effected by telling a story; she thus combines speech and vision. But in her narration, in contrast to that of Spendius, contact with the area where language affects action is lacking. For the barbarians do not understand her idiom. Her story, then, sets her apart from her immediate situation.

Salammbô can influence others only by symbolizing for them something which they do not understand; the significance of the phrase "Personne

encore ne la connaissait" extends beyond this first chapter. Doubt about her
identity is central to the whole work: in what sense is Salammbô Tanit? and
who is Tanit, as a power which the reader can believe important in controlling the action, except the idea that Salammbô has of the nature of divinity? If Tanit is simply a delusion shared with the heroine by the rest of
the characters, what is the controlling power, and what is the source of
Salammbô's influence?

This doubt is shared with the characters by the reader; and, unless the
whole problem can be dismissed ironically as a delusion, it remains unre-
solved at the end. The point is made in a recent article by Jean Rousset when
he traces the "signification seconde de l'œuvre, celle qui couvre d'un sym-
bolisme astral les rapports des deux protagonistes; le livre doit se lire éga-
lement sur le plan mythique" ("Positions, distances, perspectives dans
Salammbô"). Rousset supports this claim by analysing the way in which,
throughout the novel, objects and persons are presented first as appearance;
the recognition of the reality behind these appearances comes later, so that
the movement towards understanding dominates the object to be understood
and the real world is seen as constituted by this movement in consciousness.
The creation of metaphor is thus fundamental in the structure of the novel.
This makes it impossible to devalue one level of metaphoric comparison in
favour of the other; to read, say, Tanit as simply a way of looking at
Salammbô.

But, in the context of a work where all explanation is provisional, it
would seem to be equally impossible to detach with the clearness that Rousset
desires, the symbolism of the mythical level. Such a pattern of symbolism
must, in reading—and I have argued that the process of reading is the only
basis on which we can build a structure for this novel—be reinserted in the
text. And there any certainty as to relations between the appearance of
characters in the world of action and their significance in the world of myth
is undercut by the very emphasis on the tentative and subjective nature of
the process of classification—of making sense of things—that Rousset so
well describes.

Salammbô, then, for the reader, as for Mâtho, represents what is not
understood. This tends to make us take seriously Mâtho's exalted view of
her; his are the eyes through which we try to focus on her; and it is his
question, "Où est-elle?," that we adopt.

This question is answered, provisionally, by Salammbô herself when, in
the third chapter, she invokes the moon-goddess. In the invocation she seems
to be providing us with possible attributes of herself. Tanit is responsible for
order and harmony: "le monde . . . comme en un miroir, se regarde dans ta

figure," but also for change: "Où donc vas-tu? pourquoi changer tes formes perpétuellement?"; and Salammbô ends her prayer thus, "O Tanit! tu m'aimes n'est-ce pas? Je t'ai tant regardée! Mais non! tu cours dans ton azur, et moi je reste sur la terre immobile." The world sees itself in the goddess, but all that it can see of her is a reflection of its own changing forms, apart from these she is, like Salammbô, simply a symbol of what is not understood.

There is an unbridgeable gap between the vision of such a symbol and any means of translating its vision into the world of action. It is from this fact that the Zaimph, the sacred veil, derives its power; it represents a way of translating vision into action, of integrating vision and speech; thus it gives its possessor the power of organizing and controlling the world of the novel through the principle of narration. But the Zaimph is also taboo and it is noticeable that this taboo is never really transgressed. In the two scenes where it figures most strikingly, the characters think that they are seeing it, but what they really see is a reflection of their own illusion.

In the first scene, Mâtho sees it as a symbol of his love for Salammbô; he uses the idea of the sacred to express the power of his passion. For her, the idea of divinity has quite different associations; it is simply the veil of her tutelary goddess, the one prop that had been lacking in her re-living of the myth that was to make sense of her own experience. When she finally "gets the message" it is not from the Zaimph at all, but from Mâtho's attempt to embrace her. He tells her to look at the Zaimph: "J'ai été le chercher pour toi dans les profondeurs du sanctuaire! Regarde!"; but it is only when she looks at him that she unconsciously realizes what he is trying to use the sacred object to communicate:

> Elle s'avançait toujours . . . avec ses grands yeux attachés sur le voile. Mâtho la contemplait . . . et tendant vers elle le zaïmph, il allait l'envelopper dans une étreinte. Elle écartait les bras. Tout à coup elle s'arrêta, et ils restèrent béants à se regarder.

The lack of connexion between speech and vision in this scene is thus striking. Neither of the two characters appears to understand or even to hear what the other is saying. Mâtho's "Je t'aime" passes with no response other than Salammbô's "Donne-le!" The level of speech/action and the level of vision/attempt to expand understanding, remain completely separate, so that a possible integration in narration is suspended. We remember that the principle of narration was connected with myth and ritual as a way of making human actions coherently meaningful. Here, the impossibility of its operation appears in two parallel failures: that of the characters to communicate their ideas of divinity on the level of human speech/action and so to expand this

level to take in a fuller understanding; and also, the failure of the reader to
know how the "gods" of the novel are to be taken.

The Zaimph remains an enigmatic power for both characters and reader;
and this is underlined in the last sentence of the novel: "Ainsi mourut la fille
d'Hamilcar pour avoir touché au manteau de Tanit." We cannot take this
sentence simply as the voice of popular superstition; nor may the "common-
sense" explanation—of course her contact with the Zaimph caused her death
since it led to her contact with Mâtho, which, in turn, caused the emotional
stress that killed her—be accepted. For we do not know what it *means* to
have touched the veil of the goddess. The Zaimph remains a symbol for a
possible narrative integration which the text denies us. To this extent the
reader shares the characters' awe in the face of sacred power; and, once
again, cannot detach himself sufficiently to claim a reductive ironic understanding.

When the level of speech and the level of vision are thus disconnected
the characters can neither communicate with each other about what they see
nor fit their mute vision of each other into the world of action.

This is even more striking in the second scene with the Zaimph. In the
tent, Mâtho and Salammbô surround themselves with the apparatus of misunderstood myth. They use this, and the reader uses it with them, to plot
their positions relative to each other. They try to understand each other as
surrogates for the gods, Moloch and Tanit respectively. If the gods are taken
as symbols for the characters' need to integrate vision and speech, then the
gods are the cause of the union of Mâtho and Salammbô. This is in direct
contrast to the union, later in the same chapter, of Salammbô and
Narr'Havas, which is caused by the opposing plane of the action: politics
and war. On this plane the idea of divinity is perverted to serve ends that
are already understood, rather than being used to enlarge possible understanding.

But the union with Mâtho fails; and the reason for this is given in the
chapter immediately preceding: Salammbô's reaction to Schahabarim's narration of myth is described thus: "Elle acceptait comme vrais en eux-mêmes
de purs symboles et jusqu'à des manières de langage, distinction qui n'était
pas, non plus, toujours bien nette pour le prêtre." It is a distinction that is
not clear for the reader either; we are at a loss how to take the connexion
between such descriptive phrases as, "Quand Mâtho arriva, la lune se levait
derrière elle. Mais elle avait sur le visage un voile jaune à fleurs noires et tant
de draperies autour du corps qu'il était impossible d'en rien deviner," and
Mâtho's question "Qui est-tu?" The question is caused by physical conditions, her all-enveloping veils, and seemingly refers to physical identity; but

it has a wider significance and is never properly answered on the thematic level where identity has to accommodate the idea of the sacred.

There is the same mystery about how we are to connect speech and vision in a slightly later passage:

> La lune glissait entre deux nuages. Ils la voyaient par une ouverture de la tente—"Ah! que j'ai passé de nuits à la contempler! elle me semblait un voile qui cachait ta figure; tu me regardais à travers"

with the exclamation:

> "A moins, peut-être, que tu ne sois Tanit?"
> —"Moi, Tanit!" se disait Salammbô.
> Ils ne parlaient plus. Le tonnerre au loin roulait. Des moutons bêlaient, effrayés par l'orage.

Is the reader to use the physical details, the veils, the ordinary nightly passage of the moon, the sheep frightened by the storm, to contrast with and to undermine the characters' desire to give these details a place in their vision of each other? This is the usual critical reading; and with it is accepted the implication that the power of the Zaimph to integrate vision and action does not exist, or exists only in so far as it is a collective superstition which motivates the movement of armies and the fortunes of war.

An additional implication that there *is* nothing to see in the Zaimph, in the mystery of sacred power, except the characters' several versions of its place in their private world of illusion, accompanies this reading. Any other interpretation seems to incur the danger of sharing the characters' failure to distinguish between symbols and forms of language and the reality which they represent. But this failure is inherent in the reader's involvement with the novel which does not allow us to form a consistent picture of the relationship between language and reality. In a sense, then, the Zaimph as a symbol for potential integrated understanding, stands also for the reader's activity. So that its power and its mystery are to that degree more than illusion.

The way in which the contrast between speech and vision may be seen in a character's relation to the idea of divinity can also be illustrated in the case of Hamilcar. He is situated half-way between the world of perverted understanding in which ideas of the gods are used as tools in political intrigue and military strategy, and that other examination of the sacred which attempts to understand it as part of individual personality and which is thus included in the principle of vision.

At the beginning of the chapter entitled "Hamilcar Barca," we have: "Il s'efforçait à bannir de sa pensée toutes les formes, tous les symboles et les appellations des dieux, afin de mieux saisir l'esprit immuable que les appa- rences dérobaient." This assimilates him to the principle of vision; and the assimilation is only partly undercut by the "realistic" explanation of his need: "devenue faible tout à coup, il sentit le besoin de se rapprocher des dieux." Later on, however, he falls back to the level of perverted judgement and invokes the gods according to conventional formulae in support of his denial that Salammbô is associating with the mercenaries. Moreover the climax of this tirade is his statement that he will not even speak to her of the accu- sation. This amounts to a refusal to try to integrate his speech/action and the background of attitude that underlies speech and action. For he half- believes the accusation, and this is among the reasons for his final acceptance of military command. The misunderstanding consequent upon his refusal to speak to Salammbô is among the causes of the war. Thus refusal to integrate speech and personal vision reduces the character to the corrupted under- standing contained in the verbal formulae of others.

The same reduction occurs in the case of Schahabarim who also has intuitions of a new idea of the sacred but falls back, finally, on an explanation in the old terms: Moloch is superior to Tanit. It is significant that it should be he who, in the name of this false explanation, tears out Mâtho's heart. This scene can be read as the triumph of imperfect understanding over the attempt to transcend it. Mâtho and Salammbô, who symbolize this attempt, are unable to make the reductive move back to imperfect explanation. It is logical, therefore, that they should die; for the novel's undercutting of any final synthesis deprives them of a space in which to live.

LANGUAGE AND POWER

The use of conjunctions in the novel is bewilderingly eccentric. To take two trivial examples only: the darkness which Mâtho and Spendius contem- plate from the terrace of Hamilcar's palace is presented through their eyes as containing "de vagues amoncellements, pareils aux flots d'un océan noir pétrifié"; this is immediately contrasted with the appearance of the dawn: "Mais une barre lumineuse s'éleva du côté de l'Orient"; or again, after an account of Hamilcar's grudge against his daughter because of her sex, "Les dieux, plus tard, lui avaient envoyé un fils; mais il gardait quelque chose de son espoir trahi et comme l'ébranlement de la malédiction qu'il avait pro- noncée contre elle," we find, "Salammbô, cependant, continuait à marcher." In the second example the oddity is more striking for the presence of an ordinary use of conjunctions in "mais il gardait." One can only understand the "mais" of the first example and "cependant" here as indicating a lack of connexion between two levels of discourse: the level which presents the characters' point of view on a scene or person, and that which represents the independent physical being of such scenes and persons.

Such lack of connexion is clearly evident in Mâtho's account of his passion for Salammbô. Because he does not understand either her or his own feelings, he doubts her existence and the fact that he has seen her, that is, he doubts the connexion between his own consciousness and the objects of the external world:

> Ses yeux me brûlent, j'entends sa voix. . . . Il me semble qu'elle est devenue mon âme! Et pourtant, il y a entre nous comme les flots invisibles d'un océan sans bornes! . . . et je crois, par moments, ne l'avoir jamais vue . . . qu'elle n'existe pas . . . et que tout cela est un songe!

The physical world seems, then, to depend for its existence on the possibility of being understood. A little later, subjective point of view is directly contrasted with physical being:

> On sentait derrière elle comme l'odeur d'un temple, et quelque chose s'échappait de tout son être qui était plus suave que le vin et plus terrible que la mort. Elle marchait cependant, et puis elle s'est arrêtée.

These strange uses of conjunction are a special case of the peculiarity of causal connexions in the novel as a whole. The peculiarity is manifested in the power which certain kinds of language have to structure the action.

After Salammbô's first narration, which separates her from the surrounding situation and from the reactions of the other characters:

> Ils se demandaient ce qu'elle pouvait leur dire avec les gestes effrayants dont elle accompagnait son discours . . . ils tâchaient de saisir ces vagues histoires qui se balançaient devant leur imagination.

She produces another narration which is directly linked to the present situation:

> Elle employait simultanément tous les idiomes des Barbares. . . .
> Aux Grecs elle parlait grec, puis elle se tourna vers les Ligures, vers les Campaniens, vers les Nègres; et chacun en l'écoutant retrouvait dans cette voix la douceur de sa patrie.

We may ignore the suggested explanation for this change: that she desired to mollify the anger of the barbarians; for such explanations belong to the plane of reduction where we, as readers, are deluded into believing that we know the reality behind the characters' actions; this plane corresponds to the level of political and military intrigue, the level of perverted understanding, within the text.

The real motivating force at the thematic level is the effect of vision on speech. Both Mâtho and Narr'Havas have been watching Salammbô throughout the intervening paragraphs; and her reaction to the effect of her change in narration: "elle resta quelques minutes les paupières closes à savourer l'agitation de tous ces hommes," shows that it is the gaze of the other characters, concentrated in these two men, that has caused the change in discourse.

If we take Mâtho's gaze to symbolize the possibility of vision, while Narr'Havas represents the level of corrupted, political understanding, we may see why this narration of Salammbô's is only an imperfect incarnation of the principle. Her eyelids are closed so that she has retreated from the attempt to integrate vision and speech. She has abandoned the "sacred rhythm" of her first narration, and, though this rhythm persists in Mâtho's reaction and is recognized there when she is impelled to offer him wine from the golden cup, it is interfered with by the social explanation: "elle lui versa dans une coupe d'or un long jet de vin pour se réconcilier avec l'armée," and the social cliché—that a woman's offer of drink represents an offer of her body. The recognition is then dissipated by Narr'Havas's attack which belongs to the corrupted level of war.

The oddity of causal relations in the novel is to be understood as representing uncertainty as to the connexion between the subjective consciousness and physical reality; as such it is a further analogue for the opposition between vision and speech. This means that we interpret the relation between events in terms of this opposition. The relation is odd because it is incomplete; the framework of understanding that would integrate events with other events, speech with vision, and consciousness with the physical world, is lacking. This framework, we remember, was to be identified with the principle of narration which, in turn, is an analogue for the reader's activity in reordering the text. Hence it is the reader's language that has ultimate power to arrange the levels of language found in the novel.

But, of course, as I have already pointed out, the reader's activity can enter the novel only in terms of its metaphorical analogue, and Salammbô's second narration is a further example of failure to integrate speech and vision in a way that will be comprehensible to the collective consciousness. So many large issues depend on the possibility of communication, of finding intelligible symbols, that the thematic charge of her narration is too great to be accounted for by a single explanation in terms of realist psychology or physiology—for instance, that her change in narration and her reaction to the effect this produces are part of a syndrome of subconscious sexual desire. For one thing, such explanations reduce the reader to the level of incomplete understanding represented by the social world and lead him to ignore, not only many other elements in the text, but also the power of his own reading. Not only does the sense of mystery built up from the beginning of this section preclude our acceptance of the simplified level; when the scene finds its place in the whole work, when we know who Mâtho is and how his view of Salammbô develops, it is seen to contain a symbol for our attempt to reach complete understanding. The failure of Mâtho and Salammbô to reach understanding in the perverted political world is the failure of this symbol to organize the action of the novel.

As such Salammbô's narration in this scene contrasts with Spendius's degradation of it to an instrument of intrigue, both in his first speech and in the later "mistranslation scene" which functions as a parody of Salammbô's multilingualism. He uses the existence of many different languages to spread confusion; whereas she tries to make it an instrument of reconciliation.

There is another kind of narration which also contrasts with that of Salammbô. It is placed midway between political tool and means of reaching integrated understanding, and is exemplified in the figure of Schahabarim.

In his first narration the priest uses myth to hide the aspects of the goddess that are crucial to Salammbô's understanding, and for lack of which the understanding fails: the implications of the fact that Tanit "governs the loves of men." In this way he conceals the central mystery of the book, which is the nature and power of love and the way in which human actions may be understood in terms of the divine. His motives in this concealment are two. First, on the level of political intrigue, he has a duty to Hamilcar to keep Salammbô in ignorance of the real nature of the gods and hence of her own real nature; so that she may more easily be used as a political pawn. Secondly, on the level of vision, he regards Salammbô as a symbol for the divinity which he has been seeking and now despairs of finding. He thus does not wish to degrade her vague intuitions by allowing her to fit them into preestablished religious formulae; nor does he wish her to use these formulae to make discoveries of her own which would destroy her mystery for him.

These two motives are present again in his attempts to send her to retrieve the Zaimph. She is both a strategic tool and an experiment in religion which the priest wishes to conduct. Narration is prominent here also; he tells her many details of cosmology of which she had been ignorant. But he himself no longer believes that these are a true expression of the nature of the world: "grandissait dans sa pensée une religion particulière, sans formule distincte, et, à cause de cela même, toute pleine de vertiges et d'ardeurs." The fact that this intuition is immediately undercut by the bathos of "Il ne croyait plus la terre faite comme une pomme de pin; il la croyait ronde," does not destroy it. For we have been given enough indication that such intuitions, however ridiculous their translation into forms of belief, are a central force in the organization of the novel.

It is precisely because their translation into facts of belief and behaviour must be ridiculous that the novel is a tragedy in a fairly traditional sense. It presents the conflict of an ideal possibility of existence with the destruction of the ideal by the limitations of a world in which the power of the human mind to understand itself is limited.

The most important active attempt to organize such understanding is found in the "Salammbô" chapter in which she practises a rite whose elements are an ordered arrangement of looks ("Salammbô regarda l'étoile polaire"), speech (she invokes the goddess and thus associates herself with the principle of narration through an account of the nature and history of the sacred), and physical objects (the ground is strewn with a "poudre d'azur qui était semée d'étoiles d'or à l'imitation du firmament").

Once again the reader sees the character's activity as an analogue for his own attempt to order the kinds of discourse which represent these different thematic elements. So that we are presented with Salammbô's view that "l'idée d'un dieu ne se dégageait pas nettement de sa représentation, et tenir ou même voir son simulacre, c'était lui prendre une part de sa vertu, et, en quelque sort, le dominer," we recognize this as a symbol of our own processes of understanding the text.

It is notable that this idea recurs in the next chapter where it is used by Spendius to persuade Mâtho to steal the Zaimph: "[le voile] est divin lui-même, car il fait partie d'elle (the goddess, but also, Salammbô. Mâtho wishes to make the divinity of the veil a part of Salammbô and thus attain the level at which human actions and emotions can be made sacred). Les Dieux résident où se trouvent leurs simulacres." Spendius knows in what sense this is true: as a collective superstition that may be turned to strategic advantage. But we, along with Mâtho and Salammbô, cannot rest with this limited explanation. For, just as the veil is a metonymy for divinity, the action which centres on it is a metonymy for our process of reading. We are trying to construct a "simulacrum" of this process in terms of the novel so that we may dominate, by making objective, our forms of understanding.

Like the characters, however, we are only partially able to control the discourse with which we are confronted. We are presented here with an allegory of the limitations of the power of language. So that we identify ourselves once again with Salammbô when, reflecting on her experience in the tent, "elle n'aurait su de quelle manière, par quel discours l'exprimer." For, despite "les mots ayant par eux-mêmes un pouvoir effectif," their power to represent reality is limited by the social context in which they must operate; and in this novel we are shown a constant undermining of the power of language to connect action and understanding. This undermining cuts the ground from under our feet when we try to make such connexion on the level of critical reading.

THE ILLUSION OF IRONY

To conclude briefly: if the pattern I have tried to sketch is the most adequate means of taking account of the reader's contribution in organizing the various levels of *Salammbô,* it suggests that, when dealing with material that demands to be integrated as a metaphor for the processes of reading, the deflating kind of irony which relies on glances aside to an assumed reality, behind the action, of which the reader is aware but the characters are not, is bound to fail. For two reasons: first, this integration assumes, and must rely on, a certain structure in the process; it cannot completely undermine elements in its material which are seen as analogues for elements in this structure, since that would be to destroy itself: secondly, the reader cannot, without loss and an attenuated picture of his own part in the text as a whole, detach himself sufficiently to think that his "realistic" explanation is the finally valid integrating principle, that he understands where the characters do not. If he is made to recognize his own reading of the text as a process in constant flux, any finality of organization is an illusion.

Irony as it is usually understood relies on a complicity between author and reader to accept such an illusion. When we think, therefore, that it is the characteristic narrative method in *Salammbô* of showing the provisionality and partiality of human understanding and of conveying Flaubert's message, "ne pas conclure," we are mistaken. As Barthes puts it, "Flaubert ... en maniant une ironie frapée d'incertitude, opère un malaise salutaire de l'écriture: il n'arrête pas le jeu des codes (ou l'arrête mal), en sorte que ... *on ne sait jamais s'il est responsable de ce qu'il écrit* (s'il y a un sujet *derrière* son langage)" (*S/Z*). We may see this as a more profound kind of irony by which we are deluded into thinking that we can organize the text and are then forced to realize that this organization is only partial. But this process, as the observations quoted from Barthes indicate, is related to the wider issue of a "lack of fit" between language and the world that calls into question our concept of the relation between the subjective consciousness and physical reality; and it is impossible to look at this issue entirely ironically without self-contradiction. For we would be assuming in our forms of language the reality of the processes we set out to doubt. If, on the other hand, we deny altogether the reality of our own processes of operating with language, the consequences for our relation with literature would be even more disastrous than those which overtake our surrogates in this novel, Mâtho and Salammbô.

HAYDEN WHITE

The Problem of Style in Realistic
Representation: Marx and Flaubert

Prior to the nineteenth century, the problem of style in literature turned upon discussion of techniques of rhetorical composition and especially techniques of figuration by which to generate a secondary or allegorical meaning in the text beyond the literal meaning displayed on its surface. But the advent of realism meant, among other things, the rejection of allegory, the search for a perfect literality of expression, and the achievement of a style from which every element of rhetorical artifice had been expunged. For Flaubert, for example, style was conceived to be the antithesis of rhetoric; in fact, he identified style with what he called "the soul of thought," its very "content," to be distinguished from "form," which was merely thought's "body." Realism in the novel, like its counterpart in historiography, strove for a manner of representation in which the *interpretation* of the phenomena dealt with in the discourse would be indistinguishable from its *description;* or, to put it another way, in which *mimesis* and *diegesis* would be reduced to the same thing. Instead of mediating between two or more levels of meaning within the text, which "style" had been conceived to do during the time when "literature" was identified with "allegory," style now became a manner of translating phenomena into structures of discourse, transforming "things" into "words" without residue or conceptual superaddition.

The aim of realism, then, was literalness as against figurative expression, so much so that the difference between the style of Balzac and his successor

From *The Concept of Style,* edited by Berel Lang. © 1979 by Berel Lang. University of Pennsylvania Press, 1979.

Flaubert can be marked by the relative paucity of metaphors in the latter as compared with the former. Nonetheless, writers continued to seek to cultivate distinctive styles of representation. There was no thought, as far as I can determine, that the perfection of a realistic mimesis would result in a uniform mode of expression, with every discourse resembling every other. But the criterion for determining stylistic achievement had changed; it was no longer the manner or form of utterance that constituted style, but rather the matter or content of the discourse, as Flaubert had insisted. This meant that style had to do with cognitive perspicuity, the insight which the writer had into "the nature of things." To *see* clearly was to *understand* aright, and understanding was nothing other than the clear perception of the "way things are."

But this conflation of understanding with perception meant, obviously, that if allegory had been barred from entering the house of art by the front door, it had found entry at the back. It entered in the form of "history," no longer considered as a construction of the historian's powers of composition, as it had been considered in earlier times when historiography itself was regarded as a branch of rhetoric, but as a domain of "facts" which offered itself to perception in much the same way that "nature" did to the unclouded eye of the physical scientist. The "truth" of the realistic novel, then, was measurable by the extent to which it permitted one to see clearly the "historical world" of which it was a representation. Certain characters and events in the realistic novel were manifestly "invented," rather than "found" in the historical record, to be sure, but these figures moved against and realized their destinies in a world which was "real" because it was "historical," which was to say, given to perception in the way that "nature" was.

Now, arguably, history does not exist except insofar as a certain body of phenomena are organized in terms of the categories that we have come to associate with a specifically "historical consciousness." History does not consist of all of the events that ever happened, as the distinction between merely natural and specifically human events itself suggests. But neither do all human events belong to history, not even all human events that have been recorded and therefore can be known to a later consciousness. For if history consisted of all of the human events that ever happened, it would make as little sense, be as little cognizable, as a nature conceived to consist of all of the natural events that ever happened. History, like nature, is cognizable only insofar as it is perceived selectively, insofar as it is divided up into domains of happening, their elements discriminated, and these elements unified in structures of relationships, which structures, in turn, are conceived to manifest specifiable rules, principles, or laws which give to them their determinate forms.

The dominant view underlying early nineteenth-century historiography was that the structures and processes of history were self-revealing to the consciousness unclouded by preconceptions or ideological prejudices, that one had only to "look at the facts" or let the facts "speak for themselves" in order for their inherent meaning or significance as historical phenomena to come clear. And this view was shared by novelists and historians alike, with the former grounding their "realism" in their willingness to view history "objectively" and the latter distinguishing their work from that of the novelist by their exclusion of every "fictional" element from their discourse. Few commentators (Hegel, Droysen, and Nietzsche are notable exceptions) perceived that there were as many possible conceptualizations of history as there were ways of fashioning novelistic fictions; that there were as many styles of historical discourse as there were styles of realistic representation: that if realism in the novel could have its Constant, its Balzac, its Stendhal, and its Flaubert, realism in historical representation had its Michelet, its Tocqueville, its Ranke, its Droysen, and its Mommsen, each of whom felt himself to be representing history realistically, letting the facts "speak for themselves," and aspiring to a discourse from which every element of allegory had been expunged. In supposing that history constituted a kind of "zero degree" of reality, against which the fictive elements of a novelistic discourse could be measured, the realistic novelists of the nineteenth century both begged the question of the metaphysical base of their realism and effected an identification of style with content with which modern critical theory continues to have to contend. But this supposition, when examined critically, gives insight into the hidden allegorical elements in every realistic representation and raises the question of the problem of style in a way different from that which takes the form-content distinction for granted.

I propose to examine the problem of style which the project of realism in the novel raises by comparing a novelistic and a historical text produced at about the same time, both of which deal with the same general set of historical events and lay claims to a realistic representation of the events in question, but which are generally recognized as representing virtually antithetical ideological positions and different stylistic attributes. These texts are Flaubert's novel, *The Sentimental Education,* and Marx's history, *The Eighteenth Brumaire of Louis Bonaparte.* No two texts could be more dissimilar when viewed from the conventional standpoint of stylistic analysis that turns upon the distinction between form and content and identifies style with the former. Flaubert's discourse is cool, detached, leisurely to the point of shape-lessness in its depiction of what Lukács calls the fragmented world of its protagonist. Marx's discourse, by contrast, is shot through with an irony bordering on open sarcasm and contempt for the personalities, situations, and events he depicts; it manifestly originates in a preconceived judgment, ideological in nature, of the Second Republic, the bourgeoisie which created it, and the "charlatan," Louis Bonaparte, who overturned it. Whereas Flau-bert forebears to intervene, in his function as author, in the narrative, per-mitting his narrator's voice only a few laconic observations on the folly of human desire in a world devoid of heroism, Marx intervenes continually, alternating between the manner of the clear-eyed analyst of events, on the one side, and the ranting ideologue, on the other. If we conceive style, then, as manner of utterance, we would have to mark down Marx as a represen-tative of the ornate and Flaubert of the plain or mixed style, so different are the rhetorics of these discourses, so opposed the attitudes revealed on the level of language alone.

But if we conceive style as a perceivable strategy for fusing a certain form with a certain content, then there are remarkable similarities to be discerned between the two texts. The manifest form of both works is the mock *Bildungsroman,* in the one case, of a young French provincial seeking love and self-realization in Parisian society in the 1840s, in the other, of the French bourgeoisie itself, seeking to deal with the vicissitudes of its rise to power in a society fatally divided between contending classes, groups, and factions. This means that the content of both works is the drama of a de-velopment of a kind of consciousness—personal on the one side, and class on the other. The *Eighteenth Brumaire* is, we might say, "the sentimental education" of the French bourgeoisie, just as *The Sentimental Education* is "the eighteenth Brumaire" of a personification of a typical member of the French *haute bourgeoisie.* As thus envisaged, the respective plot-structures of the two works describe the same patterns of development: what begins as an epic or heroic effort at the implementation of values—personal on the one side, class on the other (although these reduce to the same thing ulti-mately, inasmuch as Frédéric Moreau, the protagonist of Flaubert's novel, has no values other than those given him by his historical situation)—pro-gresses through a series of delusory triumphs and real defeats, to an ironic acceptance of the necessity of abandoning ideals to the accommodation to realities in the end.

At the end of Flaubert's novel, Frédéric Moreau exists in precisely the same condition that the French bourgeoisie is depicted as having come to at the end of Marx's history, that is to say, as the very incarnation of a cynical acceptance of comfort at the expense of ideals. Even more strikingly, both authors insist—the one indirectly, the other directly—that the final condition in which their protagonists find themselves was already implicitly present in the structure of consciousness with which each embarked upon its "sentimental education." This structure of consciousness is shown to have been fractured from the beginning, fractured as a result of a fundamental contradiction between ideals consciously held at the outset and the conditions of existence in a dehumanizing society, one in which no *human* value can be distinguished from its commodity status. Frédéric Moreau's final rejection of his ideal love, Mme Arnoux, and his recognition that his life had failed at all crucial points correspond precisely with the French bourgeoisie's rejection of the ideals of "liberty, equality, and fraternity" which it had defended since the French Revolution and its acceptance of the card-sharp Bonaparte as the custodian of "order, family, property, and religion."

What is most remarkable, however, is yet a fourth resemblance between the two discourses, what I wish to name as their shared style, considered as a transformational model for marking off the phases in the development of the consciousnesses being depicted and for integrating them across a time series so as to demonstrate their progressive transumption. This model I call *tropological,* since it consists of a pattern of figurations which follows the sequence: metaphoric, metonymic, synecdochic, and ironic; and I identify this tropological model with the style of the discourses being analyzed since it constitutes a virtual "logic" of narration which, once perceived, permits us to understand why these discourses are organized in the way they are both on their surfaces and in their depths. The tropes of figuration, in other words, constitute a model for tracking processes of consciousness by defining the possible modes through which a given consciousness must pass from an original, metaphoric apprehension of reality to a terminal, ironic comprehension of the relationship between consciousness itself on the one side and its possible objects on the other. The tropes of metonymy and synecdoche function as models of transitional phases in this procession of modes of comprehending reality, the former governing the arrangement of phenomena into temporal series or spatial sets, the latter governing its integration into hierarchies of genera and species. The deployment and elaboration of experience under these modes of figuration is what I mean by style, a usage which permits us to pay tribute simultaneously to the conception of style as form and style as content, of style as the union of the two in a discourse, of style as both group and individual signature, of style as the process of composing a discourse, and of style as an attribute of the finished composition. Style as process, thus conceived, is the movement through the possibilities of figuration offered by the tropes of language; style as structure is the achieved union of form and content which the completed discourse represents.

Let us begin with a consideration of Flaubert's *Sentimental Education*. Tropological criticism directs us to look, first, not at plot, character development, or manifest ideological content (for this would presuppose that we already had an understanding of these phenomena at least as subtle as that of the author, or a better understanding of them, or that these were not problems for the author but solutions to problems), but rather at the principal *turns* in the protagonist's relationship to his milieux. Flaubert's narrative is divided into four chronological segments, three covering the years 1840–51 and ending with the coup d'état of Louis Bonaparte, and a fourth, comprising chapters 6 and 7 of part 3, which is separated by fifteen years from the last event recorded in chapter 5 of this part. In the last segment, the protagonist, Frédéric Moreau, and the woman he had loved, Mme Arnoux, meet after a fifteen-year separation in order to realize how ill-fated their love had been from the beginning; and Frédéric and his best friend, Deslauriers, meet in order to reflect on how and why their lives had gone wrong from first to last. We have no difficulty recognizing the ironic tone of these two chapters. The three characters in it display themselves the attainment of an ironic distance on their earlier passions, beliefs, ideals, follies, pride, and actions; and as Jonathan Culler points out in his reading of this passage, Flaubert himself reaches sublime heights of ironic sympathy for the attempts of the actors to ironize their own lives.

Having specified the ironic nature of the conclusion, we might be inclined retrospectively to cast the shadow of irony back over the sections preceding it. And this is legitimate enough, since we must suppose that irony (or what Freud called secondary revision) is the dominant trope of any consciously wrought fiction—and the governing, even if unacknowledged trope of all "realistic" discourse, insofar as its author supposes that he sees clearer or understands better what was "really happening" than did the agents whose actions he is describing or retailing. But here we must distinguish between the irony of the author and the consciousness he ascribes to his agents; and discriminate among the changing modes of relationship, between the protagonist and his milieux, which mark off the significant turns in the narrative. And we may say, following a Hegelian reading of the text, that here we have an allegory of desire, personified in all of the figures but condensed especially in that of Frédéric Moreau, projected into a world in which everything appears in the opaque form of a commodity, to be bought, exchanged, and consumed or destroyed without any awareness of what might be its true, its human value. It is the commoditization of reality that accounts for the melancholy tone of the whole novel, even in those moments of *hysterica passio* that constitute the most sensual scenes in the story. Flaubert has no need to set forth explicitly a theory of the true value of things; the absence of that value or its absence in the consciousness of the agents in his story is sufficiently suggested by the succession of frustrations which he recounts in the efforts of every one of them to achieve a deep union with its ideal object of desire. It is the absence of this human value, we may say, in the face of the oppressive presence of the dehumanizing uses made of others, which is the true subject of the discourse.

But that being given, what are the stages supposed to have been passed through by Frédéric Moreau in the process of realizing the discrepancy between aspiration and possibility of achievement which he comes to in the conclusion? When we ask this question in the light of tropology, the structure of and relationships among the first three sections of the book become clearly discernible.

We may say that the first part, which covers the period 1840–45, presents us with an image of desire personified in Frédéric projected in the mode of metaphor, desire seeking an object but unaware of anything but practical obstacles to its gratification. Here the object of desire is first presented to Frédéric in the mystery of Mme Arnoux's *appearance* only, as mere image rather than as image grounded in substantial reality, desire not yet individualized, and sensed to be painfully unattainable—in Frédéric's mind, simply because he is not wealthy enough to pursue it. This is the period of Frédéric's reluctant exile from Paris to the dull life of Nogent which, in retrospect, will have turned out to be no more dull, no more despiriting than Paris itself. While there, he encounters another potential object of desire, in the figure of the girl-child, half provincial bourgeoise, half savage peasant, Louise Rocque, the ambiguity of whose nature is signalled in her illegitimate birth no less than in the precociousness of the passion she feels for Frédéric from the start. But Frédéric's desire for her is still unfocused, still sublimated in the unconsummated Paolo and Francesa relationship they have and limited to caresses and fraternal kisses in Frédéric's part. This part of the novel, which opened with a leisurely journey by water from Paris to Nogent, ends with Frédéric's inheritance, by pure chance, of the fortune that will permit him to imagine that by returning to Paris, he will be able to possess whatever he wishes and achieve whatever he likes, spiritual as well as carnal.

Part 2 begins with a journey, not by paque boat, but by coach, the rapidity of the sensations of which already signals the disjunctions and discontinuities of the relationships figured in this section. Permit me to call the dominant mode of relationships figured in this section, between Frédéric and

his world as well as between the objects inhabiting that world, *metonymic,*
not only because the literal meaning of the word, "name change," suggests
the shifting, evanescent nature of the play of appearances rather than an
apprehension of any putative reality, but also because the mode of relationship supposed to exist between things in the use of this trope is that of mere
contiguity. Here desire becomes specified, fixed upon particular objects, all
of which are equally desirable but found to be in the possession of them
equally unsatisfying, frustrating, finally unpossessable in their essence. Kierkegaard would call this *desire* "desiring" (insect-like), as against *desire*
"sleeping" (plant-like); desire carnal, but desire conscious of itself as desire,
and rising to the level of technical competence and cunning in pursuit of
objects—like Don Juan in Mozart's opera, seeking the universal in the particular. Which means that all particulars become possible objects of desire,
irrespective of any considerations of intrinsic value. The image of desire is
now endowed with material substance, is apprehended as merely material in
its very consumption, is totally consumable thereby, hence in need of endless
replacement, substitution, repetition.

Frédéric now has money and a desire for women, pursues Mme Arnoux
and cunningly contrives her seduction, fights a duel for her honor, tries his
hand at law, painting, writing a novel, and finds them all equally unsatisfying.
And when Mme Arnoux fails to meet him at the room he had taken (because
of the illness of one of her children which she, stupidly, takes to be a sign
from heaven warning her of sin), Frédéric substitutes in her place, in the
same room and same bed he had reserved for Mme Arnoux, the mistress of
M. Arnoux, the dissembling and opaque, and utterly sensual, Rosanette. The
last scene of the last chapter of this section has Frédéric in bed with Rosanette, in a state of post-coital depression, weeping for his loss of Mme
Arnoux, but telling Rosanette that he is weeping because "I am too
happy. . . . I have wanted you for such a long time."

The evanescent quality of Frédéric's desire for Mme Arnoux is suggested
by his inability to fix her image in its specifically human incarnation. At
times, his lust for her is concretized in a fascination with some part of her
body, her foot, the inner side of her arm, some object that she possesses but
which, magically, seems to have taken on her essency by its physical proximity to her. At times, her essence dissolves and spreads over the whole of
the city of Paris, in such a way that she and the city become identified in
Frédéric's enfevered imagination. She remains unspecified as an individual,
however, unlocatable between the universal which she represents and the
particulars which characterize her as image. In this respect, the alternate
feelings of lust and repulsion that Frédéric feels for her, when she returns

after fifteen years, in the penultimate chapter, are perfectly consistent with the relationship which he bears to her in the second section of the book. Things fall apart because their essence is indiscernible. In the end, there are only things, and the relationships they sustain with one another are nothing but their placement side by side, nearer or further, from one another in a universe of objects. Whence the seeming ease of the displacements of desire from one object to another, the slippage of desire across a series of objects, all of which turn out to be exactly the same, however the imagination, in the service of desire, construes them.

Part 3 begins with the sound of gunshots in the streets. It signals the opening phase of the Revolution of February 25, 1848, the events of which—down to the coup by Louis Bonaparte (Napoleon III), of December 1851—form alternatively the foreground and background of Frédéric's life during that time. Frédéric has much to do in these three and a half years. He must participate in the February Revolution; attempt a political career; take care of his business affairs; squander his fortune in the process; keep Rosanette as his official mistress; continue to pursue Mme Arnoux; seduce Mme Dambreuse, the wife of a wealthy banker; witness the death of the child born to Rosanette; be betrayed by his best friend, Deslauriers; reject and then seek to win Louise Rocque; and witness the death of the only true political idealist among his friends, Dussardier, shot by another of his friends, Sénécal, a socialist in principle who, in pursuit of *his* ideals, has become a policeman. Things not only fall apart, they come apart at the seams in the process, and reveal the counteressence—the nothingness—which is the real substance behind all seemingly ideal forms.

Such, admittedly, is the moral of the story. And yet it is not the whole story. Flaubert's decision to place this grotesque series of events against the backdrop of the 1848 Revolution reflects—arguably—the despairing idealism of his vision. The absurdity of Dussardier's death is apparent enough, but so too is his goodness, decency, and humaneness. The absurdity which Flaubert finds in the events of 1848–51 does not fully hide the bitterness which he must have felt while witnessing France's last effort to construct a society on principles of social justice. To be sure, we know that he did not confuse justice with a belief in the equality of individuals, but neither did Marx. That confusion lies at the heart of Social Democratic sentimentalism and feeds the Utopian brand of socialism. True, he did not, like Marx, present the proletariat as the martyred heroes of the Revolution, but nor did he see them as more misguided and victimized by their own stupidity than Marx did. And he has his hero Frédéric participate in the events of February–March 1848 with the same enthusiasm, the same hopes, even the same bravery and idealism with which Marx credits the Parisian populace during that same period. He participates, that is, until, like the bourgeoisie itself, he becomes distracted by his own self-interest. Moreau, it is important to recall, is not a proletarian; he is a bourgeois through and through; and his life during the period 1848–51 mirrors perfectly, in microcosm, as it were, the career and betrayals, of itself and others, of the French bourgeoisie.

In part 3 of the novel, Frédéric displays a higher degree of consciousness, both social and psychological, and of conscience than he does in the rest of the book. It is as if Flaubert wished us to perceive Frédéric at this stage as one who grasps fully, even if in the end despairingly, the nature of his class, its strengths as well as its weaknesses, the disparity between its ideals and its actions, and the disillusionment which that disparity caused in that class as a result of the events of 1848–51. In this section, Frédéric's desire is—if only for a moment—generalized and idealized; it reaches out in a spirit of service and even sacrifice to the people, to the nation. He feels genuine anger when a citizen standing next to him on the barricades is shot by the soldiery, although he is as much angered by the thought that the shot might have been aimed at him as he is by the realization that it has killed a fellow citizen. He enthusiastically joins the mob in the sacking of the Tuileries and insists that "The people are sublime." Flaubert's characterization of the "carnival" mood of the days following the deposition of Louis Philippe, when "People dressed in a careless way that blurred the distinctions between classes, hatreds were concealed, and hopes blossomed" and "pride" shone in the face of the people "at having won their rights," has no irony in it at all. "Paris," he writes, was, during those days "the most delightful place."

But this pride is soon smothered in the realization, by the bourgeoisie especially, that social justice threatened private property, and the tone of the account shifts perceptibly with the narrator's remark:

> Now Property was raised in men's eyes to the level of Religion and became confused with God. The attacks made on it seemed sacrilegious, almost cannibalistic. In spite of the most humane laws that had ever been enacted, the spectre of '93 reappeared, and the knife of the guillotine vibrated in every syllable of the word "Republic"—which in no way prevented the government being despised for its weakness. France, realizing that she was without a master, started crying with fright like a blind man deprived of his stick, or a child who has lost his nurse.

The fragility of the alliance between the bourgeoisie and the people is symbolized by the pregnancy of Rosanette, the sickness of the child born of the union of a proletarian and a bourgeois, and, finally, by Frédéric's growing disgust for his mistress and his decision to take a new mistress, the aristocratic wife of the banker M. Dambreuse. This decision is as cynical on Frédéric's part as it is calculated on Mme Dambreuse's part to accept him as a lover.

The narrator tells us that, as of June 1848, the time of the infamous June Days, when the proletariat was ruthlessly suppressed, "The mind of the nation was unbalanced," a condition reflected in Frédéric's recognition that his "morality" had become "flabby" but also reflected in his choice of an antidote: "A mistress like Mme. Dambreuse," he muses, "would establish his position." We are not left with any doubts as to the nature of his attraction to her: "He coveted her because she was noble, rich, pious," and this recognition coincides with Frédéric's growing conviction that perhaps "progress is attainable only through an aristocracy," a conviction that is revealed to be as absurd as his earlier belief that "the people are sublime."

His deception of Rosanette now gives him infinite pleasure: "What a bastard I am!" he says; "Glorying in his own perversity," the narrator adds. His political interests fade, and with them his intention to stand as a candidate for the Assembly. He now luxuriates in "a feeling of gratification, of deep satisfaction. His joy of possessing a rich woman was unspoilt by any contrast; his feelings harmonized with their setting. His whole life, nowadays, was filled with pleasures." And the greatest, "perhaps, was to watch Madame Dambreuse surrounded by a group" of admirers: "all the respect shown to her virtue delighted him as an indirect homage to himself, and he sometimes longed to cry: 'But I know her better than you do. She's mine!'"

Not quite, of course. Mme Dambreuse is Frédéric's equal in venality and cunning self-servitude. The limits of his desire for her are set by his distaste for her "skinny chest": "At that moment, he admitted what he had hitherto concealed from himself; the disillusionment of his senses. This did not prevent him from feigning great ardor, but to feel it he had to evoke the image of Rosanette or Madame Arnoux. This atrophy of the heart," however, "left his head entirely free; and his ambition for a great position in society was stronger than ever." The death of M. Dambreuse, the subsequent revelation of the hatred and contempt underlying the Dambreuses' marriage, and Frédéric's growing disillusionment with Mme Dambreuse foreshadow the deterioration of the political situation, a situation laconically summed up by the narrator in a two-word paragraph: "Hatred flourished."

The death of Rosanette's child provides an occasion for the depiction of the total depravity of Frédéric's nature, his narcissism, and emotional self-indulgence, his disinterest even in desire itself, along with a correlation of

the death of realism in art (Pellerin's portrait of the dead child) and the death
of idealism in politics. Frédéric's tears at the deathwatch of his child are for
himself. He had forgotten the child while it was gestating in Rosanette's
womb. His tears are caused by the news that Mme Arnoux has left Paris
forever.

His break with both Rosanette and Mme Dambreuse is followed by a
decision to marry Louise, his "savage" and "peasant" girl-child; and he flees
to her, but this too is frustrated when he arrives to find her marrying his
best friend Deslauriers. He returns to Paris just in time to witness the coup
of Napoleon III and the murder of the communist Dussardier by the former
socialist, now policeman of reaction, Sénécal.

The interweaving of political events with the events in the life of Frédéric
in this section of the novel is highly complex and invites a host of different
interpretations. I call the mode of the whole section *synecdochic,* inasmuch
as, here, it is borne in upon Frédéric's consciousness and upon that of the
reader, the author's conviction that in the society depicted, the object of all
desire is commodity possession. Desire is generalized and universalized by
the equation of the value of every object with its value as commodity. This
generalized and universalized form of value appears, however, in two guises:
as a desire for human unity, in the first instance, reflected in the celebration
of political liberation; and in the absurd form of the commodity fetishized.
Mme Dambreuse is indistinguishable from her wealth and social position.

The melancholy tone of the last two chapters, the retrospective summing
up of this epic of disillusionment and frustration, can only derive from the
juxtaposition of the way things are in modern society and the way they ought
to be. The absent ideal is present as tacit antithesis to the painful reality.
The irony of the last two chapters is melancholic because, whether he knew
it or not, Flaubert had succeeded in representing more vividly than Hegel
himself the path of development of consciousness's encounter with reality
which leads to the condition of "the unhappy consciousness,"—that consciousness which is not only in and for itself, but also *by* itself, *beside* itself
in its simultaneous dissemblance and awareness of this dissemblance. The
melancholy of the last section is precisely similar to that which Marx depicts
as a mode of bourgeois life in France under the absurd Napoleon III. And
his analysis of the etiology of this symptom follows the same outline as that
given to us figuratively in Flaubert's novel.

You will recall that Marx opens the *Eighteenth Brumaire* with a signal
that he is about to unfold a "farce." The farcical nature of the events to be
depicted is manifested in their outcome: the elevation of the charlatan "Crapulinski," the roué, opportunist, and fool—the original Napoleon the

Great's nephew—Louis Bonaparte, to the imperial purple by a coalition of criminals, lumpenproletariat, peasants, and high bourgeois property owners. But, Marx reminds us a number of times throughout the discourse, this grotesque or absurd outcome of events—in which the least admirable man in France is hailed as the representative and defender of the interests of all classes of French society—was already implicitly present in the first, or February, phase of the Revolution of 1848, which had swept Louis Philippe from the throne and proclaimed the Second Republic.

How had this transformation, so remarkable and unforeseen by most of the actors in the spectacle, come about? Marx's answer to this question consists of an explication of the relationship between what he calls the true content of the "modern revolution" and the forms which specific revolutions take as a result of the conflict of interests which a class-divided society engenders.

The relation between the form and the content of any social phenomenon in any specific historical situation, Marx argues here and elsewhere, is a product of a conflict between specific class interests as these are envisaged and lived by a given class, on the one side, and general or universal human interests, which derive from the system of needs, primary and secondary, that are peculiar to mankind, on the other. Ideals are always formulated in terms of putatively universal human values, but since social perceptions are limited to the range of experiences of a given social class, the universally shared common interests of living men everywhere are always interpreted in a situation in which goods and political power are unevenly distributed in terms of the immediately envisaged *material* interests of the dominant class. This is why the political program of 1848, designed to establish a republic, quickly got transformed into a program designed to undermine this republic in the interest of protecting private property. The bourgeoisie in power says "Republic," against the old regime of inherited privilege and despotism, but it means "aristocracy of wealth." It says: "Justice," when it seeks to enlist the lower classes in its struggle against the old regime; but it means "Law and Order" when the aristocracy of wealth is established. It says, "Liberty, Equality, and Fraternity," when it is at the barricades or sending the lower classes to them; but it invokes "infantry, cavalry, and artillery," when the lower classes try to claim these rights in concrete terms. It comports itself on the historical stage like a tragic hero in its early phases of development, but its avarice and fetishism of commodities soon force it to abandon in practice every ideal it continues to preach in theory, and to reveal itself as the "monster" which any human being who conceives of life as an epic of production for profit alone must become.

So much is commonplace for Marxists, but exists only as a judgment still to be demonstrated. Part of the demonstration must be historical, since the process being analyzed is construed as a historical process. Marx chooses the events in France between 1848 and 1852 as a microcosm of the plot which every bourgeoisie must ultimately play out. And his demonstration of the adequacy of this judgment to the events themselves consists of a dialectical explication of those events as products of an interplay between forms and their actual contents, on the one side, and the form of the whole and its obscured universal meaning, on the other.

On the surface of the events, Marx discerns a succession of four formal incarnations of the revolutionary impulse. Each of these incarnations is simultaneously a response to socioeconomic reality (here construed as class interests) and an attempt to deny the universal meaning of the revolution in relation to ideal human aspiration. He divides the drama into four phases, each of which is signalled by a change in the form of government established on the political level. But the form of government established is itself a projection of a form of political consciousness, itself a product of either a coalition of classes, more or less self-consciously contrived, or of a specific class.

The real protagonist of Marx's narrative is neither the proletariat (its Dussardier) nor Louis Bonaparte (its Sénécal), but rather the bourgeoisie as it lives through the longings, sufferings, and contradictions of its existence that constitute its own "Sentimental Education." Its *Bildung,* like that of Moreau, consists of a progressive evacuation of ideals in order to become reconciled to a reality conceived as the melancholy consumption of commodities whose real value remains indiscernible.

Like Frédéric, the bourgeoisie and the revolution in which it will achieve its "absurd" triumph, passes through four stages of consciousness: February 1848 is metaphoric; political aspiration and social ideals are entertained in the euphoric spirit of unspecified desires and glimpsed in the image of "a social republic." Marx says of this period: "Nothing and nobody ventured to lay claim to the right of existence and of real action. All the elements that had prepared or determined the Revolution, the dynastic opposition, the republican bourgeoisie, the democratic-republican petty bourgeoisie and the social-democratic workers, provisionally found their place in the February *government.*" "It could not be otherwise," Marx continues: "Every party construed [the republic] in its own sense." Although the proletariat proclaimed a "social republic," and thereby "indicated the general content of the modern revolution," the proclamation was both naive and premature, given the interests and powers of other social groups. And this accounts for the "confused mixture of high-flown phrases and actual uncertainty and clumsiness, of more enthusiastic striving for innovation and more deeply rooted domination of the old routine, of more apparent harmony of the whole society and more profound estrangement of its elements," which characterized this phase of the whole revolutionary process.

Phase two of the Revolution, the period of the Constituent National Assembly, May 4, 1848, to May 29, 1849, represents the period of dispersion of the revolutionary impulse across a series of contending parties and groups, a period of strife and specification of contents, emblematized by the bloody street warfare of the June Days (June 23–26, 1848) and the progressive betrayal of one group by another until the bourgeois republicans accede to dictatorial power in the Legislative National Assembly, an accession which demonstrated to every observer of the event that "in Europe there are other questions involved than that of 'republic or monarchy.' It had revealed," Marx says, "that here [in Europe] *bourgeois republic* signifies the unlimited despotism of one class over other classes." Under the sign of the motto, "property, family, religion, order," every alternative party is crushed. "Society is saved just as often as the circle of its rulers contracts, as a more exclusive interest is maintained against a wider one. Every demand of the simplest bourgeois social reform, of the most ordinary liberalism, of the most formal republicanism, of the most insipid democracy, is simultaneously castigated as an 'attempt on society' and stigmatised as 'socialism.'"

With the dictatorship of the bourgeoisie, we have passed into the third phase of the Revolution, the synecdochic phase in which the interests of a specific segment of society is identified with the interest of society as a whole. This pseudo-universalization of the interests of the bourgeoisie, this incarnation of the universal in the particular, this fetishism by a class of itself, is a preparation for the absurdity represented by Bonaparte's claims to be "the savior of society" and the irony of his use of the motto "property, family, religion, order" to justify his suppression of the *political* power of the bourgeoisie.

In this, the last phase of the Revolution, bourgeois "high priests of 'religion and order' themselves are driven with kicks from their Pythian tripods, hauled out of their beds in the darkness of night, put in prison vans, thrown into dungeons or sent into exile; their temple is razed to the ground, their mouths are sealed, their pens broken, their law torn to pieces in the name of religion, of property, of family, of order. Bourgeois fanatics for order are shot down on their balconies by mobs of drunken soldiers, their domestic sanctuaries profaned, their houses bombarded for amusement—in the name of property, of family, of religion, and of order. Finally the scum of bourgeois society forms *the holy phalanx of order* and the hero Crapulinski [from Fr. *crapule* 'gluttony'] installs himself in the Tuileries as the 'savior of society.'"

What justification do I have for calling the modes of relationship among the elements of society represented in Marx's characterization of the phases of the Revolution by the names of the tropes of figurative language? The best reason is that Marx himself provides us with schematic representations of the modes of figuration by which to characterize the relation between the forms of value and their contents in his analysis of the "language of commodities" in chapter 1 of *Capital*. Most of this chapter consists of an adaptation of the traditional conception of the rhetorical tropes to the method of dialectical analysis. Here the problem, Marx says, is to understand the Money Form of Value, the "absurd" notion that the value of a commodity is equivalent to the amount of money it is worth in a given system of exchange. And just as the explanation of the "absurd" spectacle of Bonaparte's posing as the "savior of society"—while unleashing all of the criminal elements of society to an orgy of a consumption ungoverned by any respect for human values or the persons who produced by their labor the commodities being consumed—is contained in the understanding of the first phase of the Revolution which brought him to power, the February phase; so too the absurd form of value is explained by reference to the structure of the Elementary or Original Form of value, the form contained in the simple metaphorical *identification* of "x amount of Commodity A" with "y amount of Commodity B." Once the purely figurative nature of this statement of equivalency is grasped, once it is seen that, like any metaphor, it both contains a deep truth (regarding the similarity of any two commodities by virtue of their nature as products of human labor) and at the same time masks this truth (by remaining on the superficial level of an apprehension of their manifest similarity as commodities), the secret of men's capacity to bewitch themselves into believing that the value of anything equals its exchange, rather than its use, value is revealed for everyone to see. Just as irony is implicitly present in any original, primitive or naive characterization of reality in a metaphor, so too the absurdity of equating the value of a product of human labor with its money value is contained implicitly in the equating of any given commodity with any other as a basis of exchange. And so too with the other two forms of value, the Extended and the Generalized forms, which Marx analyzes in this chapter of *Capital*. They are to *metonymy* and *synecdoche*, the relationships by contiguity and putative essential identity, respectively, as the second and third phases of the Revolution are to the same tropes.

To be sure, Marx's analysis of the forms of social phenomena, whether of commodity values or of political systems, is carried forth on the assumption that he has perceived their true contents, which the forms simultaneously figure forth and conceal from clear view. The true value-content of all commodities is for him the amount of human labor expended in their production, which is precisely equivalent to their use value, whatever their apparent value in a given system of exchange. The true content of all political and social forms, similarly, is the universal human needs which they at once manifest and obscure. Marx's aim as a writer was to clarify this relation of content to form in a way which he thought, correctly I believe, was consistent with Hegel's dialectical method of analysis, although—in his view—Hegel had got the form-content distinction wrong way about. But he carried forward the method of Hegel's *Phenomenology* and *Logic* by divining the element of consciousness which was the basis and bane of humanity's efforts to grasp reality and turn it to its service. This element was man's capacity for what Vico called "creative error," a capacity of the figurative imagination without which reason itself would be inconceivable, just as prose without poetry would be unthinkable. More: he divined clearly what Hegel only in passing glimpses and in his pursuit of the secret of Being-in-General too quickly passes over; namely, that the secret of human consciousness is to be found in its most original product, which is not reason, but figurative language, without which reason could never have arisen.

What does the discernment of a common pattern of tropological representations of the modes of consciousness imply with respect to the project of "realistic representation," on the one side, and the problem of style, on the other? With respect to the former, I would suggest, it permits us to identify the "allegorical" element in realistic discourse, the secondary meaning of the events depicted on the surface of the narrative which mediates between those events and the judgment rendered on them, launched from the consciously held ideological position of the writer. The progression of these structures of consciousness permits the encodation of the process through which the protagonist is passing in his/its "education," in terms which allow the writer a judgment on its end phase as a stage of cognitive awareness. This quite apart from whatever archetypal schema may be revealed in the literary encodation of the events in generic terms, i.e., as comedy, tragedy, romance, satire or farce. The discourses of Marx and Flaubert can thus be construed as correlations of events with their mythic archetypes, on the one side, and with types of cognition, on the other. And it is the twofold encodation of these events, as satires and as reductions of consciousness to a condition of "ironic" self-reflexivity, which tacitly justifies the ideological judgment rendered on them, in the narrator's voice on the diegetic level of the discourse. To be sure, the revelation of the "farcical" nature of a given set of events constitutes a judgment on their "meaning" in itself. But merely to have emplotted a given set of events as a "farce" testifies only to the literary skill of the narrator; every set of events can be emplotted in any number of ways without doing violence to their "factuality." Every specific emplotment of a set of events, then, requires at least tacit appeal to some cognitive criterion, some notion of the way things really are, in order to establish that the emplotment in question is both plausible and illuminative of the true structure of the events in question. The theory of consciousness, which construes it as a process of passage from a metaphoric, through metonymic and synecdochic phases of development, to the condition of self-consciousness represented by irony, serves this cognitive purpose in Marx's and Flaubert's discourses. Their "realism" is thus revealed to be triply allegorical, possessing levels of elaboration corresponding to the figurative, moral, and anagogical levels discriminated in the Augustinian hermeneutic tradition. The meaning of the processes depicted on the literal level of the texts is revealed by the transcoding of the processes in generic, ideological, and cognitive terms.

With respect to the problem of style, our analysis of the discourses of Marx and Flaubert suggests that we should regard style, at least in realistic discourse, as the process of this transcoding operation. When we speak of the style of a discourse, we should not feel compelled to limit ourselves to a consideration of either the linguistic-rhetorical features of a text or to its discernible ideological posture, but should seek rather to characterize the moves made, on the axes of both selection and combination, by which a form is identified with a content and the reverse. Flaubert was certainly right when he sought to identify "style" with the "content" of the discourse, but specified that the content in question had to do with "thought" rather than with the manifest referent of the discourse, the characters, situations, and events depicted in the narrative. What he may have been pointing to here was the inexpungable element of "construct" contained in every discourse, however "realistic," however perfectly "mimetic," it might strive to be. If the linguistic sign is to be identified neither with the signifier nor the signified, but with their conjunction, then every representation of reality in language must possess, as an element of its content, the "form" of the signifier itself. Discourse turns the union of signifier and signified in the sign into the problem with which it must deal. Its aim is less to match up a group of signifiers with their signifieds, in a relationship of perfect equivalency, than to create a system of signs that are their own signifieds. To put it this way is no doubt to muddy the waters, but it at least helps to explain why every "realism" in the end fails and is supplanted by yet another "realism" which, although claiming at last to be a pure *mimesis,* is soon revealed by a vigilant criticism to be only another perspective on the ever shifting relationship between words and the things they are supposed to signify.

Finally, this approach to the problem of style, considered within the context of mid-nineteenth-century realism, as represented by Marx and Flaubert, helps us to comprehend better the seemingly substantive "modernity" of their discourses. Their embedding of the tropes of figurative language within their discourse as a model of the processes of consciousness allows them to appear to be the very types of a certain *kind* of realism, on the one side, and heralds of "modernism" in both writing and criticism, on the other. For modernism, whatever else it may be, is characterized by a hyper-self-consciousness with respect to the opacity of language, by language's demonic capacity to intrude itself into discourse as a content alongside of whatever referent may be signalled on the surface of the text. Marx's and Flaubert's identification of the stages of consciousness with tropological structures, the structures of language in its prefigurative aspect, amnestied them against the perils of literalism, on the one side, and of symbolization, on the other. Their discourses are not reducible either to the manifest forms in which they appear or to the specific ideological positions they held. On the contrary, their discourses remain eternally fresh and enduringly "realistic" precisely to the degree that their "contents" were identified as the process of their own production.

JANE ROBERTSON

The Structure of Hérodias

In spite of considerable interest shown in the *Trois Contes* in recent years, *Hérodias* still receives little individual critical attention. This comparative neglect can largely be attributed to the problems raised by the obscurity of the text. In his famous letter to Flaubert, Taine criticized five obscure points, but he thought *Hérodias* the finest of the three stories; by subsequent critics the textual difficulties have usually been considered a defect which makes *Hérodias* inferior to the other two *contes*. One critic has recently taken a different approach by suggesting that the obscurity is not so much a matter of style as of concept, and that "le conte est obsur parce qu'il doit traiter de l'obscur" (Raymonde Debray-Genette, "Re-présentation d'*Hérodias*," in *La Production du sens chez Flaubert*). Considered from this more positive point of view the richness of the work is better appreciated. The nature of the text's obscurity is essentially elliptical, arising from Flaubert's abridging or omitting explanations and from his appositional technique. The resulting density of the text means that its skilful structure is not immediately apparent.

There is even room for debate about the main subject of the story: it presents, like a classical tragedy, the twenty-four hours ending in the death of John the Baptist, but his name does not feature in the title. If the main event is indeed the death of the prophet, this event is brought about by Hérodias: she is seen as the power behind the throne, playing on the weak-

From *French Studies* 36, no. 2 (April 1982). © 1982 by the Society for French Studies.

ness of Antipas and using Salomé as an instrument to gain her ends. Yet this
is not the only perspective. Hérodias is not the subject of the story in the
way that Félicité and Julien are the subject of theirs, and she is not present
at the end. As a political intriguer she is highly competent: her plot against
Agrippa succeeds; her far-sighted plot against Iaokanann also succeeds. Hers
is, however, a hollow triumph, and we do not see her as a victorious figure.
Our last, memorable, view of her is when her desire for the execution of
Iaokanann is temporarily thwarted and she pours forth violent and vulgar
abuse, flanked by the stone lions who seem to imitate her. When her aim is
achieved she has disappeared from the story, her role in determining history
fulfilled. The text is immediately dominated by the severed head ("La tête
entra") which remains the focal point of the story to the end and attains by
this emphasis the stature of a symbol. In this way Hérodias may be seen as
an instrument unwittingly furthering the prophet's mission and the course
of history. She is not shown shaping or suffering her own destiny as Félicité
and Julien are shown; she decides the fate of someone else who knows that
his death is necessary ("Pour qu'il croisse il faut que je diminue"). We may
thus see in the published order of the Trois Contes, parallel to their progressively more distant temporal situation, a determinism progressively more
external to the characters. Félicité's personality may be considered to determine her life and death. In La Légende Flaubert seems to give as equal a
weighting as possible to individual responsibility and external forces. In Hérodias all the characters may be seen as players of predetermined roles. Hérodias has a different narrative focus: it does not chronicle a single life (in
fact the most detailed psychological portrayal is that of Antipas) but presents
a pattern of characters and events, crystallized into twenty-four hours, which
forms the author's stylized view of a historical turning-point. The figure of
Hérodias forms the thematic centre of the narrative pattern.

On the level of the characters and plot, the tension between Hérodias
and Iaokanann underlies the structure of the story, with Antipas unwillingly
between them. Most of the story is seen from the point of view of Antipas,
the character closest to the reader and probably the best understood. In many
ways he acts as l'homme moyen, who serves both as a foil and as a focus
for the other characters. With the exception of Antipas most of the main
characters fall into one of the two camps headed by Hérodias and Iaokanann.
Phanuel and Jacob appear "for" the prophet and afford a counterweight to
those who, like Hérodias, are "against" him: Mannaeï, Salomé and guests
at the banquet. The opposition of individuals from these two groups reflects
on another scale the opposition of Hérodias and Iaokanann: Phanuel is set
against Mannaeï and Jacob against other guests at the banquet. Mannaeï is

a character defined by his hatred of Jews in general and Iaokanann in particular (a hatred, however, not unmixed with awe): this epitomizes on an
individual level the tension between Samaritans and Jews. The essential contrast between the prophet and those opposed to him is between his self-
sacrifice and abstinence and their ambition and sensual indulgence. It is
Hérodias who typifies these latter qualities: ambition is her driving force
and sensuality the means she uses to achieve it (albeit by proxy). This is
stressed by the technique of Flaubert. Almost every appearance of Hérodias
is accompanied by a description in sensuous terms of her person, clothes or
surroundings. The striking and very significant exception is the central scene
in chapter 2 where she enters but is not described; here Iaokanann, in de-
nouncing her sensuality, gives the *counterpart* to these descriptions by enu-
merating her attributes in order to pronounce a curse on them. These
descriptions reach their climax in the last chapter where the appearance of
Hérodias leads to the description of Salomé. Salomé is the extension of Hérodias, an unreflecting instrument, the personification of sensuality. Mannaeï
might similarly be seen as incorporating violence, and Aulus greed: these
three elements combine in the atmosphere of the banquet which results in
the death of Iaokanann. Iaokanann himself is hardly physically present and
little description is devoted to him, with the important exception of the
description of his severed head, which greatly contributes to its symbolic
domination of the end of the text. Flaubert does no more than indicate the
simplicity of Jacob and Phanuel, their pale robes contrasting especially with
the richly coloured clothing of Hérodias and Salomé. The proportion of
description devoted to the two groups thus underlines their opposition.

The presentation of Iaokanann, however, requires a further remark. His
appearance is first mentioned by Mannaeï, who says he has "l'air tranquille
d'une bête malade." Then it is recalled by Hérodias in the first chapter as
she relates the crucial encounter between them; this is the most complete
physical description of Iaokanann: "un homme parlait. Il avait une peau de
chameau autour des reins, et sa tête ressemblait à celle d'un lion. . . . Ses
prunelles flamboyaient; sa voix rugissait." Here he is introduced simply as
"une homme," but the descriptive elements associating him with animals
tend already to separate him from the rest of humanity. The next description
occurs when he is glimpsed in his prison; from "un homme" he becomes
here: "un être humain . . . couché par terre sous de longs cheveux se confondant avec les poils de bête qui garnissaient son dos. Il se leva. Son front
touchait à une grille . . . et, de temps à autre, il disparaissait dans les profondeurs de son antre." His appearance and movements, and Flaubert's vocabulary ("antre"), isolate him even further from the rest of humanity; and

so does the later description of his face in terms of inanimate objects; "son visage, qui avait l'air d'une broussaille, où étincelaient deux charbons." Thus Iaokanann is described, however briefly or indirectly, in each of the three chapters; we may note that his eyes figure as a focal point in each description: ("ses prunelles flamboyaient"; "deux charbons"; "les prunelles mortes").

The interplay of the opposing characters will be seen more clearly when the thematic structure of the text is examined in detail. First, however, we may consider the development of the text from another point of view: that of the time presented. The twenty-four hours of the story's duration are presented in three chapters, progressing from before dawn through the early morning in the first, to the bright noonday sun when everyone listens to the voice of the prophet in the second, the torchlight of the banquet in the third, and ending with the following sunrise. The presentation of time in the story resembles that in a play, in that time is, generally speaking, continuous within each chapter (as it is within an act) while temporal ellipses occur between chapters. Also, significantly, there is an ellipsis just before the end, where the pause serves to focus attention on the significance of the death of the prophet and to put into perspective the preceding narrative. The passing of time is conveyed throughout, and strongly emphasized at the beginning. The first chapter is punctuated by descriptions which convey the passing of the morning, and the anxious waiting of Antipas creates an anticipatory tension. This waiting, together with indications of preparation both for the banquet (mentioned at the beginning and forming a temporal framework for the fateful developments of the story) and for the arrival of Vitellius, seems to hasten events to their conclusion; later, the prediction of Phanuel has the same effect. The prophecies of Iaokanann and the focus of the final paragraph imply the more distant future (outside the text), while a historical perspective is indicated in an observation on Aulus who is "emporté par cette goinfrerie qui devait surprendre l'univers." The past, however, figures much more largely in the text than the future. It is the past both distant and recent that conditions the present: from the past of the Old Testament in the allusion to the destruction of Sodom and Gomorrah and the ancestors of Antipas and Hérodias, to the more recent achievements of the father of Antipas, the ambitions of Hérodias since childhood, the marriage of Antipas and Héro-dias twelve years ago and the ensuing war, the desecration of the temple at Jerusalem by Mannaeï, the humiliation of Hérodias by Iaokanann and his imprisonment, the plot of Hérodias against Agrippa and the visit of the two men to Iaokanann a month ago. These references are in the first chapter and the early part of the second. The last chapter evokes the recent past in explanations of events already included in the text: the secret training of

Salomé by Hérodias, the meaning of the prediction of Phanuel and the retrospective identification of Salomé by means of the old woman seen with her twice before.

However, with the narration of the miracle of Jacob's daughter the last chapter also includes the perspective of the New Testament. There is thus a shift of emphasis from the Old Testament at the beginning of the story to the New at the end, while the most dramatic passage in the central chapter is transitional in that the voice of the prophet includes both. This movement reflects the importance of the story as a turning point. In the first chapter Antipas and Hérodias are crushed by the past. They are presented as ageing and careworn (a passage which stands out because it gives a poignant picture of their changed relationship and shows the effects of time on each of them) and throughout the story Antipas is worried and powerless: the age of Antipas and Hérodias is coming to an end. This impression is strengthened by the heavily decadent atmosphere of the joyless feast (celebrating, ironically, the birthday of Antipas) in the last chapter and is confirmed by the ending of the story, when Iaokanann is dead, and Hérodias and the guests have gone; there is no final scene showing Antipas alone, which would make the beginning and the end of the story pleasingly symmetrical but would at the same time imply a circular structure. In the final half-page the perspective opens out for the beginning of another era.

This evolution is emphasized by the structure of the narrative: tension increases throughout until the closing paragraph. It will be seen that the thematic structure shows in general a cumulative progression, in which narrative elements introduced separately are gradually combined. The structural pattern includes a development of narrative detail in three stages corresponding to the three chapters. An obvious example is the banquet: the reasons for it are given in chapter 1, preparations for it are indicated in chapter 2, and it takes place in chapter 3; from chapter 2 it is linked increasingly with the figure of Aulus. There is a slight but suggestive indication of the intrigue of Hérodias against Iaokanann by means of Antipas and Salomé in each of chapters 1 and 2 and this plot is put into effect in 3. Less obvious is the link between this intrigue and the one against Agrippa which foreshadows it. The development of the two by Flaubert is such that the first plot of Hérodias in chapter 1 counterbalances her second in chapter 3. In chapter 1 Agrippa is a source of anxiety to Antipas from the beginning and Hérodias announces the success of her plot against him: the ruthlessness and power of Hérodias are evident to the reader from her first appearance, as they are to Vitellius when she announces Agrippa's arrest to him. The last mention of Agrippa is on the occasion when he is again the cause of at least some of the fears of Antipas, whom Hérodias again reassures, and to whom she gives the medallion showing Tiberius. Here is the point of contact between the two intrigues and the point at which the second takes over, for when Antipas produces the medallion at the banquet Hérodias knows that the moment has come when she can turn the guests' thirst for violence to suit her own ends, and it heralds the entrance of herself and Salomé, which leads to the success of her second plot. Her two intrigues are moreover linked by Hérodias herself in a transition after her explanation of the Agrippa plot: "Rien ne me coûtait! Pour toi n'ai-je pas fait plus? . . . J'ai abandonné ma fille!"—a strategy essential for her domination of Antipas.

On the same level, a pattern may be distinguished in the division of the narrative. Indeed it is possible to consider that each chapter has a number of scenes: chapter 1 would appear to have several short scenes, chapter 2 fewer, longer ones, and chapter 3 may be seen as a single, large crowd scene (with a contrasting "epilogue"). This arrangement of the narrative in groups of increasing volume (known on the smaller scale of sentences and paragraphs as a *cadence majeure*) also contributes to the movement in gradation of the story as a whole. The four main scenes in chapter 1 show Antipas alone with the landscape, Antipas and Mannaeï, who appears when the subject of Iaokanann is introduced, Antipas and Hérodias, and Antipas and Phanuel. Within the chapter there is a cumulative movement in that Antipas becomes more burdened with each of these successive responsibilities and by the time the Romans arrive the exposition has been completed in the essential respect of the relationships between main characters. In this first chapter Antipas is seen in relation both to those "for" and to those "against" Iaokanann. His interview with Hérodias reflects the main focus of the narrative by its relative length and its position between the interviews with Mannaeï and Phanuel. This interview makes clear, moreover, the link between the ambitions of Hérodias and the fate of Iaokanann who threatens them. The presence of Iaokanann is felt throughout: he is the central topic in each of these three interviews. The final short passage of chapter 1 forms a transition to chapter 2, announcing the arrival of Vitellius anxiously awaited by Antipas at the beginning of the chapter. The major part of chapter 2 is taken up with the presentation first of the Romans and then of the voice of Iaokanann. The first part of the chapter conveys the political force and temporal power represented by the Romans (this is one of the rare sections of the work where the subject of Iaokanann does not occur). With this is contrasted the spiritual and moral power represented by the voice of the prophet in the second part as he dominates all those present. The remaining short scenes of this chapter, the prediction of Phanuel and the visit to Hérodias, contribute more directly to the development of the action towards the *dénouement,* a movement which is accelerated in chapter 3. Here the emphasis is not on encounters between individuals as in chapter 1, but, as so often in *Salammbô,* on the reactions of a crowd. The accumulation of people suggests increasing tension and violence just as the accumulation of food and drink which alternates with it conveys the degree of self-indulgence and decadence. The violence of the crowd threatens to erupt against Antipas and against the Romans before the entry of Hérodias and Salomé seems to calm the atmosphere. But the tension increases nonetheless; sensuality and violence go together, and the dance of Salomé ends with the demand for the head of Iaokanann. The execution of the prophet depends on the reaction of Antipas to the dance of Salomé: but everyone present reacts in the same way, his decision to submit to the demand takes them into account ("et le peuple attendait"); and when Mannaeï fails at the first attempt, the reactions of Antipas and of the crowd are still as one. After the execution Antipas and Phanuel remain alone in the deserted banqueting hall. Towards the end of each of the three chapters Antipas is seen in company with Phanuel: the subject of their conversation in the first two is Iaokanann, and, in the third, the head of the prophet is present. This symmetry conveys the insistent presence of the prophet's influence and forms a counterweight to those elements hostile to him. The division of the narrative is thus marked by a technique of cumulative progression and symmetry.

These same two structural features may be distinguished on a more detailed thematic level. They are obvious in the presentation of certain characters: Mannaeï is described in chapter 1, identified as executioner in chapter 2 and fulfils his function in chapter 3. Salomé is glimpsed by Antipas towards the end of chapters 1 and 2 and identified only when she enters to play her part towards the end of chapter 3. Clearly, the two glimpses of the unidentified girl are a narrative device to create suspense, like the prediction by Phanuel, initiated towards the end of chapter 1, made towards the end of chapter 2 and fulfilled towards the end of chapter 3. Less obviously, each *glimpse* of Salomé is heralded by the *mention* of the daughter of Hérodias by another character: Hérodias herself speaks of her in her appeal to the feelings of Antipas a little before Antipas catches a brief glimpse of the girl, and Eléazar refers to her during the dispute about the marriage of Antipas and Hérodias a little before Antipas glimpses her in the chamber of Hérodias. These are the only mentions of Salomé in the text before her dance in the last chapter; each appears in conjunction with the figure of Hérodias and in a context of immediate relevance to the story (the attempt of Hérodias to regain her power over Antipas, the moral and political question of their marriage). This treatment of Salomé is an example of Flaubert's richly significant use of economical detail. It also implies a certain stylization in the presentation of character: viewed in this way, characters (notably Salomé, Mannaeï and Phanuel) will be seen more as motifs in the textual pattern than as personalities.

Repetition of detail on an obvious level forms a framework to the narrative: the saying of Iaokanann: "Pour qu'il grandisse il faut que je diminue" is reported at the beginning by Mannaeï, who is puzzled by it; it is taken up again at the end by, significantly, Phanuel and this time it is understood. This *reprise* echoes the temporal framework of twenty-four hours, gives an air of fatefulness to the action and underlines the essential aspects of time and change. On a more subtle level there are symmetries of detail which reflect a different kind of progression. In each of the chapters the mention of Iaokanann in the text is followed by a dispute: between Antipas and Hérodias in 1, among Pharisees, Sadducees and Antipas in 2, and at the banquet. There is a gradual increase in the number of people involved and at the same time a broadening of the issues: from the personal level of the attack on Antipas by Hérodias to the wide-ranging historical, mythological and metaphysical questions raised at the banquet. The technique here affords a means of broadening into these wider issues, and it evokes the atmosphere of unease, hostility and latent violence brought into focus by the figure of Iaokanann and finally converging on him. There are similarly three short passages which present a moment of stillness broken by a voice. In the first chapter it is the oppressive stillness of the surroundings which is broken by the awesome voice of Iaokanann, in the second chapter it is the momentary relief from tension for Antipas which ends with the prediction of Phanuel, and at the end of the third chapter it is the silence in the abandoned banqueting hall which is broken only by the murmured prayers of Phanuel. These pauses mark stages in the narrative and contribute to the richness of the narrative pattern and to the evocative power of the text.

In most cases, however, development of details contributes directly to the movement of the narrative in progressive gradation. The religious and racial complexities and tensions basic to the work are represented in the first chapter on an individual level in the confrontation of Mannaeï and Phanuel; they are increased in the passage depicting the arrival of the Romans and in the discussion provoked by the voice of Iaokanann; while in chapter 3 these tensions become increasingly vocal, mounting throughout the chapter and ending in the explosion of violence represented by the decapitation of Iaokanann. The theme of the relationship between Antipas and Hérodias likewise develops gradually throughout the chapters. In chapter 1 Hérodias attempts to reawaken the tender feelings of Antipas towards herself and to make him nostalgic for the days when he was under her spell. In chapter 2 it is suggested that her ruse is working, as the visit which Antipas pays her is motivated in part by this: "Il la haïssait pourtant. Mais elle lui donnerait du courage; et tous les liens n'étaient pas rompus de l'ensorcellement qu'il avait autrefois subi." In chapter 3 it is the same "ensorcellement" that ensures the success of the intrigue of Hérodias from the moment when Antipas sees Salomé and thinks, in a moment of hallucination reflected by the *style indirect libre:* "C'était Hérodias, comme autrefois dans sa jeunesse." The subtle density of Flaubert's text is such that these developments are likely to be missed on a first reading; but the thematic details again contribute very largely to its suggestive power by establishing a network of echoes.

Of even more importance to the story is the presence in the text of a dimension beyond the merely human. The first discreet indication occurs in the description of the scenery. Whereas the initial passages convey the colours, geometrical shapes, grandeur, aridity and emptiness of the exotic geographical setting, once the subject of Iaokanann has been introduced the impact of their surroundings is perceived by the characters. The temple of Jerusalem is seen by Mannaeï as "quelque chose de surhumain" and the landscape offers to Antipas evidence of past destruction wrought by divine wrath. The descriptive passages throughout these pages giving the setting of the story show a progression in intensity. They reflect on one level the feelings of the characters, especially Antipas, and on another they put the narrative into perspective by indicating the scale of its significance. In a most striking juxtaposition the last of these passages is followed by the first description of Hérodias, her air of casual sensuality set against the portentous austerity of the background. There is a comparable juxtaposition in chapter 2 when the fateful prediction of Phanuel is followed by description of the perfumed chamber of Hérodias. The juxtaposition in each case implicitly links the sensuality of Hérodias with the idea of doom. The superhuman dimension is further implied in chapter 1 when Hérodias is angered by the inexplicable power of Iaokanann, shown in his survival of an attempt on his life: "On avait mis des serpents dans sa prison; ils étaient morts." This theme is taken up again in a more dramatic form just before the execution, when Mannaeï sees outside the prison "le Grand Ange des Samaritains, tout couvert d'yeux et brandissant un immense glaive, rouge et dentelé comme une flamme." It is further implied in the prediction of Phanuel, when the disaster sensed from the beginning is put into words—"la mort d'un homme considérable"—and the time, "cette nuit même," becomes tragically imminent. This prediction is made immediately after the dramatic central passage of chapter 2 when the superhuman element is implicit in the words of Iaokanann.

It is the voice of Iaokanann which shows the progressive development of most significance to the story. Throughout the three chapters his voice grows; moreover its nature evolves. In chapter 1 it is at first inarticulate, only heard as "une voix lointaine, comme échappée des profondeurs de la terre." Then it is presented indirectly, as it is recalled by Hérodias in terms which, anticipating the central scene in chapter 2, already express part of its message and associate it with a force of nature: "il cracha sur moi toutes les malédictions des prophètes . . . sa voix rugissait; il levait les bras comme pour arracher le tonnerre . . . ces injures qui tombaient comme une pluie d'orage." There is thus a prefiguration in chapter 1 of the dramatic presentation of the prophecies in chapter 2: much of the vocabulary in the first passage is amplified in the second, to which it gives added resonance. In chapter 2 the voice begins as a far-carrying sigh and grows eloquent, reaching a climax with the curse on Hérodias when Flaubert's vocabulary assimilates it to a force of nature: "La voix grossissait, se développait, roulait avec des déchirements de tonnerre, et, l'écho dans la montagne la répétant, elle foudroyait Machærous d'éclats multipliés." The voice here is inescapably powerful: echoed by the mountains, it is also repeated as it is translated into Latin for Vitellius and seems to reverberate indefinitely. In chapter 3 the voice of Iaokanann is not heard at all; but reduced, as it were, to its essence, it dominates throughout, as his message is seen to be already spreading and taken up by others.

Hérodias may thus, even in its smallest structural details, "be considered as the extreme example of the power of form to convey sense" (M. G. Tillet, "An Approach to Hérodias"). The density and complexity of the text give it the power Flaubert sought, to "faire rêver." Even the difficulty of the text may be considered to have two related advantages. Firstly, it may alert the reader to the possibility that "le conte est obscur parce qu'il doit traiter de l'obscur": the meaning of the events depicted remains obscure to the characters (except to Iaokanann, who is presented in a perspective different from the others); the initial confusion of the reader may mirror the bewilderment of Antipas. Secondly, the obscurity may alert the reader to subtle patterns within the text itself and serve to focus his attention on Flaubert's conte, which is fictitious and stylized, instead of on a chronologically accurate reconstruction of history which he could piece together himself from information derived from outside the text. The allusiveness of Hérodias arises both from the textual obscurity and from the formal organization of structural details. In the sense that it evokes what it does not express and demands considerable involvement on the part of the reader, we may see Hérodias as the least accessible but the most poetic of the Trois Contes.

ANDREW J. McKENNA

Allodidacticism:
Flaubert 100 Years After

Et d'enchaîner sur Chamfort, dont la formule qu' "il y a à parier que toute idée publique, toute convention reçue est une sottise, car elle a convenu au plus grand nombre," contentera à coup sûr tous ceux qui pensent échapper à sa loi, c'est-à-dire précisément le plus grand nombre.

—JACQUES LACAN, *Ecrits*

Vox populi, vox Dei (*Sagesse des nations*)
—GUSTAVE FLAUBERT, *Dictionnaire*
des idées reçues (epigraph)

Of all the pedagogical figures in French literature—Rabelais, Montaigne, Voltaire, Rousseau—Flaubert's Bouvard and Pécuchet are perhaps the most comical and, as I shall argue, the most disquieting. It is by the conjugation of these qualities that their educational experience, both as learners and teachers, is for our time, most instructive.

Near the term of their encyclopedic foray through Western knowledge, the two autodidacts embark on the task of educating Victor and Victorine, two orphan bastards consigned by the provincial Chavignollais community to reform school and to the convent:

> They procured several works relating to Education—and their system was decided upon. It would be necessary to banish all metaphysical ideas and, after the experimental method, follow

From *Yale French Studies* 63 (1982). © 1982 by Yale University.

the lead of Nature. There was no hurry, for the two pupils would have to forget what they had learned.

After this implicit bow to Rousseau, Pestalozzi, Lancaster, and others, the second paragraph evokes the Renaissance ideal, according to Rabelais and Montaigne, of training the body along with the mind:

> Although they had a solid constitution, Pécuchet wished, like a Spartan, to harden them more, to accustom them to hunger, to thirst, to bad weather, and even that they wear shoes with holes in them to prevent catching colds.

One imagines Pécuchet proclaiming the conundrum, *mens sana in corpore sano*. And as one might have expected, "Bouvard s'y opposa." His opposition here is as comical as it is mechanical, recalling the tic-tac of earlier debates between Bouvard and Pécuchet, and exemplifying Flaubert's most consistent tactic in his general strategy of intellectual devastation. To each thesis of Bouvard or Pécuchet the other responds by its equally authoritative antithesis; the resultant impasse goads them to grasp at another branch of the tree of knowledge until "Tout leur a craqué dans les mains" ("Everything has snapped in their hands").

The reader may thus feel advised not to take the educational adventure of the two men seriously. After all, they have, as indicated by Flaubert's notes for this tenth chapter of the novel, the last completed in manuscript form, an "idée exagérée de la puissance de l'éducation." On the other hand their experience in its entirety, as it serves as the premise for the novel's conclusion, can lead us to reflect, can educate us, according to the commonplace etymology, on the power of ideas and ideas of power in contemporary history. The issue, as posed by Flaubert's text, and as informed by events of the last hundred years since his death, is nothing less than a choice between a comic or tragic resolution of history itself.

The experiment of Bouvard and Pécuchet in the domain of education, like those essayed in all other fields hitherto, fails, and it fails, in multiple senses of the word, abysmally. The mental obtuseness and vicious conduct of the two orphans conspire with obstacles, to be examined herein, built into the tutorial undertaking, in thwarting the educational aspirations of the two men. As with their earlier ventures in the physical and human sciences, reality proves once again refractory to the constraints of system and the utopia of method. The pedagogical failure of the two "bonhommes" thus deepens the abyss of cognitive nihilism which has already engulfed everything from geology and archeology through history, esthetics and religion. At the same time, chapter 10 represents "en abîme" the entire trajectory of epistemological catastrophe that constitutes chapters 2 through 9, as the two men proceed in quest of foundations for knowledge which forever elude them. This last chapter thus stands in episodic, metonymic relation to the narrative which precedes it; it serves as well as a metaphor for their entire intellectual enterprise.

Their dilemma is everywhere the same. As the two men range pêle-mêle through language, botany, history and religion, with novel, not to say progressive forays into sex education and ecology, their experience is scanned at every turn by the same rhythm of research, essay and failure as in their other scientific ventures comprising chapters 2 through 9. The inadequacy, the incompletion, the incoherence of each field of study motivates these two researchers to pursue firmer ground in another, then another, and another, with no end in sight. There is no end in sight because there is no valid, irreducible point of departure; there is no origin which is not arbitrary in its constitution, no foundation whose probing does not reveal an abyss beneath it. Their quest brings to mind a Borgesian archeological dig, which would pulverize each layer of civilization in search of a source buried still deeper in the sand, and become one with it in its disintegration. From on high—"Quel est le but de tout cela?" ("What is the purpose of all that?")—queries the star gazing Bouvard; and Pécuchet: "Peut-être qu'il n'y a pas de but?" ("Perhaps there is no purpose?")—as from way down below—"La géologie est trop défectueuse! A peine connaissons-nous quelques endroits de l'Europe. Quant au reste, avec le fond des Océans, on l'ignorera toujours" ("Geology is too defective. We hardly know a few places in Europe. As for the rest, with the bed of the Oceans, we'll always be ignorant")—the lesson of defeat is the same, and one wonders about the novelty of our deconstructive criticism, whose tireless errand is to repeat it in the realms of sign and psyche.

Of course we are entitled to say it is not the same thing; it never is—entirely. Proust, I think, enunciates the structural laws of our intellectual passion in speaking generally, as it were indifferently, of passional attachments (I elide references to the affair with Albertine and to the Dreyfus Affair, lest we repeat the error which he describes):

> It is true that the anti- . . . would have replied to me: "But it is not the same thing." But it is never the same thing, any more than it is the same person . . . otherwise, faced with the same phenomenon as before, someone who was a second time taken in by it would have no alternative but to blame his own subjective

condition, he could not again believe that the qualities or the defects resided in the object. And so, since the phenomenon, outwardly, is not the same, the intellect has no difficulty in basing upon each set of circumstances a new theory. . . . (And yet, the subjective element that I had observed to exist in . . . vision itself did not imply that an object could not possess real qualities or defects and in no way tended to make reality vanish into pure relativism.)

(The Past Recaptured)

The possible differences between our nuanced relativism and earlier ones remain to be worked out, genetically and historically, and perhaps too with this cautionary truism in mind: "MEMOIRE. Se plaindre de la sienne—et même se vanter de n'en pas avoir mais rugir si on vous dit que vous n'avez pas de jugement" ("MEMORY. Complain of one's own—and even boast of not having one but roar if you're told you have no judgment"). For one of the most comically devastating features of Bouvard et Pécuchet is its reduction of Western scepticism, with all its demystificatory pomp fully ripened by Voltaire's time, if not Montaigne's, to the commonplace, the banal:

> Science is constituted according to data drawn from a corner of extended space. Perhaps it doesn't agree with all the rest which isn't known, which is much bigger, and which can't be discovered.

One wonders, I say, because, as anyone might observe, we are not Bouvard and Pécuchet; and we know more about space, and the ocean floor, and . . . Yet it behooves us to determine in what ways our scepticism deserves to be distinguished from theirs: not to avoid confusing their levelling and ultimately panic "bêtise" from our own rigorous intelligence of epistemological affairs—if that can be done, for some of the most penetrating readings of this novel of late, I think, are devoted to showing its author as a precursor of our intellectual aporia—but to understand what has transpired since their time, what we have learned and what, as Proust suggests, we have not, so as to boast of a more radical, more informed and more nuanced scepticism. This raises the question of the historicity of deconstruction, of the factors in intellectual, social and political history which determine its emergence in our time, roughly a century after Flaubert. It is a question of which neither its advocates nor its adversaries offer very much in the way of a genetic explanation. It is a question for which there ought to be an answer, if, when we teach Lacan and Derrida and Foucault et al., we suppose we know what we are doing. "HYPOTHESE. Souvent 'dangereuse,' toujours 'hardie'" ("HY-POTHESIS. Often 'dangerous,' always 'bold'"). It is with the question of difference, as thematized and problematized by deconstructive criticism but not as yet historicized, that we have elected to turn the corner on the scepticism of Bouvard and Pécuchet as of Voltaire and Montaigne. "DOC-TRINAIRES. Les mépriser; mais pourquoi? on n'en sait rien" ("DOCTRI-NAIRES. Despise them; but why? nobody knows").

With no end in sight, Flaubert's novel remains appropriately unfinished. It is intended to close, as the scenarios for the conclusion show, with still another "mise en abîme," the letter of Dr. Vaucorbeil recapitulating the adventures of the "deux imbéciles inoffensifs": "En résumant toutes les actions et pensées, elle doit pour le lecteur, être la critique du roman" ("While summarizing all the actions and thoughts, it should be for the reader a critique of the novel"). And a note adds: "Cette lettre résume et juge B et P et doit rappeler au lecteur tout le livre" ("This letter summarizes and judges B and P and should recall to the reader the entire book"). A representation of the novel as a whole, the letter in turn is destined to representation:

> "What are we going to do with it?" No reflections! Let's copy!
> The page must be filled, the "monument" completed.—equality
> of all, of good and evil, of Beautiful and ugly, of the insignificant
> and the characteristic. There is nothing true but phenomena. Ex-
> altation of statistics.
>
> Finish with the prospect of the two old fellows bent over their
> desk and copying.

It is in terms of this nihilistic vocation to the letter that the full significance of the pedagogical adventure of the two men emerges. This chapter constitutes an indispensable stage in this process of "mise en abîme"—the endless representation of representation—beginning as it does with language study. An unpublished note—"B et P regrettent que les enfants parlent déjà. Sans cela ils feraient des expériences sur l'origine des langues en les isolant" ("B and P are sorry the children speak already. Without that they'd do experiments on the origin of language by isolating them")—reminds us that questions of language ultimately imply questions of origin, that reflection on the one inevitably leads to reflection on the other.

Here, the very hebetude of their pupils allows us to see that the roots of the pedagogical failure on the part of the two men are seeded from well within their enterprise, deriving from a fault or fissure at the heart of the semiological system from which all formal schooling springs. It is the failure of signs to adhere to any logic at their point of origin, as the two men

experience in the instruction of the prime matter of our cultural representation, the alphabet:

> Bouvard took charge of the girl, Pécuchet of the boy.
>
> Victor made out his letters, but did not succeed in forming
> syllables. He stammered over them, stopped suddenly and looked
> idiotic. Victorine asked questions. How come *ch* in "orchestre"
> has a *q* sound and a *k* sound in archeology? Sometimes two
> vowels must be joined, other times separated. All that isn't fair.
> She grew indignant.

The allodidactic experience represents at a more primary level a dilemma
encountered in the autodidactic. The two pupils apprehend the confusion
and contradiction at the level of the phonemic signifier which their tutors
encountered at more elaborate levels of the linguistic articulation. The same
incoherence and redundancy reign in the rules of grammar as in the realm
of "idées reçues":

> The subject always agrees with the verb, except in the cases where
> the subject does not agree.
> BLONDS. Hotter than brunettes (see *brunettes*).
> BRUNETTES. Hotter than blonds (see *blonds*).
> DIPLOMA. Sign of knowledge. Proves nothing.

Victorine's indignation recalls an earlier disillusionment with the signifying system:

> Grammarians, it is true, disagree; some see a beauty where others
> discover a fault. They admit principles whose consequences they
> reject, proclaim consequences whose principles they refuse, lean
> on tradition, throw out the masters, and have strange refinements.
> Ménage instead of *lentilles* and *cassonade* approves *nentilles* and
> *castonade*. Bouhours *jérarchie* and not *hiérarchie* and M. Chapsal
> *oeils de la soupe.*
>
> Pécuchet especially was dumbfounded by Génin. How would
> *z'annetons* be better than *hannetons*, *z'aricots* than *haricots*—
> and under Louis XIV they pronounced *Roume* and M. de *Lioune*
> for *Rome* and M. de *Lionne!*
>
> Littré dealt them the final blow in affirming that there never
> had been correct spelling, and never would be.
>
> They concluded from that that syntax is a fantasy and grammar
> an illusion.

Their conclusion, we note, springs from a problematic of difference: between written and spoken language, diachrony and synchrony, principles and consequences, such that the elements of signification are ever at a difference from themselves. Once it is scrutinized, the arbitrariness governing the constitution and ordering of the linguistic sign are readily perceived by the unschooled mind, and formal language apprenticeship rightly inspires indignation. Bouvard and Pécuchet have already been frustrated by this arbitrariness, as it emerges in the unbridgeable passage between proper and common nouns in geology:

> And then the nomenclature vexed them. Why Devonian, Cambrian, Jurassic, as if the soils (terres) designated by these words were not anywhere but in Devonshire, near Cambridge and in the Jura? Impossible to make out where you are!

With "ch" and "q" and "k," Victorine perceives a more radical flaw, a split within the signifier. The word or sign does not resemble a thing, nor does it resemble itself.

Victor and Victorine's intellectual conscience remains inviolate to this literal imposture, this semiological scandal, and their tutors will not overcome it by any rational means within the signifying system. Their teachers perform this coup by another, familiar strategy informing the politics of education. Where deduction and induction are fruitless, seduction proves deplorably effective.

> They came back to the lessons; and the alphabet blocks, the copy books, the toy printing press, all had failed, when they devised a stratagem.
> As Victor was inclined to gourmandise, they showed him the name of a dish: soon he read fluently in the *Cuisinier français*. Victorine being coquettish, a dress would be given her if she wrote to the dressmaker to order it. In less than three weeks, she accomplished this prodigy. It was pandering their faults, a pernicious means but successful.

"Il n'est désir plus naturel que le désir de cognoissance," writes Montaigne, who probably learned it from reading Aristotle rather than from the book of nature. But a knowledge of desire itself seems of more primary importance. Victor's sapience is nourished by his unnatural appetite, Victorine's *libido sciendi* stems casually from her libido, if not from a more metaphysical desire. At any rate, the high-minded aims of education are in question in

Flaubert's little apologue, which serves as a parody of enlightened self-interest.

It is largely to the fundamental incoherence in the signifying process, and to the conflict emerging from diverse, incongruous orders of representation, that Bouvard and Pécuchet owe subsequent failures, which proceed in conformity to type. They conform, that is, to the incoherence of their literal, graphological or rather graphillogical archetype. Thus with Victor:

> By means of an atlas, Pécuchet explained Europe to him; but dazzled by so many lines and colors, he could no longer find the names. The basins and the mountains did not tally with the countries, the political order muddled the physical.
>
> All that, perhaps, would be clarified by studying History.

The intelligence of Victor is rudimentary, but only the more candid in its perceptions for being so; it understandably balks before such an excess of representation. The geographies of nature and culture, of physis and polis, are heterogenous. The overlay of topography and typography replicates rather than dominates the chaos of the natural. Culture emerges as a second nature, assuming its opacity and disorder, its utter facticity.

The discordant problem of mapping nature and culture is compounded by that of framing. The dilemma of whole versus part, of micro- versus macrocosmic perspectives, presents itself in both geography and history: "They differed in their opinions as to geography. Bouvard thought it more logical to begin with the township. Pécuchet by the world as a whole." Both "*logiques*" are impeccable. "*Logique*" sins against itself, which is the case too with "*pratique*": "It might have been more practical to begin with the village, then the district, the department, the province. But Chavignolles having no chronicles, it was best after all to stick to world history. So much material encumbers it that one should only take its finest flowers."

And so on: through elements of science, whose abstractions surpass the imagination of the pupils; through religion and morality, confounded by the frank carnality of the girl, the nearly pristine brutality of the boy. In the midst of all this, Bouvard and Pécuchet engage in a civic discourse which increasingly absorbs their attention while incurring the unanimous opprobrium of the community. Their political radicalization reminds us of the potentially subversive dimension of education, to which I shall attend via some general reflections on their pedagogical experience.

Granted that *Bouvard et Pécuchet* offers only a caricature, a hyperbolic representation of learning and teaching, it is not any the less radical in its critique of these activities for being so. The mental and moral refractoriness

of their pupils constitutes, without any exaggeration in many cases, a no-
torious impediment to the task of education, as mounting statistics bear out
nationwide. And it is not for any lack of erudition that the two men fail
either in their own intellectual aim or in their pedagogical experiment. Flaubert, we know, consumed over one thousand five hundred volumes in preparing their research, and it is his knowledge that they repeat in their quest
and that they seek in turn to filter down to their pupils. If anything, they
are overeducated, overqualified for the task from that point of view. We
cannot charge their failure either to the seeming randomness or incompletion
of their instruction. For we can recognize in its very selectivity from an excess
of information and overlapping of disciplines the educational construct we
designate as an academic curriculum, a choice of data, ideas and methods
whose well-roundedness, implicit in the name we give it, does not bear up
under rigorous scrutiny. The recourse of the autodidacts, for their own enlightenment, to instructional manuals and such like summary compendia
anticipates only too well the empire of the "textbook" in contemporary
education: that strange and often alienating amalgam of scanty, abridged
sources, hasty references and sketchy commentary, replete with such mne-
motechnical devices as chapter outlines, indexes, color-coded print, marginal
illustrations and rubrics, which informs our educational industry at every
level.

Nor can we simply attribute the pedagogical failure of Bouvard and
Pécuchet to a "défaut de méthode dans les sciences," as the projected subtitle
for Flaubert's novel might suggest. For that phrase is ambiguous by itself; it
allows the inference that it is in "les sciences" themselves that method is
lacking, rather than in the two autodidacts, who find themselves before contradictory imperatives in education:

> It is not an easy dilemma; if one starts from facts, the most simple
> demands over-complicated reasons, and by posing principles first
> one begins by the Absolute, by Faith.
> What to decide? Combine the two ways of teaching, the ratio-
> nal and the empirical; but a double means towards a single end
> is the opposite of method. Ah! so much the worse!

It is at least questionable whether any dimension of our academic curricula
is immune to this vicious circle, whether any method is but a "pis aller."
Flaubert, for his own part, felt that the issue was central to his chapter: "Ça
va même très lentement. Mais je *sens* mon chapitre. J'ai peur qu'il ne soit
bien rébarbatif. Comment amuser avec des questions de méthode? Quant à
la portée philosophique des dites pages, je n'en doute pas" ("It's going very

slowly. But I *feel* my chapter. I'm afraid it's quite forbidding. How to amuse with questions of method? As for the philosophical import of said pages, I don't doubt it") (*Correspondance générale* [Corr.]). It is largely out of a concern for method that modern science is launched on its stellar career. Flaubert's subtitle recalls handily that of Descartes's autobiographical and resolutely autodidactic essay, *Discours de la méthode pour bien conduire sa raison dans la recherche de la vérité.* This text has been shown by a number of readers—Descartes's rivals in quest of a rationality—to proceed by just such a duplicity as cited by Flaubert. Paul Valéry found occasion to admire the "coup de volonté," the "coup de force," rather than any inherent logic, by which the cogito is constituted ("Descartes" in *Masters and Friends*). Michel Foucault has pointed to the significant historical coincidence between its constitution and the expulsion of madness into what were to become our mental institutions (*Madness and Civilization: A History of Insanity in the Age of Reason*). Jacques Derrida, elaborating Foucault's reading of the *Méditations,* shows that the cogito in and of itself is more than hospitable to madness, that its rationality flows from an act of faith which is theological in origin ("Cogito and the History of Madness" in *Writing and Difference*). It is meet therefore that the question of the danger Bouvard and Pécuchet pose to the community should turn on the issue of madness, on whose violent expulsion reason depends for its own determination. It is to the local prefect who asks "si Bouvard et Pécuchet n'étaient pas des fous dangereux" that Dr. Vaucorbeil describes them as "deux imbéciles inoffensifs."

The situation of Bouvard and Pécuchet with respect to the community and to community authority is worth examining in all its implications. In a note to chapter 10 we read: "ils démoralisent les enfants, on vient les leur retirer." The tutors cannot fail to demoralize their pupils if they seek to anchor their curriculum in rationality, for the foundations of rationality are not in themselves rational. (This point is developed by Jacques Derrida in his address on Kant and "Le Conflit des facultés," *Diacritics* 13 [Fall 1983].) The community, alarmed by their tendencies "au nivellement et à l'immoralité" ("to levelling and to immorality") can hardly abide their presence in its midst, and as a consequence of their intrusion into public affairs they are subject to arrest: "On les accuse d'avoir attenté à la Religion, à l'ordre, excité à la Révolte, etc." ("They are accused of having attacked Religion, order, incited to Revolt, etc."), we read in Flaubert's scenario for the conclusion. As they thrust their recently acquired knowledge into civic discourse, Bouvard and Pécuchet assume the status of scapegoats with respect to official values, and their threatened incarceration reflects the dynamics of a sacrificial crisis as analyzed by René Girard (*Violence and the Sacred*). It is a crisis of difference, the matrix of value as of meaning itself. Their pedagogical adventure, undertaken as it is "tabula rasa," cannot fail to "saper les bases," even as it occasions their own political radicalization, which is their encounter with the rootlessness of values and institutions. As they do so, we can see a replay of the Enlightenment, with its consequent revolution; with Proust ever in mind, we can see our own demystifications in the offing. What violence do they clear a space for? What violence, however covert, however institutionalized, do we underwrite to fend it off?

When, owing to a local squabble, Bouvard and Pécuchet have their day in court, they utter pronouncements which seem to encapsulate the polemics of Michel Foucault, who has devoted himself to studying the complicity between an arbitrary "Savoir" and an incriminating "Pouvoir":

> "Hold on now," cried Pécuchet. "The words contravention, crime and offense are worth nothing. Taking the penalty to classify punishable actions is taking an arbitrary basis. It is as much as saying to citizens: 'Don't worry about the value of your actions. That is only determined by the punishment of the Power Structure!' What's more, the Penal Code seems to me an irrational work, without principles."

Codes, principles, rationality, these are what are at stake in the gestation of Western society, in the construction and propagation of its values, and these are what Western society, in its relentless quest for its own foundations, has unceasingly continued to undermine, to "deconstruct." Bouvard and Pécuchet embody the fundamental aspirations of our culture even as they are threatened by exclusion from it. Their protest represents the division of our culture from within; their incrimination the outward projection of its danger—to itself.

One must appreciate, therefore, the rectitude, the implacable logic of the nearly unanimous decision on the part of the community which threatens the expulsion-incarceration of Bouvard and Pécuchet. Pedagogues, intellectuals, descending from the role of scribes to the Heavenly City, are not less a danger to the establishment of its earthly counterpart than they are its assigned guardians and transmitters. The official adversaries of Flaubert in his own time, like those of Baudelaire, are far more consistent and logical in their opposition to the writer than his brilliant admirers in our humanities departments of today. Augustine and Pascal believe as little in the substantial authority of a penal code as Nietzsche. No culture can survive or perdure in the full light of the intuitions shared by Flaubert and his doubles at the projected conclusion of the novel. No education, no acculturation, no order or hierarchy, no structure, primacy or ultimacy are rationally conceivable or justifiable in the light of the radical nihilism, rooted in the senselessness of language itself, which radiates throughout the virtually endless pages of Flaubert's novel. Rather culture survives and endures by exclusion, by expulsion, by alienation. Prevalent theories regarding the religious, sacrificial origins of culture can point to the "cultus" from which it springs. They are barbarians to the Greeks who do not speak their language and acknowledge their gods. As a complex of hierarchical differences, culture marks off as utterly and otherwise different—sacred, mad or "bête"—groups or individuals which threaten to dissolve its differentiations. (Jean-Louis Bouttes writes ingeniously of the fated meeting between Bouvard and Pécuchet and Zarathustra [*Le Destructeur de l'intensité*].) This expulsion hangs over anyone who, since at least the time of Socrates, questions the inarticulate substantiality of its valuations from within. This properly sacrificial destiny is especially legible in the historical experience of French writers: from the time of the mythically outlawed Villon and of Rabelais, who was vilified by both Protestant and Catholic opponents (and whose encomium Flaubert composed in the youthful time of his aspiration to be a "démoralisateur" [*Corr.*]), to the time of Baudelaire, who subversively dialectized good and evil, and of Flaubert himself, justly tried for the immorality of *Madame Bovary* (and justly acquitted, for its profound immorality escaped its readers of his day, and is only appearing in our time).

The incarceration of the two men is only forestalled, according to Flaubert's scenario, by the offhand diagnosis of madness on the part of Dr. Vaucorbeil: "Vaucorbeil (attracted by the noise) speaks for them, 'They really ought to be hauled off to a madhouse.'" This in turn is a fate from which they are preserved perhaps only by their voluntary self-exile in the desert of letters, whereby they end up as they began: "*Copier comme autrefois.*" Thus Bouvard and Pécuchet accomplish the final, pantheistic vow of Flaubert's Saint Antoine—"*Etre la matière!*"—in a secular, atheistic mode: "*être copiste*" is to be in the only mode of being which the exhaustion of Western metaphysics has left to man. "*Etre copiste*" is to be only in the mode of representation, to be ever at a distance and a difference from oneself, of which the letter, as the mark of an absence, is the paradoxical symbol.

The investigations of Derrida suggest that the letter, writing, have emerged at critical junctures in the history of culture—Plato, Rousseau, Saussure—as a theme upon which to focus questions of cultural origins (*Of Grammatology,* and "Plato's Pharmacy" in *Dissemination*). The importance of writing is paradoxical: its specific privilege within the thematics of culture is that it is not a respecter of persons or of privilege (*privus lex*), but indifferently accessible to many. It is as such that Plato condemns it in the *Cratylus*. It is as such that it has served as a principal means of secularization and democratization in history. It is as such that Flaubert, in one of his rages against modern "bêtise," is prepared to condemn it to oblivion: "If the emperor tomorrow suppressed the printing press, I'd journey to Paris on my knees and I'd go kiss his ass as a sign of gratitude. That's how tired I am of printing and of the abuse it's put to" (*Corr.*).

Flaubert himself longed for a preponderant vocal power, of the kind to which Ioakanann, as if inspired by the Holy Spirit, gives vent in *Hérodias*. To this oratorical force the writer contrasts the mindless repetition of his century which will later be incarnate in Félicité's parrot in *Un Coeur simple:* "Je sens pourtant que je ne dois pas mourir sans avoir fait rugir quelque part un style comme je l'entends dans ma tête et qui pourra bien dominer la voix des perroquets et des cigales" ("I feel nonetheless that I should not die without having found somewhere a way to roar out a style as I hear it in my head and which could dominate the voice of the parrots and cicadas") (*Corr.*). This contrast provokes in turn an allusion to letters, and to *Don Quijote,* the novel whose antithetical doubles represent the opposition between bookish versus oral culture: "We take our country on the soles of our feet and we carry in our hearts without knowing it the dust of these dead ancestors. As for me personally, I would do a demonstration of that as simple as A + B. It's the same in literature. I rediscover all my origins in the book which I knew by heart before I could read, *Don Quijote*" (ibid.). In Flaubert's time, this antithesis collapses, this difference is erased by the advance towards universal literacy, of which the widely read Homais is the paragon. In *Bouvard et Pécuchet,* the theme of writing emerges in conjunction with the theme of the double, as if by way of demonstrating that the dissolution of meaning to which they are destined by their research brings on a dissolution of identity. Thus Flaubert's notes read:

> Their intrinsic difference must be perceived in spite of their union
> until the end where they become in the joy of Copy and in the
> community of passion the same man, down to resembling each
> other physically one and the same being doubled.

It is as a difference which is in itself insignificant that writing plays a role in Flaubert's critique of modern culture. It is as such, with Derrida and others, that it resurges at the epicenter of cultural debate today, as the symbol of a crisis on a world becoming totally, globally Western, a world in which cultural difference is on the wane. "L'humanité s'installe dans la monoculture," writes Claude Lévi-Strauss, whose *Tristes Tropiques* repeats the gesture of Plato, Rousseau and Saussure in condemning writing.

For Derrida as for Lévi-Strauss, writing is the mark of a violence suggesting a tyrannical rather than contractual order in the organization of culture. Our contemporary impasse concerning origins should not blind us to the concrete possibility of an ultimate violence, wrought by a technology which descends from writing and which owes its development unequivocally to our Western, writerly culture. On page one of the issue of *Le Monde* (April 25, 1980) containing a special section commemorating the hundredth anniversary of the death of Flaubert, a French deputy calculates that the nuclear capability worldwide is adequate to put two tons of dynamite under the feet of every one of its inhabitants. It is in terms of this possibility that the conclusion of *Bouvard et Pécuchet,* even as it concerns pedagogical imperatives, is fraught with significance.

The two autodidacts do not embark explicitly on the quest for the origins of culture, but in the concluding scenario we do find them prognosticating about its end. "Our studies give us the right to speak," they decide in announcing a program of adult education. It appears from Flaubert's notes for this episode that the author first contemplated a unified perspective: "They arrive at contemporary Socialism which is Cosmopolitanism, and absolute levelling—Auto-idolatry of humanity, the Dogma of progress; without defining it." "*Autolâtrie,*" as the logical destiny of man in a desacralized universe, is how Flaubert, judging by his correspondence, views the future of humanity. As a seeming divine capacity for destruction accrues to man, it is a view worth serious consideration. But it is when, in an effort to define progress, Flaubert outlines "leurs deux prosopopées sur l'humanité," that his text offers a most telling reading of our situation, as well as a comic lesson in reading.

When Pécuchet views the future of humanity "*en noir,*" Bouvard views the same "*en beau.*" For the former, modern man is "amoindri et devenu une machine" ("diminished and become a machine"), while for the latter he is "en progrès." The one foretells:

Final anarchy of the human race (Buchner, 1.2)
Impossibility of peace.
Barbarism through excess of individualism, and the rage of Science.

There will no longer be any ideal, religion or morality.
America will have conquered the earth.

This view is balanced in perfect equilibrium by the other's positive expectation that

> Europe will be regenerated by Asia, the law of history being that civilization goes from East to West—role of China—the two humanities will be finally fused.
>
> Disappearance of evil by the disappearance of need. Philosophy will be a religion.

Of course one can dismiss this text as still another exercise in intellectual futility, a parody of "world historical swashbuckling" (the phrase is Kierkegaard's) already in vogue in Flaubert's time. Still the text betrays an uncanny pertinence to contemporary ideological conflict, in which rival eschatologies, East and West, Communist and Capitalist, identify their cause with the future of humanity as the stakes at large.

One is tempted to suggest, according to an open-minded, liberal view of affairs, that the future lies somewhere in between, and furthermore that a modicum of common sense and generous effort would inflect matters along a hopeful, positive course, the right course—which political left and political right each identify as their proper course, the course proper to their aspirations for mankind. Such a view has ever been the Western one, which has prided itself on its optimism and good will towards mankind, and which has sought, with unprecedented missionary zeal, to educate the world in the wisdom of its liberalism. Such a view would not fail to claim its identity in the optimistic, progressive role assigned to the East, and thereby operate a change of signs, a Sino-American exchange in this instance. But this about-face or reversal of signs leaves intact the Manichean dualism of Flaubert's text, its tic-tac automatism. Rather it is necessary to abstract altogether from the historical and political referents in order to perceive the relevance of Flaubert's schema for contemporary history.

For to confide in the substantial pertinence of these rival prognostications is to succumb to the veritable folly which their symmetrical juxtaposition is designed to reveal. It is to underwrite or subscribe to a difference, to a difference in substance or to the substance of a difference, which only resides in the tension between the opposing stances. These in turn do not reflect an ideological stalemate, a static impasse of opposing views. They are antithetical valuations of a single destiny, ambi-valenced assessments of a single future, whose law of becoming is perhaps best expressed in Pécuchet's third hypothesis:

Three hypotheses. Pantheist radicalism will break all ties with the past, and an inhuman despotism will follow; 2° if theist absolutism triumphs, the liberalism with which humanity has been imbued since the Reformation succumbs, everything is overturned; 3° if the convulsions which exist since 89 continue, without and between two issues, these two oscillations will blow us away by their own forces.

The oscillatory hypothesis does not reconcile or synthesize the thesis and antithesis preceding it; it summarizes the law of their interaction. The violent outcome of the opposition represented by Bouvard and Pécuchet is thus enfolded within the logic of one of its terms, this asymmetry being the essential dynamic of a binary structure which, as such, is perfectly blind to its own rigorous symmetry.

Ideological conflict corresponds less to political, historical or socioeconomic realities than to the structural laws of binary opposition which govern language, which is, as Saussure reminds us, a form not a substance. According to these laws, the sign derives its meaning or value in terms of its difference from other signs; its value is negative, opposite, relative; words signify not by any meaning proper to them, not by any substance in them but by their difference from other words in the lexicon. It follows from this that East and West cannot significantly oppose each other until or unless they speak the same language; they are never so likely to clash as when they are competing under the same ensign, never so likely to differ as when they resemble each other. "It is then," writes Vincent Descombes, "the same song on both sides" (he is speaking of the French national anthem, of the "sang impur" whose spilling it acclaims):

> Symmetry turns a thing around an axis, and presents it thereby as *vis-à-vis*, as an adversary, in the spatial sense of the word. It thereby opposes the thing to itself, the same to the same, and it is in that identity of adversaries that we must find *adversity* in the second sense, no longer only spatial: *hostility*. It is symmetry, that is the absence of any difference other than that of rotation in space by which the same can see itself in the other, which is the ground of enmity ["le fond de l'inimitié"].
>
> (*L'Inconscient malgré lui*)

It is the comic revelation of this identity in difference which we find in Flaubert's formula, "un même et un seul être en partie double."

These same laws of language govern the composition of *Bouvard et*

Pécuchet from its inception, that is from the very first appearance of the two men on the scene of literature in chapter 1 of the novel:

> Two men appeared.
>
> One came from the Bastille, the other from the Jardin des Plantes. The taller, in a linen suit, walked with his hat cocked back, his waistcoat unbuttoned and his tie in hand. The shorter, his body enveloped in a brown frock-coat, held his head low beneath a pointed cap.
>
> When they reached the middle of the boulevard, they sat down at the same time on the same bench.

"L'un, l'autre, le plus grand, le plus petit," East, West, thema, anathema: negative, oppositive, relative. Bouvard and Pécuchet, these complementary nonentities drawn from the democratic herd and whose difference is in so many senses only nominal (*bos/pecus*), are shortly to be identified as copyists. They are in fact copies of each other, positive and negative representations of each other. They are "*repoussoirs,*" as Flaubert says of Jules and Henry of the first *Education sentimentale* (*Corr.*), like concave and convex, like "B" and "P" themselves, the latter being but an unvoiced repetition of the former, its phonemic negative, its literal, mute representation, its specular double in every sense. With these two individuals as with the ideological confrontation they configurate, we are dealing with a phony opposition which rings hollow even as we pronounce it, and of which the letter is the unsubstantial trace, the arbitrary, violent mark.

It is the vocation of B and P, as we may now spuriously identify them, to lettering, to "*la Copie,*" that reduces their "*différence intrinsèque*" to "*un même et un seul être en partie double.*" The projected resolution of Flaubert's novel conforms to the law of relativity, according to which matter-as-energy is ever at a distance from itself. This is the law which governs everything in our universe from the movement of atoms to the determination of signs, where it goes by the name of "*dissémination,*" "*différance.*" It is a law, the opposition of same to same, of the thing to itself within itself, which emerges, as if providentially, as cultural differences erode worldwide. In a world left entirely to its own all-too-human devices, difference is nowhere without and everywhere within, as humanity lines itself up "en partie double" for an intraspecific contest without parallel in the animal kingdom.

Homo sum et nihil humani alieno puto. But what is proper to humanity is the double part it plays against itself, unto possible annihilation. This is a prospect that might not have disappointed Flaubert, who reads the progress of mankind as "paganisme, christianisme, muflisme" (*Corr.*). But Flaubert's works also suggest, in a specifically educational context, a means of averting the prospect—if anything like a pedagogical imperative can do so.

The first, lamentable appearance of Charles Bovary on the scene of literature is situated in a class of students engaged in the study of Latin, a dead language known only through writing, studied only in books. *Pensums* are distributed to punish the disorderly mockery which greets the appearance of Charles, who for all his ineffectual innocence does not escape the punitive assignment of self-mockery: "Quant à vous, le *nouveau,* vous me copierez vingt fois le verbe *ridiculus sum*" ("As for you, the *new boy,* you will copy out twenty times the verb *ridiculus sum*"). The inaugural thematics of copy, repetition, "bêtise," doubtless speak for themselves at this stage. The structural dynamics of this scene, as it is narrated by an anonymous "nous," come more fully to light by contrast with its specular reversal in the opening pages of *Mémoires d'un fou.* Here we find a volatile first-person narrator exclaiming with febrile rancor against his schoolmates:

> I still see myself, seated on a class bench, absorbed by my dreams of the future; thinking what a child's imagination can dream of the most sublime, while that pedant of a teacher made fun of my Latin verse, while my snickering schoolmates looked at me. The imbeciles! Them, to laugh at me! They, so weak, so common, so narrow minded; I whose spirit was drowning in the limits of creation, who was lost in all the worlds of poetry, who felt greater than them all, who enjoyed infinite pleasures and who had heavenly ecstasies before all the intimate revelations of my soul.

Of course Charles, who is last seen by "*nous*" as "cherchant tous les mots dans le dictionnaire et se donnant beaucoup de mal" ("looking for every word in the dictionary knocking himself out"), is different from this character, whose Latin phrasing doubtless exceeds the classical measure expected by his professor. They are not the same, unless we allow that Flaubert has reversed the perspective, from strident first-person narrator vaunting his victimized singularity to the anonymous, impassive "*nous,*" in order to portray himself as incongruously other, to see himself as others might see him. For it is clear that the beginning of *Mémoires d'un fou* and of *Madame Bovary* compose the same scene "en partie double." The "eux-moi" opposition of *Mémoires* is a tragic or romantic modality of the double, of which the later "*nous*" is an ambiguous, evasive stage. In the "*sottisier*" to be compiled by Bouvard and Pécuchet, the reader would find the pride of his intellectual culture held up to ridicule, such that no one could utter a statement without fear of falling victim to (self-) mockery, without fear of evidencing his own "*bêtise*": this is perhaps the definitive stage. All, "*eux*," "*moi*," "*nous*," are summoned to copy, "comme autrefois," the *pensum* assigned to "le *nouveau*," until it is learned by heart, learned as one's very inmost truth, as access to the only possible presence of humanity to itself, the syllables of a dead language: *ridiculus sum*.

MICHAL PELED GINSBURG

Representational Strategies
and the Early Works of Flaubert

The radical change which Flaubert criticism has undergone in recent years
has as one of its effects the possibility of seeing for the first time the work
of Flaubert as a whole. Not only because certain works are finally admitted
into the canon, but mainly because it becomes more and more evident that
beyond the superficial differences which seem to oppose the *Tentation de
saint Antoine* to *Madame Bovary* or *Madame Bovary* to *Bouvard et Pécuchet*
the Flaubertian text has some constant features which give it its particularity.

I will argue that these features result from narrative strategies Flaubert
adopts in order to overcome basic problems of representation created by his
text. It should be stated from the outset that my analysis itself is inscribed
within (and even shaped by) a growing awareness in recent criticism of the
problematic nature of representation. This theoretical awareness has as one
of its "sources" the practice of certain writers, among them Flaubert, while
on the other hand it generates new readings of those writers, "creates" a
new Flaubert. This interchange between text and theory, where each can be
seen as generating and determining the other, is one of the issues at stake in
the problematization of the concept of representation. The questioning, or
"deconstruction," of the concept of the representation involves a demonstration that the opposition between experience and representation (or, in
terms of literary analysis, between text and interpretation) is generated by a
mis-recognition of the derived nature of experience and of the originative

From *Modern Language Notes* 98, no. 5 (December 1983). © 1983 by The Johns
Hopkins University Press, Baltimore/London.

character of representàtion, that is to say, the misrecognition of the impossibility to separate and oppose these terms. A similar critique would apply to the concept of the subject where not only the primacy of the self over language is put into question buf where also it can be argued that while the subject projects (or creates) an image of himself, it is this image which creates him, constitutes him as a self. These "theoretical" problems are in some way or another already thematized in the text of Flaubert, especially through his preoccupation with the relation between experience and language. What I intend, however, to show in this paper is how the problematic nature of representation and of the self dictates a certain number of narrative strategies which then determine the plot, themes, and narrative voice of his works.

These strategies can be discerned quite easily in the early works where the search for an adequate mode of narration is all too clear: the *Mémoires d'un fou, Novembre,* and the first *Education sentimentale.* Each of these works is composed of heterogeneous elements: in the *Mémoires* the fifteenth chapter, relating the story of the two English girls, is written in an ironic style that contrasts with the tone and narrative tradition of the rest of the work. In *Novembre* the confessional mode is broken by the interpolated story of Marie, and with the second narrator the narration changes from first to third person. The *Education* is narrated partially in the first person (letters), partially in the third. This absence of narrative unity is not simply the result of lack of craftsmanship in the young Flaubert. The narrative impasses which dictate the change in narrative mode result from a basic problem in generating the text and this problem lingers in Flaubert's work to the end. An analysis of the early narratives will help us understand the subsequent works of Flaubert.

I

The problem of representation which Flaubert faces is clearly formulated in the Dedication of the *Mémoires:* "Ces pages . . . renferment une âme toute entière. Est-ce la mienne? est-ce celle d'un autre?" Having completed his autobiographical text, the narrator doubts whether he is really its subject matter, and as a reader of his own text he finds himself alienated from himself. The "I" plays here the roles of narrator, character, and reader, but this fusion does not generate unity. Though he writes about himself, the narrating-I necessarily creates a character which, once created, seems to have a life of its own and hence escapes his control: "Ces pages . . . renferment une *âme* toute entière . . . peu à peu, en écrivant . . . l'*âme* remua la plume et l'écrasa" (my emphasis). The "soul," by being represented, becomes independent and different from the narrator who, hence, at the end no longer recognizes himself in it. This feeling of alienation, the loss of the self through self-representation, which the retrospective Dedication formulates so clearly, is present throughout the *Mémoires* and governs its movement.

From the beginning of the *Mémoires* one finds that writing involves externalizing part of oneself and giving that projected part a certain independence. The process of projection is made manifest by the visual nature of the act of narration. In the *Mémoires,* from the moment the narrator starts to narrate, he *sees*. And as he tells about himself, or more precisely about the writer he is trying to become, it is not surprising that he does not simply see himself, but rather sees himself seeing, that is to say, sees himself as one who sees a spectacle which his imagination has created:

> Je fus au collège dès l'âge de dix ans. . . .
>
> J'y vécus . . . seul et ennuyé. . . .
>
> Je me vois encore, assis sur les bancs de la classe, absorbé dans mes rêves d'avenir, pensant à ce que l'imagination d'un enfant peut rêver du plus sublime. . . .
>
> Je me voyais jeune, à vingt ans, entouré de gloire . . . je voyais l'Orient et ses sables immenses, ses palais que foulent les chameaux avec leurs clochettes d'airain; je voyais les cavales bondir vers l'horizon rougi par le soleil; je voyais des vagues bleues, un ciel pur, un sable d'argent; je sentais le parfum de ces océans tièdes du Midi; et puis, près de moi, sous une tente, à l'ombre d'un aloès aux larges feuilles, quelque femme à la peau brune, au regard ardent, qui m'entourait de ses deux bras et me parlait la langue des houris.

The structure *en abîme* of this passage (in which the narrator sees a school boy who sees a young man who sees an oriental scene) suggests that in Flaubert both reminiscing and imagining—autobiography and fiction— have the structure of a spectacle, are both an externalization of part of the self which the self then can watch. The difference between the two is only in the degree of differentiation and independence which the spectacle is given. The oriental scene would no longer be an "autobiographical" account of the imagining of an (imaginary) young man, and become a "story" of oriental passion if the woman—the spectacle which the self has projected—could gain some life of her own, that is to say, become independent and different from her creator. However, as the Dedication has shown, such differentiation also takes place in autobiography, so that every autobiography is to some extent fictive. This awareness jeopardizes the whole enterprise of the *Mém-*

oires, which is based on the assumption that the self can translate its own unique story into language.

Moreover, the logic of the structure is such that the more the spectacle is differentiated, the more it is independent of its creator—the more fictive it is—the more it can generate a narrative. This means that in Flaubert the intention to narrate is always in conflict with the narcissistic interest of the subject to unite with his own mirror image.

For Flaubert creating means projecting a part of the self, giving birth to an image which can be called "I," "a madman," "woman," "the world," and so on. This image, in order to live, must become differentiated from the self; it becomes actually so different that, as the Dedication has shown, it cannot be recognized as an image of the self anymore. The mirror image is hence threatening and inherently hostile since it usurps the place of the self and thus annihilates it. The creation of the spectacle entails an aggressive conflict between creator and spectacle, between the "I" and a hostile world: the fellow students who ridicule him, the father who mutilates him, the castrating woman. What is important to note is that in Flaubert the representation of the world as antagonistic is not simply the restatement of the romantic cliché of the individual singularity in danger of being destroyed by a world that does not understand it; it is, rather, a necessity of the representation.

The narrator of the *Mémoires* can see only one solution to the threat presented by the spectacle he has created: he destroys his creation, eliminates the spectacle. The sequence of the two dreams the narrator relates (chapters 4 and 5) articulates the threat which the differentiated spectacle represents for the self and the destruction of the created image which follows. In the first dream the spectacle the narrator has projected (the "vision" he sees) threatens to mutilate him. Hence, in the second dream the mother, the mirror image, is destroyed. The mother is clearly the narrator's narcissistic double: trying to see her when she calls for help he looks at his own reflection in the water: "j'étais avec ma mère qui marchait du côté de la rive; elle tomba. . . . Je me penchai à plat ventre sur l'herbe pour regarder, je ne vis rien; les cris continuaient." It is true that in this passage the elimination of the other is not represented as a deliberate murder but as an inevitable catastrophe; but its voluntary aspect will become apparent as it is repeated.

The rhythm of the *Mémoires* is that of creation, differentiation, fear of this differentiation, and elimination. As the annihilation of the created spectacle rules out continuation of the story, the whole cycle must start again.

The narrator of the *Mémoires* tries out different strategies that would allow the narration to continue without endangering him. When he evokes his past, for example, he is careful not to give the spectacle he creates so much life that he cannot control it: the past is hence presented as dead: "une série de souvenirs ... passent tous confus, effacés comme des ombres. ... souvenirs calmes et riants ... vous passez près de moi comme des roses flétries." In the main episode, that of Maria, the narrator attempts to keep a strenuous balance between existence and annihilation of the mirror image. The narrator first encounters Maria when he saves her coat from the water, the water from which he did not want to (or could not) save his mother. But Maria is "saved" only to be repeatedly in danger of drowning and her footsteps are constantly being wiped out by the waves ("La vague a effacé les pas de Maria"). In addition, though described as a rather large, dark woman, with "expression mâle et énergique" (ibid.), Maria remains a shadow because the narrator refuses to give her flesh and blood. The very thought of her as a living body, full of desire, fills him with rage. Instead of giving her a voice of her own, he simply reports that she talked and that "Maria et moi nous étions parfaitement du même sentiment en fait d'art." Giving her a voice of her own would be to establish, side by side with her similarity to himself, her complete otherness, her existence as a separate entity independent of him and hence a threat to his unity and integrity as a self. Maria remains a fleshless, voiceless figure, object of a platonic love, because the narrator cannot face making her a living creature; but, on the other hand, he cannot sustain a narrative around this spectral figure. Hence, the narrative stops and starts again with the story of the two English girls.

This episode too begins with the creation of a spectacle:

Parmi tous les rêves du passé, les souvenirs d'autrefois et mes réminiscences de jeunesse, j'en ai conservé un bien petit nombre, avec quoi je m'amuse aux heures d'ennui. A l'évocation d'un nom tous les personnages reviennent, avec leurs costumes et leur langage, jouer leur rôle comme ils le jouèrent dans ma vie, et je les vois agir devant moi comme un Dieu qui s'amuserait à regarder ses mondes créés.

The spectacle is described as both alive (the characters can act in front of him) and dead ("comme un cadavre"). We have seen that this is an aggressive measure by which the narrator protects himself against his creation. But the distinctiveness of this episode is that the annihilation of the spectacle is brought about neither by placing it on the border between existence and death, nor by characterizing it as ephemeral and insubstantial. Rather, the narrator protects himself against his narration by showing its imaginary and inauthentic character.

The main text of the *Mémoires* is based on the assumption that the self can tell its own story in language. The narrator presents himself as a madman, "image hyperbolique d'une singularité, d'une subjectivité exacerbée" (Shoshana Felman, "Modernité du lieu commun: en marge de Flaubert: *Novembre*") and in dwelling on the story of his youth, virginity, and first love, he presents himself and his desires as original and hence authentic. He trusts in the capacity of language to express his subjectivity and therefore posits an adequacy between the subject and his language: "Seulement tu croiras peut-être, en bien des endroits, que l'expression est forcée et le tableau assombri à plaisir; rappelle-toi que c'est un fou qui a écrit ces pages." The particular character of language is accounted for by the individuality of the person who uses it. In the episode of the two English girls, however, this notion of originality, in matters both of love and of literary expression, is consciously and deliberately undermined.

The audience of friends to whom the narrator tells this episode serves as an ironic deflation of the narrator's beliefs: "par hasard, j'avais du papier et un crayon, je fis des vers . . . (Tout le monde se mit à rire)"; "—Voilà que tu vas devenir bête, dit un des auditeurs en m'interrompant." The notion of spontaneity and hence originality and authenticity of expression is undermined by being exposed as in itself a literary cliché. Instead of a genuine, original desire, which can be spontaneously expressed in language, we find that self, desire, and language are inauthentic, a result of imitation and self-suggestion:

> Mais ces vers, pour la plupart étaient faux. . . .
> Je me battais les flancs pour peindre une chaleur que je n'avais vue que dans les livres; puis, à propos de rien, je passais à une mélancolie sombre et digne d'Antony . . . et je disais à propos de rien:
>
> > Ma douleur est amère, ma tristesse profonde,
> > Et j'y suis enseveli comme un homme en la tombe.

The narrator realizes that language, whether that of the poets or that of his own poems, rather than expressing his desire, creates it, bringing into being his image as a desiring self. In other words, he sees that he does not have a self that precedes its (re)presentation in language. But this (re)presentation which creates him also brings about, as he has already discovered, his death, since he cannot recognize himself in the self he has created. The precarious situation between life and death which his creation occupies is thus a necessary feature of representation. The self discovers that it is always already double, alienated from itself, aggressive and subject to aggression, in a precarious balance between life and death.

In the *Mémoires,* however, this insight remains without consequences; after a moment of lucidity the narrator falls back into mystification, claiming that doubling and fictionality are the result of representation and not features of experience itself. Hence, when he realizes that his work is a failure, he says: "quelle vanité que l'art! vouloir peindre l'homme dans un bloc de pierre ou l'âme dans des mots, les sentiments par des sons et la nature sur une toile vernie." But the insights of the episode of the two English girls are not lost; they are further developed in *Novembre.*

II

Novembre repeats in many ways the movement of the *Mémoires.* It also starts with the doubling of the self and the creation of a spectacle. On the first page of *Novembre,* for example, one reads: "ma vie entière s'est placée devant moi comme un fantôme . . . mes pauvres années ont repassé devant moi . . . une ironie étrange les frôlait et les retournait pour mon spectacle"; "la vie m'apparaissait de loin avec des splendeurs et des bruits triomphaux." But what *Novembre* makes explicit is the erotic character of the experience of doubling. The narrator externalizes a part of himself that, under its feminine form, he wants to join sexually:

> Oh! que ne pouvais-je presser quelque chose dans mes bras, l'y étouffer sous ma chaleur, ou bien me dédoubler moi-même, aimer cet autre être et nous fondre ensemble. . . .
>
> Mes lèvres tremblaient, s'avançaient, comme si j'eusse senti l'haleine d'une autre bouche, mes mains cherchaient quelque chose à palper . . . et je remuais les cheveux autour de ma tête, je m'en caressais le visage . . . j'aurais voulu . . . être la fleur que le vent secoue, la rive que le fleuve humecte, la terre que le soleil féconde.

It is this erotic-narcissistic doubling, with its rhythm of differentiation and assimilation, which generates the main part of *Novembre,* the episode with the prostitute Marie.

Marie is clearly the narrator's specular opposite: "ta vie et la mienne, n'est-ce pas la même?"; "sans nous connaître, elle dans sa prostitution et moi dans ma chasteté, nous avions suivi le même chemin, aboutissant au même gouffre; pendant que je me cherchais une maîtresse, elle s'était cherché un amant, elle dans le monde, moi dans mon coeur; l'un et l'autre nous

avaient fuis." Marie is his mirror image not only on the erotic but also on
the narrative level. She is a "narrator" who uses the cliché language of the
novels and poems that created the desire of the narrator: "'Ange d'amour,
de délices, de volupté, d'où viens-tu? où est ta mère? à quoi songeait-elle
quand elle t'a conçu? rêvait-elle la force des lions d'Afrique ou le parfum de
ces arbres lointains, si embaumants qu'on meurt à les sentir?'" She fiction-
alizes him, makes him the idealized subject of her own narration in the same
way that in the *Mémoires* he created a fiction of Maria: she creates him as
an idealized man and lover ("ange d'amour"), attributes to him a perfect
mistress ("il me semblait qu'avec ces mots elle me faisait une maîtresse
idéale"), and describes all the cliché situations of a "roman d'amour": "'Ta
maîtresse t'aime, n'est-ce pas? . . . Comment vous voyez-vous? est-ce chez
toi, ou chez elle? est-ce à la promenade, quand tu passes à cheval? . . . au
théâtre, quand on sort et qu'on lui donne son manteau? ou bien la nuit, dans
son jardin?'"

Marie then is a double in which the narrator can see himself. But she
is also a double which is well developed and alive: being a prostitute, Marie,
unlike Maria of the *Mémoires,* is necessarily given a bodily existence, and
again, unlike Maria, she has a voice and a life of her own which she herself
narrates. Thus what was desperately avoided in the *Mémoires* can take place
here: the double takes on flesh and bone to such an extent that it threatens
to annihilate the narrator. Not only on the erotic level, where Marie's desire
seems to gain frightening dimensions: "'Oui, oui, embrasse-moi bien, embrasse-moi bien! tes baisers me rajeunissent . . .' Et elle s'appuya la bouche
sur mon cou, y fouillant avec d'âpres baisers, comme une bête fauve au
ventre de sa victime," but also on the level of narration. After all, from a
certain point on, it is Marie who becomes the narrator, usurping the first
person.

Thus the double which the "I" has created, by gaining life and independence, threatens to annihilate him both erotically and verbally (both as
a hero and as a narrator). In other words, the "I" is faced with the necessity
of giving up "romantic" autobiography, which proved to be impossible, for
the sake of "realistic" fiction. During the Marie episode he is not yet ready
for this. He hastens to eliminate Marie as a vital force and keeps her as a
memory, well under his control. Though Marie is much more alive and
independent than Maria, a step forward towards "creation," the same destiny
awaits both. But the difference between them is important and influences
the course which each work takes.

In both works, after the disappearance of the desired object (in the
Mémoires this disappearance is still attributed to chance while in *Novembre*

its deliberate nature is clear), desire increases: "je ne l'aimais pas alors, et en tout ce que je vous ai dit, j'ai menti; c'était maintenant que je l'aimais, que je la désirais; que, seul sur le rivage, dans les bois ou dans les champs, je me la créais là, marchant à côté de moi, me parlant, me regardant," writes the narrator of the *Mémoires*. Similarly, in *Novembre:* "A mesure que le temps s'éloignait, je l'en aimais de plus en plus; avec la rage que l'on a pour les choses impossibles, j'inventais des aventures pour la retrouver, j'imaginais notre rencontre."

These two passages establish a dichotomy between the "real" woman and a "fictive" image which the self creates in the absence of the real object. We know, however, that the "real" object is just as much an imaginary, narcissistic projection. The difference between the "real" and the "imaginary" lies only in the degree of independence the image is granted. The "real" object has been eliminated because its potential difference threatened the integrity of the self; but its annihilation made any further narration impossible. The way the narrator tries now out of this impasse is that of preserving his creation by pretending that it is alive, and hence able to generate a story, while never losing sight of the fact that as a created image it depends on him and cannot threaten him. The same solution of any imaginary substitute is attempted in both *Novembre* and the *Mémoires,* but the imaginary substitute which has satisfied the "I" of the *Mémoires* no longer satisfies the "I" of *Novembre*. In the *Mémoires* we read:

> Un jour je revenais, vers le crépuscule, je marchais à travers les pâturages couverts de boeufs, je marchais vite, je n'entendais que le bruit de ma marche qui froissait l'herbe; j'avais la tête baissée et je regardais la terre. Ce mouvement régulier m'endormit pour ainsi dire, je crus entendre Maria marcher près de moi; elle me tenait le bras et tournait la tête pour me voir, c'était elle qui marchait dans les herbes. Je savais bien que c'était une hallucination que j'animais moi-même, mais je ne pouvais me défendre d'en sourire et je me sentais heureux.

The narcissistic-onanistic experience, result of the elimination of the other, is satisfactory. Not so in *Novembre:* "Une fois, je marchais vite dans un pré, les herbes sifflaient autour de mes pieds en m'avançant, elle était derrière moi; je me suis retourné, il n'y avait personne. . . . et je suis retombé seul, abîmé, plus abandonné qu'au fond d'un précipice." The "I" who panicked at the strength of his creation, seeing that giving life and independence to it necessarily entails his elimination as a desiring and speaking self, killed his own creation so that he could safely employ himself in imaginary pleasures. The impact, the "reality" of Marie was, however, too strong and the narrator realizes that his attempt, erotic and verbal, is a failure: "C'est pour me la rappeler que j'ai écrit ce qui précède, espérant que les mots me la feraient revivre; j'y ai échoué, j'en sais bien plus que je n'en ai dit."

Hence the end of *Novembre*. The narrator realizes that in order to exist as the other, as his narcissistic projection, the third person, he has to die as an "I." He therefore dies and out of his ashes the second narrator is born.

The second narrator begins by keeping his distance from the first narrator, the subject of his discourse. He does not use the text as an occasion to narrate his own experience or express his own feelings but limits himself to narrating, with some criticism, the life of a character, the first narrator. But gradually he discovers more and more affinity with his character and the critical attitude yields to a feeling of solidarity: "Il avait aussi trop de goût pour se lancer dans la critique; il était trop poète, peut-être, pour réussir dans les lettres." Along with this change in attitude comes a change in the mode of narration: the second narrator starts expressing his own opinions and not only reporting those of the first narrator. His own narrative voice mixes with what he reports and the "je" at times becomes ambiguous:

> Il pensait sérieusement qu'il y a moins de mal à tuer un homme qu'à faire un enfant: au premier vous ôtez la vie . . . mais envers le second, disait-il, n'êtes-vous pas responsable de toutes les larmes qu'il versera depuis son berceau jusqu'à sa tombe? sans vous, il ne serait pas né, et il naît, pourquoi cela? pour votre amusement, non pour le sien à coup sûr; pour porter votre nom, le nom d'un sot, *je* parie? autant vaudrait l'écrire sur un mur. [My emphasis.]

It is symptomatic that the fusion between narrator and character occurs in a discussion of birth and murder, creation and destruction, the two poles between which the narration of *Novembre* and the *Mémoires* oscillates.

The menacing power of Marie and the death of the first narrator indicate the dangers that representation entails for the integrity of the self. They operate within the opposition self/representation, experience/language. But *Novembre* actually undermines the opposition between language and experience, which it itself plays out, by showing that doubling and lack of originality, both of which seemed to be the result of the translation of experience into language, already exist on the level of experience. Experience itself has the structure of representation.

Like the *Mémoires*, *Novembre* starts with the illusion of the originality of experience. "Comme le premier homme créé, je me réveillais enfin d'un long sommeil, et je voyais près de moi un être semblable à moi . . . et en même temps je sentais pour cette forme nouvelle un sentiment nouveau dont ma tête était fière." This belief, however, is soon in conflict with the awareness of the non-originality of desire: "Ces passions que j'aurais voulu avoir, je les étudiais dans les livres." *Novembre* thus restates the conclusions of the episode of the two English girls which the last part of the *Mémoires* tries to obfuscate: as language (both one's readings and one's writings) creates desire, one can say that experience doubles language just as much as language doubles experience. On the levels both of language and of experience *Novembre* shows a disillusionment about the possibility of authenticity and originality. Its sub-title is "Fragments de style quelconque" because, in opposition to the *Mémoires,* style can no longer be seen as a mirror of the self. To the impossibility of original language is linked the impossibility of virgin-desire, thematized in the love episode with the prostitute Marie.

In this respect, again, the difference between the *Mémoires* and *Novembre* becomes clear when we compare two similar episodes. Towards the end of both stories the hero returns to the scene of a crucial experience. This visit dramatizes the structure of memory, the movement of autobiography, and therefore can be taken, in each case, as an emblem of the text as a whole. In the *Mémoires* the visit is an experience of sameness and difference: the place is the same and yet different because the beloved is not there: "Je revoyais le même océan avec ses mêmes vagues . . . ce même village . . . Mais tout ce que j'avais aimé, tout ce qui entourait Maria . . . tout cela était parti sans retour." The pathos of the scene emerges from this opposition between present lack and past plenitude, echoing the view of the *Mémoires* that not experience itself but its doubling in language is faulty and inauthentic. In *Novembre,* on the other hand, the narrator is struck by a more radical form of dispossession: "'O mon Dieu, se dit-il, est-ce qu'il n'y a pas sur la terre des lieux que nous avons assez aimés, où nous avons assez vécu pour qu'ils nous appartiennent jusqu'à la mort, et que d'autres que nous-mêmes n'y mettent jamais les yeux!'" There never was a place one could call one's own. Lack is not a matter of having lost something, but of never really owning anything. Experience itself, and not simply its representation in language, is the scene of loss and division.

Moreover, while the visit at the end of the *Mémoires* is to a place where the narrator-hero was, in however ambiguous and transitory way, in the presence of the "object" of desire, the visit at the end of *Novembre* is to a scene which already in its "first" occurrence was a repetition, to a place where the hero has already felt himself as double and different from himself. The alienation which seemed to characterize representation (and differentiate it from experience), exists already on the level of experience and the lack of coincidence of the self with itself is not simply the result of literary creation but the result of consciousness, which is itself a writing. From the moment there is memory, or desire, or language, that is to say, from the very moment there is a self, the self is divided from itself, double and alienated from itself, and this division is experienced as a loss, but as a loss which has always already occurred and cannot be avoided or made good.

Loss and alienation can be avoided only at the price of narcissistic sterility and destruction; they can however be accepted and manipulated as a source of production. This realization dictates the relation between narrator and character in the first *Education sentimentale*.

III

On one level the first *Education* tells the familiar story of the gradual differentiation between the self and its mirror image which the previous works acted out in spite of their creator. Starting out as specular opposites ("toi, tu voulais une pâle Italienne en robe de velours noir, avec un cordon d'or sur sa chevelure d'ébène, la lèvre superbe, l'allure royale, une taille vigoureuse et svelte, une femme jalouse et pleine de voluptés; moi j'aimais les profils chrétiens des statuettes gothiques, des yeux candidement baissés, des cheveux d'or fin comme les fils de la Vierge"), Jules and Henry end up utterly different (of a difference which is no more reducible to an economy of the same): "Ils ne pensaient de même sur quoi que ce soit et n'envisageaient rien d'une manière semblable." But the peculiarity of the *Education sentimentale* is that it has as its *starting point* the complete separation between Jules and Henry. And because Jules and Henry are from the very beginning separated, each of them is independent of the other, "free" to live as he finds fitting, and not subjected to the other. While in the previous works the assumption was that a unique self, by the necessities of consciousness, memory, and writing, gave birth to an image of itself of which, as its own creation, it could dispose as it found fitting, the *Education* posits as a point of departure a duality, a division, that is present from the beginning, prior to any act of desire, memory, or writing. This change is a radicalization of the insights gained in the *Mémoires* and *Novembre* where it was shown that the mirror image creates the self just as much as the self creates its mirror image, that a character can become a narrator and a narrator a character, and that language and experience are each the origin of the other. The point of difference between the first *Education* and the *Mémoires* is not so much that one is a novel and the other an autobiography, one in the third person, the other in the first; rather, the difference between the two lies in the fact that in the first *Education* the narrator has stepped out of the narcissistic circle and instead of contemplating his mirror image (as did the second narrator in *Novembre*) sees himself as divided into two.

As the opposition creator/created, narrator/character, self/mirror image proved to be imaginary, the relation between Jules and Henry has to be defined in different terms. As we have seen, the conflict which dictated the movement of the previous narratives is that between, on the one hand, a narcissistic attempt of self to defend its (imaginary) integrity and unity by repressing any indication of its division from itself, and, on the other hand, an awareness that this narcissistic attempt leads to sterility and death and that only by accepting and exploiting its own alienation can the self continue to live and narrate. In the *Education* these two conflicting attitudes are each developed to its logical end, the first in the figure of Henry, and the second in that of Jules. What was previously represented as different moments in the same story is now seen as two separate and independent possibilities. Through an acceptance of his division (his death as a unique and unified self), the narrator can get out of the vicious circle where projection is always followed by annihilation, creation by destruction.

Henry is the representation of the narcissistic self which refuses, in order to protect its unity, any loss of itself. He does not externalize any part of himself and hence does not see himself as other or in the other. While Jules, experiencing his alienation and the difference from himself, "sees" the world as a book where he can read his past ("Etrange sensation du sol que l'on foule! On dirait que chacun de nos pas d'autrefois y a laissé une ineffaçable trace, et qu'en revenant sur eux nous marchons sur des médailles où serait écrite l'histoire de ces temps accomplis, qui surgissent devant nous"), Henry "looks" at a world totally strange and incomprehensible to him. Arriving at Paris, at the beginning of the novel, Henry walks in the streets and looks:

> Ne sachant que faire les premiers jours, il rôdait dans les rues, sur les places, dans les jardins ... il s'asseyait sur un banc et regardait les enfants jouer ou bien les cygnes glisser sur l'eau. ... il regardait les devantures des boutiques de nouveautés ... il admirait le gaz et les affiches. ...
>
> ... il s'arrêtait, aux Champs-Elysées, devant les faiseurs de tours et les arracheurs de dents; sur la place du Louvre, il passa un jour beaucoup de temps à contempler les oiseaux étrangers. ...
>
> Il montait sur les tours des églises et restait longtemps appuyé

sur les balustrades de pierre qui les couronnent, contemplant les
toits des maisons. . . .

Il entrait dans un café et restait une heure entière à lire la
même ligne d'un journal.

This passage makes clear the difference between the act of "seeing" (of
the *Mémoires,* of *Novembre,* of Jules) and the act of "looking" of Henry.
While "seeing" is a projection, a creation of a spectacle, "looking" is a
passive fascination with external objects which seem totally incomprehensible
because they do not correspond to anything inside. But Henry is not entirely
the "idiot" who gazes at incomprehensible objects, passively, open-mouthed;
sometimes he looks actively, making sense of what he sees around him, or,
in other words, creating a world, projecting a spectacle:

Il se faisait transporter en omnibus d'un quartier de Paris à
l'autre, et il regardait toutes les figures que l'on prenait et qu'on
laissait en route, établissant entre elles des rapprochements et des
antithèses. . . .

Il allait au bois de Boulogne, il regardait les jolis chevaux et
les beaux messieurs, les carrosses vernis et les chasseurs panachés,
et les grandes dames à figure pâle . . . il rêvait, en les contemplant,
à quelque existence grasse, pleine de loisirs heureux . . . il se
figurait les salons où elles allaient, le soir, décolletées, en dia-
mants.

But these moments of imagination and creation are immediately checked
and repressed: "Mais, à chaque joie qu'il rêvait, une douleur nouvelle s'ou-
vrait dans son âme, comme pour expier de suite les plaisirs fugitifs de son
imagination." The pleasures of the imagination are forbidden for Henry, and
by censoring them he gradually eliminates them completely. This is the aspect
of annihilation of the spectacle which we have seen in the earlier works and
which is now followed to its logical conclusion.

The same repression of creation in the interest of narcissistic unity can
be seen in Henry's relation to his past. The retrospective moments in Henry's
story are never moments in which he sees his own past self, himself as
another. He sees his past in the same way that he sees the world: as a
collection of external objects that amaze or amuse him but never show him
his own face. After having spent a vacation at home Henry goes back to
Paris and passes again the route he has taken six months before, when he
first left for the capital:

Henry s'ennuya pendant toute la route. . . . il se blottit à sa place, se roula sur lui-même comme un limaçon dans sa coquille, et se mit à penser. Il se laissait aller au mouvement de la voiture, qui se balançait doucement comme un navire, au galop de ses six chevaux; il regardait les arbres qui passaient le long de la portière et les mètres de cailloux couchés au bord du fossé. Pour passer le temps, il regarda aussi la mine avinée du gros homme qui dormait et les favoris rouges de l'Anglais.

En revoyant les lieux qu'il avait vus pour la première fois il y avait six mois, il songea à ce temps passé et à tous les événements qui s'étaient écoulés depuis; cela l'amusa une grande heure.

Unlike Jules, or the narrator of the *Mémoires* or *Novembre,* who would have read in this scene their difference from themselves, Henry remains absorbed in external objects and even the regular movement of the carriage, with its lulling effect, does not create the usual movement of self-reflective doubling. The return journey of Henry and Emilie provides an even more striking example. The voyage is a repetition of the voyage to America: they come back on the same boat, take the same cabin, pass the same towns and villages. But unlike the hero of *Novembre* in his visit to X . . . , they do not read in this repetition their difference from themselves. "Du Havre à Paris ils passèrent par les mêmes villages, ils revirent les mêmes arbres, verts comme autrefois et toujours jeunes; ils avaient fleuri deux fois depuis qu'ils ne les avaient vus." Characteristically, the moments that Henry cherishes the most are "ces moments qui s'écoulent vaguement, doucement, sans laisser dans l'esprit aucun souvenir de joie ni de douleur."

Jules, as we have said, represents the other possibility, that of exploiting alienation as a creative power. He starts with the particular Flaubertian predicament of projection. In the third chapter, when he reminiscences in a letter to Henry about their past life and dreams, he evokes the image of the theater where one is in the position of "contemplant sa pensée vivre sur la scène." For Jules, as for the narrator of the *Mémoires,* love is related to the theater, and the desired woman, Lucinde, is the actress, the woman-spectacle. He is subject to auto-suggestion and his words create his desires: "il s'exaltait en écrivant, devenait éloquent à force de parler, s'attendrissait lui-même." But after the disappearance of Lucinde (which is parallel to the disappearance of the woman-spectacle, Marie and Maria, in the earlier works), things change.

In the twenty-first chapter Jules, alone, dreams: he projects his desires, makes them alive, and contemplates them. But this projection, rather than being an attempt to capture himself in the object of his contemplation, becomes an act of renouncement. The act of imagination is seen not as a way of recovering a lost unity, but as a dispersion of the self in the world it created, a loss of the self which emptied itself out in a way which prevents dialectical recuperation. This is because Jules does not arrest his attention on one particular image; his imagination proliferates and shows him different possibilities. The spectacle that Jules creates is full of life, but nevertheless he does not enter into an erotic-narcissistic relation with it as was the case with Marie. Instead, Jules shifts his attention from one image to another and creates a multiplicity of objects: as they are all his image, his projection, none can give him back a unified image of himself. The movement of creation and annihilation, life and death gives way to dispersion, a renouncement of one image for the sake of the possibility of creating another. To limit oneself to one image is to enter into the narcissistic field of love and aggression; in this chapter (which prefigures already the *Tentation de saint Antoine*) this movement is changed into one of temptation and renouncement and that guarantees the inexhaustible proliferation of creation.

Another change with respect to the earlier works can be seen in the twenty-sixth chapter of the *Education* which describes Jules's encounter with the dog. The full meaning of this passage emerges from a comparison with similar passages in the *Mémoires* and *Novembre:* In all three works we find key passages where a walk in the country, near water, in the grass, describes the act of projection, the creation of the other, mirror image and imaginary object of desire. One may cite two passages from the *Mémoires,* four from *Novembre,* and finally the episode with the dog from the first *Education:*

> Ailleurs, c'était dans une campagne verte et émaillée de fleurs, le long d'un fleuve;—j'étais avec ma mère qui marchait du côté de la rive; elle tomba.
>
> (*Mémoires*)

> Un jour je revenais, vers le crépuscule, je marchais à travers les pâturages couverts de bœufs, je marchais vite, je n'entendais que le bruit de ma marche qui froissait l'herbe; j'avais la tête baissée et je regardais la terre. Ce mouvement régulier m'endormit pour ainsi dire, je crus entendre Maria marcher près de moi; elle me tenait le bras et tournait la tête pour me voir, c'était elle qui marchait dans les herbes.
>
> (*Mémoires*)

> Je rêvais la douleur des poètes . . . des pages, où d'autres restaient

froids, me transportaient . . . je me les récitais au bord de la mer, ou bien j'allais, la tête baissée, marchant dans l'herbe, me les disant de la voix la plus amoureuse et la plus tendre.

(*Novembre*)

Je suis sorti et je m'en suis allé à X . . . ; . . . j'ai d'abord marché dans les sentiers qui serpentent entre les blés; j'ai passé sous des pommiers, au bord des haies; je ne songeais à rien, j'écoutais le bruit de mes pas, la cadence de mes mouvements me berçait la pensée. . . .

. . . l'esprit de Dieu me remplissait, je me sentais le cœur grand, j'adorais quelque chose d'un étrange mouvement, j'aurais voulu m'absorber dans la lumière du soleil et me perdre dans cette immensité d'azur.

(*Novembre*)

J'allai au bord de la rivière; j'ai toujours aimé l'eau. . . .

. . . écoutant le bruit de l'eau et le frémissement de la cime des arbres, qui remuait quoi qu'il n'y eût pas de vent, seul, agité et calme à la fois, je me sentis défaillir de volupté sous le poids de cette nature aimante, et j'appelai l'amour! Mes lèvres tremblaient, s'avançaient, comme si j'eusse senti l'haleine d'une autre bouche. . . .

L'herbe était douce à marcher, je marchai; chaque pas me procurait un plaisir nouveau, et je jouissais par la plante des pieds de la douceur du gazon. . . .

Tout à coup je me mis à fuir.

(*Novembre*)

Une fois, je marchais vite dans un pré, les herbes sifflaient autour de mes pieds en m'avançant, elle [Marie] était derrière moi; je me suis retourné, il n'y avait personne.

(*Novembre*)

A peu près dans ce temps-là, il arriva à Jules une chose lamentable; il était sorti dans les champs, il se promenait, les feuilles roulaient devant ses pas, s'envolaient au vent, bruissaient sous ses pieds; c'était le soir, tout était calme. . . .

il marchait et pas un autre bruit n'arrivait à ses oreilles.

Sa pensée seule lui parlait. . . .

Il releva la tête. . . .

Il entendit quelque chose courir dans l'herbe, il se retourna, et
tout à coup en chien s'élança sur lui. . . .

Jules reprit sa route . . . il marchait vite, le chien le suivait. . . .
Le vent soufflait, les arbres, à demi dépouillés, inclinaient leurs
têtes et faisaient fouetter leurs rameaux, les feuilles des haies tres-
saillaient. . . .

Le chien s'enfuit. . . .

"Il est encore là," se disait-il, et il entendait en effet, derrière
lui, toujours quelque chose qui sautillait et courait sur ses talons;
il se retournait, il n'y avait personne.

(Education)

In all these passages the hero is alone and enclosed within himself. His
head lowered, he is not concerned with the "real" world outside him; rather,
lulled by the sound of his own steps in the grass or by his voice, he projects
an image—his mother, Maria, loving nature, Marie—which attracts him
erotically. Thus the dog appears in the same landscape as the imaginary
other, object of desire; this is why in most of the passage it is referred to as
feminine "la bête," "elle." The appearance of the dog is the result of an act
of projection as is the appearance of the object of desire and the reaction to
it is the same as to the feminine other—fear and attraction.

But the difference between the dog episode and the scenes from the
Mémoires and *Novembre* is as striking as the similarity. If in the earlier
works the self tries to avoid or to destroy the difference between itself and
the image it necessarily has to create, in the *Education* the narrator realizes
that the most important thing is to keep this difference. This means that the
other keeps its basic quality of otherness and is thus inassimilable and unknown. Jules tries in various ways in this episode to understand the dog,
make him known, and in this way to abolish the difference between the dog
and himself. But these attempts all fail and opening the door to the dog at
the end of the chapter, Jules has to accept the dog's otherness and real
difference from himself. The dog is an independent creature; it is, one might
say, the first real *character* that Flaubert has created. One should note that
strictly speaking the dog is a character created by *Jules* and not by the
narrator. The scene in this respect announces and repeats the structure *en
abîme* which characterizes all the works of Flaubert, and which is most
evident in the *Tentation de saint Antoine*. The possibility of the created world
to proliferate and in its turn to create new worlds is a sign of its life and
independence of the self which created it. We have seen it already in *No-

vembre, when Marie became a narrator and told her story. But while in Novembre this life and creativity of the mirror image was dreaded as threatening to the self (when Marie said that she might have a child the narrator fled away), in the first Education and in later works it is embraced as the only way in which the self, aware of its doubleness, of the fact that it does not exist prior to its (re)presentation of itself as another, can assure its existence by allowing the process of creation and representation to continue.

IV

We have seen how, in his early works, Flaubert adopts certain narrative strategies in order to overcome problems of representation created by his own text. These strategies give shape to the narrative, dictating its plot, characters, themes, and narrative voice. Though we stopped short of the major works we have already seen why and how the most important features of the text come into being: the so-called "objectivity" of Flaubert—his "absence" as a subject from the narrative; the structure en abîme; the opacity, incomprehensibility, or lack of significance of his characters; the serial structure (of temptations in Saint Antoine, of lovers, in Madame Bovary, of objects of desire, in Un Cœur simple, of subjects of knowledge, in Bouvard et Pécuchet). There is thus a strong and meaningful continuity rather than a break, between the early and the late Flaubert, between the autobiographical writings and the novels, the "romantic" works and the "realistic" ones. The late "realistic" novels are the logical development, the radicalization, of the insights of the early "romantic" autobiographies. Realistic fiction in Flaubert is the (re)presentation of the self as different from itself and not entirely known or controllable.

SHOSHANA FELMAN

Flaubert's Signature: The Legend of Saint Julian the Hospitable

An uncanny superimposition of the myths of Oedipus and of Christ, *The Legend of Saint Julian the Hospitable* is the strange story of Christ the murderer and/or of Oedipus the saint: the story of a child who kills his parents only to be sainted by this very deed, which turns out to be at once his fated cross and his redeeming Calvary.

The tale, divided into three parts strictly calculated in conception and composition, does not articulate a simple chronology or succession of events, but a veritable narrative logic, a *structural necessity* that links, through the central murder of the parents (chapter 2), the initial story of the child (chapter 1) and the final legend of the saint (chapter 3). The parents' murder, by its mediate position, would appear, then, as the paradoxical transition, as the unexpected necessary juncture between the *birth of a child* and the *birth of a legend*. Through the mediating gap thus structurally produced by the murder, two underlying questions seem to be concurrently inscribed in— and articulated by—Flaubert's text:

What is a child?

What is a legend?

From *Flaubert and Postmodernism*, edited by Naomi Schor and Henry F. Majewski. © 1984 by Shoshana Felman. University of Nebraska Press, 1984. This essay was translated by Brian Massumi, Rachel Bowlby, Richard Russell, and Nancy Jones, with the collaboration of the author.

I

JULIAN'S DESTINY

What is a child? A child, the text seems to suggest, is first of all a dream: the combined dream of his two parents.

> Rejoice, oh mother! Your son will be a saint!

says the apparition of a hermit to the mother; and to the father, a beggar looming up from the mist predicts:

> Ah! Ah! Your son! . . . Much blood! . . . Much glory! . . . Always
> happy! An emperor's family.

What is the meaning of these two prophecies regarding Julian's destiny? In what way do the oracles reveal the origin, at once of the child's fate and of the legend's meaning?

We may note, to begin with, the way in which the oracle of Julian's destiny significantly differs from the oracle concerning Oedipus. In the Oedipus myth, the parents receive—by way of a divine *curse*—a *single* oracular message warning them of the *misfortune* their son will bring them. Here, the parents receive two separate messages—*two* oracles—which they perceive, not as a curse, but on the contrary as a *blessing*. Their son appears in the oracular message, not as an agent of misfortune, but as a promise of good fortune:

> He was dazzled by the splendors destined for his son, even though
> the *promise* of these splendors was not clear. [my emphasis]

The underlying Flaubertian question, *What is a child?*, here translates textually into the following question: Why does the promise of good fortune the child embodies prove to be, as such, incapable of fulfillment? Why can't Julian keep the promise he is supposed to be except by transforming its good fortune into bad? How—and why—is the blessing changed into a curse? (Only the oracle communicated to Julian appears in the form of a curse: "Accursed! Accursed! Accursed! One day, cruel heart, you will assassinate your father and your mother!" Thus the filial curse [Julian's oracle] is the obverse of the parental blessing [the parents' oracle].)

If the destiny of Oedipus—the fatal curse uttered to the parents—is here ironically believed to be a blessing, and if the divine message concerning Julian divides itself into two distinct predictions separately given to the mother and the father, it is because the Flaubertian oracle in reality only returns to each parent *his own* unconscious message, his own *desire* for the child.

In both cases, in effect, the text discreetly puts in question the objective reality of the oracle: no one but the father and the mother sees the respective apparitions.

> The next day, all the servants questioned said that they had seen no hermit.

> The good nobleman looked right and left, called out as loudly as he could. No one! The wind was whistling, and the morning mists were clearing away.

The ambiguous status of the oracle—real or fantasized—does not, moreover, escape the notice of the parents themselves, who very much suspect, each in his turn, the hallucinated, dreamlike nature of the message that so gratifies them. "Dream or reality," the mother tells herself, "it must have been a message from heaven." As for the father, "He attributed the vision to his mental fatigue from having slept too little."

Thus not only are the oracles themselves of different substance for the mother and the father, but the two parental *readings* of the oracles are in turn diametrically opposed: while the mother chooses to interpret what could be her symptom as no less than a supernatural sign, the father, for his part, chooses to interpret what could be a supernatural sign as nothing but a symptom; while the mother chooses to reduce the very ambiguity of the vision to a single, mystical meaning (religious or transcendental), the father chooses to reduce the ambiguity of the vision to a single, realistic meaning (psychological or pathological). On one side, an absolute passion for mysticism; on the other, an absolute passion for realism; on one hand, a fantastic reading, and on the other, a phantasmic reading of the legendary element of the oracle: two antithetical interpretations, mutually exclusive, and yet whose destiny it is to coexist, to coincide throughout the tale—two schemes of meaning whose contradictory dynamic fights over the text, two schemes of meaning whose dynamic contradiction fights over—and within—Julian himself.

This is, in Flaubert, the fateful secret of the oracle: the two distinct fates prophesied for Julian correspond to the two ambitions that the father and the mother secretly nurture for their son. The father, a veteran of war who regularly and nostalgically takes pleasure in "regaling . . . his old battle companions," wishes for his son heroic distinction and military fame ("Much blood! . . . Much glory!"); the mother, religiously ascetic, and whose household is "governed like the inside of a monastery," hopes her son will be "a saint": two heterogeneous ambitions, two irreconcilable parental desires whose difference is determined not just by two scales of value, by two different *ethics,* but, above all, by two distinct *self-images,* two narcissistic constellations radically foreign to each other. Each parent, in effect, projects onto the son his own idealized self-image. On both sides, the child is imagined, dreamed, desired as a double—as a narcissistic reflection.

Torn, from before his birth, between two narcissistic programmings, caught between two laws, between two unconscious minds, between two projects for his future, Julian will be called upon to satisfy two radically contradictory parental wishes. "What is a child?" asks the text. The answer, ironically outlined by the very silence of the narrator, arises out of that which can be articulated, not by words, but only by events: a child is, paradoxically enough, nothing other than the embodiment of the *contradiction between his parents.*

THE BLANK, THE SILENCE, THE GAP

The problem for Julian—the model child, "a little Jesus"—is thus the following: how can he *live* the contradiction that has begotten him? How can he conform to the double, contradictory model ordained by his two parents?

> Often, the nobleman would regale his old battle companions. As they drank, they would recall their wars, the assaults on fortresses with the clash of armor and the prodigious wounds. Julian, listening to them, would let out cries at this; then his father had no doubt that he would later be a conqueror. But in the evening, as the Angelus drew to a close, when he would pass between the bowing poor, he would dip into his purse with such modesty, with such noble air, that his mother was convinced she would eventually see him an archbishop.

> His place in the chapel was at his parents' side.

The silence of the narrator (of the story) is audible only in the blank that separates and links the two indented paragraphs so as to situate—to mark—Julian's "place." It is important to note that this paragraph immediately precedes Julian's first act of violence: the murder of the mouse. The succession of the paragraphs suggests that, in some way, the murder—as dissonant as it may be—comes out of Julian's place: Julian's place, precisely, in the chapel. But what is, strictly speaking, this place beside his parents, one of whom envisions him as an archbishop and the other—as a conqueror? It is a middle place, but a place—an *in-between space*—that is totally contradictory, impossible: a place which, like the blank of the indented paragraph that introduces it, is the silent locus of *discontinuity*, the very place of a division, of a gap. Julian's problem, his tragic dilemma, is, precisely, *how to assume the lapse* of that location, the hiatus of that place? How can he respond to the *division* between the two demands addressed to him? How can he take on, how can he realize the gap between his parents?

Two parents that the text, from its first words, simultaneously *juxtaposes* and *opposes*:

> The *father* and the *mother* of Julian lived in a castle.

Two parents that the text, once again, carefully juxtaposes and opposes in the two contiguous paragraphs that describe them for the first time. The contrast between the father and the mother is not spelled out: the opposition comes out of a concerted technique of juxtaposition. As always with Flaubert, it is the last sentence of the paragraph that *punctuates* the latter (gives it a *point*), while also making it ambiguous. That is, it at the same time gives the paragraph all its meaning and suspends the meaning: it makes the meaning veer toward the silence of the blank space, which it overloads with the unsaid. Now the parallel structure of the two paragraphs describing the parents is punctuated by two concluding sentences between which a dissonance begins ironically to resonate from one paragraph to the other:

> Always wrapped up in a fox fur, he would walk about his house, give justice to his vassals, arbitrate his neighbors' quarrels. . . . *After many adventures, he had taken as his wife a maiden* of high birth.
>
> She was very white, somewhat proud and serious. . . . Her household was governed like the inside of a monastery. . . . *By dint of praying to God, a son came unto her.*

What is striking is the *nonencounter* between the two paragraphs, both of which, however, point toward the *encounter* that will give birth to the son. "After many adventures, he had taken as his wife a maiden"; "By dint of praying to God, a son came unto her." Like the contrast that will later be brought out by both the oracles and the parental readings of the oracles, these initial descriptions already prefigure the dichotomy between the paternal order—secular, assertive, realistic, and the maternal order—mystical, religious, and ascetic.

Still, the semantic overload, the ironic tinge of the sentence which concludes the description of the mother—"By dint of praying to God, a son came unto her"—does more than just oppose the mother's religious and the father's secular disposition. By making quite plainly an allusion to the Immaculate Conception, it connotes a *nonrelation of the mother to the actual father* of her son. The mother's mystical perception thus involves not simply faith but a subtle syntax of denial, of negation: a denial—conscious or unconscious—of the sexual act that necessarily preceded the child's birth, a denial, therefore, of the mother's own sexuality as what motivated—and made possible—her maternity. Julian, then, will also have to consummate a double bind—to live out an aporia—between two paradigms of which one, the paternal, is a model of self-assertion and sensual affirmation, whereas the other, the maternal, is a model of self-denial and sexual negation.

This contradiction is, however, neither simply the result of the mother's faith nor a simple accident of psychology: it corresponds to the stereotypical sex roles of the man (Patriarch-Adventurer) and the woman (always, in some sense, Virgin-Mother) in Western culture. The mother's *mysticism* is, indeed, the *feminine mystique* par excellence. Thus the contradictions of which Julian is the incarnation are also, among other things, the symptom of a culture. However, Julian is a symptom only insofar as he is the very offspring of the gap, the very child of the discrepancy between his father and his mother: insofar as, paradoxically enough, he is *begotten by the nonrelation between the sexes.* What, indeed, could be more strikingly ironic than this vision of an *aporetic sexual act?*

The implicit motif of the nonrelation between the mother and the father is taken up again in a more explicit form in the scene of the oracular apparitions—solitary visions which the two spouses keep above all from communicating to each other. Thus the very image of the child stays with each parent as a private, unshared fantasy: the discontinuity between the father and the mother, the nonrelation between the two sexes, are thematized and sealed by the nondialogue—the silence—between the two partners of the couple whose child becomes, ironically, the figure, not of what they share, but of what they *do not share.* The child of contradiction and division, Julian is the offspring, above all, of silence.

> Dream or reality, it must have been a message from heaven; but she took care to say nothing about it, for fear of being accused of pride. . . .
>
> He attributed this vision to his mental fatigue from having slept too little. "If I speak of it, I will be ridiculed," he told himself.
>
> *The spouses hid their secret from each other.* But both cherished the child with equal love.

This silence which unites and separates the parents—and which makes the child into a *guilty secret*—is prolonged, extended, deepened, later on, by the child's own guilty silence sealing his first murder: the murder of the mouse in the church:

> A drop of blood stained the flagstone. He wiped it up quickly with his sleeve, threw the mouse outside, and *said nothing about it to anyone.*

The silence of the child about the mouse—the real murder he has committed—is in turn prolonged by the silence of Julian's wife concerning the obsession that haunts her husband: the fantasy of the murder of his parents. But it is precisely *by keeping silent* to Julian's parents about their son's imaginary secret that Julian's wife brings about the fantasy's realization:

> They asked a thousand questions about Julian. She replied to each one, but *took care to keep silent about the ominous idea concerning them. . . .*
>
> Julian had crossed the park. . . . Everywhere there hung a great silence. . . .
>
> His father and his mother were before him, lying on their backs with holes in their chests; and their faces, with a gentle majesty, seemed to be keeping an eternal secret.

From the "secret" of the oracle that the spouses hid from each other, to the "eternal secret" that the parents' corpses seem to keep, *The Legend of Saint Julian the Hospitable* can be read as *the story of a silence*. "Man," writes Freud in a formula itself oracular and lapidary, "man speaks in order not to kill." It is out of the reversal of this formula that Flaubert's narrative is written: Julian *kills because he does not speak;* in his legend, it is silence that engenders, motivates, unleashes murder.

Paradoxically, however, it is also *what withholds speech* in the legend that constitutes the very energy of its narration: it is *out of Julian's silence* that Flaubert *writes,* that the text *speaks,* that the tale is indeed *telling.*

THE INK STAIN

The symbolism of color contrast draws out at yet another level the opposition between the mother and the father. Thus the mother, who "was very *white,*" is repeatedly associated with the signifier of the color white. When the mother is by mistake all but murdered by her son, it is "two white

wings" that Julian sees and at which he throws his javelin, thinking he has
seen a stork.

> A piercing cry was heard.
> It was his mother, whose bonnet . . . remained pinned to the
> wall.

In the same way, the "little *white* mouse" killed in church—the mother's
space—is doubtless also a substitutive figure for the mother.

The father, on the other hand, is symbolically associated with the signifier black. So the prodigious stag which, "solemn like a patriarch and like
a judge," curses Julian for killing him and predicts he will one day "assassinate his father and his mother," "was *black* and monstrous in stature."

It is doubtless not by accident that the contradiction of black and white
turns out to be the very one that produces writing. As Mallarmé suggestively
puts it:

> You have remarked, one does not write, luminously, on an ob-
> scure background, the alphabet of the stars alone is thus indi-
> cated, sketched, or interrupted; *man pursues black on white.*
>
> ("L'Action restreinte")

What, then, is the *writing* which the contradiction between black and
white—between the mother and the father in Flaubert's text—in effect produces, if not Julian himself as the very *text of contradiction,* as a marked,
imprinted page?

> The spouses hid their secret from each other. But both cherished
> the child with equal love; and regarding him as *marked by God,*
> they bestowed infinite respect and care on his beloved person.

Produced by contradiction, difference, and alterity, the *mark*—at once the
counterpart and the obverse of silence—is nothing other than a written letter.
But what is, here, the page on which the mark is to be printed, the page on
which the stained destiny of contradiction is to be inscribed and literally
written down "black on white," if not, precisely, Julian's very body? Thus,
in the metaphorical deer family, while the stag-"patriarch" is "black" and
the doe-mother is "fair," the little fawn—obviously Julian's own reflection—
is significantly "spotted."

But Julian's own skin is itself literally spotted, marked. It is indeed these
very marks or spots that serve as signs of recognition by which Julian's aged
parents, who are unknown to his wife, are able to identify their son for her:

Nothing could convince the young woman that her husband was
their son.

They provided proof by describing certain *particular signs* he
had on his skin.

Julian is thus "marked by God" very much like Cain, bearing in his turn
the concrete inscription of a *writing*—of distinctive marks or signs—printed
or imprinted on his very skin.

It is therefore not surprising that this legend of marked skin—of the
epidermal stain and of writing in the flesh—should reach its pinnacle, or its
epiphany, in the dramatic figure of the leper.

Julian saw that a hideous leprosy covered his body. . . . His shoulders, his chest, his skinny arms disappeared into *slabs* of scaly
pustules. Enormous *wrinkles* dug into his forehead.

"I'm hungry!" he said. Julian gave him what he had, an old
chunk of lard and a few crusts of dark bread.

When he had devoured them, the table, the bowl, and the handle of the knife bore *the very same spots that were visible on his*
body.

Just like the spotted fawn and the signs marking Julian's skin, the leper's
spotted skin is, once again, nothing other than a metaphorical image of Julian
himself. But whereas Julian kills the fawn and plans to kill himself, he accepts—and saves—the leper: the ending of the tale marks the climactic moment at which Julian (at the actual point of dying—that is, of becoming in
effect a saint) for the first time *forgives himself*—and accepts himself: forgives himself his spotted, tainted skin; forgives himself, in other words, for
being *marked* by his own *otherness to himself;* accepts himself, therefore, as
a stained, marred text, at once black and white, innocent and guilty: a text
of contradiction he will no longer struggle to suppress (as he had attempted
through the various killings), but to which he will henceforth submit, en-
deavoring to *pass through,* to traverse, to *pass beyond.* The crossing of the
river, among other things, is also the symbolic crossing of his own division
and his own contradiction.

II

THE VOICE CAME FROM THE OTHER SIDE

Since the passage became known, travelers presented themselves.
They would hail him from the other bank. . . .

> . . . The . . . voice . . . came from the other side. . . . The shad-
> ows were deep, and here and there *torn by the whiteness* of crest-
> ing waves. . . .
>
> With each thrust of the oar, the backwash raised [the boat] in
> front. The water, *blacker than ink,* flowed furiously on each side
> of the vessel.

Why is the river's water said to be "blacker than ink"? In what way are we
meant to read the crossing of the river as a metaphor of writing? And what,
if so, is writing all about?

Navigating in the midst of "*shadows . . . torn* by the *whiteness* of crest-
ing waves," passing through the *ink-black* river, Julian, struggling to survive
division, crosses the contradiction between black and white (father and
mother, innocence and guilt, sameness and otherness, consciousness and the
unconscious). From one side of the ink-black river to the other, writing is
this passage for survival, this repeated crossing of the contradiction of black
and white, this constant shuttle movement between life and death. It is thus
that Julian struggles to *traverse the ink stain,* to survive, pass through, and
pass across the writing on his very flesh.

This struggle, this necessity of crossing, this agonizing passage through
the ink stain is, indeed, Julian's predicament. But it is also the predicament
of Flaubert who, elsewhere, writes in turn, for his part, to Louise Colet:

> I fret, I itch. . . . I've got stylistic abscesses, and the sentence itches
> and cannot be quelled. What a heavy oar the pen is, and what a
> hard current is the idea, when one digs into it!

But what, then, is Flaubert's place in the legend of the Other, in the story
of Saint Julian—which he writes?

The place from which the legend is enunciated is itself *marked* in the
last paragraph of the tale:

> And that's the story of Saint Julian the Hospitable, as one can
> find it—more or less—on a stained-glass window of a church, in
> my country.

It is out of this concluding, final sentence that the second question of the tale
emerges: What, in the last analysis, is a legend?

A double blank, a silent gap marking a break in tone and a change of
perspective, separates this final sentence from the narrative that precedes it.
However, in order to attempt to grasp the import of the final sentence and
the way it can shed light on what a legend is, we must try to look beyond—

in fact across—this gap, for the *relation*—the articulation—on the contrary, between the apparently removed last sentence and the main (narrative) bulk of the text.

What is remarkable about this sentence—which is indeed unique in Flaubert's work—is the peculiar fact that it refers the text to a *first person* ("*my* country"), which could well be not just (fictitiously) the narrator's, but perhaps also (referentially) the author's. Even aside from the specific reference to the church window whose historical existence in Rouen did in reality motivate and trigger the writing of the tale, the closing sentence—at least fictitiously—designates the narrator as the actual author. Placed just above the proper name "Flaubert," the "I" that so unexpectedly emerges in the closing sentence *in excess of the story,* so as to punctuate the text and bring it to a close, appears indeed to be, in relation to the (written) story, not just its narrator but its *signatory.* It therefore, in some sense, inscribes within the text the very signature of Flaubert.

The signature, however, says: *It isn't me,* it's not my person, that is the tale's originator: it's not from me that the narration springs, but from my homeland, from "my country." The question then becomes: what, exactly, is a country?

THE STORY OF A COUNTRY

> I have in me that melancholy of the barbarian races, with its migratory instincts and innate disgust with life that made them leave their country as if they were leaving themselves.
>
> (Flaubert, *Letters*)

> Julian crossed in this way an interminable plain, and at last he found himself on a plateau dominating a *great expanse of country.* Flat rocks were scattered among vaults in ruins. One would stumble over dead men's bones; here and there, worm-eaten crosses slanted lamentingly. But there were shapes moving about in the uncertain shadows of the tombs.
>
> (Flaubert, *The Legend of Saint Julian*)

What is a country? The answer to this question is, indeed, suggested in the tale: suggested by the way in which the signatory, final sentence implicitly rejoins the narrative's first sentence, which it remotely echoes; the ending is thus structured as a subtle counterpart to the tale's opening:

> The father and the mother of Julian lived in a castle, in the middle
> of the woods, on the slope of a hill.

Much could be said about this sentence which, like the closing sentence, is rich in implications—beyond its innocuous appearance. One could stress the opposition it draws out between the *castle* and the *wood* (the animals' space, which will grow to be important in the story): an opposition between inside and outside, between the space of nature and the protected space of culture; "the slope of a hill" foreshadows, on the other hand, the possibility of a fall; and since this spatial description does not directly situate Julian himself, the implicit question which is left hanging is that of knowing, what space will belong to Julian? Indeed, as we will later learn, Julian will turn out to be the natural inhabitant of the woods and of the slope—far more than of the castle. What I wish to stress, however, is the fact, crucial in its simplicity, that the legend's opening—the very first sentence of the tale—gives information as to *where the hero's parents live*. The first sentence speaks, in other words, of Julian's country—of Julian's homeland, whereas the last sentence speaks of Flaubert's country—of the signatory's homeland.

What, then, is a country, if not, as the text suggests, the country where one's parents live? So, too, in the closing sentence, "my country" means *my parents' country;* that is to say, the country, at the same time, of the *cultural heritage* my parents have passed on to me.

But in this text "the country of my parents" necessarily implies the country of the *contradiction* which inhabits the relationship of those who have a child: the country of the gap, of the discontinuity which, paradoxically, is enacted by the very act of procreation. "My country," therefore, is the country of the contradictions embodied by the burden of the cultural heritage within which I am born, and with which my birth afflicts me.

The question of the meaning of a country thus begins to answer the initial question, concerning the nature of a legend. A legend is, precisely, the unconscious of the contradictions that beget us: the unconscious of the cultural heritage, articulating its *discontinuity with itself* in the form of this contradiction we, in turn, have to live, and to live out.

> As if we didn't have enough of our own past, we chew over that
> of humanity in its entirety.
>
> (Flaubert, Letters)

In fact, beneath the allegoric figure of the very story of *birth into consciousness,* it is humanity's entire cultural and mythic past that Flaubert condenses into the *legend.* Almost all the myths of the Western heritage are present in it: the Greek and Latin myths of Oedipus, Narcissus, Ajax, Charon, the biblical myths of Adam, Noah, and Cain, the evangelical myths of the life of Christ and the trials of the saints. (For Narcissus, compare the scene where Julian contemplates, with suicidal desire, his own reflection in the fountain. Like Ajax, Julian massacres animals which, here as well, are in reality substitutes for humans. In his letters, Flaubert mentions Sophocles' *Ajax,* which he read repeatedly. Compare the crossing of the river, which recalls Charon welcoming passengers and taking them across the river [Acheron or Styx] to the shore of Hell. For Adam and Noah, see my analysis below. Cain, like Julian, bears a mark on his skin—a sign imprinted by God to mark him as a murderer. Julian's parents, on the other hand, after the predictions about their son's future, think he has "been marked by God.") "The story found in my country" being that of Occidental culture as a whole, "my country" is not simply France or Rouen, but rather Babel: the very Babel of the West.

But the Flaubertian inscription of this mythic Babel ruptures and subverts, for each myth, its autonomy of sense and its semantic unity and integrity. Out of the Western Babel of the myths, Flaubert's ironic writing registers precisely the contradictions which, opposing the myths to one another, oppose them—and make them discontinuous—to themselves.

Thus Julian, Christ and Oedipus ("He resembled a little Jesus. His teeth came in without his crying a single time"), is *crucified,* irreverently, not over his own death, but over someone else's death: over the corpses of two goats—prefiguring those of his parents—that the text specifically describes as his *cross.* ("At the edge, two wild goats were looking into the abyss. . . . He finally got to the first goat and plunged a dagger through his ribs. The second, terror-struck, jumped into the void. Julian leapt to strike it, and, his right foot slipping, he *fell onto the other's corpse,* his face above the abyss and *his arms stretched out.*" Compare, during the parents' burial: "During the mass he stayed *prone* in the middle of the doorway, *his arms outstretched in the form of a cross.*")

Incarnating, in this way, the very irony—the very aberration—of the contradictory coincidence of Oedipus and Christ, Julian is also, at the same time, the embodiment of the conflicting myths of Adam and of Noah:

> Sometimes, in a dream, he saw himself as *our father Adam* in the midst of paradise, among all the animals; stretching out his arms, he would make them die; or they would file two by two . . . as on the day they entered *Noah's ark.*

Adam, in the myth, did not *kill* animals: he *named* them. The Flaubertian distortion of the myths suggests, in a revealing way, a textual correlation

between *naming* and *killing*. In the case of Julian, the act of killing is suggestively substituted for the act of naming or of speaking, implying, once again,
a relationship between silence and murder. Julian *kills* because he does not
name; Flaubert, for his part, *names*—in order not to kill? Or perhaps rather
to kill *by naming* him "our father Adam," to implicate himself in turn in
the very parricide of myths? "The distortion of a text," writes Freud, "is not
unlike a murder, in its implications. The difficulty resides not so much in
perpetrating the crime, but in covering up its traces" (*Moses and Monothe-
ism*).

What is there to cover up, however, if not the fact that the murdered
father had already—from the outset—been dead, that there had always been
too many fathers, too many myths? What *The Legend of Saint Julian the
Hospitable* reveals is, paradoxically enough, that *parricide is fundamentally
impossible*.

Too many fathers, too many myths: behind "our father Adam" is already profiled, in the same breath (in the same paragraph), this other father
of the human race, whose mythic function was, precisely, to start it over:
"The animals would file two by two, . . . as on the day they entered Noah's
ark." Noah, Adam: in coupling those two fathers of humanity, what is at
stake in Flaubert's text is, once again, the inscription of a (yet another)
contradiction between our parents. Whereas Adam, perpetrator of original
sin, is the embodiment of guilt and of its irreducible human inheritance,
Noah is, in contrast, the very figure of innocence par excellence: far from
killing animals, he is rather their savior, the one who gives them life. The
superimposition of these two myths in the same paragraph suggests that
Julian—the very text of contradiction—is *at once* innocent and guilty: he
who is most guilty, he from whom descends mankind's heritage of sin, and
he who, of all mankind, is the sole innocent. Innocence is here no longer, in
effect, *opposed* to guilt.

In this way Flaubert, inscribing "black on white" the myths of stain
upon the myths of purity, writes innocence into the myths of guilt and guilt
into the myths of innocence.

> And that's the story of Saint Julian the Hospitable, as one can
> find it—more or less—on a stained-glass window of a church, in
> my country.

The story of a country: a story of the relation between Flaubert's land—
that of the closing sentence—and Julian's (parents') land—that of the opening sentence. A tale of the relationship between where Flaubert comes from
and where Julian comes from, between the country that locates the hero at

the contradictory crossroads of conflicting dreams and parents, and the country that locates the signatory or the signature—the very energy of the writing—at the contradictory crossroads of conflicting myths.

INSIDERS AND OUTSIDERS: HOSPITALITY

Since the native country of the signatory is thus related to the legendary country where "the father and the mother" live, it should be stressed that Julian, nonetheless, is by definition one who cannot say "my country": his story is that of an *exile,* endlessly renewed. Structurally, the repeated scansion of Julian's displacement—his departure into exile—in effect constitutes the very punctuation of the three parts of the tale: each chapter ends with the hero leaving. Thus, at the end of the first chapter, Julian flees the parental castle and leaves his native country; at the end of the second chapter, he flees his own castle and leaves the country of his wife, which, through the marriage, had become his own; at the end of the third chapter, he leaves this world to ascend to heaven—the wayfarer's ultimate departure.

Since Julian is, by definition, he who has no land, but who nonetheless *inhabits my land*—lives in "my country" as the host of a church window, what else is a country if not, precisely, that which is *constituted by legends of exile?* If Julian, all the same, is defined as the story of "my country," then the story of "my country" is the story of an exile situated, not outside, but, paradoxically, *inside* my land.

This commingling of the inside and the outside of the tale itself, this relation adumbrated by the closing sentence between the (intrinsic) legendary hero and the (extrinsic) narrative first person of the signatory—between the legend and Flaubert's self-referential signing of the legend—suggests that writing is itself in fact an *inside job:* a relation—far more complex than we might think—between being an insider and being an outsider, between the stance of being in and the stance of being out of what one writes about.

Writing—but also murder. Julian consummates, indeed, his destiny as murderer both by virtue of his being an insider and by virtue of his being an outsider. On the one hand, it is because Julian has left his country that he—like Oedipus—ends up unwittingly killing his parents: the tragic mistake would not have happened had Julian not exiled himself out of his home and family, had he not cast himself on the outside.

But on the other hand, ironically enough, Julian kills in order to eliminate outsiders, to *protect the inside* of his home and of his family: finding his parents in his own bed, offered them—without his knowledge—by his wife, and tragically confusing his mother and his wife—whom he believes

to have caught with a lover, Julian commits the double murder of his parents
in a fit of jealousy that is clearly, in a metaphoric manner, Oedipal. But if
Julian kills because he takes his own father for a stranger—an outsider—he
kills because he in effect radically *confuses inside and outside* and thus mis-
takenly strives to protect what is *within* against what he believes to be an
intrusion from without.

The attitude of the murderer, who endeavors to protect the inside from
the outside and hence casts on the outside what is really only an unrecognized
part of his inside, is diametrically opposed to the attitude of the Hospitable,
who opens himself up to the outside and actually welcomes the outsider into
his own home. It is not by chance, indeed, that "the Hospitable" figures in
the legend's title. Hospitality, though hardly obvious or explicit—except precisely in the title—in effect plays in the tale an absolutely crucial role: crucial
for an understanding of the way Flaubert *rewrites* the legend and of the irony
with which he writes *into* the legend his sophisticated signature.

While it is true that Flaubert's title is no more than a recapitulation of
the traditional title of the saint, as well as of the saint's title to sainthood—
Saint Julian the Hospitable—Flaubert's writing does not fail to introduce
into the very title (of the saint, as of the tale) an ironic split: the ambiguous
tension, once again, of contradiction and division.

Hospitality itself, it turns out, is ironically divided in Flaubert's text:
the title in effect refers not to just one but to *two* occurrences, to two displays
of hospitality in the tale. The most obvious is that of Julian welcoming the
leper and offering him everything he has, right down to his very body. That
is, by all accounts, the ultimate in hospitality: the kind of hospitality that
leads to sainthood. But the other textual occurrence of hospitality is when
Julian's wife generously welcomes into her own bed the two strange visi-
tors—the two impoverished and aged nomads—that the very parents of her
husband have over the years become.

The symbolic link between these two narrative occurrences of hospitality is effected through the signifier of the bed: in both cases, the hospitable
welcome is enacted by the gesture of *giving one's own bed:*

> Julian's wife persuaded them not to wait up for him. *She herself
> put them in her bed,* then closed the window; they fell asleep.

> The leper shook from limb to limb . . . and, in an almost silenced
> voice, he murmured: "Your bed!" Julian gently helped him drag
> himself to it.

Thus it is the bed which twice becomes the quintessential site of hospitality.

But to what is the bed hospitable—what does a bed host? Sleep, of course, and dreams, and desire, and the erotic mingling of bodies ("Undress, so I can have the warmth of your body!" says the leper). But in the *legend,* the bed also becomes a tomb, since it is in bed that Julian kills his parents. The bed is thus equally hospitable to the murder of one's parents.

The ultimate gesture of welcome—*offering one's bed*—leads, then, on the one hand, to the sainthood of Saint Julian the Hospitable, yet on the other hand it leads to murder.

But it is precisely to the coincidence of these two scenes—to the ironic contradiction between these two displays of hospitality *taken together* and together issuing either in murder or in sainthood—that Flaubert's writing, in its turn, means to be hospitable. Hospitable to contradiction: hospitable to the voice of the Other, to a constant *countercurrent of meaning;* hospitable to silence, sleep, to its own silence, its own sleep, to its own difference from itself—hospitable, then, to a maximal number of mutually exclusive points of view within the same narrative statement, to a maximal number of opposed, conflicting readings (maternal/paternal, religious/sexual, supernatural-fantastic and/or natural-phantasmic, and so forth) within a single enunciation.

In the story as in its narration, on the inside as on the outside, what is at stake in hospitality is, therefore, not the simple gesture of inviting the outsider in—the welcoming of the outside inside—but, much more radically, the subversion of the very limit that distinguishes them from each other: the discovery that the outside is already within, but that what is within is, in effect, without—outside—itself.

MUCH BLOOD, MUCH GLORY;
OR, THE STAINS OF THE STAINED-GLASS WINDOW

A double, triple irony: not only is hospitality what leads at once to sainthood and to murder, but the Hospitable is, paradoxically enough, a man who has, himself, no country—no home of his own ("A small table, a stool, a bed of dead leaves and three clay cups, that was all his furniture. Two holes in the walls served as windows"), a man, moreover, who is himself received or welcomed by no one, and whose narrative—or message—will elicit nothing other than an absolute refusal of hospitality:

> Out of the spirit of humility, he would tell his story; then everyone would flee him, making the sign of the cross. In the villages he had been through before, as soon as he was recognized, *the doors*

were shut, threats were yelled out at him, and stones were thrown
at him. The most charitable people set a bowl on their windowsill,
then closed the shutters to avoid seeing him.

How is that Flaubert can tell Julian's story while Julian himself *cannot
tell*—or get anyone to listen to—his story? It must be because Julian's story
is by definition the story of the Other—the story of no one: a tale in some
way without language, which can be articulated in effect only by the *silence*
of the stained-glass window. If Flaubert speaks, tells the deaf, mute story of
the stained-glass visual image, he can only read, *translate* it. For his own
protection, he is screened, precisely, by the stained-glass window, whose
function is indeed to separate him from his own tale.

It is thus the stained-glass window of the church which can, alone, be
host—hospitable—to Julian's story; but Flaubert's tale can in turn be hospitable to—host—the stained-glass window:

And that's the story . . . as one can find it on a stained-glass
window of a church, in my country.

Is the window *hosted* by the tale inside or outside? What is the significance
of the inscription of the window in the closing sentence? In what way does
Flaubert's stained-glass in effect partake of the very nature of a signature?

The tale, quite literally, is *the legend of the stained-glass window,* since
the word *legend* can also mean "any text that accompanies an image and
gives it its meaning" (*Le Petit Robert*). If the tale—like the account or interpretation of a dream—thus consists in the verbal translation of pictorial
images into narrative, the stained-glass window constitutes a *legend* in the
etymological sense as well: *legenda*—"what must be read." How, then, does
the text define—or concretize—this figure of "what must be read"?

A stained-glass window is a painting; but it is also, at the same time,
just a window; as such, it is, once more, a boundary, a limit that not only
separates what is within from that which is without but also sets up the
dependence of the inside on the outside: indeed, we could not see the painting
on the inside were it not for the light that filters in from the outside. The
stained-glass window thus enacts an ambiguous relationship of nontrans-
parency, and yet of interfusion, between what is in and what is out. The
outside—behind the painted window—is what the eye looking at the painting
does not see, but it is also, at the same time, *what enables it to see.*

All these connotations of the stained-glass window are put into play by
the tale itself. For the closing sentence, with its signatory gesture toward the
referential church window that the narrator has just translated, is not the

only mention of a stained-glass window in the legend. From within this signatory, painted window which in some sense frames the tale—apparently from outside the tale—another stained-glass window is outlined—and framed—inside the tale, in the very heart of the narrative itself. The story speaks, indeed, no less than three times of another stained-glass window: not that of Flaubert's home church, but that of Julian's castle. It must be significant that the three occurrences of this other stained-glass window all appear in proximity to the parental murder, which they literally frame.

The first appearance of the window introduces into the tale's silence a signatory note of tragic irony that mutely *signs* the parents' last sleep—the sleep from which they will never again awaken:

> Julian's wife persuaded them not to wait up for him. She put them herself in her bed, then closed the window; they fell asleep. *Day was about to break,* and *behind the stained-glass window,* little birds began to sing.

In the bedroom, *in front of the window,* the invisible narrator seems to contemplate the parents' sleep—their unawareness. But what is there *behind the stained-glass window?* Apparently, behind the window day is breaking. But in reality, day will, for the parents, dawn no more: behind the stained-glass window it is nothing other than eternal night—and death—which in effect await them. The window, then, embodies here the very ambiguity of day and night: the ambiguous borderline that at the same time separates and links sleeping and waking, death and life, without our being able to know for sure which is inside, which is outside—what, exactly, lies behind the window.

The second textual inscription of the stained-glass window can be found just before the murder, when Julian, harassed and frustrated by the final hunt, returns home:

> Having taken off his sandals, he gently turned the key, and went in. *The stained-glass windows adorned with lead obscured the light of dawn.* Julian . . . made his way towards the bed, lost in the shadows spreading deep into the room. When he was at the bedside, in order to embrace his wife, he bent over the pillow, where two heads were resting side by side. Then, he felt against his mouth the sensation of a beard. . . . Definitely it was a beard . . . and a man! A man in bed with his wife!
>
> Bursting with inordinate anger, he leapt at them, stabbing them repeatedly with his dagger.

The signifying chain of the stained-glass windows which constructs a link between the narrative and its frame, which subtly binds the windows framed by the legendary story and the framing window of the narrator-signatory, here takes on a curiously ironic tinge. For while the stained-glass window contemplated by the narrator is *what makes us see* the legend, giving the story visibility, the window at the same time turns out to be *that which obscures,* creates a blindness: it is because of the window that Julian, seeing nothing, kills his parents. The window thus maintains an ambiguous relation with light: its function is not just—by letting in the rays of light—to *produce representation,* but also—by screening them off—to *distort perception.* The stained-glass window, or "what must be read," at once gives sight and blinds.

And if, unlike those who "closed their doors" so as *not to see* Julian, so as not to look at—listen to—his story, we agree to look at the stained-glass window, to listen to the legend, is it not precisely because of the blinding power of what a stained-glass window—or a legend—lets us see? Doesn't Flaubert suggest that the property of a legend (of a window) is to make us look, to make us see, while at the same time blinding us to the way the window in effect reflects on—has to do with—us?

The third occurrence of the stained-glass window takes place right after the murder. As day breaks, the rebus of the window lights up:

> His father and mother were before him, stretched out on their backs with holes in their chests. . . . Splashes and *pools of blood* spread over the middle of their *white skin,* onto the bedsheets, onto the ground. . . . *The scarlet reflection of the stained glass window, now struck by the sun, lit up these red stains, and cast many more of them around the whole room.*

At its last appearance within the legend, the stained-glass window—hit by light—becomes itself a rhetorical figure of writing: a figure of the optical prism of language as what determines, motivates, compels, the performance of "the pen-man." ("I am a pen-man. I feel through it, because of it, in relation to it and much more with it" [Flaubert to Louise Colet].) "Style being, in itself, an absolute way of *seeing* things" (to Louise Colet), it is indeed the window that is writing: it is the window which, *multiplying stains of red* throughout the room, brings back the motif of color contrast—the textual inscription of the stain, the mark. "The scarlet reflection of the stained-glass window, now struck by the sun, lit up these red stains, and cast many more of them around the whole room."

In this way, the stained-glass window turns out to be *hospitable* to *blood:* hospitable, ambiguously, both to what in blood is most uncanny, most unsettling—the blood of mortal injury, of murder—but also, at the same time, to what in blood is most familiar, reassuring: the bloodline of the family, the very familiarity of heritage. Uncannily familiar and familiarly uncanny, the stained-glass window is inscribed throughout the text as a writing which consists, precisely, of staining white surfaces: a writing—a play of colors and a play of light, a chiaroscuro—which consists of tinting the white pages of the text with ink that, in effect, is blood, with blood that, in effect, is ink.

It is thus that, when the signatory brings the legend to a close by bringing out his own relation to the stained-glass window in his homeland, the referential, outside window is already *signed* from inside the text: signed, precisely, by the blood stain changed into an ink stain.

"Of all writing," asserts Nietzsche through the mouth of Zarathustra, "I love but that which one has written with one's blood. Write with blood, and you will learn that blood is spirit." Has Flaubert told the story of, precisely, writing with one's blood?

> It was a Bohemian with a braided beard. . . . With an inspired
> air, he stammered these disconnected words:
> Ah! Ah! . . . Much blood! . . . Much glory!

In the end, what is the connection that uncannily emerges from behind these words' apparent disconnection? In telling us, along with Julian's story, the very story of the stained (glass) signature, the tale can give a different, unexpected insight both into the Bohemian's "inspiration" and into the nature of the "glory" he predicts. If the art of disconnection here turns out, indeed, to be inspired, if blood issues in glory and if the very glory of the "inspiration" is necessarily tied up with blood, the glory—like the blood as well—is Flaubert's.

"Almost everyone dies," writes Flaubert, "without knowing his proper name, unless he is a fool." A signature, indeed, is not the simple writing down of a proper name. A signature is nothing other than the story of one's writing with one's blood: the story of how *one does not know one's own name* and how, not knowing one's own name, one signs, instead, with one's own blood.

I, THE UNDERSIGNED

It would be quite pleasant to spell out my thought in order to relieve Sir Gustave Flaubert by means of sentences; but what importance does this honorable Sir have?

(Flaubert, *Letters*)

As for disclosing my own personal opinion of the people I put on stage, no, no, a thousand times no! I don't grant myself the *right* to do so.

(Flaubert, *Letters*)

And that's the story of Saint Julian the Hospitable, as one can find it—more or less—on a stained-glass window of a church, in my country.

This highly complex signature in effect says in one breath: I am external to my text (an outsider); I am internal to my text (an insider). There is a gap separating me from my tale: the wall of the church window, for which I am not responsible. But on the other hand, it is only "more or less" that my text duplicates the stained-glass window: so I am also, at the same time, responsible for the discrepancy—the gap—that separates the stained-glass window from my tale. Just as the stained-glass window stands between my text and me, (the) "I" in turn stand(s) between the window and my text. Where, then, does the legend come from? With respect to it, I am at once responsible and not responsible, guilty and innocent.

> *To Georges Charpentier, Croisset, Sunday (16 February 1879).*
> . . . I wanted to put the stained-glass window of the Rouen cathedral after *Saint Julian*. It was a matter of adding colors to the plate that's found in Langlois's book, nothing more. And this illustration pleased me precisely because it was not an illustration, but a historical *document*. In comparing the image to the text, one would have said to oneself: "I don't understand any of it. How did he get this out of that?"
> All illustrations exasperate me, . . . and while I am alive none will be made. . . . The same is true of my portrait.

Just as Julian's "I" enacts the gap—the *relationless relation* that at the same time separates and links his parents—the signatory's "I" enacts the relationless relation that at the same time separates and links the window and the tale. "And that's the story . . . more or less": the expression of approximation—more or less (*à peu près*)—marks the "I" as the play, precisely, of the undecidability between distance and proximity.

However, the very play of undecidability is itself decided and overdetermined: it is a play the "I" does not—cannot—decide.

> One morning as he was returning through the colonnade, he saw on the crest of the rampart a large pigeon. . . . Julian stopped to look at it; since there was a breach in the wall at that point, *a splinter of stone met his fingers.* He cocked his arm, and *the stone knocked down the bird,* which fell straight into the ditch.

Just as the stone *meets* Julian's fingers—of its own accord, it seems—the stained glass window—"as one can find it" in the church—*meets* Flaubert's eye. The signatory's "I" itself is therefore nothing other than the acting out of the encounter between necessity and chance: the very writing of the unavoidable necessity of a chance encounter. Flaubert is the *instrument of the window,* just as Julian is the instrument of the stone.

> Art has but the form we can give it: we are not free. Each follows his path, despite his own will.
>
> > (to George Sand)

> I've always guarded against putting anything of myself into my works, and yet I've put in a great deal.
>
> > (to Louise Colet)

It is noteworthy that Flaubert, whose writing effort always tended toward the suppression of the "I," the effacement of the author's voice, nonetheless signs one of his last works by referring it back to the realm—discreet as it may be—of the first person, a first person, it is true, whose silent, subtle presence is denied and masked by an indefinite third person:

> And that's the story of Saint Julian the Hospitable, as *one* can find it [telle qu'*on* la trouve] . . . in *my* country [dans *mon* pays].

To understand the implications of this *mon* ("my")—beyond its contradiction, its denial by the *on* ("one")—it is revealing to relate the signatory silence of this first person ("my") to all the other instances of the discourse of an *"I"* in the legend of Saint Julian. When we extract from the legend's narrative, told in the third person, the few fragments of *direct speech*—the several quotations reported in the first person—what we come up with is a stupefying textual precipitate which reads as follows:

CHAPTER 1

(Julian's discourse)   I cannot kill them!
                              What if I wanted to, though?

CHAPTER 2

(Julian's discourse)   It's to obey you! At sunrise I'll be back.
(Julian's wife's discourse)   It's my father.

CHAPTER 3

(The leper's discourse)   I'm hungry.
                              I'm thirsty.
                              I'm cold.
                              Undress, so I can have the warmth of
                              your body.
                              I'm going to die.

This is, then, what the "I" says, what the "I" *can* say, *all* the "I" can say—
a quintessence of the discourse of the "I," an abstract of that, precisely,
which Flaubert will never say in his own name, in his own right, with his
own voice. Literature is, for Flaubert, *about the silence* of this discourse: the
art of writing, in Flaubert's conception, is, precisely, the production of such
silence.

What Flaubert will never say; what literature is all about:

> I cannot kill them. What if I wanted to, though?
> It's to obey you . . . I'll be back.
> It's my father.
> I'm hungry, thirsty, cold.
> Undress, so I can have the warmth of your body.
> I'm going to die.

This muted discourse of the "I," this summarily exhaustive spectrum of
complaint, appeal, anxiety, protest, interrogation, and demand of the first
person, is however, what the undersigned—the signatory "I" of the legend
of Saint Julian—in the very gesture of denying it his own voice, at the very
moment of his own lapse into silence, nonetheless refers back to his space—
"finds in *his* country."

> And that's the story of Saint Julian the Hospitable, as one can
> find it—more or less—on a stained-glass window of a church, in
> my country.

Flaubert's signature: I, the undersigned, have found in my country that which I can tell, but which I cannot say—that which I deny myself the right to say.

I, the undersigned, am going to die.

I am getting lost in my childhood memories like an old man. I expect of life nothing more than a succession of sheets of paper to stain with black ink. I seem to be traversing a loneliness with no end, to go I don't know where. And I myself am all at once the traveler, the desert and the camel.

(to George Sand)

I feel mortally wounded. . . . I'll soon be fifty-four years old. At that age one does not redo one's life, one does not change habits. I'm devoured by the past, and the future has nothing good to offer me. I think of nothing other than of the days past and of the people that cannot come back. Sign of old age and of decadence. As for literature, I no longer believe in myself, and I feel empty. . . . In the meantime, I'm going to begin writing the legend of *Saint Julian the Hospitable*, just to occupy myself with something and *to see whether I am still able to craft a sentence*, which I sincerely doubt.

(to Madame Roger des Genettes)

Flaubert's signature: this is what *I* will not say.

I'm cold, I'm thirsty.
I, the undersigned, am going to die.

What Flaubert will never say, he nonetheless—in his own sophisticated, silent way—will *sign:* a crafted sentence. A sheet of paper stained with black ink.

"And that's the story." The legend of Saint Julian. The story of the ink/blood stain. As one can find it in my country.

Were it necessary to be moved in order to move others, I could write books that would make hands tremble and hearts pound, and, since I'm sure I'll never lose this capacity for emotion which the pen gives me of its own accord without my having anything to do with it, and which happens to me in spite of myself in a way that's often disturbing, I don't preoccupy myself with it, and what I look for, on the contrary, is not *vibration* but *design*.
Signed: GUSTAVE FLAUBERT

(to Louise Colet)

EUGENIO DONATO

Who Signs "Flaubert"?

In telling a story I pretend to speak the dead.
—LOUIS MARIN

The Self: A cemetery guard.
—JACQUES DERRIDA

In a letter written on June 26, 1852, addressed to Maxime Du Camp who has just moved to Paris and who invites his friend to come there in order to make "a name" for himself, he whom we choose to call Flaubert protests:

> It seems to me that with regard to my situation you suffer from a *tic* or a redhibitory vice. It *does not bother me,* have no fear of that. I have long since made up my mind on the matters you mention.
> I will merely tell you that all the words you use—*hurry, this is the moment, it is now time, your place will be taken, establish yourself* and *outside the law*—are for me a vocabulary empty of meaning. It is as if you were speaking to an Algonquin—I don't understand.
> *To get somewhere*—what for? . . .
> *To be known* is not my main concern.

The site of literary fame is not the theater wherein the writer would like to inscribe his name; that others occupy the forestage does not trouble him at all:

From *Modern Language Notes* 99, no. 4 (September 1984). © 1984 by The Johns Hopkins University Press, Baltimore/London. This essay was translated by Eduardo Cadava.

187

> I don't give a damn about whether or not Augier is successful
> and I won't become frantic if Vacqueir and Ponsard so broaden
> their shoulders that they take my place, and I have no intention
> of troubling them to give it back to me.

The letter is not signed with a proper name but simply "Your Quara-fon," the nickname that Maxime Du Camp had given to Flaubert and which remained for Flaubert associated with the mimetic talents of his friend—mimetic talents which were part of a certain literary activity, precisely that which permits one to "make a name for oneself"; "Maxime has developed a great mimetic talent . . . I call him father Etienne; he calls me Quarafon." It is thus the addressee, in the process of making himself a name among other names, who determines what Flaubert chooses to sign.

Flaubert's refusal to make a literary name for himself is linked to his refusal to move to Paris and to his choice to remain in Croisset, the privileged place of his writing. If Flaubert chooses to live in the country it is not in order to do what one usually does when living in the country but because Croisset is the place of another literature, a literature different from that which is written in the capital:

> If I really led a provincial or rural existence, devoting myself to
> the playing of dominoes or the growing of melons, I could under-
> stand the reproach. But if I am becoming stupefied it is Lucian,
> Shakespeare, and writing a novel which are to blame.

We sense the error of Bouvard and Pécuchet who, within this same Normandy, cultivated melons before understanding that "happiness" in the country consists of setting oneself at a double writing-desk in order to produce there, through a pure act of writing, *La Copie*. Already in 1852, Flaubert qualifies his literary activity as "neutralizing"—"As for so bitterly deploring my 'neutralizing' life it is as though you were to reproach a shoemaker for making shoes."

But if Croisset in particular and Normandy in general are privileged places for the consummation and production of a certain literature, it is because that same literature participates in a scene of writing which implicates Flaubert the individual. Normandy is the place of Flaubert's dead and it is these dead who, by being associated with the literary act, put into play a series of texts which produce, in their turn, the space in which a form of writing which engenders the series of texts signed Flaubert becomes possible. In a letter written barely a week before the one addressed to Maxime Du Camp, Flaubert explains to Louise Colet:

We carry away . . . the fatherland on the soles of our heels and
we carry in our heart, without knowing it, the dust of our dead
ancestors—As for me, I personally rely on a demonstration by A
+ B—It is the same in literature. I recover all of my origins in
the book which I knew before I knew how to read, *Don Quixote,*
and there is still, over and above this, the agitated froth of the
Norman seas, the English malady, the stinking fog.

This fantasmatic Normandy will therefore be the place where, for Flaubert
the individual, a certain number of the dead come to be intimately associated
with a certain literature which has always carried within it the imaginary
space wherein he chooses to live. For Flaubert, the possibility of being able
to produce a certain number of texts signed "Flaubert" will depend upon
this precise choice.

And yet the condition necessary for Flaubert to be able to produce the
texts signed "Flaubert" would exclude the possibility that Croisset's recluse
could ever come to know his own name. In that same letter of June 26, 1852,
to Maxime Du Camp, Flaubert writes this extraordinary sentence: "one
almost always dies in the incertitude of one's own proper name."

But then what might be proper to that signature which we—we who?—
read as being that of "Flaubert"? The textual production which subtends
the engenderment of a proper name—whose proper meaning would consist
precisely in the production of an oeuvre signed by a name—would consequently have to constitute the representation of a subject always distinct from
that of the psychological ego of the writer and from all the identifications
and significations which the writer or the reader would come to invest in it.
By the signing of a text, the proper name produces itself, presents itself, gives
itself to be seen and to be read, simply by producing the conditions of its
illegibility. In the end, then, a signature can only engender the mark of a
necessary non-adequation or non-attribution of a representation, or more
exactly, of what represents itself in a name to the writer insofar as he is an
individual. At least, of course, insofar as we try to determine the margin of
possible exception permitted by the "almost"—"one almost always dies in
the incertitude of one's own proper name"—or insofar as we believe it possible to say what is proper to imbecility—"unless one is an imbecile."

Without pretending to offer a response to the conditions of a proper
name's legibility and without believing myself able to say what is proper to
the imbecile, I would like to weave around the proper name "Flaubert" a
fantasmatic scenario which might at least permit us to displace the proper
name "Flaubert" onto other proper names. These other proper names would

not be any more legible than that of Flaubert; nonetheless, if to try to read a proper name can only end by displacing it onto another proper name, then this transfer, this translation, this metaphorization would at least be one of the determining conditions of its illegibility. My hypothesis is the following: if the proper name "Flaubert" remains illegible, it is partly because it is engendered by another proper name which could almost be said to be that of "Loulou—Le Poittevin"; however, "Loulou—Le Poittevin," being a name of a dead person, itself remains illegible except through the proper name "Flaubert," which it renders possible by its own encryptment (*mise en crypte*).

If the signature of a certain number of titles problematizes the proper name "Flaubert" it does not do so in a unified way over a uniform corpus. On the contrary, the signature "Flaubert" divides the Flaubertian corpus in two and gives it a particular morphology. Flaubert, the writer, does not sign his works—or only expresses his intention to sign his works beginning with the first *Tentation de saint Antoine,* that is, beginning in 1849. If his refusal to publish the works of his youth remains comprehensible, we understand less his lack of interest in publishing the first *Education sentimentale* or *Novembre,* which he nevertheless allowed to circulate among his friends.

La Tentation de saint Antoine, in any case, plays a privileged role for Flaubert. It is the first of his works that he assumes without reserve, and therefore frames, through its three versions, his career as a writer and, by his own admission, constitutes the work of his entire life. For Flaubert, it is *La Tentation de saint Antoine* and *Bouvard et Pécuchet* which occupy a privileged position among his works, and not *Madame Bovary* or *L'Education sentimentale,* which are ultimately valorized by the naturalist myth of a so-called realist Flaubert.

It is precisely here, within the register of proper names, and beginning with *La Tentation de saint Antoine,* that a series of metaphorizations of the writer's ego take place in Flaubert's writing, by way of a series of proper names based on imaginary identifications which determine, in their fashion, not only the possibility of being for Flaubert's works, but also the condition of their signature. If the phrase "Madame Bovary is I" is known and cited at every turn it is important not to forget that Flaubert the writer will identify himself on several occasions with St. Anthony and that he will end by identifying himself with Bouvard and Pécuchet—"Bouvard and Pécuchet overwhelm me to such an extent that I have become them! Their stupidity is mine, I die from it." Nor should one forget that this mechanism of identification is finally based upon a more general process: "Everything that is there within St. Thérèse, within Hoffman and Edgar Poe, I have *seen.*" Or again: "My imaginary characters haunt me, or rather, it is I who am in them." If these imaginary identifications are essential to the production of the text it is because they procure for the writer an enjoyment essential to the libidinal economy which governs his writing: "good or bad, it is a delicious thing to write, to no longer be *oneself,* but to circulate within every creation of which one speaks."

"Flaubert" is thus not the proper name of the writer; the latter calls himself, by turns, St. Anthony, Madame Bovary, Bouvard, Pécuchet, etc. These names permit the engenderment of a text which, itself, will be signed "Flaubert." "Flaubert" would only be at the limit one of the names of that heterogeneous assemblage of names. The writer only lives for, and only *enjoys* himself through, a series of names which never properly return to him but which permit him to make himself a single name, the knowledge of which will always remain enigmatic for him.

A first indication of this strange dialectic between the writer Flaubert and the name of that which signs "Flaubert": sentences such as "the writer does not write in order to be published . . . I do not in any way dream of this, thank God. . . . It is necessary more than ever to make Art for itself, for itself only" recur constantly in his correspondence and express a resolution that the writer repeats in practically each one of his novels. On the other hand, the other name, the proper name "Flaubert," only exists because of publication and only as the signature of a published text. A second indication: the names of the imaginary characters with which the writer identifies himself engender, in their turn, by association, other names which the writer does not hesitate to assume; this is what permits him, for example, to sign letters with "St. Polycarpe" or "the last of the Church Fathers."

Among all the proper names which circulate in Flaubert's novels, I single out two of them, Alfred Le Poittevin and Loulou, which seem to me to be of particular interest because of their particular relationship with the name "Flaubert." The first appears only on the occasion of a dedication, the second is the name of Félicité's parrot in *Un Coeur simple.*

In 1874, Flaubert finally publishes the third version of *La Tentation de saint Antoine* and dedicates it to Alfred Le Poittevin whose name comes to be associated with the name "Flaubert" in a privileged fashion. The text of the dedication is not content simply to mention the name of his childhood friend but also indicates the date and place of his friend's death—"To the memory of my friend, Alfred Le Poittevin, who died in Neuville-Chant-D'Oisel on the third of April, 1848." Flaubert himself recognizes the importance of Alfred Le Poittevin's name to *La Tentation.* On October 30, 1872, he writes to Laure de Maupassant: "In my mind *La Tentation de saint*

Antoine has always been dedicated to Alfred Le Poittevin. I had spoken to him about this book six months before his death. I have finally finished it, this book which has occupied me off and on for 25 years!" Four months later, in another letter to Laure, Flaubert speaks again of Alfred Le Poittevin and generalizes his point: "He remains in my memory beyond all comparison. Not a day passes that I do not think of him. Besides, the past, the dead (my dead) obsess me."

The writer thus carries within himself, among his dead, the memory of his friend. If it remains true that Flaubert had spoken to the latter about his project of writing a *Tentation de saint Antoine* and if it is to Alfred Le Poittevin that he announced, before his project, his discovery of the Breughel tableau, it remains no less true that the bond of *La Tentation de saint Antoine* to the memory of his friend is more fundamental. Even on an anecdotal level, if Flaubert thinks of the project of writing a *Tentation,* it is only in May of 1848, after Alfred Le Poittevin's unexpected death on April 3 of the same year, that he begins to compose the first version.

That the possibility of beginning "the work of all his life" and of inaugurating the signed part of his work are intimately linked, for Flaubert, to the work of the mourning of his friend, is suggested to us by a letter to Maxime Du Camp in which he describes in detail the wake and burial of Alfred Le Poittevin. I cite here some extracts from it:

> Alfred died on Monday night at midnight. I buried him yesterday and I am now back. I buried him in his shroud, I gave him the kiss of farewell and I saw his coffin being sealed. I spent two very full days there. While watching over him, I read Creuzer's *Les Religions de l'antiquité.* The window was open, the night was superb, one could hear the cock crow and a night-butterfly was fluttering around the torches. I shall never forget all that, neither the aspect of his figure, nor the first night at midnight, the distant sound of a hunting horn that came to me through the woods. The last night I read the *Feuilles d'automne.* I kept coming across pieces that he liked best or that for me had some relation to the present situation. From time to time I got up and went to lift the veil that they had placed on his face, and looked at him. I was myself bundled up in a coat that belonged to my father and that he had worn only once, the day of Caroline's wedding. . . . There, my dear friend, you have what I have lived through since Tuesday night. I have had unheard-of perceptions and flashes of untranslatable ideas. Many things have been coming back to me with

choirs of music and whiffs of perfume . . . I feel the need to say incomprehensible things.

In telling of the vigil and burial of Alfred Le Poittevin, Flaubert effectively ends up creating nothing less than a fantasmatic scenario of the origin of a certain type of literary representation. At first, the presence of his friend's corpse drives the writer to read. The choice of texts is doubly marked. Flaubert begins with the French translation of Creuzer's *Symbolik und Mythologie*. Of all the readings that Flaubert will go through for *La Tentation de saint Antoine, Les Religions de l'antiquité* is not only one of his most important sources, but it is also the very book that will provide him with indispensable iconographic material. In other words, Alfred Le Poittevin's corpse will at first permit Flaubert to read one of the important sources for the work that will inaugurate his career and to allegorize the birth of a type of literature whose most extreme form will be *Bouvard et Pécuchet*. *La Tentation de saint Antoine* in effect belongs to a literature whose pre-text is no longer a "reality" or "imagination" conceived of as outside the text, but rather a pre-text which is itself textual and which affirms itself as such. In order to be able to write *La Tentation de saint Antoine* or *Bouvard et Pécuchet* Flaubert will have to be able to say: "I have gotten indigestion from books; I burp in-folio."

Flaubert then reads the *Feuilles d'automne:* if in this case the question is not that of a text which will be part of the literary genesis of one of Flaubert's works, the choice of texts is nevertheless dictated to him by the preferences of the dead man. What the corpse gives him to understand and to feel—"choirs of music," "whiffs of perfume"—does not belong to a system of textual representation. The only possible translation of the intuitions produced by the presence of the dead man will be a series of contradictory metaphors—"unheard-of perceptions," "flashes of untranslatable ideas." Flaubert's ultimate desire to say "incomprehensible things"—what he will elsewhere call the Idea—will end by opening an unbreachable gap between what is written and the intended meaning which will be the very space of Flaubertian prose—a prose which "is never finished" and which condemns him "no longer to expect anything from life but a series of sheets of paper to scribble upon in black." In order to pass from the wish to say "incomprehensible things" to writing, "one must undertake a kind of permanent translation, and what an abyss that creates between the absolute and the work." In other words, if the corpse of Alfred Le Poittevin determines the literary practice which will produce the texts signed "Flaubert," it will engender as well the aesthetic which sub-tends such a practice.

We might be tempted, because of the way in which Flaubert represents his literature to us as a thanatography, to conclude that what is proper to the Flaubertian signature belongs to Alfred Le Poittevin. Such a conclusion is more incomplete than false. On the one hand, it neglects the fact that there are other names apart from that of Alfred Le Poittevin which belong to that fantasmatic scenario of the origin of Flaubertian writing; yet on the other hand, it forces us to ask what is theoretically at stake when we declare that, in last analysis, the signature of Flaubert belongs to one or several corpses.

The conditions under which Flaubert composes the end of *Un Coeur simple* are well known. He borrows a stuffed parrot from the Museum of Natural History at Rouen which he places in front of him on his work table: Félicité's parrot is a textual transposition of the representation of the dead parrot that the writer has in front of him. Félicité's parrot is named Loulou, an unusual name for a parrot: "Many are surprised when it does not answer to the name of Jacquot, since all parrots are named Jacquot." Félicité's parrot will die and in turn become a stuffed bird. Yet, this is not the essential point.

For the author of *Un Coeur simple* thus summarizes his tale: "She [Félicité] successively loves a man, the children of her mistress, a nephew, an old man whom she cares for, then her parrot; when the parrot dies, she has it stuffed and when she in turn is dying she confuses the parrot with the Holy Spirit." Flaubert's tale is based upon the series of Félicité's libidinal objects, a good part of which disappear in her dying. The series is itself engendered by the double death of Félicité's parents and Mme Aubain's husband. The parrot, the last object of the servant's affection, suspends the play of substitutions among which it is the privileged term since it is the only one which in being dead continues to "live" stuffed in the form of a simulacrum and the only one which will eventually be transformed into the Holy Spirit by Félicité's death.

Now Loulou has a very particular relationship to language. Alive, the parrot utters only pure signifiers that are indefinitely repeated by a voice that the deaf Félicité hears and understands; dead, it will be transformed into the symbol of the only name that we can say is truly proper, the transcendental signifier of all signification, the proper name of what is proper to the name, namely, the Holy Spirit. But it is within this last transformation that the role of the parrot becomes paradoxical for, if *in principium erat Verbum*, at the origin the parrot is also the endless babble of language, the indefinite repetition of a signifier without signification. If the Holy Spirit calls itself Loulou, then the only properly proper name is itself only composed from the repetition of the insignificant signifier "lou." In other words, through Félicité's death, the dead parrot divides language in two; on the one side, an indefinite babble of "sonorous inanities," on the other side, an always inaccessible transcendental signified.

We have often approached the description of Virginie's corpse in *Un Coeur simple* through the description that Flaubert gives us of his dead sister, Caroline. We must not forget, however, that the daughter of Mme Aubain is named Virginie (and her son, Paul) and that her name is only a reference to a literary antecedent. Moreover, Loulou is also one of the names that Flaubert gives to his niece Caroline, the daughter of his sister Caroline. It is also important to note, as Philippe Bonnefis has emphasized (in "Exposition d'un perroquet"), that during the entire period of the writing of *Un Coeur simple*, in all of his letters addressed to his niece, he calls her only by the name of Loulou. If *Un Coeur simple* returns us to the death of Caroline Flaubert, it does so through a series of transpositions which puts into play Félicité's parrot and the name of Loulou. If, for Félicité, the parrot replaces the lost object, Virginie, the name of the parrot remains associated, for Flaubert, with that of his niece which, in turn, repeats and replaces the name of his dead sister. *Un Coeur simple* evokes the corpse of Caroline Flaubert by transposing it into that of a parrot, that is to say, by inscribing it into a textual problematic of the proper name.

The description of Caroline Flaubert's corpse, dead in 1846, two years before the death of Alfred Le Poittevin, is itself significant insofar as it also proposes to us a fantasmatic scenario of the genesis of Flaubert's literary production. In a letter to Louise Colet in 1847 Flaubert describes the vigil of his sister in the following manner:

> When my sister died, I stood vigil over her at night; I was on the edge of her bed; I was looking at her lying on her back in her wedding dress with a white bouquet.—I was reading Montaigne and my eyes were going from the book to her corpse; her husband was sleeping and breathing heavily; the priest was snoring; and I was saying to myself, in contemplating all this, that forms pass and that only the idea remains, and I had shivers of enthusiasm from the way in which the author worded some of his sentences.—Then I thought that he too would pass; it was freezing, the window was open because of the odor and from time to time I got up to see the stars, calm, caressing, sparkling, eternal; and I told myself that when, in turn, they should become pale, when they should send, like the eyes of those in agony, lights full of anguish, all will be said and everything will be even more beautiful.

Again we have a scene of reading created by the displacement of a libidinal investment in a dead object into the literature that Flaubert proposes to us. In front of his sister's corpse, the writer, who will in the future sign "Flaubert," reads Montaigne. But it is precisely this transposition of a dead body into a written representation, this *translatio,* this metaphorization of the corpse into a text which positions language between the already-said of a literature to be read and the text to be written, between plural forms and effects of style, between the source of the writer's enjoyment and the Idea— the transcendental signified. As in *Un Coeur simple,* this play of oppositions works only to announce an eschatology within the indefinite future of an eventual end of time. It is only when the speakable [*le dicible*] has used up the time engendered by the anteriority of the corpse and the aftermath of the text, when "everything has been said," and when the corpse has finally recuperated the textual representations that belong to it, that a final epiphany will be possible.

A few sentences before the description of the dead Caroline, Flaubert had written: "Perhaps I am only a violin." What he will not say, or more exactly what he will not name, is the name of whoever holds the bow or the name of the melody which is being played. We might be tempted to say that what holds the bow is nothing other than the corpse, to name the corpse Caroline Flaubert, Loulou, or Alfred Le Poittevin, and to recognize, within the melody, the work signed "Flaubert." However, we must leave to the corpse the capacity to remove the limits of our discourse and to determine the theoretical stakes of attributing the name "Flaubert" to "Loulou Le Poittevin."

In order to try to explain the relation of the corpse to the subject, we have no theoretical vocabulary other than that proposed by psychoanalysis and no model other than that which psychoanalysis offers us in order to think the work of mourning. It is thus a question of understanding the relation of the lost object to the representations that it might engender in terms of the notions of incorporation and introjection.

For Freud the normal work of mourning should consist of detaching one's libidinal investments from the lost object. In one sense, a normal mourning should end in forgetting the dead or, in the wording of Lagache, in "killing the dead." It is with the maladies of mourning that the notion of incorporation comes into play. Again, according to Freud, this notion implies that the ego, regressing to a phase of oral and cannibalistic development, incorporates the lost object by devouring it. Following the commentary of Laplanche and Pontalis (in *The Vocabulary of Psychoanalysis*) for whom the Freudian notion of incorporation and the Ferenczian notion of introjection are equivalent, the incorporation of an object into the ego by way of a fantasmatic form implies three processes: the possibility of giving oneself pleasure either by having an object penetrate into oneself, by assimilating the qualities of the object, or finally by assimilating the qualities of the object by conserving them within oneself. It would not be difficult to show that taken together these three processes constitute a psychoanalytic version of Hegelian sublation. Through incorporation the ego "destroys" the object by recreating and maintaining an ideal representation of the object within itself. It is precisely this sublation of the object which renders it readable in a psychoanalytic context.

Abraham and Torok have returned to the Ferenczian notion of introjection, defined as "a mechanism which allows primitive auto-erotic interests to extend to the exterior world by absorbing into the ego the objects of the outside world," in order to oppose it to that of incorporation, which they qualify as "occult magic to recuperate the object of pleasure" (*L'Ecorce et le noyau*). According to Abraham and Torok, it is the notion of introjection and not that of incorporation which is of concern within the maladies of mourning, for the introjected object remains encrypted in the ego and is not dialecticized in its relation to the representations that it engenders. Consequently, the object does not give itself to be read within ordinary psychoanalytic work. In fact it is almost by accident that a psychoanalyst happens to bring a malady of mourning to light and to divine the existence of an encrypted object within the ego. Without putting into question the clinical good faith of Abraham and Torok, we might ultimately ask ourselves if the notion of introjection, as they conceive it, is an operative concept since an object encrypted within the ego should be by definition unreadable.

This brief summary claims neither to want to account for psychoanalytic discussions of the notions of incorporation and introjection, nor to take a stance on the question of the identity or difference between these two concepts. What I simply want to emphasize is that, if we accept the possibility of their being two distinct concepts, they differ precisely in their conditions of reading: if the incorporated object is always readable, the introjected object never is.

It is Derrida who deserves credit for having, in "Fors," radicalized the notion of crypt and marked the problems of reading that this notion poses. A crypt would be a fantasmatic, hermetically sealed space which surrounds and hides a corpse introjected by the ego. The status of the corpse is a peculiar one for we cannot say whether it is dead or alive. According to Derrida, the inhabitant of the crypt is always "a living dead, a dead entity we are perfectly willing to keep alive, but *as* dead, one we are willing to

keep, as long as we keep it, within us, intact in any way save as living." But
the fantasmatic space of the crypt is also a linguistic space. As such, it
encloses an occulted name through the elaboration of a cryptic code whose
function is to displace and to translate, by *misreading it,* every sign which
tries to penetrate it or to read the name that it hides: "Nothing there can
be perceptible or verbalizable from the first, through and through. Without
this general 'hieroglyphia,' we could never even understand the mere possibility that a crypt could take place."

Following Derrida, we might say that every attempt to unseal a crypt
and read the name of the living dead which it dissimulates can only reduce
the introjection to an incorporation, the crypt to a funerary monument, the
living dead corpse to a dead person, the name to a metaphor. Such a reading
then is itself only an effect of the crypt. In fact, Derrida compares the text
of Abraham and Torok to a "narrative, a novel, a poem, a myth, a drama,
the whole thing in a plural translation." ["Fors" was written as an introduction to N. Abraham and M. Torok's *The Wolf Man's Magic Word.*] In
other words, to propose a concept in order to read the proper name of an
encrypted corpse, a corpse which is properly attended by a certain literary
representation, would be equivalent to recreating a fantasmatic scenario of
the genesis of literature, as Flaubert has already left us to understand.

Let us return to Flaubert one last time. To try to read "Loulou Le
Poittevin" as the proper name of "Flaubert," to say that what is proper to
his name belongs to one or several names or introjected corpses is a necessary,
but ultimately derisory, critical enterprise. For if such is the case—and we
have every reason in the world to believe that this is in fact the case—it is
neither readable nor sayable.

Flaubert, "stuffed by funerals," vomits the names which in turn permit
him to retell their stories. However, the texts thus engendered always hide
from us their ultimate signatories. We can always read the signature "Flaubert" as being that of "Loulou Le Poittevin." But this deciphering, this
decrypting, this archaeological restoration is itself only the trace left by the
impossibility of a translation without remainder of that which a proper name
gives us to read of what properly belongs to a proper name.

The attempt to read a proper name always ends by problematizing the
proper name which serves us within our own signatures. I have chosen the
name "Flaubert," but what if in its place I had substituted mine or yours?
Can we ever know who signs our sayings or our writings? It is he who
writes, in the third person, his impossible autobiography: an autobiography
which, as Louis Marin has admirably shown, is always a thanatography.

PETER STARR

Science and Confusion: On Flaubert's Temptation

Flaubert spoke often in his letters of a desire to make criticism, literary style, and even politics "scientific." Recent critics have tended to assume that the meaning of Flaubert's "science" lies always elsewhere than in practices of the natural sciences as he and his contemporaries knew them. When Raymonde Debray-Genette writes, for example, "Flaubert n'emprunte véritablement à la science que l'idée d'une généralité probable," she implicitly subsumes science to an aesthetic category, to a "documentary *vraisemblable*" which justifies—or better *authorizes*—prior acts of the imagination ("Flaubert: science et écriture"). Likewise there has long been a tendency among readers of the *Bovary* to see in science a threatening but ridiculous discourse of power inscribed in the young Gustave's Oedipal conflict with his father, the doctor (Sartre, *The Family Idiot*).

Ultimately Flaubert's rhetoric of science must be brought to bear on the process of writing itself, if not also on the real-life vicissitudes that conditioned that process. But I will argue in this essay that only by *postponing* the subsumption to aesthetics or personal history, only by looking first at the nineteenth-century science behind Flaubert's rhetoric, can you see how Flaubert was at once tempted by science as an institution of power and drawn to confusion, the very negation of science and its ruses. My reading of the motley bustle that is *La Tentation de saint Antoine* will show how Flaubert actually wrote the contradictory temptations of science and confusion into

From *Modern Language Notes* 99, no. 5 (December 1984). © 1984 by The Johns Hopkins University Press, Baltimore/London.

the final, 1874 version of that text. And it will argue for the inevitability of the temptation of confusion, given the model of science to which Flaubert in his middle years actively subscribed.

This reading starts with chapter five, and with the march of the idols and gods which Antoine's one-time student, Hilarion, orchestrates as a demonstration of the ephemerality of religious belief. When a mourning Isis says of Osiris, torn to bits by the hideous Typhon: "We have found all his members. But I don't have the one that made me fertile,"

> ANTOINE est pris de fureur. Il lui jette des cailloux, en l'injuriant. "Impudique! va t'en, va t'en!"
> HILARION "Respecte-la! C'était la religion de tes aïeux! tu as porté ses amulettes dans ton berceau."

Antoine's immediate and violent denial of the phallus, and of the Egyptian cult of fertility for which it here stands, is presented as the denial of that which is heretical and "shameless" to the Christian mind. At the same time it is a denial of Antoine's personal history, intended as a synecdoche for the history of Christian belief as a whole. Hilarion's response is perfect. What he seems to see is that Antoine's surprisingly violent condemnation of Isis is not so much a reaction to an apparent shamelessness as an effort to put distance between himself and an unchristian belief which nonetheless belongs to his personal past; ethical rejection here masks the effort to purify the history of a belief.

Good Christian that he is, Antoine must qualify as monstrous or unnatural all pre-Christian beliefs, all idolatries. To him, the history of his belief is a history of revelations; revelations and history itself all originate in the truth of the divine intervention. Hilarion, on the other hand, has profited from the nineteenth century's continuing interest in comparative religion, historical anthropology and (as we shall see) natural history; he knows that Antoine's truth resembles—and probably originated in—so-called error:

> Tu retrouveras la Trinité dans les mystères de Samothrace, le baptême chez Isis, la rédemption chez Mithra, la martyre d'un dieu aux fêtes de Bacchus. Proserpine est la Vierge! . . . Aristée Jésus!

One would misunderstand the *Temptation* if one failed to see that Flaubert intended Hilarion's argument to be irrefutable. In the battle between historiography on the comparative model and a history based on myth and revelation, the former will always win. To Hilarion's brilliant display of erudition, Antoine can only give what appears as the stupidest of responses:

he says the Nicene Creed, "le symbole de Jérusalem . . .—en poussant à chaque phrase un long soupir."

SCIENCE

Consider the following two passages from the correspondence. The first dates from 1863, the second was written ten years earlier; yet one can read in the margin of both the future, final version of the *Saint Antoine:*

> L'histoire, l'histoire et l'histoire naturelle! Voilà les deux muses de l'âge moderne. C'est avec elles que l'on entrera dans des mondes nouveaux. Ne revenons pas au moyen age. *Observons,* tout est là. . . . Chaque religion et chaque philosophie a prétendu avoir Dieu à elle, toiser l'infini et connaître la recette du bonheur. Quel orgueil et quel néant!

> Qui est-ce qui, a jusqu'à présent, fait de l'histoire en naturaliste? A-t-on classé les instincts de l'humanité et vu comment, sous telle latitude, ils se sont développés et *doivent* se développer? Qui est-ce qui a établi scientifiquement comment, pour tel besoin de l'esprit, telle forme doit apparaître, et suivi cette forme partout, dans les divers règnes humains? Qui est-ce qui a généralisé les religions? Geoffroy Saint-Hilaire a dit: le crâne est une vertèbre aplatie. Qui est-ce qui a prouvé, par exemple, que la religion est une philosophie devenue art, et que la cervelle qui bat dedans, à savoir la superstition, le sentiment religieux en soi, est de même matière partout, malgré ses différences extérieures, correspond aux mêmes besoins, répond aux mêmes fibres, meurt par les mêmes accidents, etc.?

> (*Correspondance*)

Both the character of Hilarion and the comparative tactic by which he tries to overcome Antoine's faith in the uniqueness and necessity of Christianity are new to the 1874 text. My thesis here is that "Hilarion" stands in the final *Temptation* as a fictionalized answer to the question Flaubert had posed twenty-one years earlier, "Qui est-ce qui a généralisé les religions?" For this reason, I cannot help but think that the name "Hilarion"— particularly when applied to a character who explicitly doubles the protagonist-*saint*—was associated in Flaubert's mind with the name "Geoffroy Saint-Hilaire," on the model of whose work he had conceived the project of generalizing the religions in the first place. I do not, however, intend to use

the correspondence, and its mentions of a specific natural historian, as a key
to the "truth" of the literary work, as if the *Temptation* were a *roman à
clef* and the character of Hilarion a thinly veiled Geoffroy Saint-Hilaire. My
purpose is rather to let the letters and novel/drama read each other. I hope
to show that the text of the final *Temptation* glosses the earlier letters as
thoroughly and convincingly as the letters themselves gloss that text.

In considering the exemplarity of natural history as one of the "muses
to the modern age," let us start with the principle of the "unity of organic
composition" (or more precisely, the "theory of analogues") for which
Etienne Geoffroy Saint-Hilaire was best known and to which Flaubert's letter
of July 7–8, 1853 implicitly refers. In his *Philosophie anatomique* Geoffroy
presented that principle in this way:

> La nature emploie constamment les mêmes matériaux et n'est
> ingénieuse qu'à en varier les formes. [Cf. Flaubert's "le sentiment
> religieux en soi est de même matière partout, malgré ses diffé-
> rences extérieures. . . ."] Comme si, en effet, elle était soumise à
> de premières données on la voit tendre toujours à faire reparaître
> les mêmes éléments en même nombre, dans les mêmes circon-
> stances et avec les mêmes connexions.

Unlike Cuvier who distinguished four "principal forms" of animal life (*animaux vertébrés, animaux mollusques, animaux articulés, animaux rayon-
nés*), Geoffroy Saint-Hilaire propounded a single "general plan" for all the
animals. To this end he published articles, for example, comparing the op-
ercular series of the fishes to the ossicles of the middle ear in the terrestrial
vertebrates or arguing that insects "live within their spinal columns as mollusks live within their shells." In the course of his celebrated debate with
Cuvier in February and March of 1830, Geoffroy conceded that the expression "the unity of composition" could better be rendered as "the unity of
the system in the composition and arrangement of the organic parts"; by
"the unity of the system" he means the unity of nature itself such as the
anatomist can deduce it. Geoffroy posited a law of "organic balance"
whereby the hypertrophy and atrophy of an organ in a given region of an
organism would necessarily lead to the atrophy or hypertrophy respectively
of other organs in that same region. This law of "organic balance," together
with the idea that a species' circumstances account for the hypertrophy or
atrophy of given organs, allowed him to account for the fact of difference
while still attempting to reproduce,

comme un fait acquis *a posteriori,* l'idée *a priori,* l'idée-mère et fondamentale de la philosophie de Leibnitz; l'idée que ce vaste génie renfermait dans cette expression, la variété dans l'unité.

(Philosophie anatomique)

It would be quite impossible to perceive such a unity of the system of nature without recourse to a process of comparison that sought to reduce the apparent diversity of natural phenomena to a more fundamental sameness. You may recall that the first explicit comparison between religions in chapter five comes from Antoine himself: "—et cela [the Barbarian idols] n'est pas plus criminel que la religion des Grecs, des Asiatiques et des Romains!" For Antoine, error is error and no one error is more criminal than another; to say that one non-Christian belief is closer to the truth than another is to admit that the truth can be shared and that Christianity itself is not absolute. Hilarion of course rejects the distinction between truth and error but he maintains the logic of the formula by which the Christian relativizes the other: religious sentiment is religious sentiment and no one practice is more criminal than another. His first interventions in the march of the gods serve purely to make this point:

Mais les dieux réclament toujours des supplices. Le tien même a voulu . . .

Pourquoi fais-tu des exorcismes?

Père, Fils et Saint Esprit ne font de même qu'une seule personne!

When Hilarion murmurs lines of Scripture as a running commentary to the Buddha's life-story, he enacts the style of reading that the *défilé* demands; from inside the text he creates that text's proper interpretation. Thus, as the march continues, the function of comparison can become more implicit and more beholden to information given directly by the gods (e.g., Ormuz saying of his cult, "On se purifiait avec de l'eau, on s'offrait des pains sur les autels, on confessait à haute voix ses crimes") or by the curiously narrativized stage directions which Jeanne Bem has called the counter-text (the Buddha's "halo"; "Antoine songe à la mère de Jésus") (*Désir et savoir dans l'oeuvre de Flaubert*). Comparison becomes, as it were, embedded in the very fabric of the text.

To this point, however, there appears no reason to privilege the comparative gestures of natural history over those of comparative religion or mythology. Why then was the project of generalizing the religions associated with the anatomical work of Geoffroy Saint-Hilaire and not with the historical relativism, say, of Quinet's *Le Génie des religions*?

It was Balzac's "Avant-propos à *La Comédie humaine*" which, in 1842, definitively introduced the theories of Geoffroy Saint-Hilaire to the world of French letters. After presenting the theory of the unity of composition and singing the praises of Geoffroy Saint-Hilaire, Balzac writes:

> Pénétré de ce système bien avant les débats auxquels il a donné lieu, je vis que, sous ce rapport, la Société ressemblait à la Nature. La Société ne fait-elle pas de l'homme, suivant les milieux où son action se déploie, autant d'hommes différents qu'il y a de variétés en zoologie? . . . Il a donc existé, il existera donc de tout temps des Espèces Sociales comme il y a des Espèces Zoologiques.

At the risk of schematizing a complex essay, we may say that Geoffroy's "unity of composition" allows Balzac to treat society as a totality, as a unified system on the order of nature, and that the idea of the Social Species lets him claim for literature an ease of representation long accorded to the natural historian on the basis of the recognizable, structural distinction between one species and the next. Balzac wants to write the one work about the one society that is Restoration France; he wants to paint "le tableau de la Société, *moulée,* pour ainsi dire, sur le vif "; the writer's task is that of "*copying* all Society" ("Avant-propos à *La Comédie humaine*").

In his pronouncements on the exemplarity of natural history, the young Flaubert clearly shared Balzac's interest and faith in the possibility of representing in language phenomena of the seemingly extra-linguistic world. When he says (in a passage we shall consider shortly), "Il faut faire de la critique comme on fait de l'histoire naturelle, *avec absence d'idée morale,*" Flaubert assumes that the process of representation is not inherently problematic, even though particular representations may be tainted by the "moral idea." Even as late as 1863, at a time when his novelistic practice increasingly questions the delimited unity of the object-in-the-world upon which classical representation depended, Flaubert still conceives of natural history as a domain of pure, untainted representation. Thus the injunction, "*Observons, tout est là,*" is a call above all to a certain kind of writing, that same *writing with one's impartial eye* that had made natural history a "muse to the modern age."

From the beginning, however, Flaubert's claims for the impartiality of natural history give as much the impression of a will to believe as that of real conviction. Consider what follows the "absence of the moral idea" claim in his letter to Louise Colet of October 12, 1853:

> Il faut faire de la critique [Flaubert has in mind his project for a

Histoire du sentiment poétique en France] comme on fait de l'histoire naturelle, *avec absence d'idée morale.* Il ne s'agit pas de déclamer sur telle ou telle forme, mais bien d'exposer en quoi elle consiste, comment elle se rattache à une autre et *par quoi* elle vit (l'esthétique attend son Geoffroy Saint-Hilaire, ce grand homme qui a montré la légitimité des monstres). Quand on aura, pendant quelque temps, traité l'âme humaine avec l'impartialité que l'on met dans les sciences physiques à étudier la matière, on aura fait un pas immense. . . . Eh bien, je crois cela faisable. C'est peut-être, comme pour les mathématiques, rien qu'une *méthode* à trouver. Elle sera applicable avant tout à l'Art et à la Religion, ces deux grandes manifestations de l'idée.

That Flaubert was not wholly comfortable with his claim of exemplary impartiality for natural history is clear from his recourse here to the "physical sciences" which study "matter," and later to mathematics, as the ultimate methodological examples. Natural history as it is presently done ("comme on fait de l'histoire naturelle") must serve as the model for a new historical criticism because natural history has a *method* of representation; it eschews judgments of value in favor of "impartial" description, contextualization and functional explanation. Yet behind this model there are—inevitably it would seem—the models of the more justifiably "impartial" physical and mathematical sciences. What the Flaubert of 1853 perhaps already knows, but seeks to deny in deference to a certain will to believe ("Eh bien, je crois cela faisable"), is that the writing of history as a causally linked series of events is an invitation to be partial, and that the best of geological histories—to take an example from *Bouvard et Pécuchet*—can easily turn into "une féerie en plusieurs actes, ayant l'homme pour apothéose." Interestingly enough, this particular history is signed "Cuvier."

Let us bracket for a moment Flaubert's will to believe in the impartiality of the methods of natural history in favor of a closer look at the particular method which proved the "legitimacy of monsters." Etienne Geoffroy Saint-Hilaire and his son Isodore were not the first, as Flaubert implies, to have shunned the moralizing rejection of the monstrous for the sake of a scientific study of the monster's place in a natural order. Nor were they first to suggest that monstrosities resulted from abnormalities in the process of embryonic differentiation. What the Geoffroy Saint-Hilaires did was to demonstrate that the monstrous organism grows according to the same complex but regular developmental system as its normal counterpart. In other words, starting from the assumption that accidents of development such as improper

adhesions of the embryo to the placental wall or abnormal deliveries of blood
to specific regions of the organism lay at the heart of the problem of mon-
strosity, they went on to devise experiments showing that the monstrous
growth was a regular and natural response to an initial accident. The Geoffroy Saint-Hilaires could therefore reintegrate the monstrous organ into the
system of nature by knowing three things: 1) "what it consists of " (i.e., the
organ's present state as visible to the examining eye); 2) "how it is attached
to another" (what connections or relationships of balancing it maintains with
other organs); and 3) "how and by what it lives" (what nourishes it and for
what function).

Hilarion, it is true, gives no explanations as to why given practices
develop necessarily in given circumstances (under certain "climates," given
certain "needs of the spirit"). But he does legitimate the monstrous belief
by showing that what seems unnatural to Antoine belongs in fact to a natural
system with its own profound unity. He does to Antoine's belief in the
godlessness of idolatry exactly what Geoffroy implicitly does to the traditional Christian belief that monsters are "créations sans Dieu" (Chateau-
briand). He neither divinizes nor rejects the monstrous; he naturalizes it. For
understanding alone mitigates the scandal of the "criminal form":

> Rappelle-toi dans l'Ecriture toutes les choses qui te scandalisent,
> parce que tu ne sais pas les comprendre. De même, ces dieux,
> sous leurs formes criminelles, peuvent contenir la vérité.

At the same time, Hilarion shows that the apparently natural beliefs of Christianity carry still within them the unnatural idolatries from which they
sprung. From the "scientific" point of view, therefore, it makes no sense to
speak of the naturalness or unnaturalness of specific practices. All historical
phenomena are in themselves mixed, heteroclite, even monstrous. Nature
resides in the system as a whole. It is not the phenomenal world either wholly
or in part. Rather, like the religious sentiment in itself, nature stands above
the obvious diversity of phenomena as a creation of a scientific intelligence
which in the pursuit of impartiality effectively validates its will to power.

Notice in passing that science's greatest ruse is also its most stringent
demand. The pursuit of a scientific impartiality can satisfy an individual's
will to power only so long as that will to power never in fact announces
itself as such. At the end of the défilé, though, the very figure of Science
reveals its will to power for all to see:

> Et Hilarion est devant lui, mais transfiguré, beau comme un ar-

change, lumineux comme un soleil,—et tellement grand, que pour
le voir ANTOINE se renverse la tête. "Qui donc est-tu?"
HILARION "Mon royaume est de la dimension de l'univers, et
    mon désir n'a pas de bornes. Je vais toujours, affranchissant
    l'esprit et pesant les mondes, sans haine, sans peur, sans pitié,
    sans amour, et sans Dieu. On m'appelle la Science."
ANTOINE se rejette en arrière. "Tu dois être plutôt . . . le
    Diable!"
HILARION en fixant sur lui ses prunelles. "Veux-tu le voir?"
ANTOINE . . . "L'horreur que j'en ai m'en débarrassera pour
    toujours.—Oui!"
Un pied fourchu se montre.
Antoine a regret.
Mias le Diable l'a jeté sur ses cornes, et l'enlève.

CONFUSION

Hilarion names himself Science at the moment of his triumph over the
last of the gods, "le Seigneur Dieu"; he is "beautiful as an archangel, luminous as the sun." But the eminent sublimity of this victory is undercut by
the fact that, at the moment of his transfiguration, the moment of his *naming*,
he takes on a divine and absolute character, a character precisely equivalent
to those which all his previous statements and demonstrations had sought
to relativize. In other words, Hilarion victorious becomes immediately subject to scrutiny on the basis of those principles that had assured his victory
in the first place. They are: 1) that no one system of belief has an absolute
monopoly on truth to the exclusion of other systems; 2) that all absolutisms,
like all organic objects in a vitalist universe, are subject to an exhaustion
(*épuisement*) inherent in the notion of life itself; and 3) that the true discourse never contradicts itself. We have examined already the first of these
principles; the pages that follow consider the second and third.
    Prior to Virchow's elaboration in the late 1850s of a cellular theory of
reproduction and growth, so-called vitalist biology explained animal procreation by hypothesizing a process whereby brute matter was imbued with
mysterious "vital principles." As a result of that hypothesis, vitalists concerned themselves first and foremost with the fate of individual organisms
as manifestations of the "vital properties," and especially with the struggle
against death that characterizes the particular life. "If life is a matter of
death," wrote Cabanis in 1830, "death in turn gives birth to and immor-
talizes life." In other words, those this time of François Jacob, "if the vital

properties are worn down in each individual being, they are conserved throughout the living world" (*La Logique du vivant*). For the vitalist then, the life and death of particular organisms functioned dialectically to assure the continuity of Life as an attribute of the system as a whole.

In the final version of the *Temptation*, and in that version alone, Death and Lust take each other by the waist and sing a hymn to the vitalist dialectic:

> —Je hâte la dissolution de la matière!
> —Je facilite l'éparpillement des germes!
> —Tu détruis, pour mes renouvellements!
> —Tu engendres, pour mes destructions!
> —Active ma puissance!
> —Féconde ma pourriture! . . .
> ANTOINE "Ainsi la mort n'est qu'une illusion, un voile, mas-
> quant par endroits la continuité de la vie."

Just such a dialectic of life and death lies at the heart of the march of the gods. Like natural historians watching the generation and dissolution of living beings, Hilarion, Antoine and we as readers consider a sequence of religious beliefs and practices caught in the ebb and flow of vital properties. Just as the vitalist dialectic assures the continuity of Life itself, so too do the successive destructions of individual expressions of the religious senti-ment serve to demonstrate the unity and continuity of that sentiment in itself. Several pages into the march, Hilarion explains the multiple aspects and rapid transformations of the Indian gods by saying, "la vie s'épuise, les formes s'usent, et il leur faut progresser dans les métamorphoses." It is difficult to read the *Temptation* without reading "la vie s'épuise, les formes s'usent" as an explanation *en abyme* for the dissolution which overtakes all the gods the fiction presents, and which is explicitly thematized as dissolution in the case of the Latin gods (e.g., Apollo). It is equally difficult to imagine that "Science" later might be exempt from that very process of exhaustion it here proves to be inherent in the assumption of religious power.

As if to underscore science's new-found status as religion, Flaubert shows its spokesman in chapter six succumbing to the "pride and nothing-ness"—elsewhere reserved for "religion" and "philosophy"—of "claiming to have God to itself, to measure the infinite and to know the recipe for happiness." The chapter begins with the Devil whisking Antoine away and up into the skies. Freed of weight and suffering, Antoine learns—or re-learns—the secrets of the Newtonian cosmos:

> LE DIABLE l'emporte au milieu des étoiles. "Elles s'attirent en

même temps qu'elles se repoussent. L'action de chacune résulte des autres et y contribue,—sans le moyen d'un auxiliaire, par la force d'une loi, la seule vertu de l'ordre."

But Antoine suddenly lowers his gaze and asks, "Quel est le but de tout cela?" The Devil answers, "Il n'y a pas de but! Comment Dieu aurait-il un but? Quelle expérience a pu l'instruire, quelle réflexion le déterminer?"

By using the denial of finality as a simple point of transition between Newtonian physics and a bastardized version of Spinozist metaphysics, the Devil sets up the first of many contradictions which will riddle his *discours savant.* In classical, mechanist physics, "il n'y a pas de but" denotes the workings of nature as a closed system of inviolable laws; nature's order is the creation of a hypothetical Prime Mover who retired from the field once the initial act of creation was accomplished. Spinoza of course denies the God/nature dualism upon which this mechanist scenario is predicated. "God" and "Nature" are simply two names for the same infinite substance, the *natura naturans;* God is thus the world's immanent and perpetual cause, not just its transient first cause. Or, as the Devil himself says of God: "puisqu'il existe éternellement, il agit éternellement." In other words, the God of the Spinozist Devil is an "auxiliary force" such as the Newtonian Devil had denied on the previous page.

At the end of the chapter the Devil changes his tune again, denying philosophic access to the thing in itself:

> Mais les choses ne t'arrivent que par l'intermédiaire de ton esprit.
> Tel qu'un miroir concave il déforme les objets;—et tout moyen
> te manque pour en vérifier l'exactitude.

What follows is a syllogistic hodge-podge of Cartesian doubt, Heraclitian flux and Renanian relativism whose conclusion—"Peut-être qui'il n'y a rien"—evidently contradicts the Spinozist Devil's certainty that "le néant n'est pas! le vide n'est pas!"

We must not here denigrate contradiction per se. Indeed to contradict oneself was for Flaubert the prerogative both of God and of the rare artistic genius who, as if "penetrated" by the objective world, was able to reflect that world in all of its multiplicity. Contradiction was the sine qua non of Flaubert's political pronouncements, the cornerstone of an aesthetics based on "contradictory ideals" and the "harmony of disparate things," and a dominant strategy of his humor (*Corr.*) Still the Devil is undone by his contradictions because earlier, as Hilarion, he had cited the contradictions of Christian Scripture as proof of its fallibility:

> Cependant l'Ange annonciateur, dans Matthieu, apparaît à Jo-
> seph, tandis que, dans Luc, c'est à Marie. L'onction de Jésus par
> une femme se passe, d'après le premier Evangile, au commence-
> ment de sa vie publique, et, selon les trois autres, peu de jours
> avant sa mort [etc.].

In short, the Devil's discourse *repeats* the Book. "Science" in the *Temptation* is not stupid because contradictory; it is stupid only by dint of its pretense to absolute power over a doctrine it in fact doubles. And thus "Science" foreshadows its own dissolution by proving itself just one more religious belief subject to the vitalist dialectic and its twilight of the gods.

CONNAISSANCE

From the moment at the end of chapter three when Hilarion offers to lead Antoine to a land where wise men live beneath gigantic trees, nourished by a "warm air," the temptation of knowledge appears preeminent among the temptations. "Tu les écouteras," Hilarion promises, "et la face de l'Inconnu se dévoilera." No one figure in the *Temptation* better incarnates the temptation of *connaissance,* in all of that word's senses, than Apollonius of Tyana. Antoine himself resumes the attraction of this half sage and magician, half tour guide and pimp when he says, "Sa manière de parler des dieux inspire l'envie de les connaître," and thereby sets into motion the march of the idols and gods. One offer of acquaintance particularly troubles Antoine, and particularly exemplifies the ambivalence of Apollonian *connaissance:*

> APOLLONIUS "Quel est ton désir? ton rêve? Le temps seulement
>   d'y songer. . . ."
> ANTOINE "Jésus, Jésus, à mon aide!"
> APOLLONIUS "Veux-tu que je le fasse apparaître, Jésus?"
> ANTOINE "Quoi? Comment?"
> APOLLONIUS "Ce sera lui! pas un autre! Il jettera sa couronne,
>   et nous causerons face à face!"

The reference is naturally to Paul's first Letter to the Corinthians:

> A présent nous voyons confusément dans un miroir, mais nous
> verrons alors face à face. A présent, partielle est ma science, mais
> je connaîtrai alors comme je suis connu.   (13:12)

Apollonius wreaks havoc with the subtle metaphorics of the biblical text. An image that in Paul stands for the perfect coincidence of knowledge and acquaintance ("face à face") becomes for Apollonius the mark of familiarity and a certain submission. If Christian history is a voyage with Christ to the perfect knowledge of Christ and the Father, the Christ-like magician can offer that voyage too, albeit in the most absolute spirit of parody. Not the end of history, the appearance of Jesus here would have been just one adventure among others, the diversion of a moment which quickly passes. For Apollonius, the voyage to knowledge is nothing more than a series of fantastic *acquaintances,* a project of exotic adventure endlessly rejuvenated for the pleasure of the voyage itself, and for the fundamentally equivalent pleasure of the narration:

> Nous avons rencontré, sur le bord de la mer, les Cynocéphales gorgés de lait, qui s'en revenaient de leur expédition dans l'île Taprobane. . . . La terre, à la fin, se fit plus étroite qu'une sandale;—et après avoir jeté vers le soleil des gouttes de l'Océan, nous tournâmes à droite, pour revenir.
>
> Et maintenant nous recommençons le pèlerinage!

The Devil of chapter six succeeds where Apollonius had failed. He guides Antoine on a voyage of knowledge through a marvellous universe, but he does so as heir to a conception of knowledge as acquaintance that dates from the intervention of the Quixotic sage. Blithely assuming a perfect analogy between books and the world, the Devil reads and represents physical and metaphysical systems as Apollonius read and represented the fantastic phenomena he had seen on his travels. What the Devil doesn't see, or doesn't *wish* to see, is that philosophical discourse is subject to a principle of non-contradiction foreign to the travelogue. This blindness makes him as ridiculous in his high seriousness as Apollonius, that prophet of the eternal return, was serious in his ridiculousness.

If Hilarion's comparative tactics are more subtle than the tactics of Apollonius and the Devil, they are nonetheless based on a similar, anti-theological and decidedly anti-mystical notion of knowledge as acquaintance. Once again a text of Geoffroy Saint-Hilaire helps to render explicit a conception that Hilarion's reticence must leave implicit. In his *Fragment sur la nature* of 1829, Geoffroy presents the following account of the origin of human knowledge:

> Mais enfin, appliqué à *connaître* et soi-même et ce qui existe autour de lui, [l'homme] en vint à s'établir *en maître* au sein de la création. Car bientôt on le vit concevant et poursuivant l'au-

> dacieuse entreprise de *prendre une à une toute chose créée;* de
> façon que ce qui forme l'avoir et les richesses de la nature, il *se
> les soumit,* il les *enregistra,* il les *inventoria* en quelque sorte,
> comme s'il se les donnait à titre de pièces de son mobilier.

For Geoffroy the acquisition of knowledge is a process composed of three
stages, the first two of which—the consideration "one by one of all created
things" and the establishment of records and inventories—he evokes here.
In the third and final stage one "arrives at a deduction, a general idea which
includes and explains (observed) coincidences"; by an effort of "intellectual
reduction" one discovers the "general laws of nature." The essay mentions
two such laws: Kepler's law of universal gravitation and Geoffroy's own
principle of the unity of organic composition.

Knowledge for Geoffroy Saint-Hilaire is the appropriation and domestication of one's self and one's circumstances; the world is mastered when
it is shown to be saturated with analogy, and this on two levels. Above and
beyond the play of similarity and difference which allowed for the inventory,
for the establishment (in the best Linnaean tradition) of a "tableau de tous
les faits de l'univers," Geoffroy perceived "philosophic resemblances"; organisms that were marked by the sign of difference on the level of classification—vertebrates and mollusks, for example—could be shown analogous
by the intellectual effort of a "philosophical anatomy" capable of distinguishing an underlying uniformity of organization. I have shown how the Hilarion
of the *défilé* manipulates a comparable notion of the uniformity of religious
sentiment, originally suggested to him by Antoine himself. At the same time
it is Hilarion who appears most responsible, within the diegesis, for the
work of classification that characterizes those chapters in which he plays a
specifically demonstrative role. Thus he is responsible for introducing Antoine first to problems of biblical exegesis, then to the heresies, and finally
to the "false" gods (in chapters three, four, and five respectively). Hilarion
should also be credited, in his capacity as knowing guide to the chaos of
Antoine's phantasms, with the implicit order perceptible within certain of
these chapters. The heresies of chapter four, for example, appear in topical
groups treating the dualism of matter and spirit, devotions and mortification,
the problem of evil and its origin, the humanity or divinity of Christ, per-
secution, and so on.

In another of his midnight letters to Louise Colet Flaubert wrote:

> Il faudrait tout connaître pour écrire. . . . Les livres d'où ont
> découlé les littératures entières, comme Homére, Rabelais, sont

des encyclopédies de leur époque. Ils savaient tout, ces bonnes
gens-là; et nous, nous ne savons rien.

La Tentation de saint Antoine is both encyclopedia and anti-encyclopedia.
It continues in the long tradition of encyclopedic narratives from the Bible,
Cervantes and Rabelais to Buffon and Goethe, borrowing heavily from each
of these; yet it deconstructs the mechanism for the transfer of knowledge
upon which the encyclopedia is predicated. When Hilarion organizes the
panoply of human superstitions along thematic lines he carries out an essentially encyclopedic task. As the book progresses, however, such implicit structure gives way more and more to an anarchic comprehensiveness that makes
the gesture of being encyclopedic without really fulfilling the predicative
conditions for the appropriation of knowledge. Such empty gestures of predication are particularly noticeable in the book's final chapters. When in one
such list, for example, the text tells us that a "Mirag" is a "hornèd hare
that inhabits the isles of the sea," it strictly speaking fulfills the promise of
predication but without rendering the proper name perceptibly less strange
and thus less resistent to assimilation into the field of the reader's knowledge;
it does not *tame* the hornèd hare.

Knowledge, according to Geoffroy, is like furniture; it clearly belongs
to you only when every piece of it has been recorded and inventoried. The
lists that fill the *Temptation*'s final chapters play on this reassuring function
of the inventory yet—with the possible exception of the classically emblematic list of the Olympians—all tend to be as unappropriable as the objects
they contain, as resistent to domestication as "alligators on roe-deer feet,
owls with snakes' tails, pigs with a tiger's snout," etc. If on the one hand
the plot of the *Temptation* charts a path of knowledge and science from the
first century to Flaubert's day, from exegetical disputes through Newtonian
physics to the cellular theory which informs the book's final pages, on the
other hand it enacts a progressive disintegration of the possibility of knowledge's formation and transfer; Science's apparent victory is nearly contemporaneous with the noise of the lists and the indifferentiation of monsters
in the book's final pages. As the earliest incarnation of "Science," Hilarion
represents both the second and third stages of knowledge in Geoffroy's
scheme; he creates orders of identity and difference and still masters the
"philosophic resemblance." His method is silent but efficient. The Devil
follows Hilarion in the time of the diegesis, yet marks a curious regression
to Geoffroy's first stage; he takes cosmologies and epistemologies "one by
one," establishes analogies between them which allow him to fill the silence
of the heavens with a discourse that is explicitly (but inefficiently) scientific.

He cannot see "philosophic resemblances" for his science has not passed through the stage of the inventory; because he cannot yet see difference (between Newton and Spinoza, for example), he cannot perceive the "philosophic resemblances" which may surmount it. His analogies are the simple, uncritical analogies of Geoffroy's primitive antiquarian. Rather than demonstrating that the philosophic sentiment is "of the same stuff everywhere" by observing philosophies from a critical distance, the Devil unwittingly parodies such a demonstration by enacting the indifferentiation of philosophies. Bouvard and Pécuchet themselves are never more stupid. Or rather, they are never more enamored of the notion that knowledge is a matter of acquaintance, and as such can lead nowhere, can serve no purpose except to generate text.

The monster that is Flaubert's final novel exists already preformed in the germ of the Devil's discourse. What other passage of the *Temptation* better argues that writing is simply a processing or transposition (nearly a *copying*) of the already written? what other seems better to illustrate *Bouvard*'s hypothetical subtitle, "Du défaut de méthode dans les sciences"? In short, who but the Devil could have written *Bouvard et Pécuchet?*

DESIRE

You will recall that, at the moment he comes into his inheritance, Frédéric Moreau faces a crucial choice. Should he buy stock, and thereby accede to the power of that network of capital—epitomized by M. Dambreuse—which quietly but effectively subtends *L'Education sentimentale?* Or should he follow his inclination and buy furniture?

Read in conjunction with Geoffroy Saint-Hilaire's theory of knowledge, the *Temptation* implies that a similar choice lies on the route to cognitive power. You can strive for science, for a strategy of control masked by its fundamental reticence to say that it controls. Or you can, as it were, get stuck as a primitive antiquarian of uninventoried knowledge; you can remain in Geoffroy's first stage. Supposing one might willingly pass through that first stage, what might be the overriding appeal of undifferentiated *connaissance?* Why would the Devil, or Antoine, *choose* confusion?

In the aftermath of the dance of Death and Lust, Antoine exclaims:

Ainsi la mort n'est qu'une illusion, un voile, masquant par endroits la continuité de la vie.

Mais la Substance étant unique, pourquoi les Formes sont-elles variées?

> Il doit y avoir, quelque part, des figures primordiales, dont les
> corps ne sont que les images. Si on pouvait les voir on connaîtrait
> le lien de la matière et de la pensée, en quoi l'Etre consiste!

He goes on to say that he has seen such "primordial figures" painted on the
wall of the temple of Bélus in Babylon, that those who cross the desert
encounter animals beyond description. . . . The Sphinx and Chimera then
surge into view. But Antoine has made a phantasmatic mistake; these "primordial figures" are not those which can help explain why the Forms of a
unique Substance are varied, nor in what Being itself consists. The Sphinx
and Chimera episode is interesting as spectacle, but it is of little consequence
in the process of temptation.

Flaubert once wrote to Edmond de Goncourt that Antoine's "final defeat" was due to the "scientific cell." The scene is uncanny; Antoine participates in a fantastic journey back through time where plants and animals
start to resemble humans and the products of human artifice:

> Et puis les plantes se confondent avec les pierres.
> Des cailloux ressemblent à des cerveaux, des stalactites à des
> mamelles, des fleurs de fer à des tapisseries ornées de figures.

"At the end," as a marginal note from Flaubert's scenarios for the *Temptation* tells us, Antoine

> est trop loin, dans un pays abstrait, ayant regardé tout, n'ayant
> plus nulle conscience de lui-même, et n'étant *qu'une machine à
> regarder, une contemplation vivante.* . . . Il ne sait pas distinguer
> les Ordres de la Nature.
> ("Scénarios de *La Tentation de saint Antoine*")

Antoine has been witness to all creation; he has quite literally *become* the
Impartial Eye. In fact, his status as an observer appears so plainly "scientific"
that critics have been known to ask whether, in the passage that follows,
Antoine might not be looking through a microscope:

> Il se couche à plat ventre, s'appuie sur les deux coudes; et retenant
> son haleine, il regarde.
> Des insectes n'ayant plus d'estomac continuent à manger; des
> fougères desséchées se remettent à fleurir; des membres qui man-
> quaient repoussent.
> Enfin, il aperçoit de petites masses globuleuses, grosses comme
> des têtes d'épingles et garnies de cils tout autour. Une vibration
> les agite.

ANTOINE délirant: "O bonheur! bonheur! j'ai vu naître la vie,
j'ai vu le mouvement commencer. Le sang de mes veines bat si
fort qu'il va les rompre. J'ai envie de voler, de nager, d'aboyer,
de beugler, de hurler. Je voudrais avoir des ailes, une carapace,
une écorce, souffler de la fumée, porter une trompe, tordre
mon corps, me diviser partout, être en tout, m'émaner avec les
odeurs, me développer comme les plantes, couler comme l'eau,
vibrer comme le son, briller comme la lumière, me blottir sur
toutes les formes, pénétrer chaque atome, descendre jusq'au
fond de la matière,—être la matière!"

There are countless ways for a reader to feel uncomfortable about this
scene, many of them no doubt intended by Flaubert himself. To minds attuned to the idea of scientific progress, the contemporaneity of the represented science—cellular theory dates from the late 1830s; Haeckel's theories
of creation, upon which Flaubert particularly draws, appeared in 1867—
would have coincided disturbingly with the breakdown of the promise of
predication upon which the transfer of knowledge depends. But the mythic
journey back to the origin clearly fulfills Antoine's search for "[ce] en quoi
l'Etre consiste" since he reads the material cell in terms traditionally reserved
for the soul, or for God: "Je voudrais . . . me diviser partout, être en tout,
m'émaner avec les odeurs [etc.]." A new Spinoza, he has found "the link
between matter and thought." It is tempting to claim that Antoine's plunge
to the origin also dramatizes a presupposition of all unity-of-plan theories,
viz. the possibility of *speculatively* reconstructing an original moment when
the unique Substance appeared indeed unique, a moment prior to the development of the so-called various Forms. Of Geoffroy Saint-Hilaire, Cuvier
once wrote:

Il y a derrière cette théorie des analogies une autre fort ancienne
réfutée depuis toujours mais que quelques Allemands ont repro-
duite au profit du système panthéiste appelé philosophie da la
nature, celle de la production de toutes les espèces par le déve-
loppement successif de germes *primitivement identiques entre
eux.*
(Report of April 5, 1830; in Théophile Cahn's *La Vie et
l'œuvre d'Etienne Geoffroy Saint-Hilaire*)

But in the *Temptation*'s return to a hypothetical primitive state, everything
seems naturally to resemble everything else. Such a primitive metaphoricity
is in fact the death of metaphor as a willed *rapprochement* of fundamentally

different entities, as the perception of "philosophic resemblances." Antoine takes joy therefore in becoming the Impartial Eye precisely because the indifferentiation of what he sees *precludes* the possibility of a scientific inventory on the basis of similarity and difference. At the origin, the text suggests, willed analogy and the indifferentiation of phenomena are necessarily one and the same:

> Délire d'Antoine qui découvre *ce rapprochement ou plutôt cette confusion,* car, à la fin, on ne distingue plus.
>
> ("Scénarios")

Antoine yields to a frenzied joy when circumstances force him to abdicate his judgment. Or in other words, he becomes a scientist on the model of Geoffroy Saint-Hilaire (the Impartial Eye) just as science on that same model becomes impossible.

In this final scene the temptation of knowledge itself goes marvellously awry. Antoine's wanting to become the cell is indicative of a desire for maximum *connaissance* that paradoxically kills the desire for *connaissance* in the stupidity of pure being. Not only does he want to know all, be acquainted with every remote corner of the material world, he wants to *be* all materiality ("me blottir sur toutes les formes, pénétrer chaque atome"); he wants therefore to die to his own desire. Christ's superbly anti-climactic appearance in the book's final paragraphs constitutes for Antoine no real acquaintance in the Christian sense; His appearance is no milestone of history. But it does reestablish the desire for knowledge *as desire:*

> Le jour enfin paraît; et comme les rideaux d'un tabernacle qu'on relève, des nuages d'or en s'enroulant à larges volutes découvrent le ciel.
>
> Tout au milieu, et dans le disque même du soleil rayonne la face de Jésus-Christ.
>
> Antoine fait le signe de la croix et se remet en prières.

Antoine returns to the same endless cycle of chores, prayers and temptations with which the book began. Perhaps he has learned nothing. But we as readers at least have seen that what matters in temptation is not whether one resists or succumbs—Antoine in fact repeatedly gives in to his temptations, only to be saved by an act of grace. What matters in temptation is that the structure of temptation itself be preserved, that desire itself persist.

We have examined a series of specific additions to the third and final version of *La Tentation de saint Antoine* which allow that version to enact the consolidation and disintegration of the power of a scientific method.

Those additions include: Hilarion and his comparative tactic, the vitalist dialectic, "Science's" transfiguration, and the spectacle of cells. The letters tell us that the Flaubert of 1869–1872 was disillusioned with the anti-aesthetic tendencies of French positivism and disgusted, even nauseated, by the bellicose behavior of the Prussian "savants." But above all, I would argue, the disintegration of science enacted in the 1874 *Temptation* stands as an implicit recognition that the appeal of what Flaubert in 1853 called "a method to be found" was precisely that it was too Promethean, too ideal, and never would be found. By their every action Bouvard and Pécuchet show that the truth of science is a will to believe in it, a resolve to say with Flaubert, "Eh bien je crois cela faisable," and that the lack of an infallible method is actually a precondition of that truth. But Hilarion already implies as much. For while proving that there is no singular truth, Hilarion admits: "Nous n'avons de mérite que par notre soif du vrai." As a quest for truth and method, science must fail in the *Temptation* because science, truth and method are all unreachable desiderata. And as Flaubert himself wrote, "le désir fait vivre" (November 10, 1877; *Corr.*)

LAWRENCE ROTHFIELD

From Semiotic to Discursive Intertextuality: *The Case of* Madame Bovary

Over the past twenty-odd years, semiotics has established itself as a powerful, rigorous and at times elegant technique for the close reading of literary
texts. Until recently, of course, the semiotic undertaking tended to remain
within the text itself, leaving the issue of the relation between literature and
society to more traditional kinds of criticism—whether of the liberal or
Marxist kind. In the last several years, however, semiotics has begun to make
some tentative moves towards coming to grips with the social contextuality
of literature. On the one hand, some Marxist academics have attempted to
use semiotics to support a critique of ideology; Fredric Jameson's *The Political Unconscious* is the most interesting and successful example of this. On
the other hand, there has been a movement from within semiotics itself to
try to define a text's social existence through the elaboration of a concept
of "intertextuality."

One of the most prominent contemporary literary semioticians is Michael Riffaterre, whose recent work, which seeks to define "intertextuality"
in a methodologically fruitful way, illustrates this change in emphasis. Following a line of investigation originally suggested by Jonathan Culler, Riffaterre argues that literary texts can best be understood as specific
"actualizations" of cultural "presuppositions." Culler's definition of presupposition—as "that which must be revealed by another, or by an effort of
dédoublement: of thinking from the point of view of the other" ("Presup-

From *Novel: A Forum on Fiction* 19, no. 1 (Fall 1985). © 1985 by Novel Corporation.

position and Intertextuality")—is heavily tinged with a Hegelianism that Riffaterre rejects, substituting the more Kantian (or Chomskian) formulation of presuppositions as simply "the implicit conditions of an explicit statement" ("Flaubert's Presuppositions"). The advantage of Riffaterre's redefinition is that it guides him to look for sets of conditions rather than Culler's less easily delimited "point of view." In any given instance the conditions governing statements will constitute a system, and it is this system of presuppositions which the Riffaterrean student of intertextuality hopes to be able to disengage from the sociolect.

In trying to extend the semiotic project beyond the frontiers of the text itself into its context, Riffaterre is certainly moving in the right direction. But because his methodology for elucidating systems of statements within the sociolect remains rather undeveloped, Riffaterre runs into major problems when he attempts to realize his theoretical claims in particular interpretations, most tellingly in the reading of *Madame Bovary* that he gives in support of his approach. The only prerequisite Riffaterre stipulates for declaring a set of statements to be a system of presuppositions is that they derive from a "matrix sentence" supplied by the dictionary or some other anonymous source. For *Madame Bovary,* the matrix sentence is found in a popular dictionary of Flaubert's time in the entry on adultery: the cliché that "all evils stem from adultery." As a system, an "encoded ideology," adultery entails a number of subordinate consequences, all of which, it turns out, are played out in the course of Flaubert's narrative. Riffaterre concludes that the adultery-system thus "entails the whole fictional text."

Apart from this highly dubious claim to account for *total* textual production in terms of a single system, Riffaterre's approach leaves two questions unanswered. The first question is whether it is accurate to describe the literary performance that takes place in *Madame Bovary* as a straightforward actualization of the system of presuppositions about adultery. Of all writers, Flaubert is perhaps the most sensitive and resistant to the simple rehearsal of received ideas; when he does make use of such ideas, it is to struggle *against* their simplistic actualization. Flaubert's entire effort, in fact, seems to have been directed toward showing that what constituted the literary had nothing to do with the writer's overt subject, that even the most clichéd subject would do. And as Baudelaire pointed out in his review of *Madame Bovary,* "the tritest theme of all, worn out by repetition, by being played over and over like a tired barrel-organ," is adultery. Flaubert's is a repetition with a difference, but that kind of artistic difference from ordinary actualization is only vaguely gestured toward by Riffaterre, who dismisses it as an *écart stylistique*. Between dictionary and text, presupposition and actualization, Flaubert (and, one presumes, other artists) must be doing something extraordinary, and the nature of this deviation needs to be specified.

This leads us to the second question about Riffaterre's method: how does one find one's way from the text to the dictionary entry containing its most important presuppositions? Adultery is looked up by Riffaterre because it seems a good guess, but Baudelaire, in the review quoted earlier, argued that Flaubert was using hysteria, not adultery, to "serve as the central subject, the true core" of his novel. Unfortunately, instead of going on to interpret *Madame Bovary* in terms of hysteria, Baudelaire chose to guard the artistic value of Flaubert's text from historical inspection by arguing that "the Academy of Medicine has not as yet been able to explain the mysterious condition of hysteria." This was not quite true; it turns out that nineteenth-century medicine did have an explanation for hysteria as for other diseases. That explanation, however, was not to be found in a general dictionary; the system of medical presuppositions about hysteria did not exist as an encoded ideology based on a cliché (as in the instance of adultery), but as a part of a coherent discourse.

In order to deal effectively with the hysteria-system, Riffaterre would have to develop a method of discursive analysis. As a first step, of course, he would have to look for some equivalent to the popular dictionary, some repository of medical knowledge. Even if Riffaterre managed to find some such equivalent and describe the discourse on hysteria, however, he would then have to explain how medical presuppositions about hysteria inform, are actualized in, *Madame Bovary*. And given the fact that discourse is so much more complex than Riffaterre's ideological codes, the relation between discourse and fiction is likely to be more complicated than one of simple actualization.

Luckily, these problems are not insuperable in the case of hysteria and *Madame Bovary*, for two reasons. First, a methodology of discursive analysis already exists, and has been used by its inventor, Michel Foucault, to describe the presuppositions behind nineteenth-century medicine. Second, it turns out that there was in fact a medical equivalent (at least in the nineteenth century) to the general dictionary—the *Dictionnaire des sciences médicales*. This dictionary provides us with an entry on hysteria, as we shall see. But it also serves as an emblem of medical discourse as a whole, and Flaubert himself uses it symbolically in the novel in order to thematize the relation between medical discourse and the world of fiction—or, to use Riffaterre's terminology, between a presuppositional system and a text in which it is actualized.

This thematization occurs in the midst of a typically exhaustive catalogue of the contents of Charles Bovary's study, when Flaubert pauses to note the characteristics of Bovary's "Dictionary of Medical Science":

> Volumes of the "Dictionary of Medical Science," uncut, but the binding rather the worse for the successive sales through which they had gone, occupied almost alone the six shelves of a pine-wood bookcase.

If Charles's dictionary may be taken as emblematic of nineteenth-century medical discourse, this description exemplifies the strangely double status of that discourse in *Madame Bovary*. On the one hand, the medical dictionary (and medical discourse) is shown both to exist and to have cognitive authority; on the other hand, this source of cognitive power is never tapped by any of the central characters in the novel. Instead of being put into practical effect, the set of medical rules and commands symbolized by these volumes is treated only as an object, successively received and passed from hand to hand. Flaubert's description emphasizes the commodification of the dictionary ("successive sales"), the social indifference to its content ("uncut pages"), and its purely formal wear and tear ("suffering of its binding"), as if to underline the pathos of distance between discursive knowledge and *bêtise*.

While this condition of simultaneous presence and inaccessibility is a general condition of all knowledge in Flaubert, in *Madame Bovary* the inaccessibility of *medical* knowledge in particular turns out to be crucial, a matter of life and death. When Charles discovers that Emma has taken poison, he turns to the medical dictionary for the first time since it was originally mentioned early in the novel. Faced with the task of discovering an antidote, "Charles tried to look up his medical dictionary, but could not read it; the lines were jumping before his eyes." Canivet and Homais, Bovary's consultants on the case, are also unqualified to treat Emma properly—the former because his knowledge of internal medicine is scant and the latter because he is a quack. The lack of professional competence at this point is critical: Canivet's prescription of an emetic actually hastens Emma's death, as we learn from Dr. Larivière's "severe lecture" to the surgeon after the event.

Charles's dictionary, then, thematizes the determinate absence of medical knowledge in *Madame Bovary*. This knowledge, constituted as a system of *discursive* presuppositions about illness and death, seems to be precisely what the novel excludes. But the strange and innovative fact about Flaubert's novel is that, if Baudelaire's insight is correct, Emma's life is shaped by medical discourse's assumptions about hysteria, even though her death is caused by the discourse's absence. But what are these assumptions? More generally, what is their systematic form, and how does this discursive formation differ from the presuppositional, *ideological* systems that Riffaterre describes?

Taking the second question first, we can say that one broad difference between ideology and discourse is that while ideological presuppositions are a part of everyday knowledge available to anybody, discursive assumptions are specialized. It is thus often difficult to pin down the location of an ideology, which exists as what Terry Eagleton calls "a consensus of unconscious valuations"; discourse, on the other hand, tends to nest within an institutional framework that at once delimits and supports it. If we wish to understand the extent to which discourse is actualized in a literary text, we must thus look for two kinds of presuppositions: those conceptual presuppositions which constitute the discourse proper, and those institutional presuppositions that attend the discourse.

In the case of medical discourse, a very specific institutional environment—a new intellectual and professional hierarchy, a new disposition of duties and status—emerges during the early years of the nineteenth century. The question is how, and to what extent, these kinds of presuppositions affect Flaubert's imagination of the world of *Madame Bovary*. While they may seem merely sociological, I shall try to show that such presuppositions do in fact structure *Madame Bovary* to a great degree, providing the novel with what might be called a double template of relations. In the first instance, explicit relations between characters within the text are determined by the disciplinary and institutional constraints of the medical profession at this time. But institutional presuppositions also inform a more fundamental, tacit relation in Flaubert's work—that between knowledge and *bêtise*.

The inept Charles Bovary is probably the most spectacular example of a character both socially and intellectually determined by the medical institutions of the time. To understand his peculiar mediocrity, we must recognize that it is a function of his position within a complex professional hierarchy. Despite his honorific title, Doctor Charles Bovary is not a fully-fledged doctor, but an *officier de santé*—a category of medical practitioner created during the early years of the Napoleonic era under the direction of the Ideologue physician and philosopher Cabanis. During the Revolutionary period there had been both a rapid growth in the number of poorly trained army surgeons (for obvious reasons), and the abolition of the older, theoretically oriented *Facultés*. The latter were replaced, by 1795, by new learned societies like the *Societé d'émulation*, which counted Bichat, Cabanis, and Pinel among its members. Under the external pressure of public demands for commissions to screen out quack surgeons, and the internal pressure of a newly emerging institutional structure of medical authority, a general reorganization of the profession occurred. It followed a path leading to greater centralization and technocratic efficiency. Cabanis was in the forefront of this drive toward rationalization. He proposed that because medicine was an industry whose products' value could not be gauged by the public—"what price health?"— the government should ensure the value of treatment by controlling the producers but not the product. Under his plan, access to the profession was to be limited and less qualified physicians were to be supervised by an elite group of clinicians belonging to the learned societies.

As a result of these reforms, the terms of medical authority shifted as it expanded its jurisdiction. The old and bitter conflict between Parisian *Faculté* doctors and practical surgeons (a rivalry epitomized by the old surgeon Canivet's bitter remark in *Madame Bovary* about "the fads from Paris" propagated by "these gentlemen from the capital!") gave way, in 1803, to a new consolidation in the division of duties between experienced clinicians (usually located in a large city) and trained *officiers de santé*. The latter were certified, as is Charles, by department juries on the basis of a shorter course of study, and were allowed to practice only "simple procedures" in specified and restricted areas of the country. In effect, this was the first nationalized health planning, the first attempt to ensure minimal standards of care through a whole society by the controlled deployment of medical technique. It marked the first penetration of a centralized medical bureaucracy into the areas of social life that novelists like Balzac, George Eliot and Flaubert were attempting to penetrate as realists.

Charles Bovary is genealogically caught up in the transformation of the medical profession—his father, we recall, was an assistant-surgeon-major under Napoleon—so that Charles's choice of career (made by his mother, to be sure) is logical: he is simply following in his father's footsteps. But the intellectual landscape itself has changed, along with the change in title from surgeon to officer of health. Charles, unlike his father, cannot get by only on the strength of his "devil of an arm for pulling teeth," nor can he confidently espouse the brutal surgical egotism of Canivet, who rejects the advanced medical procedures of "strabismus, chloroform, lithotrity" without having the slightest understanding of them. (Canivet's surgical background is evident even in his name, which derives from *canif*, "penknife.") Charles, as an *officier de santé*, must have the slightest understanding, but that is all. Permitted to treat only "primitive accidents" and "simple indispositions" but required to pass an examination in order to do even that, the *officier de santé* is a subordinate within the new medical institution.

Above all, he is an intellectual subordinate in the new diagnostic and therapeutic paradigm represented by the medical dictionary. His is an empirically-oriented training, a closed circuit of perception and treatment; as Foucault points out, for the *officier de santé* it is "a question of knowing what to do after seeing; experience was integrated at the level of perception, memory, and repetition, that is, at the level of the example" (*The Birth of the Clinic*). The words Charles is stunned by when he begins his studies—physiology, pharmacy, botany, clinical medicine, therapeutics, hygiene, *materia medica*—remain "names of whose etymologies he was ignorant, and that were to him as so many doors to sanctuaries filled with magnificent darkness." Instead of entering into the sacred temple of medicine (whose "godlike" authority is Charles's old master, the clinician Larivière), Charles enters into the profane hovels of the peasantry: "He poked his arm into damp beds, received the tepid spurt of bloodletting in his face, listened to death-rattles, examined basins, turned over a good deal of dirty linen." The senses—sight, sound, touch, and smell—are at work here, but little else.

It should be clear from all this why it would be absurd to expect Charles to grasp the higher mysteries of medicine. His very mode of perception, one grounded in repetition yet linked to a knowledge that transcends such activity, goes with the job created by the medical profession. It should be emphasized here that Charles's mediocrity is not useless; in fact, his docile repetition, emblemized by Flaubert very early on in the book by the image of "a mill-horse, who goes round and round with his eyes bandaged, not knowing what work it is grinding out" *does perform work*. It is important to point this out, because deconstructive readings of Flaubert like those of Tony Tanner and Eugenio Donato have taken the repetition and turning in the text as purely degenerative processes that reduce all difference to indifferentiation. As I have tried to show, however, Charles's repetition is part of a regularization of professional behavior, a process which is useful to both the profession and its clients, despite its often destructive and dehumanizing effect on the individual involved in it. Charles does succeed, for instance, in setting Farmer Rouault's leg even though he is simply repeating by rote: on arriving at the farm, "Charles awoke with a start, suddenly remembered the broken leg, and tried to call to mind all the fractures he knew." Even his bedside manner is an imitation—"calling to mind the devices of his masters at the bedside of patients, he comforted the sufferer with all sorts of kindly remarks"—and yet he gains Rouault as a patient for official medicine, a small victory for the profession.

The military connotations of the word "victory" are applicable here, for if Charles, as an *officier de santé,* is a subordinate within the medical hierarchy, he is by the same token a footsoldier in the campaign to extend medical authority throughout the provinces of France. By the time Charles enters the profession, medicine has reorganized itself internally and received some official backing for its project of controlling the national health care market. But state support is not absolute, and especially at the local level, the standard-bearers of official medicine during this period find themselves competing with several other authorities for legitimate control over many of the same aspects of human behavior. More traditionally-sanctioned authorities—in particular religious healers and unaccredited folk doctors—as well as the more recently established legal functionaries, all claim some responsibility for the same deviants. The story told by Emma's maid—about a fisherman's daughter whose "fog in the head" was treated by priest, doctor, and customs officer—shows the professional polyvalence of illness (especially mental illness) in the nineteenth century.

Given this crowded field, it is easy to understand the creation during the period of a mythical history propagated by the medical profession itself. In such accounts, "the contest between the physicians and their rivals sometimes appears as the heroic phase of professionalization, pitting medical enlightenment against popular superstition" (Matthew Ramsey, "Medical Power and Popular Medicine: Illegal Healers in Nineteenth-Century France"). For the *officier de santé,* however, this mythical clarity has little to do with reality at the local level, where lines are not so clearly drawn. To consolidate his own position in the community, a country doctor like Charles is forced to develop a series of alliances, accommodations and defensive tactics.

With respect to the Church, the country doctor is faced with a rival who, like Abbé Bournisien with Hyppolite in *Madame Bovary,* promises a cure in exchange for vows of prayer and pilgrimage. Having little hope of winning in head-on anticlerical attacks of the kind made by the pharmacist Homais, the country doctor tends instead to accommodate the priest, accepting the notion that, as Bournisien remarks to Emma when she seeks help, Charles "is doctor of the body . . . and I of the soul." The result is a therapeutic regime in which, as Jacques Donzelot has pointed out, priest and doctor "occupied two clearly separate registers" (*The Policing of Families*) while attending to the same problem of pathology, whether physical, sexual, or mental.

With respect to the other two authorities, legal and pseudo-medical, the *officier de santé* faces a more serious problem. The law, in the form of the medical police, is supposedly allied with him in a joint effort to crush illegal healers. In fact, this program for achieving a professional monopoly remains largely unrealized at the local level: folk healing and charlatanism do not constitute regular targets for the police, despite the official mandate. Thus, the officer of health often finds himself in a dangerous economic struggle for patients with an opponent who tends to operate underground. To make matters worse, there is not that much of a difference in the level of skills possessed by doctors like Charles and quacks like the chemist Homais, even though the officer of health's knowledge is sponsored by official medicine with its more advanced cognitive base. Minimally accredited practitioners and "charlatans" use many of the same basic therapeutic techniques.

Homais's relation to Charles, of course, graphically illustrates this situation and its hazards for the *officier de santé*. The apothecary, we learn early in the novel, "had infringed the law of the 19th Ventôse, year xi, article 1 [Cabanis was one of the principal architects of this legislation] which forbade all persons not having a diploma to practice medicine." Homais is summoned to Rouen, but instead of being incarcerated he is merely reprimanded. Although the apothecary fears the power of the law ("he saw the depths of dungeons, his family in tears, his shop sold, all the jars dispersed"), Flaubert emphasizes the merely symbolic nature of medicine's legal power by focusing on the trappings of authority: the prosecutor receives Homais "in his private office," "standing up, ermine on shoulder and cap on head." These signs are without content, however, a fact that Flaubert underlines by adding that "it was in the morning, before the court opened."

Unfortunately for Dr. Bovary, the apothecary is not deterred for long by the scare he has received. He adapts to the reality of his position and undertakes a guerrilla war against a series of *officiers de santé* who attempt to occupy his territory in the name of official medicine. In this he is remarkably successful: Charles's predecessor runs away. Charles himself is ruined, and on the last page of the novel, Flaubert informs us that "since Bovary's death three doctors have succeeded one another in Yonville without any success, so effectively did Homais hasten to eradicate them."

Riffaterre's method, that of looking directly to the dictionary in order to find a set of elemental ideological presuppositions, remains blind to these kinds of sociological and institutional determinants of textual situations. Riffaterre's approach, of course, is more elegant and rigorous, with its semiotic insistence that context is another kind of text, and its demand that textual presuppositions be studied as purely linguistic entities embodied only in the dictionary. But, as the example of medicine shows, some kinds of linguistic presuppositions—those of what Foucault calls a discourse—are tied to a discrete social and institutional practice, as well as being found in a dictionary.

Having pointed this out, we can now use the medical dictionary to try
to understand the presuppositions of medical discourse operating in *Madame
Bovary*. Following Riffaterre's directions and Baudelaire's intuition, we can
cut the pages of the *Dictionnaire de médecine* and turn to the entry on
hysteria. There we can find a long article containing the following information:

> The circumstances that most predispose a patient to hysteria are
> . . . a nervous constitution, her female sex and her age, between
> twelve and twenty-five or thirty years of age. . . . A majority have
> from a young age shown a disposition toward convulsive ail-
> ments, a melancholic, angry, passionate, impatient character. . . .
> Exciting causes, more specifically, are morally powerful ailments
> [including] unrequited love, . . . acute disturbances of the soul,
> . . . a violent fit of jealousy, . . . powerful grief, . . . acute disap-
> pointment. . . . The nervous constitution and the unhealthy con-
> dition that precede and facilitate the development of the attacks
> are caused by excessive masturbation.

The content of this entry is striking, for it describes Emma Bovary's condition
quite accurately: her tendency to convulsive affections from an early age is
shown by Flaubert in the flashback to her convent days, when "her nature,
positive in the midst of its enthusiasms," had led her to devotional excesses;
every word used to define the "hysterical character" is also used at some
point in the novel to refer to Emma; she falls into fits after she suffers various
emotional shocks—for example, her violent chagrin at Rodolphe's letter or
her dread of imminent bankruptcy after he turns down her request for
money; and her nervous constitution, while not directly attributable to mas-
turbation, is directly referred to by herself, by Charles, and even by Charles's
old master Dr. Larivière.

To point out that Emma acts like a hysteric, however, is to do no more
than Baudelaire did a hundred years ago. We need to find out whether in
his realistic characterization of Emma, Flaubert appropriates only thematic
elements of hysteria which would be available to anyone, or whether he also
makes use of the logical and rhetorical structure of presuppositions peculiar
to medicine. In order to do so, however, we must first take a detour to
elucidate this structure, with its complex interplay—evident in the entry we
have just cited—among terms like "predisposition," "character," "constitution," and "exciting causes."

The particular figure of hysteria, together with the conceptualization of
disease in general, undergoes a profound transformation between 1780 and

1810, the period coinciding with the emergence of the twin disciplines of modern clinical medicine and morbid anatomy under the leadership of the great anatomist Xavier Bichat. The key conceptual development for the emergence of modern medical discourse is the elaboration of the concept of "sensitivity." Defined as the involuntary but active response by an organism to a positive stimulus, sensitivity becomes for nineteenth-century clinicians the sine qua non for gauging the condition of a living being. Bichat's contemporary Cabanis sums up the new centrality of this concept by paraphrasing Newton: "Vivre, c'est sentir" (*Rapports du physique et du moral de l'homme*).

When sensitivity becomes the primary property of living beings, the central terms of eighteenth-century pathology—"temperament" and "constitution"—are semantically transformed. Temperament, which previously referred to a quantitative balance of fluids or spirits, is redefined as the spatial organization of sensitivity, the three-dimensional relationship between "centers" of sensitivity within the body. "The difference of temperaments," according to Cabanis, "depends upon the difference of centers of sensitivity, of relationships of strength, weakness or sympathetic communications among various organs."

In medical discourse, the temperament thus comes to be the expression of "primitive functions" of sensitivity at work inside and between organs, in what Bichat calls the "organic life" of the individual. But sensitivity is not limited to the internal viscera, the organic life, alone; it is also affected by the relations established between a creature and its environment. This second set of relations constitutes what Bichat christens "animal life." Animal life differs from organic life in that its condition is open to some change under the control of the creature. Unlike organic life, which allocates its forces of sensitivity at birth, animal life has at its disposition a "somme déterminée de force," a vital force which can be channeled by the will or by external stimuli into the development of sensitivity of one organ or another (*Recherches physiologiques sur la vie et la mort*).

Finally, in Bichat's new framework, the term "constitution" ceases to refer to a sympathetic or qualitative similarity between the body's fibers and the external environment (think of Rameau's nephew's complaints about the weather). Instead, an individual's constitution is to be understood as the total structure of sensitivities—a complex, constantly evolving web of "rapports" between the fixed temperament of the organic life and the variable pressures of the animal life.

The idea that an individual should be viewed as a complex constitution having two distinct lives is, as I shall try to show, common to both the medical view of the patient and Flaubert's view of his characters. It has one particularly important implication that we can find in medical theories of hysteria as well as in Flaubert's characterization of Emma. This implication is that the development or formation of a constitution must take place through a long-drawn-out, incremental process of stimulation from within or without. Stimuli or desires may act upon the individual, but they cannot act directly and cataclysmically. A kind of "interior distance" (to borrow a phrase from Georges Poulet) exists within us all, but this medical interiority is a highly organized and evolving system, not a pure, phenomenologically certain locus for the Cogito. Every impulse of vital force from the will or stimulus from the environment is disseminated through a network of various centers of sensibility and thus each stimulus can modify the whole only slightly.

In the case of hysteria, the constitution is thought to undergo four distinct steps in its slow process of pathological formation. These steps can perhaps best be described as analogous to the four tropes of metaphor, metonymy, synecdoche, and irony, whose progression has been shown by Hayden White to structure the broader narrative movement in *L'Education sentimentale* ("The Problem of Style in Realistic Representation: Marx and Flaubert," in *The Concept of Style*, Berel Lang, ed.). In the first stage, a stimulus from either passion or the environment is transmitted to the cerebral cortex, in a kind of metaphorical translation. Next, the force of sensation, having arrived in the brain, is relayed to the brain's different centers of sensibility, as significance would be relayed metonymically. Third, the organs of the brain in turn affect the whole range of bodily organs by means of what one important physician terms "interior sensibility," a radiating effect similar to what is said to occur semantically in synecdoche. Gradually, the various parts of the body accumulate sensitivity, until they are saturated, reaching a state of "hyperexcitability" in which any stimulation whatsoever is intolerable. At this point, in the fourth and last stage of the development of a hysteric's constitution, the system of rapports connecting the nervous system has become a collection of "hyperexcitable" components, a sort of ironic dissociation of sensibility that predisposes the patient to suffer hysterical attacks at the slightest provocation.

Emma's development follows these steps, and more generally, all Flaubert's characters exhibit complex constitutions. Flaubert, of course, does not use the medical terms I have been describing. Rather, he translates these terms into metaphysical and psychological ones more appropriate to the novel, while retaining the structure of medical discourse. For the physical constitution he substitutes memory; for the centers of sensibility or intellectual functions deployed through the body or brain, he substitutes the representations that memory consists of; and for vital force, he substitutes desire.

The Flaubertian self, in other words, is a complex psychological constitution, a constantly evolving relation between present sensation and an always already existing set of memories. At moments when the interchange between sensation and memory becomes problematic—for example, during the transition between consciousness and sleep, or during a hallucination—the Flaubertian self can disintegrate into independent sets of memories (equivalent to the different functions into which the hysteric's constitution ironically breaks down during a fit). Flaubert is deeply interested in showing that such states are part of the human condition; they affect all his characters, even if they are as dull as Charles Bovary:

> Charles from time to time opened his eyes but his mind grew weary, and sleep coming upon him, he soon fell into a doze wherein his recent sensations blending with memories, he became conscious of a double self, at once student and married man, lying in his bed as but now, and crossing the operation theatre as of old.

The constitution of the self, like the constitution of the patient, is thus neither simply given nor unitary in Flaubert's realism. And, as in the medical constitution, the Flaubertian self is capable of slow decomposition or transformation. As memory erodes or shifts, the identity of the various characters shifts as well, sometimes even in spite of their efforts to avoid such a change. Charles, for example, finds that "while continually thinking of Emma, he was nevertheless forgetting her. He grew desperate as he felt this image fading from his memory in spite of all efforts to retain it." Beyond and sometimes in spite of individual intention, memory (like the physical constitution) adjusts and reconstitutes itself.

Such are the vicissitudes of every constitution of memory. For those who become ill, however, memory does not merely adjust; rather, the structure of memory of the patient develops in the same way that a patient's physical constitution does. In the case of hysteria, Emma, in the Flaubertian twist on the medical paradigm, does what Freud and Breuer will later say all hysterics do: she "suffers mainly from reminiscences" (*Studies in Hysteria*). Flaubert, who once described his own disorder (diagnosed as hystero-epilepsy) as "an illness of memory," anticipates Freud in psychologizing the disease, but Flaubert's presuppositions are rooted in nineteenth-century medicine, and Emma's illness follows a different course than that of Dora. Emma's stages of consciousness correspond at a mental level to the four-stage series described earlier. These four steps occur again and again in a kind of cyclical spiral, each time preparing Emma's mental constitution for its recurrent disintegration in hysterical fits.

Because the first three steps in the formation of constitution tend to resolve themselves in most instances without causing any dramatic breakdown of the self, these formative or predisposing steps are best observed in local instances such as paragraphs and brief episodes. A close reading of such passages shows how the kind of language employed by Flaubert to describe Emma's tug of war between sensations and memories coincides with the expected psychological trope for that moment in the development of her memory-constitution. Emma, like all of us, incorporates experience into memory by first metaphorically converting her sensation into feeling, then extending that feeling metonymically in imagination, and finally dissipating it in a plethora of representations stretching synecdochically through her memory as a whole.

Metaphors are used most often and sown most thickly in *Madame Bovary* during Emma's primary reception of sensations by her sensibility. One good example of this trope-clustering is the following gorgeous paragraph, whose metaphors imitate Emma's consciousness during the first moments after love-making:

> The shades of night were falling; the horizontal sun passing between the branches dazzled the eyes. Here and there around her, in the leaves or on the ground, trembled luminous patches, as if humming-birds flying about had scattered their feathers. Silence was everywhere; something sweet seemed to come forth from the trees. She felt her heartbeat return, and the blood coursing through her flesh like a river of milk. Then far away, beyond the wood, on the other hills, she heard a vague prolonged cry, a voice which lingered, and in silence she heard it mingling like music with the last pulsations of her throbbing nerves.

Within the space of three sentences, Flaubert has set three distinct metaphors, each addressing a different sense. A similar instance of such transfusion of perception, and one which is more clearly followed by a psychological retrenchment, occurs with Emma's incorporation of her experience at the Vaubyessard ball. In her first encounter with luxury, she is overwhelmed by the vivid sensations, which cancel (or at least obscure by their intensity) her previous memories:

> In the splendor of the present hour her past life, so distinct until
> then, faded away completely, and she almost doubted having lived
> it. She was there; beyond the ball was only shadow overspreading
> all the rest.

On her return home, "she devoutly put away in her drawers her beautiful
dress, down to the satin shoes whose soles were yellowed with the slippery
wax of the dancing floor. Her heart resembled them: in its contact with
wealth, something had rubbed off on it that could not be removed." This
simile signals the onset of an obsession: "The memory of this ball, then,
became an occupation for Emma." In medical terms, what has happened is
that a sensation has been successfully transported into Emma's cerebral centers and has begun to act upon her intellectual faculties.

Once Emma's sensation has been received, medical discourse tells us,
its force need not remain bound to the representation that originally carried
it. Like all direct impressions, this one soon fades, as we saw Charles's image
of Emma fade: "little by little the faces grew confused in her remembrance.
She forgot the tune of the quadrilles [like the music that mingles with her
nerves during her seduction by Rodolphe in the passage quoted earlier, this
music has been absorbed into her very nervous system]; she no longer saw
the liveries and the guest-houses so distinctly; some of the details faded but
the wistful feeling remained with her." Emma's desire, like the power of
sensibility or vital force that can be aroused by a stimulus, then becomes
capable of being metonymically redirected onto other memories, that is, other
images. In this second phase, Emma seeks imaginary satisfaction for her own
desires. Like her lover Leon, who in her absence displaces his passion for
her onto other objects, Emma applies this wistful feeling—the echo of her
sensation, as it were—to substitute objects like the Vicomte's cigar-box,
whose odors and needlework reactivate sensation on an imaginary plane.
This strategy of metonymic displacement of psychic force onto imaginary
objects is effective in the short run:

> The memory of the Viscount always cropped up in everything
> she read. She made comparisons between him and the fictional
> characters in her books. But the circle of which he was the centre
> gradually widened round him, and the aureole that he bore, fad-
> ing from his form and extending beyond his image, lit up her
> other dreams.

Unfortunately, Emma's psychic energy has been invested in mere representations which, in being extended synecdochically, always dissipate that en-

ergy: "At the end of some indefinite distance there was always a confused spot, into which her dream died." In the same way, the vital force of a future hysteric remains unfocused and simply fans out into the confusion of the body's or brain's organization, where it raises the general level of hyperexcitability. The prolongation of imaginary investment, that is, leads to what Flaubert describes in Emma as "an expansion of selfishness, of nervous irritation," as her stock of energy is exhausted without return in the form of any new sensation: "each morning, as she awoke, she hoped it would come that day; she listened to every sound, sprang up with a start, wondered that it did not come; then at sunset, always more saddened, she longed for the next day." As Emma's extreme responsiveness to the slightest sound shows, her constitution has become saturated with hyperexcitability. Given her condition, Flaubert's next two sentences come as no surprise: "Spring came round. With the first warm weather, when the peartrees began to blossom, she had fainting-spells."

What *is* surprising about Flaubert's description of Emma's breakdown is Flaubert's insistence, at a moment of crisis for his heroine, on noting even the most minute specifications of the environmental conditions ("when the peartrees began to blossom") attending this event. It is no doubt true that a certain pathos is thematized by such a detail: Spring, which should bring love, instead yields only a nervous breakdown. But the obsession with detail *qua* detail represented in this example is a central characteristic of Flaubert's realistic style. As Jonathan Culler has argued, Flaubert's details, unlike those of his predecessor Balzac, do not lend themselves to symbolic recuperation, at least not exhaustively. I would only add that Flaubert's attitude toward description can be understood as a second major consequence of his adoption of the medical point of view. For to accept the notion of a complex constitution means to also accept an extreme difficulty in determining which specific stimulus causes a predisposed constitution to go over the edge into actual breakdown. When all the centers of sensibility have become hyperexcitable, the threshold of sensibility is lowered so much that even sound or odor can trigger an attack. In such cases, as one prominent physician of the time cautions, it is often impossible to find the immediate cause of the breakdown.

Because of this proliferation of possible exciting causes, the physician is forced to deepen his observation and analysis of the patient's environment to include the most trivial and perhaps insignificant details, if he wishes to fully understand how the disease progresses. The new epistemology of diagnosis expresses itself in medical discourse with the appearance of the modern case study, which replaces the older, eighteenth-century record that correlated disease and statistical information about environmental conditions. In the case study, as opposed to the earlier mode of analysis, details provide the doctor with a web of possible connections, some spurious, some significant, that he must weave and unweave in order to make sense of the patient's illness.

The purely empirical accumulation of details would of course be useless if the physician had no epistemological guide to the pathways of illness within the body. Fortunately, such a guide is provided by the new discipline of pathological anatomy, whose founder, Bichat, catalogues the various ways in which different "concatenations of phenomena" can lead to death, or more generally to the onset of an illness. In his masterpiece, *Recherches sur la vie et le mort* (a text that Flaubert was familiar with) Bichat illustrates this point with an example that is strikingly appropriate to *Madame Bovary:*

> The simple action of a poisonous substance on the nerves of the lungs can have a very marked effect on the [physical] economy, and is even capable of disturbing its functions in a palpable way: somewhat like an odour, which striking simply on the pituitary, acts sympathetically upon the heart, and determines the occurrence of a fit; just as the view of a hideous object produces the same effect.

A good doctor, Bichat concludes, must carefully collect his details and observations if he hopes to distinguish between attacks caused by odor and those that are psychically induced by the view of an object arousing strong emotions. This lesson, with the identical example Bichat uses here, is taught us by Flaubert in *Madame Bovary*. In the episode which culminates in Emma's hysterical fit, she receives a farewell letter from her lover Rodolphe hidden in a basket of fruit sent to the Bovarys as a going-away present. The shock of discovery about Rodolphe's infidelity raises Emma's sensitivity to its height, but she controls herself enough to come down to dinner. At the dinner-table, however, Charles encourages her to taste the fruit, unaware of her hyperexcitability at this moment:

> "Smell them! Such perfume!" he insisted, moving it back and forth under her nose.
> "I am choking," she exclaimed, leaping up.
> By sheer willpower, she succeeded in forcing back the spasm.
> "It is nothing," she said, "it is nothing! Just nerves. Sit down and eat."

For she dreaded most of all that he would question her, try to help and not leave her to herself.

Charles, to obey her, sat down again, and he spat the stones of the apricots into his hands, afterwards putting them on his plate.

Suddenly a blue tilbury passed across the square at a rapid trot.

Emma uttered a cry and fell back rigid on the floor.

Like Bichat, Flaubert offers us two alternative causes of Emma's fit—odor or the view of a hideous object (the tilbury is Rodolphe's). What is more, Flaubert's laconic transcription of the events leading up to Emma's syncope follows the epistemological rules of a good case history: it does not attempt to judge causes, but only to describe as faithfully as possible the events, both psychic and physical, which might be taken as causes of Emma's attack. Although here, as usual, Flaubert weights the evidence in favor of a psychic causation by making the physical apricots themselves into psychically "horrifying objects" for Emma, who links them with the letter she has just received, the novelist is careful to record the temporal proximity linking the smell of fruit with Emma's sensation of choking (a symptom that marks the preliminary stage of a hysterical paroxysm), so that we are forced to consider the odor as data. Just as in the passage quoted earlier, which associated the blossoming of peartrees with Emma's fainting spells, but only did so by contiguity, so here Flaubert registers the possible exciting causes, leaving to the reader the task of determining which details are significant.

I could go on to show how Flaubert's treatment of Emma parallels the prescriptions of Charles's Medical Dictionary. But from the foregoing discussion, it should be clear that Flaubert integrates medical presuppositions about hysteria into his writing, to an extraordinary and quite complex degree. Flaubert's medical presuppositions, however, are not actualized in Riffaterre's sense. They do not provide a linear series of consequences forming the *plot* of *Madame Bovary* (as Riffaterre's presuppositions about adultery do); rather, these medical presuppositions are taken up by Flaubert as directives about technique. Flaubert's method of characterization is dominated by the medical presupposition that the individual develops as a complex constitution, and Flaubert's method of description is dominated by the medical presupposition that alternative causes must be considered during diagnosis of hysterical attacks. More generally, we can, I believe, speak of a *medicalization* of realism occurring with Flaubert, the emergence of a mode of writing in which the relation between author and text is modeled on medical precepts, with the author viewing his characters as a doctor views his patients (or alternatively, in Proust's work, adopting the perspective of the patient himself).

Insofar as this interpretation has been fruitful, it shows the advantages of treating intertextuality as a locus of discourse rather than simply a repository of ideological codes. Looking for discursive affiliations between text and society has one other advantage, however: it raises questions about the role and status of the author, questions that cannot be easily broached by semiotics. Why, for example, does Flaubert choose *medical* discourse to work through? More specifically, why make Emma a hysteric? And why write about a situation in which that discourse is unavailable, so that Emma is not treated effectively?

I will conclude by sketching out two broad answers to these questions. Both involve the internal hierarchy and social status of medicine discussed in the first half of the article. One answer is biographical, concerning Flaubert's personal encounter with hysteria and with the medical profession; the other is sociological, concerning the historical situation of the profession of literature within a society in which the profession of medicine was also evolving.

One fact about the concept of hysteria that I have failed to mention thus far is that in nineteenth-century medicine, hysteria and epilepsy are thought to be gender-variants of the same basic disorder of the constitution; the major difference between the two is that hysteria is thought to affect only women, while epilepsy attacks both sexes. This supposed affinity between the two diseases is of great biographical importance in Flaubert's case, for the novelist suffered from a nervous condition that was diagnosed at the time as epilepsy. The problem of determining what Flaubert was "really" suffering from, an old and hoary issue in Flaubert criticism, need not concern us here. It is sufficient to know that Flaubert perceived his own illness in the terms provided by nineteenth-century clinical medicine, and in particular by his own father, Dr. Achille-Cléophas Flaubert, who studied under Bichat as well as under the great surgeon Dupuytren.

Flaubert sees his own form of hysteria in clinical terms, as we can see from a letter he writes to Louise Colet. Here he describes one of his fits, using words and phrases that echo his fictional description of the splitting of the self discussed earlier in this article:

> Each attack was like a hemorrhage of the nervous system. Seminal losses from the pictorial faculty of the brain, a hundred thousand images cavorting at once in a kind of fireworks. It was a snatching of the soul from the body, excruciating. (I am convinced I died

several times.) But what constitutes the personality, the rational essence, was present throughout; had it not been, the suffering would have been nothing, for I would have been purely passive, whereas I was always concious even when I could no longer speak.

In another letter, Flaubert repeats the same image used here, describing how "sometimes, within the space of a single second, I have been aware of a thousand thoughts, images and associations of all kinds illuminating my brain like so many brilliant fireworks" (letter to Louise Colet, July 6, 1852). The grafting of medical or scientific terms like "seminal losses" or "pictorial faculty of the brain" with psychic terms (images, thoughts, associations) is noteworthy. More important, however, is the fact that such passages provide direct evidence that Flaubert understands Emma by projecting his own experience onto her. The metaphor of fireworks, for example, is used by Flaubert to describe Emma's hallucinations as well as his own:

> She remained lost in stupor, and only conscious of herself through the beating of her arteries, that seemed to burst forth like a deafening music filling all the fields. The earth beneath her feet was more yielding than the sea, and the furrows seemed to her immense brown waves breaking into foam. All the memories and ideas that crowded her head seemed to explode at once like a thousand pieces of fireworks. She saw her father, Lheureux's closet, their room at home, another landscape. Madness was coming upon her.

Emma's hallucination, we should note, involves an inverted, ironic return of the kind of metaphorizing we saw earlier in her perception after intercourse with Rodolphe. Here, the music and her veins seem to explode from within, and the hyperconsciousness implied by the earlier metaphors gives way to its opposite, stupor. In the present context, however, what is most striking about this passage is that Emma's symptoms are an almost verbatim transcription of Flaubert's.

Perhaps this symptomatic identification between novelist and character is what Flaubert had in mind when he remarked that "Madame Bovary, c'est moi." Certainly Flaubert was eminently qualified to portray Emma's fate from the point of view of a patient. Yet, at the same time, we have seen that Flaubert also takes the point of view of a doctor, with respect to both his own illness and that of his characters.

Flaubert's experience of illness as both delirium and knowledge thus enables him to produce the peculiar realism of *Madame Bovary*, and in a more general sense, may be said to be the phenomenological root of the bifurcated style that Albert Thibaudet, among others, sees as the essence of Flaubertian realism. The novelist himself recognized that in the act of writing he became, in his own words, "literarily speaking, two distinct persons: one who is infatuated with bombast, lyricism, eagle flights, sonorities of phrase and lofty ideas; and another who digs and burrows into the truth as deeply as he can, who likes to treat a humble fact as respectfully as a big one, who would like to make you feel almost physically the things he reproduces." Given what we now know about Flaubert, the distinction between romantic and analytic style may be redefined as a tension between hysterical and medical perspectives. The hysterical aspect of Flaubert's prose appears in what he calls the "throbbing of sentences and the seething of metaphors," stylistic events which, like the river of milk Emma feels in her veins, "flow from one another like a series of cascades, carrying the reader along." The medical side of Flaubert's style is evident from the anatomical and surgical implications of the second half of the quotation above. Elsewhere Flaubert speaks about a style that would be precise as the language of the sciences, "a style that would pierce your idea like a dagger."

Prescient in this as in so many other things, Sainte-Beuve was the first to recognize the anatomical basis of Flaubert's style, in the now-famous remark that "M. Flaubert wields the pen as others do the scalpel." The critic also recognized that to write in that way was "a sign of enormous power." We can now specify the nature of that medical power and the way in which it is exercised. It is the power to act upon, to control, and ultimately to constitute its object—human life—without coming into direct contact with it or even being visible to it. Flaubert's ideal of stylistic power is exactly this kind of medical panopticism: "An author in his book must be like God in the universe, present everywhere and visible nowhere. Art being a second Nature, the creator of that Nature must behave similarly" (letter to Louise Colet, December 9, 1852).

Certainly, as the plight of Charles Bovary's unread medical dictionary shows, the medical perspective of the author is visible nowhere in the world represented in *Madame Bovary*. There is, however, one god-like medical figure who does appear at the end of the novel, although too late to redeem the world and save the doomed Emma with his healing power. That figure is Dr. Larivière, and as we might expect, there are many affinities between him and Flaubert. Larivière's relation to those outside the profession is similar to that between Flaubert and the characters he portrays: both doctor and writer assume the status of deities. As Flaubert remarks about Larivière's arrival in town, on the eve of Emma's death, "the apparition of a god would not have caused more commotion."

A second similarity between Larivière and Flaubert is in their personalities. The doctor is described as one of those "who, cherishing their art with a fanatical love, exercised it with enthusiasm and wisdom. . . . Disdainful of honors, of titles, and of academics, hospitable, generous, fatherly to the poor, and practicing virtue without believing in it, he would almost have passed for a saint if the keenness of his intellect had not caused him to be feared as a demon. His glance, more penetrating than his scalpels, looked straight into your soul, and would detect [the French word is "desarticulait," *i.e.,* disarticulate] any lie, regardless how well hidden." Like Larivière, Flaubert is fanatical in his devotion to his art; he, too, disdains academies and honors, as is evident from his sarcastic award of the Cross of the Legion of Honor to Homais as well as from comments in his correspondence (for example, "how honors swarm where there is no honor!" [letter to Louise Colet, January 15, 1853]); he, too, feels that he acts charitably to the poor; he, too, is interested in burrowing and penetrating into the truth. And like Larivière, who "belonged to that great school of surgeons created by Bichat," Flaubert claims to "feel at home only in analysis—in anatomy, if I may call it such" (letter to Louise Colet, July 26, 1852).

Both Emma and Dr. Larivière, hysteric and physician, thus may be seen as projections of Flaubert's own personality. In this sense, *Madame Bovary* is a kind of disarticulated autobiography. A normal autobiography would be structured by a stylistic tension between what Jean Starobinski, following Emile Benveniste, describes as the historical and discursive subjects. This tension between being and (self)knowledge, according to Starobinski, is usually resolved by some radical change in the life of the autobiographer, such change most often taking the form of a conversion into a *new* life ("The Style of Autobiography," in *Literary Style: A Symposium,* Seymour Chatman, ed.). In *Madame Bovary,* on the other hand, the stylistic tension is between hysterical and discursive subjects, between being and medical knowledge. Instead of finding resolution in a new life, this tension is only resolved in death. Both pathological anatomy and Flaubertian realism are based on the premise that, as Bichat puts it, life is that which resists death. Flaubert, in a letter of March 31, 1853, to Louise Colet, echoes this sentiment: "How annihilation stalks us! No sooner are we born than putrefaction sets in, and life is nothing but a long battle it wages against us, ever more triumphantly until the end—death—when its reign becomes absolute" (Steegmuller translation). The corollary of this premise, as Bichat points out, is that while the truth of life can only be fully seen in death, when the anatomist disarticulates the body, illness is itself a form of dissection. In this sense, Emma is dead even before the novel begins, and the novel itself is a patient anatomization.

This seems somewhat sadistic, and the reader may well wonder why, after all, Emma is denied medical treatment. Why does Larivière come too late? For Jean-Paul Sartre, the reason is clear: Larivière's knowledge—and medical knowledge more generally, is irrelevant to Emma's existential pain, as it is to Flaubert's art. The doctor, according to Sartre, "*knows* the horror scientifically but does not *feel* it," because his medical knowledge is grounded in utilitarianism (*The Family Idiot*). Sartre's reading is interesting, but it is a philosopher's strong misreading: Larivière is less a representative of utilitarianism than of the medical philosophy—the discourse—of the clinic and comparative anatomy; Bichat is his mentor, not Bentham. Moreover, Larivière's professional *impassabilité,* imposed on him by the requirements of his way of knowing, does not destroy all feeling in him, as Sartre claims. The great physician's objective veneer cracks just enough at the sight of the horror to reveal Larivière's human interior: "this man, accustomed as he was to the sight of pain, could not keep back a tear that fell on his shirt front."

While this tear is similar to those that Flaubert claimed to have himself shed over Emma while writing *Madame Bovary,* it also points toward a more complicated biographical connection. Like Larivière weeping over Emma, Flaubert's father, Dr. Achille-Cléophas Flaubert, wept over Gustave during the early days after his son's first "epileptic" attack. Several other characteristics are shared by Larivière and Achille-Cléophas—both served under Bichat, both wear cloaks that identify them as somewhat eccentric, both attempt to maintain a stern late-Enlightenment moral stance. These similarities have led critics to argue that Larivière is a fictional depiction of Flaubert's father. The autobiographical problem of reconciling one's knowledge and one's being, thematized in *Madame Bovary* by the relation between Larivière and Emma, is thus complicated by the Oedipal problem of the relation between father and son.

Sartre's mammoth biography of Flaubert has dissected in great detail the intimate tensions between Gustave and his father, showing how Achille-Cléophas refused to allow his younger son to follow in his footsteps and become a doctor. Flaubert's eventual breakdown, Sartre contends, was due to his medical disinheritance, and provided him with the freedom to write. Flaubert then used this freedom to gain his revenge against his father by portraying him in what Sartre considers a less than flattering way, as Larivière in *Madame Bovary*. This interpretation of the filial tie as one of *ressentiment* relies to a great extent upon Sartre's claim that Larivière's portrait is laden with sarcasm, a claim based on what I believe to be an over-subtle reading of the evidence. A less elegant but perhaps clearer interpretation accepts Larivière as a representative of Flaubert's father and of the heritage of medical knowledge—but also recognizes that Larivière is to some extent a representative of Flaubert himself. The son would thus accede to his father's place, in that he performs—as a writer—all the functions of a doctor.

In addition to its simplicity, this interpretation of the father/son relationship has another advantage over Sartre's: it is able to account for not just two, but three generations of medical genealogy in Flaubert's life as well as in his text. If the first medical generation is that of Bichat (recall Flaubert's description of a "great line of surgeons that sprang from Bichat"), the second generation is that of Flaubert's father and Larivière, both of whom studied under Bichat. The third generation, then, belongs to Flaubert . . . and, surprisingly enough, to Charles Bovary. No wonder Flaubert feels that Larivière's kind of surgeon is now extinct. Neither Charles nor Flaubert, to be sure, is a successful physician. In this sense, Charles may be seen as the projection of Flaubert's failed ambition to become a doctor—and indeed one can trace many of the signifiers of failure borne by Charles (stuttering, falling into stupors, etc.) back to Flaubert, the idiot of the family. At the same time, however, Charles's medical ineptitude is what makes it possible for Flaubert the writer to act as a doctor in following the progress of Emma's illness. As we have seen, in the gap left by Charles's incompetence the novelist can note Emma's symptoms, elicit her delirium, supervise her fantasies, and probe the constitution of her memory. Indeed, Flaubert may be considered the true heir to Bichat's anatomical insights. By extending the anatomico-clinical concepts of constitution and diagnosis into the psychological domain, Flaubert may be said to have secured his own position within the Bichatian genealogy.

Flaubert's choice of a novelistic situation in which medical knowledge is not available is therefore explicable in biographical terms as a response to both his personal experience of illness and his family ties to medicine. We are left with the sociological issue: given the literary power of Flaubert's medical realism, why should the medical point of view become such an appropriate one, at this moment in history, for the task of representing reality? In short, why does realism become medicalized so completely in its techniques?

The answer to this question has to do, I think, with the development of the professions—including both the profession of letters and the profession of medicine—during the first half of the nineteenth century. This is an extraordinarily complicated process, but a few major points can be made about it. The first is that by the 1850s both literature and medicine are emerging from a period during which both sought professional status from the public. While the doctors succeeded in gaining control over their market, the writers failed to control the vast new market for literature that opened up during the 1820s and 1830s. By the time Flaubert begins to write, it has become clear that instead of a unified reading public under the domination of men of letters, a stratified market has formed, with some writers creating what Sainte-Beuve disdainfully refers to as "industrial literature" intended for consumption by the newspaper-reading public, and a small elite group of novelists writing for Stendhal's "happy few." The change can be measured by the fact that Balzac is one of the first to write in the new large-circulation journals, and is eager to conquer that market, while Flaubert disdains and despises journalism.

In turning away from the mass reading public, Flaubert in effect accepts literature's marginal status as a profession. Unlike Balzac, he makes no ideological appeals to his readers—he does not loudly assert, as Balzac does, that he is a "doctor of social medicine" ready to heal the wounds of post-Revolutionary French society. Instead, Flaubert focuses on technique. But with this new emphasis in realism on a medicalized style (rather than on the persona of the doctor) is not Flaubert now appealing to doctors, and indeed to the professional class as a whole, to become his readers? If this is so, then we can understand the adequacy of Flaubert's medical realism to the conditions of French society in the 1850s and later. For the professional class—which would include both literary and medical men, as well as lawyers, engineers, etc.—is the rising class during this period.

Reading Flaubert in this way, as discursively affiliated with a rising professional class, would not be possible if we did not extend Riffaterre's concept of intertextuality. But our reading also allows us to explain something about Flaubert that a Marxist reading cannot. The classic Marxist reading of Flaubert is that of György Lukács. In Lukács's Marxist aesthetic, literary texts are successful insofar as they accurately project the coming-to-power of an emerging dominant class. For Lukács, however, the only possible progressive class is the proletariat, and this class is hardly seen at all in Flaubert, much less blessed by the artist. The fact that the proletariat fails to materialize historically merely excuses Flaubert from responsibility for what Lukács must call an artistic failure, while denying him the possibility for success. We can accept Lukács's aesthetic principles, however, and still claim that Flaubert is a successful novelist. Flaubert may not be representing the power of the proletariat, but he is projecting the power of professionals—in his technique, his point of view, and his control of knowledge.

Semioticians might not accept the idea of biographical or sociological concomitants to intertextual presuppositions, while Marxists (or at least Western Marxists) might disagree with my definition of the professionals as constituting a class or with my distinction between ideology and discourse. But between semiotics and Marxism, Riffaterre or Culler and Sartre or Lukács, there has been too little discussion. By picking arguments with both sides on the basis of a discursive analysis, I hope I have at least shown how such a discussion might proceed.

MILAD DOUEIHI

Flaubert's Costumes

INTRODUCTION

> "Si le but et l'origine de l'introjection sont d'ordre érotique, si elle se produit elle-même dans le plaisir, son destin de déboucher sur la culpabilité ne pourra qu'aliéner le vrai sens du plaisir dans lequel elle s'est accomplie. Là gît peut-être l'explication du mystère qui accouple l'amour et la mort."
>
> (Nicolas Abraham: "Le 'crime' de l'introjection" in *L'Ecorce et le noyau*)

Frédéric Moreau, the perverse hero of Flaubert's *L'Education sentimentale*, is an *amant manqué*. He is also an *auteur manqué*. The novel is, in a sense, the story of these two failures. Writing, for Frédéric, is an impossible act because it is constantly obstructed by reading. Love, on the other hand, is informed and modeled on literary representations. Frédéric's love for Mme Arnoux is organized around his relationship to her clothing. Her dresses function as the insurmountable obstacle denying him access to the woman he loves. In this essay, I will develop a reading of the novel in which writing and Mme Arnoux's clothing constitute the two most important referents in terms of which Frédéric's itinerary can be explained. This reading will bring into play two psychoanalytical notions, introjection and incorporation.

From *Modern Language Notes* 101, no. 5 (December 1986). © 1987 by The Johns Hopkins University Press, Baltimore/London.

My basic claim is that Frédéric's position in the text can be accounted for as the result of a fantasm of incorporation, a fantasm that is produced in response to the failure of introjection. This failed introjection and the subsequent incorporation explain Frédéric's inability to express his love for Mme Arnoux as well as his fixation on her clothing. Therefore, in the following, I will limit myself to a brief abstract description of the fantasm of incorporation. (In this introduction, I rely on Nicolas Abraham and Maria Torok's work in *L'Ecorce et le noyau*.) At the end of the reading of Flaubert's text, I will return to this question in order to evaluate the import of this theoretical scheme as an appropriate tool for the interpretation of the text.

Introjection, as its etymology indicates, means a throwing inside. In its technical sense, it denotes the inaccessibility to a meaningful language and the inability to express through discourse a founding lack. The introjected language is, therefore, the negation of a fundamental lacuna to the extent that it is the failed articulation of an experience located by the subject outside the possibility of metaphorical naming and representation. Introjection gives rise to a process of figuration through which is accomplished a substitution, by means of representation, that is designed to allow a meaningful discursive production. In the case of the *Education sentimentale,* as we shall see, it will not be a question of a real mourning. Instead, the failure of introjection will be the result of a simulated mourning, a simulation that is as powerful as a real instance of mourning. For Frédéric it is necessary to posit this artificial moment in order to sustain and support his effort to persuade and seduce Mme Arnoux without ever declaring his passion. This fictitious instance of mourning, however, will contaminate the text of the novel to give rise to a system of symbols of which Mme Arnoux's dresses are only a partial and revealing (re)presentation. The failure of this imaginary discourse to grant access to that which is desired, namely the overcoming or the normalization of an instance of mourning, makes necessary and inevitable, because of the prohibitive factor of language, the introduction of a fantasm of incorporation.

In other words, incorporation constitutes the limit and the closure of introjection. The radical duality grounding introjection, that is to say the failure to identify and to identify with the object of mourning, accounts for the illusory and artificial qualities of introjection and points to its secretive nature. The failure of the work of introjection and the subsequent interiorization calls for the intervention of incorporation. In this perspective, the fantasm of incorporation is called upon to establish a discursive universe that allows communication, however momentary. Thus, in brief, incorporation transforms the dead and inactive symbol into an operating one. This transformation is achieved through the demetaphorization of discourse and the decondensation of the visual. For the fantasm (from the Greek "phantazô," to make visible, and "phaino," to show) is nothing but the visual animation of an essentially linguistic moment.

Visualization in the fantasm hides or covers up the inaccessible object and substitutes for this radically evasive state of affairs a camouflaged representation. A smoke screen separates the subject, in disguise, from his nostalgia over the absolute loss of identity of the object. The fantasm of incorporation is perhaps, in certain cases, the most efficient stratagem deployed by the subject in the face of mourning (or, more precisely, what Freud calls the "normal mourning") over the radical absence designated by his desperate linguistic situation. What cannot be said because of the lack of a name and the breakdown of metaphor is thus recuperated in an inalterable and irreversible proliferation. Such a proliferation, in its specific textual configuration, constitutes a powerful representation of the exterior of the representational machine as a loss or a deprivation. Through a discursive excess supporting this abundance of lack, the resulting discourse turns out to be a movement linking absence with death in order to remove that which is not yet and to defer that which is already. The work of incorporation is thus animated by a nostalgic vocation and a hidden mourning.

FRÉDÉRIC'S NOVELS

"Elle ressemblait aux femmes des livres romantiques."
"Il me semble que vous êtes là, quand je lis des passages d'amour dans les livres."

Frédéric's love for Mme Arnoux is inscribed throughout the text of the *Education sentimentale* in terms of reading and literary representations of romance. Whenever he decides to stop visiting her, either because of his inability to express to her his love or because of his usually misguided perception of some signs confirming her love for her husband and thus the futility of his passion, he decides to write a book. His literary ambition often appears to substitute for his lack of words in front of Mme Arnoux:

Cependant, Frédéric conservait ses projets littéraires, par une sorte de point d'honneur vis-à-vis de lui-même. Il voulut écrire une histoire de l'ésthétique, résultat de ses conversations avec Pellerin, puis mettre en drames différentes époques de la Révolution française et composer une grande comédie, par l'influence indirecte de Deslauriers et d'Hussonet. Au milieu de son travail,

souvent le visage de l'une ou de l'autre passait devant lui; il luttait
contre l'envie de la voir, ne tardait pas à y céder; et il était plus
triste en revenant de chez Mme Arnoux.

The project of writing is presented by Flaubert as the direct effect of
the influence of the circle of Frédéric's friends. Frédéric is merely the vehicle
through which the different, if not conflicting, tendencies of his friends will
articulate themselves. At the same time, writing, here the confused and multi-
layered grandiose design, the amalgam of "idées reçues," functions as a
withdrawal and a retreat on Frédéric's part to the extent that it compensates
for romance. Writing, however, brings back the desire for the loved one
and ultimately results in a return to the original state of affairs. Frédéric's
indecision as to his subject corresponds closely to his inability to forget and
to overcome his desire for Mme Arnoux. The curious thing in the passage
just quoted is that, despite the apparent conflicting desire between Mme
Arnoux and La Maréchale ("le visage de l'une ou de l'autre passait devant
lui"), Frédéric struggles only against his impulse to visit the Arnoux ("il
luttait contre l'envie de la voir").

A similar scenario, with slight but significant changes, is replayed later
on in the story. After a period of repeated visits to Mme Arnoux and his
failure to declare his love, Frédéric turns once again to his literary projects
in order to compensate for his failed romance:

Frédéric ne retournait point chez eux; et, pour se distraire de sa
passion calamiteuse, adoptant le premier sujet qui se présenta, il
résolut de composer une Histoire de la Renaissance. Il entassa
pêle-mêle sur sa table les humanistes, les philosophes et les poètes;
il allait au cabinet des estampes, voir les gravures de Marc-An-
toine; il tâchait d'entendre Machiavel. Peu à peu, la sérénité du
travail l'apaisa. En plongeant dans la personnalité des autres, il
oublia la sienne, ce qui est la seule manière peut-être de n'en pas
souffrir.

Reading and compiling notes for the projected History succeed this time
in making Frédéric forget his passion. This success, however, will not last.
For the compensatory work of writing will be again interrupted by the appearance of Mme Arnoux. Significantly, this time it is not Frédéric's imagination but Marie Arnoux herself who will appear on the scene to put an
end to his escape. Perhaps the reason for that is that Frédéric is actually
involved with the preliminary work and not simply meditating on his project.
In any case, the work will be soon forgotten: "Un jour qu'il prenait des

notes, tranquillement, la porte s'ouvrit et le domestique annonça Mme Arnoux."

The oscillation on Frédéric's part in the early stages of the novel between
writing and his relationship with Mme Arnoux is symptomatic of his overall
perception of Marie, a perception that is highlighted by his failure to face
up to the reality of his situation. The detour through fiction, or, more precisely, the effort to produce fiction that is nothing more than the compilation
of selected items derived from various sources, corresponds to the effects of
Marie Arnoux's dresses on Frédéric. His reaction to Mme Arnoux's clothing
follows a pattern similar to the one dictating the writing of fiction. Writing
and clothing form the material of a (mis)reading that is at the basis of the
constant digressions intervening in the text. These digressions serve to reinforce the representations of Mme Arnoux. Both operations involve the
dissolution of Frédéric's identity in that they allow him to forget his own
desires and motivations for the benefit of social influence in the case of
writing or physical appearance in the case of Mme Arnoux. Both tendencies
signal a withdrawal that is in fact a projection in the direction of a vaguely
defined exteriority.

As I will try to show in this essay, a textual network organized around
Frédéric's interpretation of the significance of Mme Arnoux's dresses plays
a determining role in shaping his character and informs the development of
their relationship. Moreover, this problematic mode of relating to the desired
person (or body), in its primarily visual concentration, calls for a new reading
of the relationship between Frédéric and Mme Arnoux.

Before going any further, I should like to point out that my reading of
the role of the female characters of the novel does not rely on the social or
cultural symbolism embodied in the different fashions they represent. Instead, my reading aims at exposing an internal context in which the costumes
take on a special significance to the extent that they punctuate and determine
Frédéric's actions as well as his imaginary representations of these actions.
Furthermore, this internal context will concentrate on the complex structure
according to which the inaccessibility of the body of Marie Arnoux is the
direct result of the failure to see through her clothing. The opacity of her
physical appearance goes hand in hand with the roundabout courtly discourse of Frédéric. Behind this determining complex there will be Frédéric's
imaginary identification of the sexual act (with Mme Arnoux) with the possibility of his own death. Mme Arnoux's clothing constitutes for Frédéric a
fetish, that is to say an erotic image and a fantasmagoric representation of
happiness and satisfaction. Underlying this fetish is the fear of a catastrophic
effect or a taboo. This taboo is in turn a screen covering a recollection of

an earlier moment in Frédéric's life, in this instance his first encounter with
Mme Arnoux, and the (im)possibility of its return in its purity and entirety.
The fear resulting from the potential loss of this experience and its repetition
determines the close connection between the significance of the dress-fetish
and Frédéric's own death. This identification, as I will argue, derives from
another identification-substitution between Mme Arnoux and Frédéric's
mother and, therefore, is grounded in the fear of a potential incest.

The initial encounter between Frédéric and Mme Arnoux in the opening
pages of the novel sets the machinery of the fantasmagoric representation in
motion. This first encounter deploys all the elements that will constitute the
various stages of his relationship with Marie Arnoux. Therefore, a close
reading of this episode will pave the way towards our appreciation of the
specificity of the fixation that controls Frédéric and of the elements upon
which it draws.

Flaubert's description of this scene is framed by an ironic and revealing
qualification. In the boat taking him back to Nogent-sur-Seine, Frédéric
despairs over the lack of romance in his life and dreams of affairs to come:

> Frédéric pensait à la chambre qu'il occuperait là-bas, au plan
> d'un drame, à des sujets de tableaux, à des passions futures. Il
> trouvait que le bonheur mérité par l'excellence de son âme tardait
> à venir.

Romance and writing are associated in the mind of the wishful young
man. The lament over his uneventful life leads him to dream about what he
deserves and what he desires. The split between the desires of the inexperi-
enced young man and the reality of his situation is put into relief by Flaubert
through the double designation, a designation that will become more significant later on in the novel, of Frédéric as "un jeune homme" and
"M. Frédéric Moreau." The introductory descriptive passages of the novel
prepare the appearance of Mme Arnoux in that they signal a tendency by
Frédéric to fill the gap he perceives in his life through dreams or imaginary
representations. Indeed, the moment Frédéric notices Mme Arnoux is presented by Flaubert as if it were in a world of dreams or a magical moment:
"Ce fut comme une apparition." This magical quality, I think, accounts for
the nature of Frédéric's reaction to Mme Arnoux and determines her status
as an inaccessible object:

> Il souhaitait connaître les meubles de sa chambre, *toutes les robes*
> *qu'elle avait portées,* les gens qu'elle fréquentait; et le désir de la

possession physique même disparaissait sous une envie plus pro-
fonde, dans une curiosité douloureuse qui n'avait pas de limites.

Frédéric's initial fascination with Marie Arnoux goes beyond sexual
desire; it points to the need to know and to be part of a different environment, a romantic setting that will correspond to the desires of the young
man. (This romantic setting is primarily textual; it ties in with Frédéric's
literary ambition: "Elle ressemblait aux femmes des livres romantiques." The
first encounter is a scene of reading, of reading perhaps an imaginary book
written by one Frédéric Moreau.) Moreover, Mme Arnoux herself is represented in this scene as if she were in a dream: "Quand la musique s'arrêta,
elle remua les paupières plusieurs fois, comme si elle sortait d'un songe."
The dream-like representation of Mme Arnoux is echoed by her representation as in a dream. Frédéric's problem in the novel will consist precisely
in his inability to overcome the initial determining moment and to deal with
Mme Arnoux in her real environment. His misreading and over-determination of Mme Arnoux will lead him constantly to fail in his efforts to consummate his love. Frédéric's imagination works from the onset of the novel to
displace Mme Arnoux from her real environment and to place her in a unique
and fantasmagoric context. Marie Arnoux is a part of the book(s) Frédéric
will never write, and therefore she will never be fully accessible to him.
Indeed, Frédéric's first action following his meeting Mme Arnoux is to start
writing a novel:

> Il se mit à écrire un roman intitulé: *Sylvio, le fils du pêcheur.* La
> chose se passait à Venise. Le héros, c'était lui-même; l'héroïne,
> Mme Arnoux. Elle s'appelait Antonia;—et, pour l'avoir, il as-
> sassinait plusieurs gentils-hommes, brûlait une partie de la ville
> et chantait sous son balcon, où palpitaient à la brise les rideaux
> en damas rouge du boulevard Montmartre. Les réminiscences
> dont il s'aperçut le découragèrent; il n'alla plus loin, et son dé-
> sœuvrement redoubla.

Mme Arnoux is a palimpsest of the second order, a palimpsest of a
palimpsest, which Frédéric is constantly deciphering and erasing for the sake
of his own survival. In his imagination, she is part of a fictional universe that
is itself constructed on the model of romantic fiction. Her name, the power
she has on him are derived from her uniqueness as well as her disguise. Mme
Arnoux is the prototype of all representations since she functions as an
originary representation herself. She provides Frédéric with an exemplary
model that allows him to indulge in his misguided ambition. In the restricted

context of *Sylvio,* the curtains signal the desired shift needed for Frédéric to break through the veils of Mme Arnoux's dresses. The curtains do not grant access to that which they cover, even though they are subject to natural effects. The wind, or Frédéric's singing, opens up the doors to Mme Arnoux. This fictional setting represents one of the few instances where Frédéric's words are efficacious.

Mme Arnoux is a palimpsest of the second order because she occupies a dual position for Frédéric. On the one hand, she—her body—is an inaccessible object, a secret. On the other hand, her clothing represents her body and, as we shall see, requires deciphering. As such, he will only be able to relate to her clothing, to her dresses, for he is only capable of dealing with that which veils the unknown he is seeking. In this perspective, Mme Arnoux's dresses correspond to the unwritten histories and dramas of Frédéric. We will recall that the desire for Mme Arnoux or for her physical presence functions as an obstacle to writing. In a similar fashion, her dresses will have a dual function. On the one hand, they will act as veils hiding the desired object and standing in the way of a transparent communication between the two lovers. On the other hand, Marie's clothing will also serve as a protective shield for Frédéric in that they direct his attention to her covered body instead of her face, and thus maintain and support his imaginary representation of the woman he loves.

Frédéric's first effort at writing a novel involves the representation of his quest for Mme Arnoux in a highly romanticized context. This imaginary representation carries itself in a curious way into reality. Immediately following the end of this first fictional detour, Frédéric sees Jacques Arnoux at the Palais-Royal in the company of two unidentified women. The description of this scene recalls an important "episode" of the *Sylvio:*

> Un soir, au théâtre du Palais-Royal, il aperçut, dans une loge d'avant-scène, Arnoux près d'une femme. Etait-ce elle? L'écran de taffetas vert, tiré au bord de la loge, masquait son visage. Enfin la toile se leva; l'écran s'abattit. C'était une longue personne, de trente ans environ, fanée, et dont les grosses lèvres découvraient, en riant, des dents splendides. . . . Puis une jeune fille blonde, les paupières un peu rouges comme si elle venait de pleurer, s'assit entre eux. . . . A la fin du spectacle, il [Frédéric] se précipita dans les couloirs. La foule les remplissait. Arnoux, devant lui, descendait l'escalier, marche à marche, donnant le bras aux deux femmes. Tout à coup, un bec de gaz l'éclaira. Il avait une crêpe à son chapeau. Elle était morte, peut-être?

In *Sylvio,* Frédéric sings under Mme Arnoux's window without seeing her ("[il] chantait sous son balcon, où palpitaient à la brise les rideaux en damas rouge du boulevard Montmartre"). At the Palais-Royal, he misreads the situation and is led to the suspicion that Mme Arnoux is dead. This is a very comic situation indeed. For if Jacques Arnoux was in mourning (as his "crêpe" would indicate), what in the world is he doing in the theatre with two beautiful ladies? The fact that Mme Arnoux is missing from both scenes leads Frédéric to unlikely conclusions. Furthermore, his inability to interpret correctly what he sees is highlighted by the emphasis on screens and veils. In a sense, his misreadings result from his incapacity to account for the screens, from the failure on his part to see through clothing and masks. There is also another aspect that is brought to light by this episode. His hasty suspicion of Mme Arnoux's death indicates his fixation on the fact that she is a married woman. He cannot imagine her outside the company of her husband. This naiveté will remain with him until the end of the novel. He wants to seduce a married woman. (He will only seriously get involved with Mme Dambreuse around the time of the death of her husband. He rejects Mlle Roque because she is a virgin!)

From what we have seen so far it is evident that Frédéric is a bad yet imaginative reader. His creative imagination grows out of the need to ignore the reality of observed reality for the benefit of an imaginary order. This substitution results in the general decondensation of the visual order as well as of the visible as such so as to avoid the longed for and yet somehow mystified encounter with the desired object. For Frédéric the decondensation of the visual gives rise to interminable discourses, to an endless struggle with his own language. His inability to articulate his love for Mme Arnoux stems from the effects of her physical presence on him and on his language. The paradoxical attitude is present from the beginning of the novel and it is not the effect of Frédéric's failure to address his love to Mme Arnoux:

> Plus il la contemplait, plus il sentait entre elle et lui se creuser des abîmes.

Frédéric, in his effort to overcome this irrevocable loss, and instead of speaking directly to Mme Arnoux, tries to communicate visually, with his eyes: "[il] lui envoya un regard où il avait tâché de mettre toute son âme." Mme Arnoux, however, does not seem to get the message: "comme s'il n'eût rien fait, elle demeura immobile." The original experience, thus, is that of the failure of communication between the two. Frédéric, in a desperate gesture, tries to express his fascination to Marie. His discourse, or rather, his message fails to reach its destination. This failure of visual communication, of the communication of the eyes and of the soul, will contaminate the whole text. Furthermore, Frédéric compensates for this failure by placing Mme Arnoux at the center of his world: "elle était le point lumineux où l'ensemble des choses convergeait." Marie Arnoux is thus the privileged object of observation and contemplation at the center of Frédéric's world. Yet this all-powerful center is beyond his reach. This contradictory situation resulting from the split or the discrepancy between the central position of Mme Arnoux and her inaccessibility through language gives rise to a fantasmagoric universe in which the desired object (or the ultimate destination, Mme Arnoux) is fragmented and reduced to a mere fetish. Frédéric's world is without a center; it rests on an imaginary point that is itself a visual representation of the missing center.

Frédéric's system in the *Education sentimentale* will consist in a constant translation and transfer of (mis)readings between the visual and the discursive. This systematic distortion will be tentatively reversed in his readings of Mme Arnoux's dresses. Before looking at this reversal, it is relevant to discuss here an example that shows the translation machine at work.

Frédéric's first dinner at the Arnoux's provides us with such an instance. In Mme Arnoux's presence, Frédéric is silent, content with observing his ideal woman. He is most interested in getting close to her, in getting to know what interests her. Thus, he roams around her, pretending not to be there:

> Frédéric, en écoutant ces choses, regardait Mme Arnoux. Elles tombaient dans son esprit comme des métaux dans une fournaise, s'ajoutaient à sa passion et faisaient de l'amour.

Frédéric's passion transforms the most trivial of conversations into a love scene. This process of "translation" goes on the length of the evening:

> Chaque mot qui sortait de sa bouche semblait à Frédéric être une chose nouvelle, une dépendance exclusive de sa personne. Il regardait attentivement les éffilés de sa coiffure, caressant par le bout son épaule nue; et il n'en détachait pas ses yeux, *il enfonçait son âme dans cette chair féminine;* cependant, il n'osait lever ses paupières, pour la voir, face à face. . . . Mme Arnoux s'était avancée dans l'antichambre; Dittmer et Hussonnet, la saluaient, elle leur tendit la main; elle la tendit également à Frédéric; et *il l'éprouva comme une pénétration à tous les atomes de sa peau.*

The sexual connotation of the passages above leaves no doubt as to the nature of the fixation of Frédéric. His blind passion, coupled with his inability to look Mme Arnaux in the face, account for his obsessive over-determination of certain moments in his life. The metaphor of penetration, used twice in the paragraphs just quoted, indicates also a reversal in Frédéric's attitude. In the first instance, he is the penetrator. Through the power and the concentration of his gaze, he penetrates into the body of Mme Arnoux. It is perhaps not a coincidence that the text reads "il enfonçait son âme dans cette chair féminine." This moment of penetration is an inversion of the first instance of exchange between Mme Arnoux and Frédéric. We recall that Frédéric "lui envoya un regard où il avait tâché de mettre toute son âme." In the present instance, he penetrates with his soul into her feminine flesh, without looking at her. It is as if, in order to avoid having the message lost before it reaches its ultimate destination, Frédéric, the operator of a translation machine, chooses to incorporate the message in the body of the destinator. In both cases, however, the sender of the message expects no answer, for he in effect leaves no room for any return. When Mme Arnoux "gives" him a part of her body, he represents this offering as an act of penetration. In other words, Frédéric stands at both ends of the exchange.

The visual exchange Frédéric initiates proliferates throughout the text and completely replaces linguistic expression. The silence of this exchange, its inanimate nature spill over and color Frédéric's self-perception. One evening, after some persistent questioning by Jacques Arnoux, Frédéric admits that he has no mistress. The reason behind his admission is his underlying fear that affirming otherwise would jeopardize his position with Mme Arnoux. Disgusted with himself, Frédéric leaves Arnoux accompanied by Deslauriers. Deslauriers wagers Frédéric that he will take home the first woman he encounters on the street, an achievement which he gloriously accomplishes. Frédéric, shocked and dismayed at the ease with which his friend accomplishes his aim, wanders in the streets of Paris. (Deslauriers's theory is quite simple: "Mais le clerc avait des théories. Il suffisait, pour obtenir les choses, de les désirer fortement.") Strengthened by the performance of his friend, Frédéric returns to the house of Mme Arnoux:

> Une espèce de colère le poussait. Il arriva devant la porte de Mme Arnoux. Aucune des fenêtres extérieures ne dépendaient de son logement. Cependant, il restait les yeux collés sur la façade,— *comme s'il avait cru, par cette contemplation, pouvoir fendre les murs.* Maintenant, sans doute, elle reposait, tranquille comme une fleur endormie, avec ces beaux cheveux noirs parmi les dentelles de l'oreiller, les lèvres entre-closes, la tête sur un bras. Celle d'Arnoux lui apparut. Il s'éloigna, pour fuir cette vision.

Frédéric's fear stems from the power of the visual scene he imagines.

He is haunted by the fact that Mme Arnoux is a married woman, for his ideal woman is detached from reality, she is the product of his fantasmagoric imagination, a fictional invention assembled from literary models. The presence of a husband spoils Frédéric's perverse pleasure and robs him of the power to speak. (Arnoux's presence resembles Mme Arnoux's quasi-magical "apparition" in their first encounter.) His desperation in front of the marital scene at the Arnoux's leads him to recall the effects of his first visit to their house in revealing terms:

> Alors, il se ressouvint de ce soir de l'autre hiver,—où, sortant de chez elle, pour la première fois, il lui avait fallu s'arrêter, tant son cœur battait sous l'étreinte de ses espérances. Toutes étaient mortes, maintenant! Des nuées sombres couraient sur la face de la lune. Il la contempla, en rêvant à la grandeur des espaces, à la misère de la vie, au néant de tout. Le jour parut; ses dents claquaient; et, à moitié endormi, mouillé par le brouillard et tout plein de larmes, il se demanda pourqoi n'en pas finir? Rien qu'un mouvement à faire! Le poids de son front l'entraînait, *il voyait son cadavre flottant sur l'eau;* Frédéric se pencha. Le parapet était un peu large, et ce fut par lassitude qu'il n'essaya pas de le franchir.

In opposition to the enclosed space of Mme Arnoux's bedroom, Frédéric here contemplates the wide-open space. In his nightmare, half-asleep, he sees his own corpse floating in the water. The image of his own death, curiously enough, precedes its logical possibility. In the same way that he thought his contemplation would demolish the walls separating him from Mme Arnoux, his contemplation of a natural spectacle, of a scene without the principal actor—Mme Arnoux—turns out to be the representation of his own death. The power invested in vision, both as contemplation and observation, constitutes an autonomous universe that excludes language and action. The penetrating gaze capable of reaching Mme Arnoux, once placed out of its "natural" context, so to speak, becomes a reflecting gaze that returns to Frédéric the figurative representation of his desperate situation. The image of his dead and inactive body personifies his mortified and inanimate discourse and his inability to act. Thus, the penetrating and prohibitive function of the gaze plays a fundamental role in the organization of Frédéric's fantasmagoric universe.

Having established the textual network informing the structure of Frédéric's relationship with Mme Arnoux, we can now turn to the analysis of the scenes in which his encounter with her is framed by his reaction to her dresses. The first time Mme Arnoux visits Frédéric in his apartment provides us with an example of the significance of her clothing. After having sent her children out of the room with the maid, she exchanges a few polite words with Frédéric. Then:

> Ils échangèrent deux ou trois mots sur leur santé, puis l'entretien tomba. Elle portait une robe de soie brune, de la couleur d'un vin d'Espagne, avec un paletot de velours noir, bordé de martre; cette fourrure donnait envie de passer les mains dessus, et ses longs bandeaux, bien lissés, attiraient les lèvres. Mais une émotion la troublait, et, tournant les yeux du côté de la porte:——Il fait un peu chaud, ici! Frédéric devina l'intention prudente de son regard.

The description, in the *style indirect libre,* of Mme Arnoux's dress comes immediately after the brief exchange of words between the two characters as if to continue the conversation. Frédéric's desire is invested with the suggestive qualities of the dress, qualities that substitute the dress for the body it covers. In this substitution, the conversation is in effect carried through. Marie's "émotion" suggests that she can read Frédéric's intentions in his eyes and therefore, for the first time in the novel, receives his "visual" message. This first instance of a successful yet incomplete exchange paves the way for more. The reason for its failure is explained by the dress itself, or, more precisely, by the connotations of the dress. Even though, as evidenced in the description, it liberates some of Frédéric's desire, it is still not the perfect seductive medium. Later on in the novel, after the mutual declaration of love between Marie and Frédéric, after the beginning of their platonic affair, we are told that Marie stopped wearing exciting dresses:

> *Elle ne faisait rien pour exciter son amour,* perdue dans cette insouciance qui caractérise les grands bonheurs. Pendant toute la saison, elle porta *une robe de chambre en soie brune, bordée de velours pareil,* vêtement large convenant à la mollesse de ses attitudes et à sa physionomie sérieuse. D'ailleurs, elle touchait au mois d'août des femmes, époque tout à la fois de réflexion et de tendresse, où la maturité qui commence colore le regard d'une flamme plus profonde, quand la force du cœur se mêle à l'expérience de la vie, et que, sur la fin des épanouissements, l'être complet déborde de richesses dans l'harmonie de sa beauté.

The "soie brune" and the "velours" go hand in hand with the normalization of Marie Arnoux. She is no longer the ideal woman, the romantic and inaccessible figure. Instead, she is like any other woman. Once Frédéric's love is recognized, Marie becomes the exemplification of the woman of her age and her beauty. The reversal in Marie's status hinges around the declaration of love, around the institution of a viable and mutual exchange between her and Frédéric. Even then, their dialogue is not always successful. For what is lacking is the unsaid and unsayable, the sexual drive behind their devotion to each other:

> Bientôt il y eut dans leurs dialogues de grands intervalles de silence. Quelquefois, une sorte de pudeur sexuelle les faisait rougir l'un devant l'autre. Toutes les précautions pour cacher leur amour le dévoilaient; plus il devenait fort, plus leurs manières étaient contenues. Par l'exercice d'un tel mensonge, leur sensibilité s'exaspéra.

Sexual desire, in fact, never appears in connection with Mme Arnoux's dresses except indirectly. During one of his visits to Marie after she and her husband have moved from Paris, Frédéric encounters a different dress and goes through a different experience. This experience is framed by a reference to literature as a model and an escape from the unbearable reality, unbearable for Frédéric in any case, marked by his constant failure to get Mme Arnoux openly to recognize his love:

> Frédéric était déterminé à poursuivre. Un volume de Musset se trouvait par hasard sur la commode. Il en tourna quelques pages, puis se mit à parler de l'amour, de ses désespoirs et de ses emportements. Tout cela, suivant Mme Arnoux, était criminel ou factice. Le jeune homme se sentit blessé par cette négation; et, pour la combattre, il cita en preuve les suicides qu'on voit dans les journaux, exalta les grands types littéraires, Phèdre, Didon, Roméo, Des Grieux. Il s'enferrait.

Marie's negation of the legitimacy of "love," her rejection of Frédéric's literary models leads him to despair. In his blindness, he gives himself to her, he surrenders his love to her mercy. At the same time, this surrender constitutes, for Frédéric, a continuation of his imaginary affair. For the verb "s'enferrer" means both to believe one's own lies and to throw oneself onto the adversary's sword. This double movement enclosed in Mme Arnoux's rejection encapsulates the structure of Frédéric's love. It is as if his imaginary love for her can be maintained only at the expense of his own life. There is no room for a "real" affair between the two, a fact that is constantly enforced in the text. Furthermore, Frédéric's figurative suicide and surrender will actualize itself in the association between death and Mme Arnoux's dress:

Le feu dans le cheminée ne brûlait plus, la pluie fouettait contre les vitres. Mme Arnoux, sans bouger, restait les deux mains sur les bras de son fauteuil; les pattes de son bonnet tombaient comme les bandelettes d'un sphinx; son profil pur se découpait en pâleur au milieu de l'ombre. Il avait envie de se jeter à ses genoux. Un craquement se fit dans le couloir, il n'osa. Il était empêché, d'ailleurs, par une sorte de crainte religieuse. *Cette robe, se confondant avec les ténèbres, lui paraissait démesurée, infinie, insoulevable; et précisément à cause de cela son désir redoublait.* Mais la peur de faire trop et de ne pas faire assez lui ôtait tout discernement.

Marie's dress is here perceived as an excessive and unspeakable secret. It stands in the way of his satisfaction by denying him access to that unknown it covers. The dress veils an unnamed object. This denial, however, reinforces and excites his desire. He thrives on the fascination provided him by the veil. It is as if the dress, in its figurative configuration, by hiding her body, constitutes Mme Arnoux as the ideal woman. The dress functions as the object of desire in that it provides Frédéric with the only possible representation of his secret and of the imaginary woman he seeks. Furthermore, the association of the dress with "ténèbres," with secrecy, damnation and ultimately death, recalls the earlier scene in which Frédéric sees the image of his own corpse floating in the water. In this instance, Frédéric will temporarily lose his identity, as if in a dream. After a silent farewell to Mme Arnoux, Frédéric, heartbroken, returns to the city. On his way, he experiences shock and bewilderment:

Ce qu'il éprouva d'abord, ce fut une stupéfaction infinie. Cette manière de lui faire comprendre l'inanité de son espoir l'écrasait. Il se sentait perdu *comme un homme tombé au fond d'un abîme,* qui sait qu'on ne le secourra pas et qu'il doit mourir.

Il marchait cependant, mais sans rien voir, au hasard; il se heurtait contre les pierres; il se trompa de chemin. Un bruit de sabots retentit près de son oreille; c'étaient les ouvriers qui sortaient de la fonderie. *Il se reconnut.*

Whereas Mme Arnoux was, when Frédéric first met her, the luminous point at the center of all objects ("le point lumineux où l'ensemble des choses convergeaient"), she has now become the darkest and most obscure object.

In the course of the narrative depicting the failed conquest of this privileged center, she turns out to be, in effect, the absorbing darkness that engulfs all objects, Frédéric included. This apparent transformation in Mme Arnoux's status in the text accompanies the change in Frédéric's reactions to her physical presence. In the first instance, Marie played the role of the illuminating element supporting Frédéric's contemplation of the fictional spectacle he produces. She functions, in this context, like a mirror reflecting Frédéric's fantasmagoric projections. In the second instance, after her resistance and rejection of his love, she becomes a figure of erasure and effacement. Thus, the subsequent momentary loss of vision, accompanied by Frédéric's own dissolution and disappearance in a natural spectacle, follows from the shift in Mme Arnoux's status.

The different roles taken by Mme Arnoux's clothing correspond, in the text, to the rhetorical deployment of a set of figurative inversions whose function is to maintain Frédéric's fantasmagoric projections of Marie's status. On the one hand, the effort to represent the body as a function of the dress, or, in other words, as an exteriority framed and formed by the veil covering it grounds the prohibitive aspects of the dress. The body, unrepresentable and inaccessible, is thus translated in the representational system at work in the novel as that which obstructs its presence, namely the clothing. On the other hand, the dress presents Frédéric with a visible exteriority covering an undefined and infinite object. The body, in this context, is associated with an open space constituting a spectacle where the contemplating gaze loses itself and ultimately fails in its quest to identify the desired object and to achieve the necessary identification (or union) with that object. The dress, therefore, operates as the central mediator between Frédéric and Mme Arnoux's body while at the same time obstructing any access to the body it promises and represents. Mme Arnoux's clothing constitutes the support of the representational machine underlying Frédéric's quest for pleasure. Yet, this machine collapses precisely because of the dual and contradictory roles of the dress.

The unique role played by Mme Arnoux's dresses in Frédéric's imaginary world is partially the result of the situations in which the encounters with Mme Arnoux take place. In almost all of the instances where Frédéric perceives Marie's dress as a problematic agent of seduction, the two characters are alone. Marie is thus detached from the social and natural environment and placed in the context of Frédéric's fantasmagoric representation of her uniqueness. This strategy of detachment reinforces Frédéric's illusion about his love for Mme Arnoux and strengthens his own withdrawal from the world. A clear indication of this is illustrated by his reaction to other women's clothing in a social gathering. For instance, during a dinner party given by the Dambreuses, Frédéric invests dresses with quite a different function:

> Des femmes le [Mme Dambreuse's boudoir] remplissaient, les une près des autres, sur des sièges sans dossier. Leurs longues jupes, bouffant autour d'elles, semblaient des flots d'où leur taille émergeait, et les seins s'offraient aux regards dans l'échancrure des corsages. Presque toutes portaient un bouquet de violettes à la main. Le ton mat de leurs gants faisait ressortir la blancheur humaine de leurs bras; des éffilés, des herbes, leur pendaient sur les épaules, *et on croyait quelquefois, à certains frissonements, que la robe allait tomber. Mais la décence des figures tempérait les provocations du costume;* plusieurs même avaient une placidité presque bestiale, et ce rassemblement de femmes demi-nues faisait songer à un intérieur de harem; il vint à l'esprit du jeune homme une comparaison plus grossière.

The provocation of the dresses is undermined by the partial nudity of the body. Clothing, in this instance, does not function as an obstacle barring the access to the body. The anonymity of the women along with the specific setting in which they appear neutralize the effects of their clothing. The spectacle they offer is a social scene, a normalized and conventionalized staging that lacks the emotional investment Frédéric perceives in Mme Arnoux's dresses. In fact, the social norms of seduction almost dehumanize the women in Frédéric's eyes ("plusieurs même avaient *une placidité presque bestiale*"). Mme Arnoux's unique position in the novel derives precisely from her detachment from the social environment. In other words, her status as the ideal woman is the effect of her representation in fictional terms and as the personification of a fictional model. The power of this fictional representation stems from the fact that it allows Frédéric to overcome the prohibitive association of Mme Arnoux with his mother (or, more precisely, the fantasmagoric representation of Mme Arnoux as a mother figure).

Early on in the novel, Frédéric receives a letter from his mother questioning him about his relationship with M. Dambreuse and urging him to use this connection in order to become a minister. Encouraged by his mother's insistence, he mentions the letter to Mme Arnoux, hoping to get her involved in his private affairs. Her response converges with his mother's wishes: "Mais je croyais que M. Dambreuse devait vous faire entrer au Conseil d'Etat? Cela vous irait très bien." Frédéric interprets her suggestion as a wish ("Elle le voulait donc. Il obéit"). The surreptitious displacement of the mother's wishes into Mme Arnoux's desires signals a substitution and an identification between the two women. At the end of the text, however, this identification becomes explicit. On their last encounter, Frédéric experiences a strange feeling in the presence of Mme Arnoux:

> Frédéric soupçonna Mme Arnoux d'être venue pour s'offrir; et il était repris par une convoitise plus forte que jamais, furieuse, enragée. Cependant, il sentait quelque chose d'inexprimable, une répulsion, *et comme l'effroi d'un inceste*. Une autre crainte l'arrêta, celle d'en avoir dégoût plus tard. D'ailleurs, quel embarras ce serait!—et tout à la fois par prudence et pour ne point dégrader son idéal, il tourna ses talons et se mit à faire une cigarette.

Frédéric's strong desire for Mme Arnoux is obstructed by a repulsion that is expressed in the text in terms of incest. Accompanying this inexpressible feeling is the desire to preserve the unique status of Mme Arnoux as the ideal woman. In fact, incest and idealization of Mme Arnoux are two sides of the same coin. For behind the illusory and inaccessible representation of Mme Arnoux lies her secret identification with his mother, her representation as the mother, and perhaps the woman par excellence. (Mme Arnoux's last action as a woman is a "motherly" kiss: "Je ne vous reverrai jamais! C'était ma dernière démarche de femme. Mon âme ne vous quittera pas. Que toutes les bénédictions du ciel soient sur vous! Et elle le baisa au front comme une mère.")

The identification of Mme Arnoux with Frédéric's mother takes on another twist when he decides to fight with Cisy to defend the honour of Sophie Arnoux. The night before the duel, Frédéric imagines the fight:

> "Je vois me battre. Tiens, je vois me battre! C'est drôle." Et, comme il marchait dans sa chambre, en passant devant sa glace, il s'aperçut qu'il était pâle. "Est-ce que j'aurais peur?" Une angoisse abominable le saisit à l'idée d'avoir peur sur le terrain. "Si j'étais tué, cependant? Mon père est mort de la même façon. Oui, je serai tué!" Et, tout à coup, il aperçut sa mère, en robe noire; des images incohérentes se déroulèrent dans sa tête. Sa propre lâcheté l'exaspéra. Il fut pris d'un paroxysme de bravoure, d'une soif carnassière. Un bataillon ne l'eût pas fait reculer. Cette fièvre calmée, il se sentit, avec joie, inébranlable. Pour se distraire, il se rendit à l'Opéra, où l'on donnait un ballet.

This scene reproduces partially an event described by Frédéric in his abandoned novel *Sylvio* in which he assassinates a number of men for the sake of Mme Arnoux. Here, however, Frédéric's fear brings back the memory of the death of his father and the effect of his death on his mother. This recollection is brought about by a narcissistic identification with the dead father. Although the precise context of the father's death is not specified, the passage allows us to make an analogy between the current situation and the one leading to the father's death. In other words, behind Frédéric's fear there lies perhaps another important identification between Mme Arnoux and his mother. It is as if his father had to defend his wife's honour in the same way Frédéric is compelled to defend Mme Arnoux. Thus there is room to suppose that his mother's reputation as a faithful wife was put in question. In this context, then, Frédéric's fear of incest is grounded in the similar positions occupied by the two women. Furthermore, this situation intensifies the paradoxical situation of our hero in that it points to the impossibility of his ever seducing Mme Arnoux. For in doing so he would be, in the context of his fantasm, responsible for his father's death. To seduce a married woman is, for Frédéric, to seduce his own mother and to kill his father. This fantasmagoric logic accounts for the persistent equation of Mme Arnoux's body with death.

Another possible interpretation of the father's death is that he himself had an affair with a married woman and was challenged by her husband. This possibility strengthens Frédéric's identification with his father. It is interesting to note, in this context, that the title of Frédéric's abandoned novel is *Sylvio, le fils du* pêcheur. Sylvio, the son of the fisherman may also be Sylvio, the son of the sinner.

FRÉDÉRIC AND THE GUILT OF REPRESENTATION

"La culpabilité naît dans la volupté."

Frédéric's consistent failure to express unambiguously his love to Mme Arnoux necessitates a detour through fiction and results in a fixation on her visual appearance. In other words, Frédéric experiences his love as something unnamable, beyond words. In order to compensate for this lack, he turns to fiction and a roundabout discourse that fails to articulate his intention and, moreover, produces a set of imaginary substitutions replacing the original and now lost object. The investment of Mme Arnoux's clothing with the power of representation of the desired object accomplishes the evacuation of the founding lack. Thus, the illusory connotations associated with the dresses give place to a totally new problematic whose primary function is to eliminate the original failure and to require the subject's involvement with this secondary situation. This scenario reproduces the failure of introjection and the subsequent introduction of a fantasm of incorporation. The proliferation of situations where Frédéric seems to be able to deal only with Mme Arnoux's clothing puts into relief two effects of incorporation. First, the demetaphorization of discourse. This demetaphorization perpetuates the pleasure derived from incorporation, a pleasure resulting from the negation of the original lack (here the lack of words). This demetaphorization of discourse, paradoxically, is grounded in an original metaphor, in a hypothetical metaphor that defies articulation because it haunts the subject and forces him to reproduce it in a deformed state.

Second, the objectification of the original moment prompting the intervention of incorporation. This objectification is articulated in the novel in terms of the effects of Frédéric's discourse on Mme Arnoux and ultimately on his own situation. In other words, instead of representing the discourse made possible by the fantasm of incorporation, a discourse that is organized around the visual representation of the desired object, as a sign of a fragmentation of the subject, objectification represents this discourse as the result of the effect of the loss of the object. This loss, however, is only an effect of representation. For, in fact, the lost object, the object of desire is preserved as such, it is preserved as that which defies representation and yet, at the same time, as that which makes representation possible. This object is an object of designation that designates the exteriority inaccessible to the subject as and through representation. The paradox of incorporation and the accompanying objectification stem from the need to cover up the survival, in its original form, of the supposedly dead object. Hence, the contradictory roles taken by the clothing. On the one hand, Mme Arnoux's dresses represent the tomb for Frédéric because they signal the impossibility of interiorization and thus operate as the remainder or the memory of the effect of the otherness Frédéric is striving to assimilate and ultimately neutralize. On the other hand, Marie's clothing functions as the original and originary instance of production of his fantasmagoric representation of his situation. Marie's dresses are located precisely on the borderline separating and uniting representation and its other. The dress is a name grounding representation in its irreducible other; it is the name of this otherness that Frédéric is constantly trying to reproduce in a discourse that is incapable of pronouncing it.

The dress, the exterior cover of the body, carries with it the inscription of Frédéric's desire in an impossible domain. It functions as the kernel that evacuates the body, a surface that denies any access to the interiority it has evacuated once and for all. Mme Arnoux's clothing produces a space where a primitive scene takes place, a scene into which the actors disappear in order to allow Frédéric to survive. Thus, the dress, as the locus of incorporation, makes possible the forgetting of the father, of the name of the father in as much as it symbolizes his death and the instance leading to his death. Marie Arnoux becomes, in this perspective, both the father and the mother. She represents, through her clothing, the death of the father and the survival of the mother. In other words, she stands for the disappearance of the obstacle and the trace of a forgotten yet determining scene for Frédéric. Mme Arnoux is not only identified with the mother as mother, but also with the father in that she symbolizes the indetermination of the status of the mother for Frédéric. As the locus of the phantasm of incorporation, Mme Arnoux, through the power invested in her clothing, becomes the producing agent of a discourse that is both necessary and unacceptable. This dual function gives rise to a triangular relationship between Frédéric, Mme Arnoux, and her dresses.

In this perspective, the question of incest in the text has to be considered not as a literal and suppressed desire but rather as the product of the fantasm of incorporation, a production that recapitulates, through an equivalent substitution, the originary introjection. The prohibitive effect of incest achieves the partial identification, for Frédéric, of a network of exterior relations that reproduce his secret inhibitions. Frédéric's secret lies in the inadmissible fact that he perhaps ultimately desires to be able to speak to Mme Arnoux as a lover and not to love her. This would explain the association of love with death in the novel. For instance, Frédéric describes his affair with Rosanette as a suicide ("S'il l'avait eue, c'était par désespoir, comme on se suicide"). Frédéric's education is perhaps his training in the secrets of substitutions and identifications, in the magical work of language.

In the novel, Frédéric's encounters with Mme Arnoux's clothing function as both a revelation of his inner desires as well as the revelation of the enigma standing in the way of these desires. The secret behind the dress is the haunting death of the father and the problematization of the mother's status as mother. The scene preceding the duel establishes the only reference to the father in the text. The import of this reference to the dead father is to transfer the conflict from the object to the body (Frédéric's body) and ultimately to his "moi." The dead father constitutes the object of the failed mourning and therefore determines the fantasm of incorporation to the extent that it undermines the failure of the symbolic work deployed by Frédéric's constant efforts to seduce Mme Arnoux. The father and the circumstances surrounding his death, not clearly specified in the text, are incorporated by Frédéric. They are part of himself, a part of himself that is nevertheless alien, other,

and in effect dangerous. The father's relation to the mother is the trap Frédéric walks into in his relationship with Mme Arnoux. Thus the persistent
efforts by Frédéric to forget himself, to avoid encountering himself and the
alien shadow of his father that haunts him. Mme Arnoux's dresses represent,
in this context, the false return of the repressed, the eruption of the primitive
scene Frédéric is seeking to avoid. Frédéric's solution to this dilemma will
consist in maintaining the conflict, in localizing it, unconsciously, in another
object, namely the clothing of Mme Arnoux. He transforms his inability or,
more precisely, his unwillingness, to decipher and to see through the veils
into a figurative misreading that aims at maintaining and protecting his
innocence while providing him with the only pleasure he knows. His pleasure
is the pleasure of designating the object of his desire without ever naming
it. Frédéric is the product of what Proust called the "hermétique continuité
du style."

Chronology

1821   December 13 Gustave Flaubert is born to Achille-Cléophas, a surgeon, and Caroline Fleuriot.

1834   At the lycée, Flaubert edits the journal *Art et progrès* and begins to write fiction.

1836   Writes a number of stories and novellas. Falls passionately in love with a woman much his senior, Madame Schlésinger, and begins to write *Mémoires d'un fou.*

1837–39   Continues to write many short stories and novellas, including *Smahr,* as well as some nonfiction works.

1840   Flaubert receives his Baccalaureate and then travels through the Pyrenees and Corsica.

1842   Moves to Paris to study law, meets Maxime Du Camp, and writes *Novembre.*

1843   Meets Victor Hugo, sees the Schlésingers often, and begins the first *Education sentimentale.*

1844   Has his first attack, probably epileptic, at Pont l'Evêque. Abandons studies and lives at home as a semi-invalid. The Flaubert family buys Croisset, the estate where Gustave will spend the rest of his life. He devotes himself completely to literature.

1845   Travels with his sister Caroline and her husband on their honeymoon to Italy. There, Gustave sees the painting by Brueghel which will inspire *La Tentation de saint Antoine.* Finishes the first *Education sentimentale.*

1846   On January 15 Achille-Cléophas dies, seven days before the birth of Caroline's daughter Caroline. A month later, the elder Caroline dies. Gustave begins *La Tentation de saint Antoine*. In June, he meets Louise Colet, a poet living in Paris. They become lovers in July.

1847   Beginning on May 1, Flaubert and Du Camp take a three month walking trip through Brittany and Normandy. Upon their return, Flaubert writes the odd and Du Camp the even chapters of *Par les champs et par les grèves*, published after Flaubert's death.

1848   February 23 Flaubert goes to Paris with Bouilhet to see the demonstrations, and briefly, joins them.

1849   Finishes *La Tentation* on September 12 and reads it, for three days, to Du Camp and Bouilhet. They declare it "unpublishable." Flaubert and Du Camp depart for a voyage to the Orient. They leave Marseilles on November 4 and go to Malta, Alexandria, and Cairo, where they remain until February of the following year.

1850   The voyage continues up the Nile, to Thebes, the Red Sea, Beirut, the Holy Land, Rhodes, Constantinople, and Athens.

1851   Flaubert and Du Camp travel through Sparta, Thermopylae, Patras, Naples, and Rome, where they are met by Flaubert's mother. Flaubert continues on to Florence, Venice, Cologne, and Brussels, and returns to Croisset in June. In July, he resumes his affair with Louise Colet, and later begins *Madame Bovary*.

1852–55   Works intensively on *Madame Bovary*. The relationship with Louise Colet ends in 1854, communication with her ends the following year.

1856   *Madame Bovary* is completed and appears, in six somewhat censored installments in *La Revue de Paris* between October 1 and December 15. Fragments of the second *Tentation* are published in the *Artiste*.

1857   Trial and acquittal of *Madame Bovary*. Flaubert is made famous and the novel appears in book form. Flaubert begins to work on *Salammbô*.

1858–62	Writes *Salammbô,* which is published on November 4, 1862.
1863	A year of great social activity. Flaubert is often at Princess Mathilda's salon, he meets Turgenev at the Maghy dinners, visits Taine, and begins his correspondence with George Sand.
1864–69	Writes and publishes *L'Education sentimentale.*
1870	Flaubert is ill and works on *La Tentation.* The Franco-Prussian War breaks out, Prussian troops are quartered at Croisset, and Flaubert and his mother take refuge in Rouen.
1871–72	Completes *La Tentation de saint Antoine.*
1873	Friendship with Guy de Maupassant. Later in the year, writes *Le Candidat,* a four-act comedy.
1874	Production and failure of *Le Candidat* and publication of *La Tentation.* Flaubert travels to Switzerland and Normandy to do research for *Bouvard et Pécuchet.*
1875	Works on *Bouvard et Pécuchet,* but later, due to poor health and finances, temporarily abandons it to work on *La Légende de saint Julien l'hospitalier.*
1876–77	Completes *Saint Julien, Un Coeur simple,* and *Hérodias.* The three pieces are published as *Trois Contes.* Flaubert returns to his work on *Bouvard et Pécuchet.*
1878–79	Continues to work on *Bouvard et Pécuchet.* In June 1879, the government grants Flaubert a commission of three thousand francs a year.
1880	Begins the last chapter of *Bouvard et Pécuchet.* On May 8, as he is working, Flaubert dies suddenly, perhaps of a cerebral hemorrhage.
1881	Posthumous publication of *Bouvard et Pécuchet.*
1884	Publication of Flaubert's letters to George Sand.

Contributors

HAROLD BLOOM, Sterling Professor of the Humanities at Yale University, is the author of *The Anxiety of Influence, Poetry and Repression,* and many other volumes of literary criticism. His forthcoming study, *Freud: Transference and Authority,* attempts a full-scale reading of all of Freud's major writings. A MacArthur Prize Fellow, he is general editor of five series of literary criticism published by Chelsea House. During 1987–88, he served as Charles Eliot Norton Professor of Poetry at Harvard University.

HUGH KENNER, Professor Emeritus of English at The Johns Hopkins University, is the leading critic of the High Modernists (Pound, Eliot, Joyce) and of Beckett. His books include *The Pound Era, The Stoic Comedians, Dublin's Joyce,* and *Ulysses.*

VICTOR BROMBERT is Henry Putnam University Professor of Romance Languages at Princeton University. His works include *The Romantic Prison, The Novels of Flaubert,* and *Victor Hugo and the Visionary Novel.*

MICHEL FOUCAULT held the chair in the History of Systems of Thought at the Collège de France in Paris and was a Visiting Professor at the University of California, Berkeley. Among his books are *Madness and Civilization, The Order of Things, The Birth of the Clinic, Discipline and Punish, Death and the Labyrinth* (on Raymond Roussel), and *This Is Not a Pipe.*

NEIL HERTZ is Professor in the Humanities Center and the English Department at The Johns Hopkins University. He is the author of essays on Longinus, Wordsworth, George Eliot, and Freud collected in *The End of the Line.*

VERONICA FORREST-THOMSON taught at Cambridge University. Her book, *Poetic Artifice: A Theory of Twentieth Century Poetry,* was published posthumously in 1974.

HAYDEN WHITE is Professor of the History of Consciousness at the University of California, Santa Cruz. He is the author of *Metahistory, The Tropics of Discourse,* and *The Content of the Form: Narrative Discourse and Historical Representation.*

JANE ROBERTSON is Senior Lecturer in French at Cape Town University, South Africa. She has written on nineteenth century French literature.

ANDREW J. McKENNA is Professor of French at Loyola University in Chicago. He has published essays on Flaubert, Baudelaire, Rimbaud, and Borges.

MICHAL PELED GINSBURG is Professor of Comparative Literature and Chairman of the Department of French and Italian at Northwestern University. She is the author of *Flaubert Writing: A Study in Narrative Strategies.*

SHOSHANA FELMAN is Thomas E. Donnelly Professor of French and Comparative Literature at Yale University. She has edited *Psychoanalysis and Literature* and written *The Literary Speech Act, Writing and Madness,* and *Jacques Lacan and the Adventure of Insight.*

EUGENIO DONATO taught at the State University of New York, Buffalo, and at the University of California, Irvine. He was the author of essays on French literature, on the relation of philosophy and literature, and on literary theory and criticism.

PETER STARR is Assistant Professor of Italian at the University of Southern California in Los Angeles.

LAWRENCE ROTHFIELD is Professor of English at the University of Chicago. He has published articles on Augustine and Sainte-Beuve, and is the author of the forthcoming *Signs and Symptoms: Illness as Discourse in the Realistic Novel.*

MILAD DOUEIHI is Professor in the Humanities Center at The Johns Hopkins University. He was the special editor of the issue of *Diacritics: The Métis of the Greeks,* and is the author of the forthcoming *Reading Shadows: On Incorporation in French Literature.*

Bibliography

Alden, Douglas W. "Proust and the Flaubert Controversy." *Romanic Review* 28 (1937): 232–36.

Auerbach, Erich. "In the Hôtel de la Mole." In *Mimesis: The Representation of Reality in Western Literature,* translated by Willard R. Trask, 454–92. Princeton: Princeton University Press, 1953.

Barbey d'Aurevilly, Jules. *Le XIXᵉ siècle: Les hommes et les oeuvres.* Paris: Amyot, 1860–1903. 17 vols.

Bardèche, Maurice. *L'Oeuvre de Flaubert.* Paris: Les Sept Couleurs, 1974.

Barnes, Julian. *Flaubert's Parrot.* New York: Alfred A. Knopf, 1984.

Barron, J. D. "La Première *Education sentimentale* de Flaubert." *Bulletin des amis de Flaubert* 12 (1958): 3–18.

Bart, Benjamin F. *Flaubert.* Syracuse: State University of New York Press, 1967.

———. "Flaubert and Hunting: *La Légende de saint Julien l'hospitalier.*" *Nineteenth Century French Studies* 4 (1975–76): 31–52.

———. "Psyche into Myth: Humanity and Animality in Flaubert's *Saint Julian.*" *Kentucky Romance Quarterly* 20 (1973): 317–42.

———, ed. Madame Bovary *and the Critics: A Collection of Essays.* New York: New York University Press, 1966.

Bart, Benjamin F., and Robert Francis Cook. *The Legendary Sources of Flaubert's* Saint Julian. Toronto: University of Toronto Press, 1977.

Bart, Heidi Culbertson, and Benjamin F. Bart. "Space, Time and Reality in Flaubert's *Saint Julien.*" *Romanic Review* 59 (1968): 30–39.

Barthes, Roland. "L'artisanat du style." In *Le degré zéro de l'écriture.* Paris: Seuil, 1953: 89–94.

———. "L'Effet du réel." *Communication* 11 (1968): 84–89.

———. "Flaubert et la phrase." *Word* 24 (1968): 48–54.

Baudelaire, Charles. "*Madame Bovary* par Gustave Flaubert." *L'Artiste* (18 October 1857). English translation in *Baudelaire as a Literary Critic,* edited and translated by Lois B. Hyslop and Francis E. Hyslop, 138–49. University Park: Pennsylvania State University Press, 1964.

Bem, Jeanne. *Désir et savoir dans l'oeuvre de Flaubert: Etude de* La Tentation de saint Antoine. Neuchâtel: La Baconière, 1979.

Berg, William J., Michel Grimaud, and George Moskos, eds. *Saint/Oedipus: Psychocritical Approaches to Flaubert's Art.* Ithaca: Cornell University Press, 1982.

Bersani, Leo. "Flaubert and the Threats of Imagination." In *From Balzac to Beckett: Center and Circumference in French Fiction*, 140–91. New York: Oxford University Press, 1970.

———. "The Narrator and the Bourgeois Community in *Madame Bovary.*" *The French Review* 32 (1958): 527–33.

Bertand, Marc. "Parole et silence dans les *Trois Contes* de Flaubert." *Stanford French Review* 1 (1977): 191–204.

Bloom, Harold, ed. *Gustave Flaubert:* Madame Bovary. New Haven: Chelsea House, 1987.

Bollème, Geneviève. *La Leçon de Flaubert.* Paris: Les Lettres Nouvelles, 1964.

Bonnefis, Philippe. "Exposition d'un perroquet." *Revue des sciences humaines* 181 (1981): 59–78.

———. "Flaubert: Un déplacement du discours critique." *Littérature* 2 (1971): 63–70.

Bopp, Léon. *Commentaire sur* Madame Bovary. Neuchâtel: La Baconière, 1951.

Borges, Jorge-Luis. "Défense de Bouvard et Pécuchet" and "Flaubert et son destin exemplaire." In *Discussion.* Buenos Aires: Emece, 1957. French translation: Paris: Gallimard, 1966.

Bouvier, E. "L'Original de *Salammbô.*" *Revue d'histoire littéraire de la France* 37 (1930): 602–9.

Brombert, Victor. *Flaubert par lui-même.* Paris: Seuil, 1971.

———. *The Novels of Flaubert.* Princeton: Princeton University Press, 1966.

———. "La Première *Education sentimentale.*" *Europe* 485–87 (1969): 22–31.

Brown, James W. "Aesthetic and Ideological Coalescence in the Alimentary Sign: *Madame Bovary.*" In *Fictional Meals and Their Function in the French Novel: 1749–1848,* 131–70. Toronto: University of Toronto Press, 1984.

Bruneau, Jean. *Les Débuts littéraires de Gustave Flaubert 1831–1845.* Paris: Armand Colin, 1962.

Buck, Stratton. *Gustave Flaubert.* New York: Twayne, 1966.

Canu, Jean. *Flaubert: Auteur dramatique.* Paris: Les Ecrits de France, 1946.

Carlut, Charles, ed. *Essais sur Flaubert en l'honneur du professeur Don Demorest.* Paris: Nizet, 1979.

Caws, Peter. "Flaubert's Laughter." *Philosophy and Literature* 8 (1984): 167–80.

Chambers, Ross. "Simplicité de coeur et duplicité textuelle: Etude d'*Un Coeur simple.*" *MLN* 96 (1981): 771–91.

Coleman, A. "*Le Roman de la momie* and *Salammbô.*" *French Quarterly* 4 (1922): 183–86.

———. "Some Inconsistencies in Flaubert's *Salammbô.*" *MLN* 27 (1912): 123–25.

Cortland, Peter. *A Reader's Guide to Flaubert.* New York: Helios Books, 1968.

———. *The Sentimental Adventure.* The Hague: Mouton, 1967.

Crouzet, Michel. "Le Style épique dans *Madame Bovary.*" *Europe* 485–87 (September-November 1969): 151–72.

Culler, Jonathan. *Flaubert: The Uses of Uncertainty.* Ithaca: Cornell University Press, 1974.

———. "The Uses of *Madame Bovary.*" *Diacritics* 11, no. 3 (Fall 1981): 74–81.

Dahany, M. "The Esthetics of Documentation: The Case of *L'Education sentimentale.*" *Romance Notes* 14 (1972): 61–65.

Debray-Genette, Raymonde. "Du mode narratif dans les *Trois Contes.*" *Littérature* 2 (1971): 39–62.

———. *Flaubert*. Paris: Firmin-Didot Etude et librairie Marcel Didier, 1970.

———. "Flaubert: Science et écriture." *Littérature* 15 (October 1974): 41–51.

———, ed. *Flaubert à l'oeuvre.* Paris: Flammarion, 1980.

Demorest, D. L. *L'Expression figurée et symbolique dans l'oeuvre de Gustave Flaubert.* Paris: Les Presses Modernes, 1931.

Derrida, Jacques. "An Idea of Flaubert: 'Plato's Letter.'" *MLN* 99 (1984): 748–68.

Diamond, Marie J. *The Problem of Aesthetic Discontinuity.* Port Washington, N.Y.: Kennikat, 1975.

Donato, Eugenio. "Flaubert and the Question of History: Notes for a Critical Anthology." *MLN* 91 (1976): 850–70.

———. "The Idioms of the Text: Notes on the Language of Philosophy and the Fictions of Literature." *Glyph* no. 2 (1977): 1–13.

———. "A Mere Labyrinth of Letters / Flaubert and the Quest for Fiction / A Montage." *MLN* 89 (1974): 885–910.

Dumesnil, René. *Gustave Flaubert: L'homme et l'oeuvre.* Paris: Desclée de Brouwer et Cie, 1932.

Durry, Marie-Jeanne. *Flaubert et ses projets inédits.* Paris: Nizet, 1950.

Europe 485–487 (September–November 1969). Special Flaubert issue.

Fairlie, Alison. "Flaubert et la conscience du réel." *Essays in French Literature* 4 (November 1967): 1–12.

Felman, Shoshana. "Gustave Flaubert: Living Writing, or Madness as Cliché." In *Writing and Madness,* translated by Martha Noel Evans, Brian Massumi, and Shoshana Felman, 78–100. Ithaca: Cornell University Press, 1985.

———. "Modernité du lieu communien marge de Flaubert: *Novembre.*" *Littérature* 20 (1975): 32–48.

Ferrère, E. L. *L'Esthétique de Gustave Flaubert.* Paris: Louis Conard, 1913.

Flaubert, Gustave. *Gustave Flaubert's* Madame Bovary. Edited and translated by Paul De Man (Norton Critical Edition). New York: Norton, 1965.

Gans, Eric. "*Education sentimentale:* The Hero as Storyteller." *MLN* 89 (1974): 614–25.

Genette, Gérard. "Flaubert par Proust." *L'Arc* 79 (1980): 3–17.

———. "Flaubert's Silences." In *Figures of Literary Discourse,* translated by Alan Sheridan. New York: Columbia University Press, 1982.

Giraud, Jean. "La Genèse d'un chef-d'oeuvre: *La Légende de saint Julien l'hospitalier.*" *Revue d'histoire littéraire de la France* 26 (1919): 87–93.

Giraud, Raymond. *The Unheroic Hero in the Novels of Stendhal, Balzac, and Flaubert,* 132–84. New York: Octagon Books, 1969.

———, ed. *Flaubert: A Collection of Critical Essays.* Englewood Cliffs, N.J.: Prentice-Hall, 1964.

Girard, René. *Deceit, Desire and the Novel.* Translated by Yvonne Freccero. Baltimore: The Johns Hopkins University Press, 1965.

Godfrey, Sima. "The Fabrication of *Salammbô:* The Surface of the Veil." *MLN* 95 (1980): 1005–16.

Gothot-Mersch, Claudine. "Le Dialogue dans l'oeuvre de Flaubert." *Europe* 485–87 (1969): 112–21.

———. *La Genèse de* Madame Bovary. Paris: José Corti, 1966.

———. "Introduction." In *Madame Bovary,* v–lxiii. Paris: Garnier, 1971.

Green, Anne. *Flaubert and the Historical Novel:* Salammbô *Reassessed.* Cambridge: Cambridge University Press, 1982.

Guillemin, Henri. *Flaubert devant la vie et devant dieu.* Paris: Plon, 1939.

Haig, Stirling. "Flaubert's Theolocutives." *Rivista di letterature moderne et comparate* 38, no. 2 (April–June 1985): 165–74.

———. "The Substance of Illusion in Flaubert's *Un Coeur simple.*" *Stanford French Review* 7 (1983): 301–15.

Hanouelle, Marie-Julie. "Quelques manifestations du discours dans *Trois contes.*" *Poétique* 9 (1972): 41–49.

Hansen, Kirsten Lund. "*Saint Julien l'hospitalier* ou l'Oedipe de Flaubert ou encore: Le bestiaire de *Trois contes.*" *(Pré)Publications* (Aarhus), 1973: 7–18.

Humphries, Jefferson. "Flaubert and the Fable of Stable Irony." In *Losing the Text: Readings in Literary Desire.* Athens: University of Georgia Press, 1986.

Huss, Roger. *The Early Work of Gustave Flaubert up to and Including the First* Education sentimentale *(1845).* Ph.D. diss., Cambridge University, 1972.

James, Henry. "Style and Morality in *Madame Bovary.*" In *Notes on Novelists with Some Other Notes,* 59–66. New York: Charles Scribner's and Sons, 1914.

Jameson, Fredric. "Sartre in Search of Flaubert." *New York Times Book Review,* (27 December 1981), 5, 16, 17.

Jasinki, René. "Sur le *Saint Julien l'hospitalier* de Flaubert." *Revue d'histoire de la philosophie* (April 15, 1935): 350–77.

Johnson, William A. "*Madame Bovary:* Romanticism, Modernism, and Bourgeois Style." *MLN* 94 (1979): 843–50.

Kadish, Doris Y. "Transcending History: *Salammbô* and *L'Education sentimentale.*" In *The Literature of Images. Narrative Landscape from* Julie *to* Jane Eyre. New Brunswick: Rutgers University Press, 1986.

Knight, Diana. *Flaubert's Characters: The Language of Illusion.* Cambridge: Cambridge University Press, 1985.

LaCapra, Dominick. Madame Bovary *on Trial.* Ithaca: Cornell University Press, 1982.

LeBlanc, Georgette (Madame Maeterlinck). *Un Pèlerinage au pays de* Madame Bovary. Paris: E. Sansot et Cie, c.1928.

Levin, Harry. *The Gates of Horn: A Study of the French Realists.* New York: Oxford University Press, 1963.

———. "A Literary Enormity: Sartre on Flaubert." In *Memories of the Moderns,* 135–44. New York: New Directions, 1980.

Lombard, Alfred. *Flaubert et saint Antoine.* Paris: Victor Attinger, 1934.

Lowe, Margaret. "'Rendre plastique . . .': Flaubert's Treatment of the Female Principle in *Hérodias.*" *Modern Language Review* 78 (1983): 551–58.

———. *Towards the Real Flaubert: A Study of* Madame Bovary. Oxford: Clarendon Press, 1984.

Lubbock, Percy. "The Craft of Fiction in *Madame Bovary.*" In *The Craft of Fiction,* 77–92. New York: Viking, 1957.

Lukács, Georg. "The Historical Novel and the Crisis of Bourgeois Realism." In *The*

Historical Novel, translated by Hannah and Stanley Mitchell. London: Vision Press, 1962.

Mason, G. M. *Les Ecrits de jeunesse de Flaubert.* Paris: Nizet, 1961.

Maynial, Edouard. *A la gloire de Flaubert.* Paris: Editions de la Nouvelle Revue Critique, 1943.

Mitzman, Arthur. "Roads, Vulgarity, Rebellion and Pure Art: The Inner Space in Flaubert and French Culture." *Journal of Modern History* 51 (1979): 504–24.

Murry, John Middleton. *Countries of Mind,* 203–22. New York: Oxford University Press, 1931.

Nadeau, Maurice. *The Greatness of Flaubert.* Translated by Barbara Bray. New York: The Library Press, 1972.

Nykrog, Peter. "Les *Trois contes* dans l'évolution de la structure thématique chez Flaubert." *Romantisme* 6 (1973): 55–66.

O'Connor, John R. "Flaubert: *Trois contes* and the Figure of the Double Cone." *PMLA* 95 (1980): 812–26.

Pater, Walter. "Correspondance de Gustave Flaubert." *The Athenaeum,* 3 August 1889, 155–56.

———. "The Life and Letters of Gustave Flaubert." *The Pall Mall Gazette,* 25 August 1888, 1–2.

Poulet, Georges. "Flaubert." In *The Metamorphoses of the Circle,* 249–65. Baltimore: The Johns Hopkins University Press, 1966.

La Production du sens chez Flaubert. Edited by Claudine Gothot-Mersch. Paris: Union Générale d'Editions, 1975.

Richard, Jean-Pierre. "La Création de la forme chez Flaubert." *Littérature et sensation,* 119–219. Paris: Seuil, 1954.

Riffaterre, Michael. "Flaubert's Presuppositions." *Diacritics* 11, no. 4 (Winter 1981): 2–11.

Rousset, Jean. "*Madame Bovary* ou 'le livre sur rien.'" In *Forme et signification: Essais sur les structures littéraires de Corneille à Claudel,* 109–33. Paris: José Corti, 1962.

———. "Positions, distances, perspectives dans *Salammbô.*" *Poétique* 6 (1971): 145–54.

Sainte-Beuve, Charles Augustin. "*Madame Bovary* par Gustave Flaubert." In *Causeries du lundi* 13, 4 May 1857, 283–97. Paris: Garnier.

———. "*Salammbô.*" In *Noveaux lundis* 4; 8, 15, 22 December 1862, 31–95. Paris: Garnier.

Sarraute, Nathalie. "Flaubert le précurseur." *Preuve,* February 1965, 3–11.

Sartre, Jean-Paul. *L'Idiot de la famille,* 3 vols. Paris: Gallimard, 1971/1972. Vol. 1, *The Family Idiot: Gustave Flaubert: 1821–1857,* translated by Carol Cosman. Chicago: University of Chicago Press, 1981.

———. "Sartre's Notes for the Fourth Volume of *The Family Idiot.*" Translated by Phillippe Hunt and Philip Wood. *Yale French Studies* 68 (1985): 165–88.

———. *Search for a Method.* Translated by Hazel E. Barnes. New York: Vintage Books, 1963.

Schor, Naomi. *Breaking the Chains: Women, Theory, and French Realist Fiction.* New York: Columbia University Press, 1985.

———. "For a Restricted Thematics: Writing, Speech, and Difference in *Madame*

Bovary." Translated by Harriet Stone. In *The Future of Difference,* edited by Hester Eisenstein and Alice Jardine, 167–92. Boston: G. K. Hall, 1980.

———— and Henry F. Majewski, eds. *Flaubert and Postmodernism.* Lincoln: University of Nebraska Press, 1984.

Seznec, Jean. "Flaubert, historien des hérésies dans *La Tentation de saint Antoine.*" *Romanic Review* 36 (1945): 200–221.

————. *Nouvelles Études sur* La Tentation de saint Antoine. London: Warburg Institute, University of London, 1949.

————. "Saint Antoine et les monstres." *PMLA* 58 (1943): 195–222.

————. *Les Sources de l'épisode des dieux dans* La Tentation de saint Antoine. Paris: Vrin, 1940.

Shepler, Frederic. "La Mort et la rédemption dans les *Trois contes* de Flaubert." *Neophilologus* 56 (1972): 407–17.

Sherrington, R. J. *Three Novels by Flaubert: A Study of Techniques.* Oxford: Clarendon Press, 1970.

Sherzer, Dina. "Narrative Figures in *La Légende de saint Julien l'hospitalier.*" *Genre* 7 (1974): 54–70.

Shoenholtz, Andrew I. "The Temptations of Truth: Imagination, Doubt, and the 'Imposing Completeness of a Delusion' in Keats and Flaubert." *MLN* 96 (1981): 1051–65.

Shroder, Maurice. "On Reading *Salammbô.*" *L'Esprit créateur* 10 (1970): 24–35.

Smith, Sheila M. *Les Sources de* La Légende de saint Julien l'hospitalier *de Gustave Flaubert.* M.A. Thesis, Manchester University, 1944.

Starkie, Enid. *Flaubert: The Making of the Master.* London: Weidenfeld and Nicolson, 1967.

————. *Flaubert the Master.* New York: Atheneum, 1971.

Steegmuller, Francis. *Flaubert and Madame Bovary: A Double Portrait.* New York: Viking, 1939.

Tanner, Tony. "Flaubert's *Madame Bovary.*" In *Adultery in the Novel: Contract and Transgression,* 233–367. Baltimore: The Johns Hopkins University Press, 1979.

Terdiman, Richard. "Flaubert and After: Failure Formalized." In *The Dialectics of Isolation: Self and Society in the French Novel from the Realists to Proust,* 60–90. New Haven: Yale University Press, 1976.

————. "Counter-Humorists: Strategies of Resistance in Marx and Flaubert," and "Ideological Voyages: On a Flaubertian Dis-Orient-ation." In *Discourse / Counter-Discourse: The Theory and Practice of Symbolic Resistance in Nineteenth Century France.* Ithaca: Cornell University Press, 1985.

Thibaudet, Albert. *Gustave Flaubert.* Paris: Gallimard, 1935.

Thorlby, Anthony. *Gustave Flaubert and the Art of Realism.* London: Bowes and Bowes, 1956.

Tillett, Margaret G. *On Reading Flaubert.* London: Oxford University Press, 1961.

————. "An Approach to *Hérodias.*" *French Studies* 21 (1967): 24–31.

Ullman, Stephen. *Style in the French Novel.* Oxford: Basil Blackwell, 1960.

Valéry, Paul. "La Tentation de (saint) Flaubert." Preface to the *Tentation de saint Antoine.* Paris: Daragnès, 1942.

Verstraeten, Pierre. "The Negative Theology of Sartre's Flaubert." *Yale French Studies* 68 (1985): 152–64.

Vinaver, Eugène. "Flaubert and the Legend of Saint Julian." *Bulletin of the John Rylands Library* (Manchester) 36 (1953): 228–44.

Warning, Rainer. "Irony and the 'Order of Discourse' in Flaubert." *New Literary History* 13 (1982): 253–86.

Wetherill, P. M. *Flaubert et la création littéraire*. Paris: Nizet, 1964.

———. "*Madam Bovary*'s Blind Man: Symbolism in Flaubert." *Romanic Review* 61 (1970): 35–42.

Williams, D. A. *Psychological Determinism in* Madame Bovary. Yorkshire: The University of Hull Press, 1973.

Acknowledgments

"Gustave Flaubert: Comedian of the Enlightenment" by Hugh Kenner from *Flaubert, Joyce and Beckett: The Stoic Comedians* by Hugh Kenner, © 1962 by Hugh Kenner. Reprinted by permission.

"*Madame Bovary:* The Tragedy of Dreams" by Victor Brombert from *The Novels of Flaubert: A Study of Themes and Techniques* by Victor Brombert, © 1966 by Princeton University Press. Reprinted by permission of Princeton University Press.

"Fantasia of the Library" by Michel Foucault from *Language, Counter-Memory, Practice,* edited by Donald F. Bouchard and translated by Donald F. Bouchard and Sherry Simon, © 1977 by Cornell University. Reprinted by permission of the publisher, Cornell University Press. This essay originally appeared in *Cahiers Renaud-Barrault,* no. 59 (1967), © 1967 by Francine Fruchaud, published by Editions Gallimard. Reprinted by permission.

"Flaubert's Conversion" by Neil Hertz from *Diacritics* 2, no. 2 (Summer 1972), © 1972 by Diacritics, Inc. Reprinted by permission of The Johns Hopkins University Press, Baltimore/London.

"The Ritual of Reading *Salammbô*" by Veronica Forrest-Thomson from *Modern Language Review* 67, no. 4 (October 1972), © 1972 by the Modern Humanities Research Association. Reprinted by permission.

"The Problem of Style in Realistic Representation: Marx and Flaubert" by Hayden White from *The Concept of Style,* edited by Berel Lang, © 1979 by Berel Lang. Reprinted by permission.

"The Structure of *Hérodias*" by Jane Robertson from *French Studies* 36, no. 2 (April 1982), © 1982 by the Society for French Studies. Reprinted by permission.

"Allodidacticism: Flaubert 100 Years After" by Andrew J. McKenna from *Yale French Studies* 63 (1982), © 1982 by Yale University. Reprinted by permission.

"Representational Strategies and the Early Works of Flaubert" by Michal Peled Ginsburg from *Modern Language Notes* 98, no. 5 (December 1983), © 1983 by The Johns Hopkins University Press, Baltimore/London. Reprinted by permission of The Johns Hopkins University Press.

"Flaubert's Signature: *The Legend of Saint Julian the Hospitable*" by Shoshana Felman from *Flaubert and Postmodernism,* edited by Naomi Schor and Henry F. Majewski, © 1984 by Shoshana Felman. Reprinted by permission.

"Who Signs 'Flaubert'?" by Eugenio Donato from *Modern Language Notes* 99, no. 4 (September 1984), © 1984 by The Johns Hopkins University Press, Baltimore/London. Reprinted by permission of The Johns Hopkins University Press.

"Science and Confusion: On Flaubert's *Temptation*" by Peter Starr from *Modern Language Notes* 99, no. 5 (December 1984), © 1984 by The Johns Hopkins University Press, Baltimore/London. Reprinted by permission of The Johns Hopkins University Press.

"From Semiotic to Discursive Intertextuality: The Case of *Madame Bovary*" by Lawrence Rothfield from *Novel: A Forum on Fiction* 19, no. 1 (Fall 1985), © 1985 by Novel Corporation. Reprinted by permission.

"Flaubert's Costumes" by Milad Doueihi from *Modern Language Notes* 101, no. 5 (December 1986), © 1987 by The Johns Hopkins University Press, Baltimore/London. Reprinted by permission of The Johns Hopkins University Press.

Index

Abraham, Nicolas, 197, 198, 245, 246
Aristophanes, 20
Aristotle, 127
Arnoux, Mme. *See Education sentimentale, L';* Moreau, Frédéric
Augustine, 131

Balzac, Honoré de, 43, 91, 93, 204, 234, 243
Barthes, Roland, 76, 77, 89
Baudelaire, Charles: adversaries of, 131; dialectic of good and evil of, 132; ennui of, 42; on *Madame Bovary,* 1, 220–21, 228; poetry of, 38
Beckett, Samuel, 1
Bem, Jeanne, 203
Benveniste, Emile, 240
Bichat, Xavier, 229, 235, 236, 237, 240–42
Bonnefis, Philippe, 195
Borel, Petrus, 1
Borges, Jorge-Luis, 48
Bouilhet, Louis, 23, 31
Bouttes, Jean-Louis, 132
Bouvard et Pécuchet: aping of commercial formulas in, 17; characters in, described, 11–13, 137; characters' names in, 10; cognitive nihilism in, 122–25, 132; community's judgment of, 130–32; compared with *La Tentation de saint Antoine,* 45, 58–61, 193; copying of texts in, 61, 132, 133; and encyclopedic approach to knowledge, 7–13, 21–22; the Enlightenment's nature in, 9–10; as farce, 10–13, 21–22, 138–39; Flaubert on the writing of, 129–30; future of humanity in, 134–36; geography and history in, 128; identification of Flaubert with characters of, 190; language of, 125–27; pedagogy in, 9, 121–23, 125–29; sainthood and stupidity in,

60–61, 214; science in, 18–19, 205, 218; serial structure of, 159; temptation in, 58–61; writing in, 133
Bovary, Charles: after Emma's death, 30; confusion of, 40–41; courtship of, 26–27, 36; escape images of, 38; in final pages, 26, 27, 34; Flaubert's relationship to, 242; love of, for Emma, 27; consults medical dictionary, 222; medical knowledge of, 222–27; monotony of experience of, 35–36; nature of self of, 231; numbness and drowsiness of, 42; in opening scene, 25–28, 138; view of fate of, 34; window symbol and, 36–37. *See also Madame Bovary*
Bovary, Emma: bitterness of marriage of, 36, 40; bourgeois nature of conversations of, 14–18; breakdown of, 231–36, 238; burial of, 42; Charles's love for, 27; confusion of, 41; convent education of, 34–35, 43, 228; courtship of, 26–27, 36; death of, 2, 4, 33, 222–23; disintegration of, 41, 42–43; first view of, 29; Flaubert's attitude toward, 3; hyperexcitability of, 234; and hysteria's nature, 228–32; identification of Flaubert with, 190; images of confinement and escape of, 35, 38–40; Henry James's view of, 2; manner of speaking of, 29; monotony of experience of, 30–33, 35–36; narrow consciousness of, 2; numbness and drowsiness of, 41–42; personality of, 1–4, 29; on poetry, 14–15; relationship of, with Léon, 39–40, 42, 233; relationship of, with Rodolphe, 37, 39, 41–42, 235–36, 238; repressed drives of, 2; sensations and memories of, 232–34; sensuality and ardor of, 3–4, 29–30; after sexual intercourse, 232, 238; at Vaubyessard ball, 232–33; window

DAVID GLENN HUNT
MEMORIAL LIBRARY
GALVESTON COLLEGE